Korea-US-China Trilateral Relations in the Xi Jinping Era

Korea-US-China Trilateral Relations in the Xi Jinping Era

Complexity, Conflict, and Interdependence

Edited by
Duck-Koo Chung and Byung-se Yun
with the NEAR Foundation

ROWMAN & LITTLEFIELD
Lanham • Boulder • New York • London

Published by Rowman & Littlefield
An imprint of The Rowman & Littlefield Publishing Group, Inc.
4501 Forbes Boulevard, Suite 200, Lanham, Maryland 20706
www.rowman.com

86-90 Paul Street, London EC2A 4NE

British Library Cataloguing in Publication Information Available

Library of Congress Cataloging-in-Publication Data
Names: Chung, Duck-Koo, 1948– editor. | Yun, Byung-se, editor.
Title: Korea-US-China trilateral relations in the Xi Jinping era: complexity,
    conflict, and interdependence / edited by Duck-Koo Chung and Byung-se
    Yun with the NEAR Foundation.
Other titles: Korea-United States-China trilateral relations in the Xi Jinping era
Description: Lanham, Maryland : Rowman & Littlefield, 2025. | Includes bibliographical
    references and index.
Identifiers: LCCN 2024032929 (print) | LCCN 2024032930 (ebook) |
    ISBN 9781538199534 (cloth) | ISBN 9781538199541 (paperback) |
    ISBN 9781538199558 (epub)
Subjects: LCSH: Korea (South)—Foreign relations—21st century. | Korea (South)—
    Foreign relations—China. | China—Foreign relations—Korea (South) | Korea
    (South)—Foreign relations—United States. | United States—Foreign relations—
    Korea (South)
Classification: LCC JZ1747 .K665 2025 (print) | LCC JZ1747 (ebook) |
    DDC 327.51073—dc23/eng/20240826
LC record available at https://lccn.loc.gov/2024032929
LC ebook record available at https://lccn.loc.gov/2024032930

Contents

Contributors

Duck-Koo Chung, Founder and Chairman of the NEAR Foundation; Former South Korean Minister of Trade, Industry and Energy

Byung-se Yun, Former South Korean Minister of Foreign Affairs (2013-2017); Chairman of Seoul International Law Academy (SILA); Co-Chair of REAIM Global Commission

Jun-Young Kang, Professor of Chinese Studies at the Graduate School of International Studies and Head of the Center for International Area Studies at the Hankuk University of Foreign Studies

Chaesung Chun, Professor at the Department of Political Science and International Relations, Seoul National University

Heungkyu, Kim, Director, US-China Policy Institute, Ajou University, and President, Plaza Project

Pyeong Seob Yang, Senior Research Fellow at Korea Institute for International Economic Policy (KIEP)

Sangchul You, Director of China Studies Center of the JoongAng

Heungchong Kim, Former President, Korea Institute for International Economic Policy (KIEP)

Gabyong Yang, Deputy Director at the Department for International Relations of Institute for National Security Strategy (INSS)

In-Hee Kim, Director of the Institute of History of Korea-Chinese Relations at the Northeast Asian History Foundation

Young Hee Chang, Research Professor at Center of Peace and Security Studies, Chungnam National University

Nam Suk Ha, Professor of Chinese Cultural Studies at the University of Seoul

Author's Copy Editor
Benedict Yim, Attorney at Law

NEAR Foundation

Established in 2007, the NEAR (North East Asia Research) Foundation stands as South Korea's foremost privately funded, independent think tank, specializing in global affairs, Indo-Pacific studies, and China studies, as well as analyzing Korea's strategies for geopolitics, geoeconomics, and geotechnology in Northeast Asia.

NEAR actively engages with international affairs, exploring a wide range of topics including international relations, politics and diplomacy, security, and the economy. The foundation places particular emphasis on critical matters concerning US-China relations, delving into the intricate strategic dynamics and matrix with the trilateral relations among Korea-US-China and Korea-Japan China. NEAR's research also focus on the Indo-Pacific regions, including North Korea's nuclear issue, the Taiwan contingency, the South China Sea contingency and more. Recently, the NEAR Foundation has been researching the emergence of global disorder and fragmentation in the arena of international relations and politics.

Duck-Koo Chung, the Founder and Chairman of the NEAR Foundation, has taught Chinese students at Peking University and Renmin University in China. Chung served as a policy advisor at the Chinese Academy of Social Sciences (CASS).

The NEAR Foundation's previous publications include "QUO VADIT MUNDUS: Competing for Order in a Fragmenting World: 2023 NEAR Global Survey Report on the World Order" (NEAR Foundation, 2023), "Why is Xi Jinping's New Era a Challenge for Korea? (Book 21, 2023), "South Korea's Grand Strategies to overcome China" (Kimyoungsa, 2021)", "The Revival of Korean Diplomacy: Alliances, Coalitions, Coexistence, and Self-Reliance" (Joongang Books, 2021), "The Power Matrix of Northeast Asia" (Isae Books, 2017), "North Korea-China Relations at a Crossroads: China's Policy Dilemma Towards North Korea" (Joongang Books, 2013).

Preface

Duck-Koo Chung

The modern history of Korea is intricately intertwined with those of the United States and China. The rhythms of their histories have left indelible marks on Korea's own narrative and will continue to do so into the unknowable future. Since the Deng Xiaoping era, China has experienced a spectacular economic rise and modernization, emerging as the greatest beneficiary of the globalism facilitated by the US-led liberal international order, eventually becoming a G2 power. During this period, erstwhile adversaries of the Korean War, Korea and China, normalized their diplomatic relations in 1992 and have since enjoyed a close and mutually beneficial economic relationship.

This all changed with the arrival of President Xi Jinping in 2013. Korea and the United States found themselves facing a grave challenge from Xi Jinping's China. He contested the US-led liberal international order, advocating instead for a Sino-centric international order as a viable alternative. Along the way, China began pursuing an aggressive—at times even belligerent—form of diplomacy.

Over the past decade or so, the United States and China have become embroiled in a full-spectrum strategic competition, precipitating a downward spiral of the international order into disorder and fragmentation. Amid this turmoil, no outstanding leader has emerged in the international community to tame the conflicts and wars breaking out across the globe. Against this backdrop, Korea has been thrust into a profound geopolitical, geoeconomic, and geotechnological dilemma, and must, once again, struggle to protect and preserve its sovereignty, identity, and survival.

This book delves into the dynamics of US-China relations, Korea-US relations, and Korea-China relations during Xi Jinping's third term in office and beyond. It examines the convergence and divergence of national interests and objectives within the matrix of the triangular relationship among these three nations and explores their far-reaching ramifications. The book poses the critical question of how Korea-China relations will evolve as the US-China strategic competition continues unabated and as the Korea-US alliance effectively transforms into the Korea-US-Japan trilateral security framework. What strategy should Korea adopt for survival, wedged between two giants exhausting themselves in a titanic struggle for supremacy?

WHAT IS SPECIAL ABOUT THIS BOOK?

This book focuses on the trilateral relationship between the United States, China, and South Korea in the face of Xi Jinping's dream of ushering in a new era stretching beyond three consecutive terms, built upon the pillars of authoritarianism, Chinese socialism, and Chinese exceptionalism. Primarily, the book underscores the imminent shifts that may impact the cooperative bond between Korea and China, which has remained steadfast over the last three decades since diplomatic normalization in 1992. It delves into the future trajectory of this relationship in light of the ongoing strategic competition between the United States and China, compounded by the menacing back-drop of the North Korean nuclear threat.

First, this book offers a unique contribution to the existing literature on the dynamics of international relations by presenting a fresh perspective through the lens of a trilateral relationship rather than focusing solely on bilateral part-nerships. Considering the rapidly changing international political landscape and the deepening economic interdependence between countries, efforts to address issues solely through the lens of bilateral relationships among countries may prove limiting. Viewing the landscape through a triangular perspective can offer valuable insights, revealing new dimensions and opportunities.

Second, the book thoroughly analyzes Xi Jinping's ideological frame-work, personality traits, and deterministic worldview, all of which influence China's decision-making patterns and mechanisms, both in domestic politics and international diplomacy. This investigation is particularly meaningful as it delves into the weak points within the Communist Party in the Xi Jinping era, analyzing how these vulnerabilities, coupled with public dissatisfaction, anger, and cynicism, could lead to cracks in the Xi Jinping regime. Through this examination of internal dynamics, the book sheds light on the potential fissures within Xi Jinping's rule amid ongoing global transformations.

Third, the book provides a unique lens in interpreting the different per-spectives of the United States and China. Concerning the sensitive issue of Taiwan, it diverges from the traditional military perspective, arguing that China's tactics are more nuanced, alternating between coercion and co-opta-tion, especially when managing relations with neighboring countries. There is a notable absence of in-depth research exploring how China perceives Taiwan in the existing literature on this subject, especially from the perspective of a third-party observer.

The formulation and execution of domestic and international strategies and policies are carried out under Xi Jinping's one-man authoritarian rule. Consequently, it is imperative to conduct in-depth research on Xi Jinping himself.

Therefore, a significant portion of the book is dedicated to examining Xi Jinping as an individual and exploring his ideological background. His persona, shaped by his early experiences, influences the trajectory of the US-China competition, as well as China's strategies for Taiwan and neighboring countries in Northeast Asia, notably Korea. In essence, Xi Jinping is fundamentally a nationalist, possessing a strong autocratic disposition while tactically adapting to varying circumstances. These chapters delve into how Xi Jinping's ideologies and personality traits interact with the Communist Party's structural dynamics, ultimately affecting the way decisions are made. They then examine the ramifications and repercussions of such decision-making on international conflicts and contingencies.

Korea has achieved its socioeconomic development within the framework of the international free market system, while simultaneously developing an ecosystem of coexistence with China since the Deng Xiaoping era. However, should China fully commit itself to the Chinese brand of socialism envisioned by Xi Jinping, a sudden and drastic realignment in this ecosystem of coexistence may be unavoidable. Korea will then be confronted with the daunting challenge of negotiating the conflicts emanating from this seismic shift.

This book analyzes such challenges and proposes potential solutions. However, one overarching constraint cannot be ignored: Korea must find a formula for continued coexistence with China despite the divergence in national interests, perspectives, and values. This enduring geopolitical imperative defines Korea's strategic landscape. Therefore, the primary focus of this book is conveying the complex and often contradictory dynamics in Korea-China relations. As such, it examines the evolution of the Korea-US alliance toward the broader Korea-US-Japan trilateral security framework, as well as the emergence of technology alliances extending beyond the traditional confines of security in the wake of the Camp David Declaration of August 18, 2023.

Lastly, it is anticipated that the relationship between the United States and China will exhibit a simultaneous blend of tension, particularly on security issues, and cooperation, especially on economic issues. The great power competition between the United States and China is fundamentally different from previous great power standoffs due to extensive economic entanglement between the two countries. However, this economic interdependence also means that China is a significantly wealthier competitor than any other the United States has faced before. This book offers an analysis of US-China relations that highlights the complexity, risk of confrontation, and economic interdependence inherent within this dynamic relationship.

CORE ARGUMENT OF THE BOOK

This book is more than an academic dissertation; it presents an overarching analysis of the Korea-US-China trilateral relationship as outlined below:

(1) This book conducts a comprehensive survey of China's changing politics, society, public sentiment, and diplomacy. It delves into the internal workings and machinations within the Chinese Communist Party (CCP), with particular emphasis on how Xi Jinping's personality traits shape the decision-making process.

(2) It traces the recent economic turmoil in China and its impact on Xi Jinping's China Dream and the market system that has existed since the Deng Xiaoping era. It further explores the necessary reforms within Xi Jinping's socialist economy to facilitate China's recovery from the economic challenges it currently faces.

(3) Due to the prolonged strategic competition, both the United States and China are exhausted and grappling with domestic political and economic challenges. As such, this book addresses the loss of leadership in the international community, which must be restored to manage the conflicts and wars breaking out in various parts of the globe. The book urges the United States and China to work together to bring about a shift from unmanaged rivalry to managed rivalry, thus contributing to the restoration of global peace and stability.

(4) Korea's survival strategy will face increasing challenges if US-China relations continue to deteriorate. The resulting intensification of North Korean nuclear provocations, tensions in the Taiwan Strait, and disputes in the South China Sea will necessitate Korea to engage in complex geopolitical and diplomatic calculations to hedge against risks and manage crises.

(5) Ultimately, this book provides a roadmap for Korea, wedged between two competing giants, to navigate the path ahead.

These issues have long been discussed in both bilateral and multilateral settings, but there is now a pressing need for both the United States and China to reassess their relationships with Korea. Korea is no longer an impoverished developing nation; it is now a middle power, with the capacity to contribute to addressing global challenges. It is imperative that China recognize Korea's transformation. As long as China's perception of Korea remains stuck in the past, it will be challenging to forge a path toward mutually beneficial coexistence.

Korea has relied on the Korea-US alliance for its survival and prosperity for many decades. However, the new realities of the twenty-first century require the two nations to "sail in the same boat with shared values based on balanced national interests." In other words, it is essential for the two nations to cultivate a stronger alliance relationship, with the most urgent task being to reaffirm their mutual trust.

Meanwhile, China possesses a vast population and territory. Its military power, technological prowess, and colossal domestic market have made it a G2 nation. However, its economy is in decline, potentially heading toward a full-blown depression. As such, China is seeking a competitive yet complementary economic relationship. It is time for Korea to dig deep to find a way toward a mutually beneficial coexistence with China.

BOLD, WHILE CAUTIOUS AND BALANCED

In publishing this book, the NEAR Foundation has made a concerted effort to address all relevant issues, whether positive or negative, as transparently as possible. Korea, the United States, and China all face their own realities and challenges that may not be easily discussed openly. Moreover, navigating discussions about politics and power structures within academia, let alone proposing solutions, presents inherent difficulties. In addition, in analyzing Xi Jinping's personality or the inner workings of the CCP, authors must be extremely careful to protect their sources. Despite these limitations, the authors of this book displayed little reservation in discussing their analysis as they perceive it. They have boldly offered their diagnoses and prognoses while maintaining a cautious and balanced approach.

The NEAR Foundation emphasized the importance of impartiality and cautioned all authors to avoid engaging in biased analysis or making statements about any particular country or individual. Each author has made his or her best effort to comply.

As the chairman of the NEAR Foundation, I consider it a great honor and privilege to have helped publish this book. I sincerely hope that many readers from America, Europe, and other parts of the world find valuable insights within these pages, gaining a deeper understanding of the geopolitical realities Korea is navigating at this moment in history.

We thank Rowman & Littlefield for their expertise in making this publication possible. We also express our deepest appreciation to the authors who contributed their invaluable scholarship and insights. Our heartfelt thanks go to Mr. Benedict Yim, a California attorney, for his work as the copy editor for the English version of this book. Last but not least, we thank Jung-A Chelsea Pyun, our project team leader, for her tireless efforts and unwavering commitment in bringing this book to publication.

Introduction

Duck-Koo Chung

This book is structured into three parts. Part I surveys China's changing politics, society, and public sentiment, together with the recent economic turmoil and its impact on the Xi Jinping regime and world politics. Part II surveys the current landscape of international disorder and fragmentation, exploring the challenges faced by Korea, the United States, and China in the realms of geopolitics, geoeconomics, and geotechnology. Part III introduces the "Trilateral Matrix," an analytical tool composed of trilateral matrices that represent the dynamics of Korea-US-China relations. Utilizing these matrices, which help conceptualize the multidimensional realities of Korea-US-China relations, this section conducts a thorough examination to identify intersecting interests and competing policies among the three nations.

XI JINPING'S CHINA: DREAMS, STRATEGIES, AND LURKING PERILS

Xi Jinping's Fatalistic Dream

Shortly after becoming China's leader in November 2012, Xi Jinping unveiled the concept of the "China Dream." According to Xi, the China Dream aims "to realize the great revival of the Chinese people." While many nations call for the revival of their people, Xi's vision appears to go beyond mere rhetoric. He appears to be banking on this grand dream to legitimize his indefinite authoritarian rule. Alternatively, he may perceive that long-term rule is a necessary condition to achieve the China Dream. Whatever the case may be, this slogan has alarmed China's neighbors, and indeed the world, for the unmistakable message is that China is now ready and eager to reclaim the former glory of the Chinese Empire from before the Opium Wars. Whether the China Dream is attainable remains uncertain, but Xi is determined to realize it for his beloved China. Former prime minister of Singapore, Lee Kwan Yew, a renowned Sinophile statesman, remarked of Xi Jinping, "He is resolute in his belief that the China Dream is China's destiny; this dream cannot be compromised." However, before China can become a hegemonic power once again, it must surpass the United States. Hence, confrontation between the United States and China appears inevitable.[1]

Let's now take a moment to reflect on how the Deng era emerged from the tail end of the Mao era, and how the "Rise of China" followed thereafter. We must also contemplate the historical significance of the past ten-plus years under Xi Jinping, juxtaposed against this breathtaking diorama.

Xi Jinping rose to power at a time when absolute poverty had become a thing of the past and China had grown to become the second-largest economy in the world. Against this backdrop, Xi Jinping did not place his focus on free and happy people, but rather perceived a communist rule that had grown lax and inept. He resolved to tighten the reins once again and reaffirm that China was a country of the Chinese Communist Party (CCP), not of the people. In doing so, Xi Jinping broke with CCP tradition and protocol, establishing a one-man authoritarian system reminiscent of the Mao era. By the time he was elected for his third consecutive term as the secretary-general of the CCP at the 20th Party Congress in October 2022, he had succeeded in surrounding himself with loyal supporters, consolidating his position as the undisputed leader of a authoritarian state. Indeed, his ambition appears to be to see his own era surpass the achievements of the Deng era and rival the greatness of the Mao era.

The commencement of his third term in office in March 2023 signaled the onset of an era of one-man totalitarian rule under hard-line socialism, projected to endure over the next ten years and perhaps even longer. On the grand chessboard of international politics, the United States and the West underestimated China's centuries-old hidden potential and actively encouraged its modernization efforts. As a result, foreign investment and trade skyrocketed, and China steadily narrowed the gap with the United States. All the while, the US economy and the Chinese economy became increasingly dependent on each other. However, amid these dynamic developments, the implications of China's ascent went unnoticed. Like a rose hiding its thorns, China's rise hurt many nations that embraced it. Today, the United States and the West are making belated efforts to contain China's role on the global stage.

Geopolitically, Xi Jinping represents a significant challenge: he hopes to position China at the center of the world stage as the preeminent economic and military power, surpassing the United States. His stated intention is to establish an alternative international order to compete with the liberal international order that the world has grown accustomed to and thrived in.

Deng Xiaoping and Xi Jinping: Antithetical Governance Experiments

Deng Xiaoping led China out of the Maoist nightmare and launched it toward the "China Rise." He accomplished this by integrating capitalist market principles into a socialist political system. He sought solutions to China's chronic shortfalls in capital, food, and energy in the international marketplace. Paradoxically, he also implemented a nuanced firewall, delineating boundaries between politics and the economy to ensure cooperation without interference. In short, Deng Xiaoping was a revolutionary, intent on establishing a new governance model for a new China. The world welcomed Deng Xiaoping's China with enthusiasm and goodwill. His grand experiment worked, propelling China to the status of a G2 member state by the turn of the twenty-first century.

Then came Xi Jinping, with a decidedly backward-looking perspective. He aspired to restore the absolute and ubiquitous authority of the CCP in China, thereby bolstering its position to confront the US-led liberal international order and capitalist market economy with "socialism with Chinese characteristics." However, Xi Jinping's greatest setback was his failure to destroy Deng Xiaoping's firewall between politics and the economy.

The consequences of this decision became apparent with the onset of the COVID-19 pandemic. Even casual observers began to notice the sharp decline of the Chinese economy, accompanied by the emergence of popular discontent and protest movements. Following the outbreak of COVID-19, China implemented strict quarantine measures over all affected regions under the draconian "zero-COVID policy," effectively confining people to their homes and suffocating the economy. This policy lasted until the Chinese populace began to display their growing impatience and suffering, culminating in nationwide protests like the blank paper protest. The appearance of slogans calling for Xi and the CCP to step down during some of these protest rallies reignited a deep-seated fear of the CCP—popular uprising. There were growing fears that, if the government continued to restrict people's freedom under the zero-COVID policy, even the fervent nationalism that Xi had been relying on to prop up his authoritarian rule may turn against him. When the CCP lifted the zero-COVID policy in December 2022, many expected the Chinese economy to roar back to life. This was not the case. COVID-19 may have hastened the downturn of the Chinese economy, but it was not the root cause.

At the time of this writing, the Chinese economy is experiencing a tumultuous upheaval. President Xi Jinping has attempted to impose socialist ideology on the market, triggering a collapse and sending the economy into a tailspin. The next few years will be pivotal for China. The question at the heart of this crisis is to what extent China will persist in integrating "socialism with Chinese characteristics" into its economy in pursuit of Xi Jinping's China Dream and socialist identity. Here, Xi Jinping's path clearly departs from China's path. His path and the path of the Chinese people appear to be increasingly divergent.

What the Chinese people demanded were livelihood, life, and survival. These demands translated into daily necessities, adequate healthcare, and a reliable pension system—a far cry from Xi Jinping's ambitious socialist agenda aimed at global dominance. These are what the Chinese people demanded in their "blank papers." If these demands remain unmet, the "blank papers" may start crying out, "Down with the CCP. Down with Xi Jinping."

Furthermore, without the economic might and national power to back it up, Xi Jinping's challenge to the United States, and indeed the world, can only be viewed as a hollow proposition. Xi Jinping himself will face a moment of truth where he will have to choose whether to adopt more cooperative policies or to remain unyielding. However noble and patriotic Xi Jinping may perceive his socialist China Dream to be, it cannot be achieved at the expense of his people's way of life.

China's Economic Crisis: Cyclical or Structural?

The depth of this crisis and its ramifications can be diagnosed by examining three aspects of the unique position China's economy occupies in the world and history. First is whether China is indeed falling into the "middle-income trap." Second is whether China has missed the opportunity to overtake the US economy as a result of its liquidity trap and deflationary trend. Third is whether the Chinese economy has indeed "peaked" and is now headed toward a recessionary spiral and possible collapse.

The most severe demographic collapse in the history of mankind, the alarming increase in debt, the largest real estate bubble and bust the world has ever witnessed, and drastically weakening consumer confidence in China would certainly raise eyebrows among economists. The resulting liquidity trap, falling growth rate, diminishing growth potential, shrinking number of producers, reduced consumer base, falling prices, extreme income polarization, and near nonexistent social safety net may well justify a conclusion that China is indeed headed toward the dreaded middle-income trap. China is literally growing old before becoming rich. If China's slow growth becomes chronic, the inevitable conclusion would be that China has indeed "peaked." The most remarkable geopolitical phenomenon of the latter part of the twentieth century—the "China Rise"—may be coming to an end. Consequently, China may have missed its chance to surpass the US economy.

However, such judgments must not be made hastily; two long-term economic indicators must first be considered. If China's growth rate remains below the global average of 3.6 percent (according to the IMF, 2004-2023), China's share of the global economy will indeed decrease. Similarly, if China's growth rate remains below the US average of 2.1 percent (according to the IMF 2004-2023), the size of China's economy is expected to reach 90 percent of that of the United States but then decline thereafter. The question then arises whether the Chinese economy will remain below these benchmarks over the next decade. According to an analysis by the Asian Development Bank, China's potential growth rate will reach 2.0 percent sometime between 2036 and 2040. Any assessment of the potential demise of the Chinese economy will depend on whether its growth can get on a trajectory toward a virtuous cycle in the intervening years. The performance of the Chinese economy over the next three to five years will provide valuable insights. Thus, the Chinese Peak theory may yet be premature.

3Ps (Policy, Property, and Perception)

The question in every China observer's mind is whether Xi Jinping will be able to reverse the loss of growth potential, thus pulling China out of economic stagnation. The Chinese propaganda machine speaks of a bright economic future, but the Chinese people and the rest of the world remain skeptical—so long as Xi Jinping's hard-line socialism remains in place. Economists speak of 3Ps (Policy, Property, Perception) in assessing the likelihood of China pulling itself out of the dire economic woes it is currently facing. The market's response, however, is negative: the market does not trust CCP policies, the real estate sector cannot return to health, and Xi Jinping's perception remains adamantly steeped in socialist ideology. The CCP authorities have also declared the "New Three Industries" (electric vehicles, batteries, and renewables) as the new growth engine for the Chinese economy and are allocating resources into these industries accordingly. However, their collective share of the Chinese economy stands at only 11 percent, half of the 20-25 percent occupied by the real estate sector. Moreover, the protectionist measures implemented by the United States and other technologically advanced countries targeting China are making any significant progress in the New Three Industries an uphill battle. Meanwhile, consumption remains dismal in the midst of a continuing deflationary spiral. As such, the outlook for the Chinese economy, with or without the 3Ps, remains gloomy.

What Xi Jinping must do is rather simple: take his foot off the pedal of socialist ideology and give back freedom to the market. Let the energy and ingenuity of the Chinese people soar, and let the market adjust itself. It is precisely here, however, where Xi Jinping's unyielding insistence on a "socialist market economy" stands in the way, putting politics and national identity above economy. Xi Jinping's socialist ideology and belief in the predestined China Dream render all his economic policies inherently market-averse. The inevitable result will be the declining growth potential of the Chinese economy.

Xi Jinping Regime, Will It Be Smooth Sailing?[2]

If the Chinese economy fails to regain its virtuous cycle by 2027, millions of unemployed Chinese may rise up against Xi Jinping, regardless of his calls for the China Dream or socialism. It is imperative that he go beyond his ideology to make the necessary adjustments. The world is waiting to see what choice he will make. Some feeble attempts by the CCP to prevent grievances from escalating into a challenge to Xi's rule or a call for political freedom have recently been observed, such as limited freedoms for life, livelihood, and survival. However, many within and outside China still doubt whether Xi Jinping has amassed sufficient achievements to justify his legitimacy, whether by bettering the lives of the Chinese people or elevating China's prestige on the world stage.

In recent years, Xi Jinping's China has been battered by wave after wave of adversities: the war in Ukraine, the catastrophic effects of the zero-COVID policy, the global supply chain crisis, worldwide inflation, the US Federal Reserve's unilateral monetary policy, and the emergence of minilateralism led by the United States, exemplified by CHIP-4. Added to this, Xi Jinping's stated goals of "national capitalism" and a "socialist economy" under the "Pivot to the State" policy, characterized by the emphasis on the manufacturing sector, common prosperity, constraints on private enterprises, and the expansion of state-owned enterprises, are strangling China's economy.

In this regard, General Secretary Xi Jinping's rallying cry to the Chinese people for a determined struggle against the United States—citing the prospect of the Chinese economy overtaking that of the United States by 2030—is beginning to ring hollow. In fact, Xi Jinping has recently been observed making statements hinting at the reevaluation of China's global strategies, as though he senses the realistic limits of China's ability to meet his dreams. It is yet unclear, however, whether this restraint is a reflection of the global economic downturn, the power of the US dollar, and the limitations of the Chinese-style socialist economy, or if it signifies his recognition of the limitations of the Chinese political system.

Cracks are also beginning to appear on the facade of the CCP. The harsh enforcement of the Zero-COVID policy sparked civil unrest among students and citizens, hinting at a refusal to acknowledge the legitimacy of the CCP. This, in turn, led to an abrupt about-face by Xi Jinping, who suddenly and without adequate preparation abandoned the zero-COVID policy and all its enforcement mechanisms. This decision resulted in a surge of COVID-19 cases among the unprotected Chinese citizenry in December 2022 and thereafter, laying bare one of China's weakest sectors: healthcare. This is likely to be the Achilles' heel of the Xi Jinping era: the lives of citizens are more important than warships, and modern healthcare is the most fundamental of all social infrastructures. It is a basic right of the people to seek medical assistance when needed, to have food when hungry, and to expect acceptable sanitation and living conditions. This issue of deteriorating national medical infrastructure will undoubtedly be an urgent policy demand facing the Xi Jinping government over the next five years.

The Future of Xi Jinping, the Big Nation China, and Its People

For now, Xi Jinping's priorities seem to revolve around ensuring domestic stability and navigating a way out of the international isolation China increasingly faces. Going forward, however, we should pay close attention to the workings and maneuvers within the Xi Jinping regime. There are already noticeable signs of fragmentation along factional lines within the regime and a sense of confusion in foreign policy direction, alongside ever-worsening hardships in people's lives.

If China insists on embracing isolationist tendencies in its worldview and socialist norms in its economic policies, it risks ending up with a shrinking and lopsided economy. Worse yet, people may be forced to seek alternative options if the Chinese government remains steadfast in its focus on the manufacturing sector in the digital era and in repressing people's rights to life and livelihood within the framework of a state-controlled socialist market economy. The world is already witnessing an exodus of capital, talent, and foreign investors out of China. If such trends continue, the Chinese economy could contract, and the once vibrant Chinese society may revert to its Maoist past.

Added to this are the intensifying checks courtesy of the Trump administration and the Biden administration. The United States has exerted its full might to contain the expansion of the Chinese communist state and gain an edge in the strategic competition. As Xi Jinping's ideological grip strengthens, the conflict and friction between the United States and China will likely escalate, casting a long shadow over the future of both China and the world.

Xi Jinping's China appears destined to face profound challenges across all aspects of statecraft beyond mere economics in the coming years. Crucially, the trajectory of the Chinese economy will determine whether Xi Jinping's rule will extend into a fourth term in 2027. How will he navigate the economic challenges facing China? Will he insist upon seeking a way to revive the Chinese economy within the confines of socialist ideology? Or will he compromise his ideological stance to accommodate the demands of the market? Can Xi Jinping's China Dream still come true? The answers to these questions rest in the hands of one man, the maestro of the dream. If President Xi Jinping, trapped by his own inflexibility, fails to escape the trap of his own making, his magnificent dream will wither. On the other hand, if Xi demonstrates intellectual agility and instead opts to alter the course he has set for China, the China Dream may once again become attainable. China's future hinges on the personality and decision-making style of one man.

Xi Jinping's Choice

Ideological Dream versus Pragmatism

History teaches us that a nation's top decision-maker confronts a crucial choice when shaping the future of their country: national pride or pragmatism. A leader's choice between these two principles determines the fate of their people. In 1991, British prime minister Margaret Thatcher signed the Maastricht Treaty to join the EU but chose not to adopt the Euro, the EU's common currency. This was perhaps a skillful compromise between national pride and pragmatism. Later, however, under Prime Minister David Cameron, Britain opted to withdraw from the EU in a surge of national pride and now appears to have entered a long period of decline.

What lesson can Xi Jinping learn from Britain's story? Community of common destiny, US-China strategic competition, state capitalism, the Moscow-Beijing subtle relationship, the blank paper protests, and the exodus of foreign investment—What will sway Xi Jinping's choice going forward: pride or pragmatism? Such actions are likely to further isolate China in the international community. Xi's assault on China's market economy under the banner of state capitalism risks constricting, if not permanently corroding, China's growth potential. As it stands now, it is up to one man, Xi Jinping, to chart a wise course between his dream and pragmatism for the sake of China's future.

Good Medicine Tastes Bitter

For China to revive its economy, it must embrace a flexible approach to the changing winds of the domestic and international economic landscapes. Since the Deng era, the Chinese economy has mainly operated on market principles and has been tethered to the global economy. Consequently, the economy may not be the right vehicle with which to realize Xi Jinping's vision of "modernized socialism." In other words, China's current economic crisis is, in fact, predestined—an unmistakable clash between the market economy and the communist/socialist political system.

Xi Jinping's one-man authoritarian system is now facing an existential challenge resulting from the failure of his own state-led economic governance experiment. To resuscitate the floundering economy, Xi Jinping needs to revert to a more market-friendly economic governance model. His perspective on the economy must become more flexible if the current contracting and imbalanced economy is to make a turn toward an expanding and balanced economy. Many economists have suggested that such flexibility would mitigate Xi Jinping's domestic political risks by improving the life and livelihoods of the Chinese people. This will take courage—a mark of leadership in a statesman. However, Xi Jinping may find it difficult to swallow this pill. The old adage "good medicine tastes bitter" has never rung truer.

Xi's Personality Trait and China's Future

The ultimate question then becomes whether Xi Jinping, the Paramount Leader in a one-man authoritarian system he himself has built, is likely to take the necessary steps. Here, Xi Jinping's innate personality may very well determine China's future. While Xi Jinping initially appears decisive and reserved, he also displays occasional flexibility—a willingness to compromise. This trait, however, often serves as a pragmatic tool to navigate obstacles blocking his path, with the core of his belief system remaining unchanged. For instance, he may roll out stimulus packages to revive the faltering real estate sector, but he will not endorse an economic model centered around real estate. As such, Xi Jinping, by simply being himself, may inadvertently hinder economic recovery.

The prospect of China returning to its former high-growth economy may be all but impossible. Accordingly, Xi Jinping's global objective may also shift from surpassing the US economy to building a new Sino-centric international order supported by China's Xi Jinping-style socialist economy, aimed at competing with the US-led liberal international order. This would effectively signify the end of Xi's original China Dream. Already, many countries that participated in the Belt and Road Initiative (BRI) are withdrawing, and the Asian Infrastructure Investment Bank (AIIB) is heavily burdened with bad debt. China's aspiration to internationalize the RMB has stalled at 2.5 percent of international settlement. This is not the time for China to contemplate involvement in the Russia-Ukraine war or an invasion of Taiwan. Instead, China must address the people's demands for simple livelihood and the creation of a pension system for the aging population. Xi Jinping must also adopt a more conciliatory and cooperative approach in his foreign policies.

The trajectory of the Chinese economy will determine whether Xi Jinping's rule will extend into a fourth term in 2027. However, Xi Jinping alone remains the sole decision-maker in China, making his personality and decision-making style pivotal factors in shaping the country's future. How will he navigate the economic challenges facing China? Will he insist upon seeking a way to revive the Chinese economy within the confines of socialist ideology? Or will he compromise his ideological stance to accommodate the demands of the market?

WORLD DISORDER IN A FRAGMENTING WORLD

Most geopolitical thinkers and policymakers agree that the world is in a state of flux, and yet, there is a notable absence of global leadership capable of taking the helm. The international community is like a ship adrift with a broken rudder. There are fires everywhere with no firefighter in sight.

The United States and China are locked in a titanic struggle for strategic supremacy, with neither side able to offer a viable resolution to the standoff. This "new type of major power relationship" suffers from fundamentally divergent value systems, perspectives on international relations, and interpretations of history. As a result, both sides have miscalculated, pursuing unrealistic strategic objectives and underestimating each other's capabilities.

Former US secretary of state Henry Kissinger, in an interview with *The Economist* in May 2023, remarked that the United States and China find themselves in a "classic pre-World War I situation" that could lead to conflict, noting that the presence of artificial intelligence (AI) makes this "not a normal circumstance."[3] Similarly, Council on Foreign Relations president emeritus Richard Haass stated, "Challenges around the globe, the responses thereto, and possibility of a war among major powers in Europe and Indo-Pacific are all on the rise. In the Middle East, Iran is acquiring abilities to disrupt the precarious peace. The world is now living through the most perilous period since WWII."[4]

When ambition begins to flirt with despair, the risk of war increases. If the Chinese economy fails to turn around by 2027, the discontent among the Chinese masses will likely escalate, and politics will become frayed. Such a state of affairs may spell the end of Xi Jinping's ambitions, heightening the risk of war. Forced into a corner, Xi Jinping may make an error in judgment. It is imperative that we remain alert of this entirely possible scenario and begin discussions now on how to prevent a war. Above all, the discussions must focus on managing US-China relations and the triggers that could push the two powers to the brink of war: the Russia-Ukraine war, the North Korean nuclear threat, and tensions in the Taiwan Strait and South China Sea.

The United States and China: Exhaustion from Protracted Strategic Competition

China is "growing old before becoming rich," characterized by an aging society despite being stuck at about the $10,000 per capita income milestone. China owes its $10,000 per capita income to Deng Xiaoping's reform and opening-up economic governance experiment. Xi Jinping, however, rejected Deng's experiment in favor of his own new global power experiment and socialist economy experiment. In the process, China quickly lost the trust of the international community, and with it, its economic growth potential.

Until recently, China appeared poised to achieve middle-income status, thanks to its long-term high economic growth, advancement in economic structure, and increased consumption. It has now become clear, however, that China has found itself in a difficult economic predicament characterized by falling into a liquidity trap, falling growth potential, declining investment, and waning consumption, all indicating a deflationary trend.

If China fails to pull itself back to a virtuous cycle of economic growth and falls into the dreaded middle-income trap over the next two to three years, the "Peak China" theory could become a reality, turning the "China Rise" into a broken dream consigned to history. Meanwhile, the United States is experiencing problems of its own. With its global leadership eroding and its domestic politics becoming increasingly polarized, the United States may be losing its esteemed position as the undisputed global leader.

The multipolar international order, marked by the rise of China, the reemergence of Russia, and the growing assertiveness of Middle Eastern oil-producing countries, is fragmenting in the midst of a general chaos. The world is now facing a disconcerting international landscape where there is nothing the international community can address without the United States, yet the United States cannot address anything unilaterally. Some liken the United States's role in today's international arena to that of the largest minority shareholder. As such, the greatest source of power for the United States now lies in its web of alliances. However, this network sustained significant damage during the Trump administration, and the Biden administration's efforts to restore its resilience have had limited success. Traditional allies like the EU and Saudi Arabia, along with the Global South, have become accustomed to being fence-sitters, straddling the line between the United States on one side and China and Russia on the other. In such circumstances, it would be wiser for the United States to prioritize strengthening its relationships with its friends and allies rather than solely focusing on containing China.

In short, without the critical factors of (1) sailing in the same boat, (2) with a shared dream, (3) along with balanced national interests, America's alliance network will continue to wither. This holds true regardless of who is elected as America's next president this coming November.

The time is ripe for both the United States and China to recognize that they are like exhausted eagles with broken wings after a prolonged struggle. They must choose not to breach each other's guardrails and instead pursue dialogue and compromise.

Xi Jinping believes that the "Great Revival of the Chinese Nation" will be his legacy. Unfortunately for Xi, the liberal democratic world, including the West, perceives him and his "China Dream" as a profound threat to the liberal international order. Consequently, Xi's China finds itself confronted with the challenges and limitations of its own making. It has been a year since the start of Xi Jinping's third term in March 2023, and many China observers anticipate that China will remain an uncompromising socialist country under one-man authoritarian rule for at least the next five to ten years.

For decades, the West underestimated China's latent potential and actively encouraged China's industrialization. As a result, Western capital poured into China, leading to exponential growth in trade between the West and China and allowing China to narrow the gap between itself and the United States. However, this period also saw a corresponding increase in mutual interdependence. Amid these historical developments, Korea and the United States failed to see China's hidden claws. Its rosy image hid sharp thorns, and many countries that embraced China's rise ultimately got pricked. Today, the West is engaged in belated efforts to suppress China's rise and contain its ambitions. Many geopolitical thinkers wonder whether United States sanctions on China have already missed the optimal timing. The initial decoupling strategy pursued by the United States at the crossroads of free trade and protectionism had a rhetorical ring to it, but it lacked realistic prospects for success. Many in the United States and the rest of the world expressed reservations, if not outright doubts. The exhaustion of the two powers will only grow with time. When coupled with the challenges of the COVID19 pandemic, the Russian invasion of Ukraine, the global supply chain crisis, and the Israeli-Palestinian conflict, the resilience of the international order diminishes with each passing day.

Peak China versus the US, Largest Minority Shareholder?

What is particularly noteworthy is that the Chinese economy is also showing its limits. China is likely on the verge of stumbling into a classic middle-income trap. In a December 2023 *New York Times* column, American economist Paul Krugman posited that the Chinese economy, which had been sustained by investments and a real estate bubble, had reached its limit, and without rapid gains in productivity, China would soon enter into the middle-income trap.

In August 2024, the IMF projected China's 2024 growth rate to be 4.6 percent, which is 0.4 percent higher than the IMF's 2023 projection but lower than China's own projection of 5.2 percent. However, the IMF's long-term growth projections for China are more pessimistic, anticipating a drop to 3.6 percent by 2027 and a further fall to 3.3 percent by 2029. The IMF pointed out that China's ability to reverse the falling labor productivity in the midst of population collapse and diminishing returns on investment will determine the future of China's economic growth. The IMF further cautioned that without sweeping structural reforms of China's state-owned enterprises, the growth rate could dip below 4 percent within five years.[5] The Chinese economy is now facing a crisis of massive scale and complexity due to the precipitous drop in potential growth rate, grave demographic decline, pronounced economic polarization, and near-total lack of a social safety net.

Signs of Xi Jinping's faltering China Dream can be observed elsewhere too. The countries that participated in the Belt and Road Initiative are withdrawing one by one, and the AIIB is struggling under a massive debt burden. Furthermore, the ambitious internationalization of the renminbi seems dead in the water, with the share of the yuan in international settlement remaining at only around 2.5 percent.

The world is witnessing the onset of a clash between market capitalism and state capitalism. The United States is closely monitoring China as it accelerates the transition of the Chinese economy into one of state capitalism, even in the midst of a severe economic recession. It is difficult to tell whether this transition is cyclic, structural, or a combination of both. However, China is undergoing the first phase of structural reform and appears to be grappling with the dilemma between long-term socialist reform and short-term responses to market downturn. It is anticipated that the CCP, under the guidance of Xi Jinping socialism, will refuse to intervene in the market, opting instead to rectify the losses incurred by the failing market. Ironically, if China falls into the middle-income trap and its economic crisis worsens, the Xi Jinping regime may resort to adventurism, potentially including an armed invasion of Taiwan. A declining China can be more dangerous than a prosperous China.[6]

Meanwhile, there is the looming question of how well the United States can restore the strength of its industrial sector. The key factors will be the ultimate effectiveness of the "friend-shoring" strategy, along with efforts to restore domestic manufacturing and mass-production capacity to sufficient levels. Currently, the United States and the West are employing the de-risking strategy vis-a-vis China. This strategy has three components: reducing dependency on China, restricting technology exports to China, and simultaneously encouraging trade with China of nonrestricted goods and services. The overarching aim of the strategy is to maintain non-hostile relations with China while gradually mitigating potential flashpoints.

"De-risking" is inherently more ambiguous compared to "decoupling." The scope of the US de-risking policy depends on how the term is interpreted. As a result, each nation must make educated guesses as to what it means and respond as best they can. Some may perceive it as limited economic distancing, while others may view it as something more akin to decoupling.[7]

The United States appears to have adopted "de-risking" as a conciliatory response to the grievances of its friends and allies amid the protracted US-China competition. This approach has also had the added benefit of reviving high-level dialogues with China. De-risking has a softer tone than decoupling, making it easier for the United States to communicate its intentions to China. The adoption of this term indicates that US policies pertaining to the global supply chain, next-generation cutting-edge technology, and national security will be more nuanced.

The Chinese leadership perceives the intentions behind de-risking as aimed at suppressing the development of Chinese technology and minimizing the impact of the US-China competition on the US economy. The United States is drawing a clear line around technologies it deems critical to its national security ("small yard") to impose firm restrictions on Chinese access to such technologies. By setting this strategic perimeter ("high fence"), the United States seeks to mitigate the risks resulting from Chinese growth and development. However, this does not signal a shift in the fundamental structure of the US-China competition.[8]

China is expected to respond to the US de-risking strategy with an "eye for an eye" approach, seeking to minimize the impact of the US sanctions through aggressive diplomacy. However, in view of the conspicuous disparity between the comprehensive national powers of the two countries, along with China's need to maintain good relations with Europe and secure direct foreign investments to keep its economy afloat, China lacks the means to sustain an aggressive response to US containment policies.[9]

UNITED STATES ON A CRITICAL PATH

How can the United States persuade its fence-sitter allies to return to being strong allies?

The United States increasingly finds itself on a lonely footing. The US-led rule-based international order is under threat from authoritarian powers such as China, Russia, Iran, and Saudi Arabia. Some old friends of America are becoming "fence-sitters" in the competition between the United States and China, and even allies are recalculating their national interests, despite their shared values with America. Their cost of survival is the decisive factor in determining whether to remain faithful to the US-led liberal international order.

To some extent, the United States has brought this state of affairs on itself. During the era of Pax Americana in the post–Cold War world, the United States sought to shape the world in its own image. However, this resulted in strategic setbacks and weakened alliances. The once formidable power of the United States, based on military might, the dominance of the dollar, techno-logical prowess, and soft power, began to wane relative to other global play-ers. In the process, the United States lost its credibility in the international community, largely due to domestic political polarization and the resulting uncertainty in its foreign policy. Especially concerning is the prospect of Donald Trump returning to the presidency. Such an outcome could plunge the international community into uncharted territory. A second Trump presi-dency would likely exacerbate the fragmentation of global leadership, leading to chaos within the international order. The world will watch anxiously to see whether Trump will reorient his policies toward order and away from the tumultuous approach that characterized his first term. Ultimately, the impli-cations are disconcerting: there are few international issues that the United States can unilaterally address anymore, nor are there any that can be resolved without US involvement.

Dr. Richard N. Haass, the president emeritus of the Council on Foreign Relations, was asked during his retirement interview with the New York Times in 2023 about what keeps him up at night and what seems to be the most serious danger to the security of the world right now. He answered rue-fully, "It is us, the US itself." When I met Dr. Haass in the fall of last year, I asked whether he still loses sleep at night worrying about the state of world affairs. He answered:

America used to involve itself as a mediator in disputes all over the world and fight to protect the world order America believes in, but it is now time to worry about America itself. Our domestic politics is failing to provide the direction America should aspire to go, and America is losing its capabilities to solve global problems. America elected President Trump, and despite the fact that his policies and behaviors were not becoming of America, many Americans still support him. I lose sleep at night desperately hoping America can recover from the realities it is facing. Whichever path China takes, it will remain America's competitor for many years into the future, and unless our domestic politics regains its balance, we will find it difficult to contain China. That the liberal international order America has been leading is descending into chaos and disor-der is regrettable, but more importantly, if America wishes to restore it, America must revamp its strategic thinking.

China in Peril

What made China's spectacular economic growth possible was a governance structure that was both willing and able to adopt a market economy. The symbiosis between China's socialist political structure and capitalist market economy made its historic economic growth possible, with the CCP promoting the market economy while the latter bolstered the stature of the CCP. However, during his second term in office, Xi Jinping began dismantling the foundation of the separation between socialist politics and the market economy, a promise that the rest of the world had trusted in since the days of Deng Xiaoping. In its place, he began implementing his "China Dream," a unique amalgamation of Chinese aspirations and determinism. The result has been a growing instability in China's politics, economics, society, and foreign policy.

Xi Jinping's narrow focus on reviving China's identity has hindered his ability to address the true perils within the Chinese economy with the necessary flexibility. Moreover, locked into a silo mentality fixated on identifying the US' weaknesses, Xi's China has spent the last decade under the illusion that it would soon surpass the US economy. As a result, China has pursued unrealistic US policies and is now inevitably heading down the path toward a liquidity trap, middle-income trap, and low-growth trap.

Now, as the Korea-US-Japan trilateral pact becomes increasingly institutionalized, China finds itself in an increasingly difficult position. China is becoming a lonely player in East Asia, having failed to mend relations with Korea after the 2016 THAAD crisis. Added to this is the US strategy to expand the Korea-US alliance beyond military cooperation to encompass economy, industry, and technology. This has inevitably led to broad restrictions on the export of semiconductor products and technology to China, despite semiconductors being Korea's single most important export item to China. From the Korean perspective, the difficulties are twofold: China is also limiting the export of scarce materials and other items to Korea.

KOREA-CHINA RELATIONS AT THE CROSSROADS

Economic and Industrial Complementarities under Duress

Korea-China relations, which have been based on Korea's simultaneous fear of and reliance on the Chinese market over the past two decades, are now undergoing a fundamental transformation. The Korea-China industrial complementarity is weakening, and competition is on the rise. China's share of Korean exports, which once stood at 25 percent, has fallen to 19 percent and is expected to further drop to 15 percent in the foreseeable future. How and where will Korea make up the difference? This is the central question in Korea-China relations going forward.

Nevertheless, the Chinese economy will continue to influence the future of the Korean economy. China will also continue to exert sizable influence on any future developments regarding the denuclearization of North Korea, or conversely, the potential nuclearization of South Korea. However, China is expected to adopt a relatively neutral stance within the China-North Korea-Russia trilateral relationship, serving as a counterweight to the Korea-US-Japan trilateral pact. If this is the case, it would be wise for Korea to uphold the notion of coexistence in its relations with China.

China's Infiltration and Intrusion Offensive against Korea

Following the expansion of the security environment over the Korean Peninsula from the Korea-US military alliance to the Korea-US-Japan trilateral pact, Korea-China relations have noticeably cooled. Outwardly, China is applying pressure on Korea by flaunting its close relationship with North Korea and by jointly exercising its veto power with Russia at the UN Security Council. China is also turning a blind eye to North Korea's rabid rhetoric about going beyond nuclear provocations and preparing for war. At the same time, however, China is continuing its efforts to entice Korea to remain in the no man's land between itself and the United States. All the while, China's efforts to infiltrate and influence Korean society and political circles continue.

China's strategic offensive against Korea is comprehensive. Its infiltration and intrusion efforts span the entire spectrum, encompassing aspects of national identity such as ancient history, culture, and even food, to economy and national security. Koreans are left wondering what China's motives might be: Is China merely seeking to bring Korea into its sphere of influence, or does it aim to assimilate the Korean Han (韓) race under the Chinese Han (漢) race as it did with the Manchus, Tibetans, and Uighurs? We must remain vigilant and keep a close eye on every word or action that comes out of China. Considering China's state-sponsored initiatives like the Northeast Project of the Chinese Academy of Social Sciences (東北工程, since 2002) under the umbrella of the CCP's "cultural engineering" (文化工程) program, it would be naive to regard Chinese advances as benign.

Despite its seemingly charming allure, Xi's "Community of Common Destiny" forms the theoretical basis for China's exercise of "sharp power," which is most evident in its infiltration and intrusion campaigns. This wave of offensives is undeniable, especially when it comes to the economy. China's economic crisis was what drove Korea-China diplomatic normalization in 1992, and the economy remains central to China's geopolitical calculations vis-a-vis Korea. China's strategy toward Korea appears to be centered around solidifying Korea's economic reliance on China—a structure where China can do without Korea, but Korea cannot survive without China. Korea experienced this strategy in action in the aftermath of the 2016 THAAD crisis. In imposing economic sanctions against Korea, it is said that China selected items of Korea-China trade that would not adversely impact the Chinese economy.

Another target of China's infiltration and intrusion offensive is the Korean people themselves. China is actively recruiting the support of key figures in Korea, adhering to Sun Tzu's adage, "Know your enemy." The methods employed by China in trying to influence the Korean people are expansive and meticulously executed. China targets movers and shakers in politics, business, academia, and the media. In the business world, priority is given to those with technological expertise. It is not surprising that the technology sector is a prime target considering the precarious state of China's semiconductor technology. As a result, the Korean technology sector is rife with Chinese industrial espionage activities, carried out through local human intelligence assets. In politics, China's top priority is to weaken the Korea-US alliance and draw Korea into China's orbit. It is no secret that China approaches members of the Korean National Assembly with patience and diligence. China's interest in Korean academia is even more pervasive. High-profile academics have access to valuable intelligence and wield substantial influence over Korean public opinion.

Korea's Choice: Strengthening Korea-US Alliance While Seeking Long-Term Coexistence with China

Korea aims to strengthen the Korea-US alliance and enhance trilateral security and technological cooperation among Korea, the United States, and Japan, departing from its traditional "security with America, and economy with China" strategy. This new policy direction is intended to safeguard Korea's sovereignty, survival, and identity while also pursuing mutually beneficial policies with China.

Korea's Long-term Strategies toward China

In pursuing this new strategic direction, Korea remains firm on the following six principles:

1. Korea will no longer tolerate China's treatment of present-day Korea as a subordinate state, reminiscent of its vassal status from past centuries. China should not resort to economic coercion as it did during the THAAD deployment incident.

2. Korea will firmly reject unjust demands from China that contradict the essence of the Korea-US alliance. This is a given in Korea-China relations. Both countries need to respect each other's red lines.

3. Korea will strongly object if China chooses to turn a blind eye to or collaborate in North Korea's nuclear provocations. Korea expects China to remain neutral in inter-Korean relations.

4. Economic interdependence between Korea and China shall not be weaponized against Korea, whether diplomatically or otherwise. China should uphold its commitment to the separation of politics and business.

5. Korea will firmly safeguard its sovereignty, survival, and identity. It will oppose any and all Chinese policies that challenge these core interests.

6. Korea and China shall jointly pursue the common goal of long-term coexistence, thereby contributing to peace and prosperity in Northeast Asia.

Distinguish China and Xi Jinping

Imagine a China beyond Xi Jinping. Much of the world, Korea included, is familiar with the China of the Deng Xiaoping era, and disheartened by the China of the Xi Jinping era. Even if Xi Jinping manages to bring the current economic crisis under some semblance of control, the people of China will likely be more forward-thinking than what Xi Jinping envisions. Under this scenario, not even Xi Jinping himself can predict how long the Xi Jinping era will last.

One way or another, the Xi Jinping era will come to a close. The new leader who emerges from the tumult is likely to be much more responsive to the demands of the Chinese populace. They will likely refrain from ideological control and diplomatic isolation, potentially guiding China toward a per capita GDP of USD20,000 by the 2030s. Therefore, we must not make the mistake of equating China with Xi Jinping. In the long run, CCP rule will inevitably become more flexible and friendly to the people, with a foreign policy geared toward greater cooperation. As such, both Korea and the United States should formulate strategies for long-term coexistence with China beyond the era of Xi Jinping.

If and when such a time arrives, Korea will face heightened competition, which may be friendly but existential in nature. The global value chain competition between Korea and China is expected to intensify, particularly as Chinese high-tech industries increasingly vie for dominance in the global arena. However, at the very least, neither Korea nor the United States will be competing with a big, bad bully.

Korea and China: Managing the Three Differences

Three fundamental gaps characterize the Korea-China relationship. The first is the difference in values and identity. If this gap widens, economic complementarity alone will not support cooperation on the question of national survival.

The second is the gap in technological advancements. Korea and China are entering into an intense value chain competition. China, which was once situated downstream in the global value chain (GVC) in the 1980s, has now turned the tables; its technological advancements are beginning to challenge Korea's position in the GVC upstream. If this challenge succeeds in upending Korea's GVC position, China may be able to exert overwhelming influence over Korea in all areas, even beyond the economy. Thus, it is critical for Korea to maintain an advantage in cutting-edge technologies and niche proprietary technologies to ensure peace in Korea-China relations.

The third is that the relationship between Korea and China moves inversely to that of the United States and Korea. Whatever happens in the trilateral relationship among Korea, the United States, and China inevitably exerts an oversized impact on Korea-China relations. Naturally, worsening US-China relations put pressure on Korea-China relations. China vehemently opposes Korea leaning toward the United States. If Korea-US relations strengthen, China is likely to attempt either appeasement or coercion to pry Korea away from the United States. Conversely, if Korea-US relations sour, China may either become more friendly toward Korea or revive its historical view of Korea as its vassal state, displaying disrespect by interfering with Korea's internal affairs or foreign policy. Either way, Korea faces the risk of bullying and disrespect from China.

Therefore, to effectively manage Korea-China relations within acceptable bounds, Korea must safeguard its identity and values, stay a step ahead of China in cutting-edge technology, and expand the Korea-US alliance based on mutual trust. At the same time, Korea should reject antagonistic impulses and instead adopt a patient and cautious approach to facilitate long-term coexistence with China.

In this multifaceted and interconnected framework, maintaining an "arm's-length relationship" will support the future of Korea-China relations. This entails a careful balancing of respective national interests to ensure coexistence. The key challenge for the Korean industry and government is how to preserve or replace the complementarity that has existed between the two nations. Korean industry must remain one step ahead of Chinese industry in cutting-edge technology and niche proprietary technology. Meanwhile, China must refrain from any further attempts at bullying or interfering with Korean sovereignty or foreign policy.

KOREA-US ALLIANCE: BEYOND THE CAMP DAVID DECLARATION

The most significant achievement in recent diplomatic and security efforts was the trilateral summit between the United States, Korea, and Japan, leading to the Camp David Declaration in August 2023. While its significance was not fully appreciated at the time, the agreement and declaration made by the leaders were a stroke of genius, revealing their foresight and wisdom in the field of diplomacy, especially given the current global situation.

This will serve as the cornerstone, the shield safeguarding the liberal world order led by the United States. The KORUS alliance of the past seventy years is the fruit of countless sacrifices and enormous costs. The United States can take pride in today's Korea, having played a crucial role in Korea's journey to where it is now. But in the next seventy years, the two countries face grave global challenges together. They must join hands as equal partners and stand together in defending the liberal international order from the challenges of authoritarian communism, most seriously, China's Xi Jinping regime and the North Korean nuclear threat.

The essential prerequisites for a sustainable, strong Korea-US alliance are as follows.

a. Sailing in the Same Boat with a Shared Dream

Korea and America have lived through the past seventy years side by side. But more challenges and adversities lie ahead. The two countries will continue overcoming all such difficulties together, sailing in the same boat with a shared dream.

As the two countries move forward in strengthening the KORUS alliance for the next seventy years, we must now undertake qualitative changes that differ from what has been done thus far. However, the United States is increasingly finding itself in a position where it must become a partner of coexistence with Korea in various fields. This partnership extends well beyond security issues pertaining to the North Korean nuclear threats, encompassing a wide range of areas. In reality, US policy toward Korea is evolving from a *variable* among tactical choices to a *constant* in the equation for America's future strategy.

b. Trust Building

For the hallowed Korea-US alliance, shaped in the crucible of the Korean War, to persist into the twenty-first century, both Korea and the United States must continue to build trust assets by upholding the promises made between the two nations. It is a prerequisite to convince the Korean people that US' commitment to its security guarantee is ironclad. US domestic politics also require a strong commitment toward the KORUS alliance, and legislative confirmation is necessary. In short, Korea and the United States must build and maintain an unshakable trust asset between the two countries.

Partisan politics in the United States have occasionally spurred demands for the withdrawal of American troops from Korea, inciting fears among Koreans that the US commitment to defending Korea could waver at any moment. US domestic politics necessitates a steadfast commitment to the Korea-US (KORUS) alliance, with legislative ratification being imperative. Conversely, it is also true that some experts in the United States voice significant frustrations regarding the shifting stance of the Korean government, which tends to fluctuate with the political ascendancy of either liberals or conservatives.

Foreign policies are subject to sudden gusts of domestic politics, public sentiment, and especially populism. However, the existential importance of the KORUS alliance for both Korea and the United States is too great to be left exposed to the changing winds of domestic politics. This alliance must be understood as a bipartisan imperative, which does not change, regardless of which administration comes into power in both Korea and the United States.

In the context of America's national security amid the threats posed by China and Russia, Korea is firmly on the front lines. The United States operates the world's largest and most advanced military base in Pyeongtaek, positioned directly at China's doorstep. Furthermore, the security cooperation among the United States, Korea, and Japan needs to be intensified, given the volatile security environment in Northeast Asia.

The United States needs to understand why a large majority of the Korean people want a revision of the ROK-US nuclear agreement. This issue goes to the heart of the trust between the two nations. Koreans feel that North Korea is a de-facto nuclear power, and they believe that the US "nuclear umbrella" alone does not guarantee protection. They are calling for nuclear weapons capability for Korea, akin to the "nuclear sharing" arrangement between the United States and NATO, or at a minimum, a "non-weaponized (nuclear) deterrence" similar to the Japanese and German models. Above all, Koreans are anxious about the shifting nature of the US nuclear guarantee with each new US administration. Koreans are hopeful that the activities of the Nuclear Consultative Group (NCG) established between Korea and the United States in July 2023 will lead to concrete measures that they can rely on for deterrence and protection against the North Korean threat.

c. Balancing of National Interests

Korea and the United States must strike a "balance of respective national interests" rooted in "shared values." Enhanced trilateral cooperation among Korea, the United States, and Japan will inevitably affect Korea's trade relations with China. Particularly, if Korea aligns with US policies to restrict exports and imports to and from China, the consequences could be profound and far-reaching.

Most crucially, immediate geopolitical benefits might lead to significant geoeconomic risks for Korea. Should Korea's trade dependence on China decrease from 25 percent to 15 percent, the country will urgently need to compensate for this 10 percent shortfall in some manner. Hence, it is vital not to become engrossed solely in security concerns but to address the geoeconomic dimensions of the alliance with adaptability and practicality.

Ultimately, the alliance between Korea and the United States will excel in the advanced semiconductor market. By combining the US leadership in advanced scientific and technological development with Korea's high productivity and mass production capabilities, the synergy effect of a technology alliance in cutting-edge semiconductors, quantum computing, and AI will be remarkable. The realization of such economic complementarity represents the next frontier for the Korea-US alliance in the twenty-first century.

d. Economic Complementarity

The Korea-US alliance, born as a military alliance, should now be expanded to encompass the economy, industry, and technology. Korea has enjoyed economic complementarity with China for nearly forty years. However, as China's industrial structure undergoes a fundamental shift, this complementarity is becoming increasingly irrelevant. Korea remains deeply apprehensive about China's domestic issues and maneuvers, as well as its international behavior.

In the context of the durability of the future KORUS alliance, the industrial complementarity between the two nations is becoming a critical strategic issue. Korea's national interest is directly linked to US national interests in the context of America's global strategy. This is no longer a matter of choice but an indispensable consideration.

Furthermore, Korea's industrial and technological advancements have positioned it as an ideal partner in building a fundamentally new level of cooperation anchored by the Korea-US alliance. The revival of the manufacturing base is at the forefront of US economic policies, and it is here where Korea emerges as a perfect partner, with its industrial technology, high-productivity manufacturing ecosystem, and mass production capability.[10] In this process, the United States and Korea are likely to foster the most productive and effective partnership. Many thinkers and policymakers in Washington agree on this observation, and this complementarity is rapidly becoming the center of US foreign policy discussions.

This complementarity is becoming the key for the continuation of the Korea-US alliance into the twenty-first century. Therefore, the term "complementarity" is poised to become a new keyword in the KORUS alliance. Over the next seventy years, the KORUS alliance will evolve into a closer complementary relationship. By fully leveraging this complementarity, the Korea-US alliance will evolve into an expanded alliance relationship as the two nations set sail together toward another seventy years of shared dreams.

Reinforcing Self-Strength for Korea's Future[11]

It is erroneous to think that Korea and China are "like-minded" neighbors, either historically or culturally. It is also unwise to assume that the United States will be Korea's ultimate "guardian" or "lender of last resort." All nations prioritize their respective national interests. If Korea adopts a posture contrary to its core interests, neither the United States nor China will hesitate to turn its back on Korea. What Korea must do, then, is to escape from between a rock and a hard place and become a nation indispensable to both powers.

The demands of the era are driving Korea to shape its own destiny. However, it must be recognized that Korea cannot determine its own fate without the cooperation of both the United States and China. This is the stern reality. First and foremost, Korea must maintain sufficient power to protect its territory and sovereignty, and to check and defend against major powers. Taking cues from the likes of the Netherlands, Israel, and Switzerland, Korea should carve out a unique role for itself as an indispensable nation. Korea should also seek to strengthen cooperation with potentially hostile powers. It is imperative for Korea to refrain from allowing its security and foreign policy to be dictated by fragmentary frames of domestic political conflict. Korea must keep a finger on the pulse of international diplomatic and security developments. Finally, the Korean people must remain united; even the threat of China's might will be futile against them.

In navigating this journey, Korea must effectively communicate its red lines to China. Korea must ensure that China recognizes Korea's national sovereignty and identity and that it does not mistake Korea as the "weakest link" in the web of US alliances. On the other hand, Korea must not make the mistake of losing sight of China's core national interests or offending its national pride. Korea must engage with China on equal terms, demonstrating respect while upholding firm principles. On a practical level, Korea should cultivate relationships with the upper echelons of the CCP and the inner circle of the Xi Jinping administration. These will be the critical tasks in the future management of Korea-China relations.

Regarding the United States, Korea needs to clearly express its principles regarding its national interests. Korea must persuade the United States of Korea's geopolitical and geoeconomic imperatives. Korea must cultivate and maintain high-level channels of communication in Washington. This will determine the success or failure of future Korean-US policy.

Matrix of Korea-US-China Trilateral Relationship

Korea-US-China trilateral relations are characterized by a delicate balance of convergent and divergent interests among the three actors. These interests are intricately intertwined, creating numerous points of potential conflict. However, the presence of economic interdependence has thus far prevented such points of potential conflict from escalating into physical confrontations. As such, an oversimplified approach based solely on power comparison fails to capture the complexity of the relationship.

As the US-China competition becomes increasingly structured and protracted, Korea, the United States, and China are all looking for ways to maximize their own national interests and values. It is here where a lack of comprehensive understanding of the crisscrossing interests and demands among the three actors can lead to a narrow strategy of attacking others' vulnerabilities and failure to explore opportunities for cooperation and fair competition.

Part III, therefore, starts from a perceived need for a structured analytical tool to understand the complexities of Korea-US-China relations—a trilateral analytical tool dubbed the "Matrix." The Matrix provides a bird's-eye view of the intersecting lines of interests, competition, conflict, interdependence, demands, and cooperation in geopolitics, geoeconomics, and geotechnology among the three nations involved. It facilitates mathematical and detailed analysis while also highlighting latent conflicts and future areas of competition, thereby helping formulate policies proactively.

Using the Matrix, Part III seeks to identify the intersecting demands and policies in Korea-US-China trilateral relations as well as the interwoven latent conflicts that result from them. Security concerns, economic interests, and guardrails against potential clashes will be included in this analysis. By comparing the intentions and capacities of the three actors, the goal is to help prevent strategic miscalculations by any one actor.

Utilizing the trilateral matrix analysis can help mitigate the pitfalls of strategic imbalance that often result from binary analyses by identifying how such analyses affect the third actor. It can also help prevent oversimplification of trilateral relations by identifying the changes in alliance dynamics, potential risks, and areas of contention in the trilateral relationship. The objective is to construct a composite three-dimensional picture of evolving alliances, emerging strategic challenges, and latent risks, thereby facilitating the development of proactive policies to avoid or mitigate security dilemmas, alliance disintegration, and economic catastrophes.

This section examines the demands each country is placing on the other two and what points of conflict exist among them. Korea-US-China trilateral relations consist of 3x2 dual relationships: US-China, US-Korea, China-US, China-Korea, Korea-US, and Korea-China. The objectives of this analysis are to determine strategies to avoid conflicts and catastrophes, as well as discover pathways toward coexistence and productive competition.

Faced with Xi Jinping's China, Korea and the United States need to delineate areas of conflicting interests, competition, and cooperation, and to share their respective strategic visions. By identifying the shared and divergent interests between the two nations vis-a-vis China, they forge a path toward a sustainable future for their alliance.

The overriding objective behind using the Matrix analysis is to maximize the benefits of convergent interests and minimize the negative effects of divergent interests by examining the complexity, conflicts, and interdependence inherent in the trilateral relations. A simplistic approach to Korea-US-China relations may lead to more uncertainties and damage the credibility of the United States among its allies, which China could exploit to its advantage. It is hoped that the trilateral matrix analysis introduced in Part III will enable Korea and the United States to make more nuanced strategic calculations and uncover pathways for coexistence within the framework of the Korea-US alliance into the future.

Overview

World Order and Indo-Pacific Challenges (Contingencies) in the Xi Jinping Era

Byung-se Yun

POLY-CRISES AND THE FRAGMENTATION OF THE WORLD ORDER

"Fire everywhere." This was the expression used by a senior EU official at the Korea–Europe conference in Brussels late last year to assess the world situation following the Hamas attack on Israel. It echoed my remarks to the same audience the day before concerning the poly-crises unfolding on multiple fronts—geopolitical, geoeconomic, and geotechnological.

This convergence of views, however, only partially captures the ongoing debates among policymakers and opinion leaders around the world aiming to diagnose the current state of world affairs and offer a prognosis for the future. Some focus on the symptoms, while others search for the root causes of what may be termed tectonic changes in the world order or *Zeitenwende*, where conflict and confrontation tend to prevail over cooperation. It is no coincidence that the 2024 World Economic Forum (WEF) held in January even chose "permacrisis" as the overarching question for leaders this year.

In particular, key stakeholders in the current international order, such as the United States, the EU, China, the G7, and G20, along with various like-minded groupings, as well as institutions like the IMF and the European Central Bank, have in recent years offered their official stances on the state of the fragmenting world and outlined their strategies to address it.

These strategies have ranged from unilateral, bilateral, and minilateral to collective responses, manifested in the form of national reports, joint declarations, new concepts or perspectives, and resolutions in regional and global institutions. Paradoxically, many of these stakeholders do not dispute the historical juncture we are currently facing. For example, the United States

formally stated in its 2022 National Security Strategy (NSS) that the post–
Cold War era has ended, defining the current state of the world as a historical
inflection point. Similarly, Germany declared that the world had reached a
Zeitenwende after the Russian invasion of Ukraine. China formally adopted
the phrase "great changes unseen in a century." EU leadership declared that
"happy globalization" is over.

In essence, there is an apparent consensus that the old order—the post–
Cold War era—is over. However, regarding the nature and causes of the
current disorder or fragmentation, there is a significant divergence of views,
including on the notion of a rules-based international order. This divide is
particularly evident when it comes to our future trajectory. No one is certain
when a new order will take shape and what form it will assume—bipolar or
multipolar, a power shift or a transition of order, unavoidable yet manageable
competition, or full-blown catastrophic conflicts.

Uncertainty seems to be the key word, with the only exception centering
around the hard-nosed projection that US-China strategic competition will be
a long game or prolonged process lasting several decades and that the next
decade will be decisive. This may also be the case with other conundrums,
such as the Russia-Ukraine war, the Israel-Hamas war, the North Korean
nuclear and missile threat, and a possible conflict over the Taiwan Strait.

Depending on their position—whether in the Global West, Global East,
or Global South—stakeholders tend to rely on their own prisms to view the
divided world. The fragmentation of the regional and global order into camps
or like-minded coalitions is rapidly becoming a "new normal" across various
domains, as we witness a proliferation of minilateral, plurilateral, subregional,
and cross-regional groupings. The Global West and its partners have become
more united than ever over the last two years, especially in the wake of the
Russia-Ukraine war. The Biden administration has formed new coalitions, such
as the Quad, AUKUS, IPEF, and the US-Korea-Japan trilateral mechanism, and
has strengthened the G7, NATO, and Indo-Pacific networking. The EU, Japan,
Korea, and Australia are also assuming greater roles in these groupings.

However, the Global East and some key players in the Global South, such
as BRICS, are no less active in seeking global redistribution of influence and
resources and the reconfiguration of the world, with China at the helm. Many
other countries in the Global South remain unaligned with any specific power
group but are rather multialigned, positioning themselves as swing states or
fence-sitters. This behavior was well manifested in the voting patterns of
UN General Assembly resolutions on Russia's aggression against Ukraine in
recent years, as well as in the surge of new applications and countries on the
waitlist to join the expanded BRICS.

Whether we call this situation the end of Pax Americana or not, we are
witnessing a steady yet complex diffusion of power among major powers, as

well as between major powers and new centers of power, including middle powers. This new reality is being increasingly recognized by many US policymakers and opinion leaders. Ambassador William Burns, director of the CIA, wrote an article in *Foreign Affairs* this January titled "Spycraft and Statecraft: Transforming the CIA for an Age of Competition," stating that China's rise and Russia's revanchism pose daunting geopolitical challenges "in a world of intense strategic competition in which the United States no longer enjoys uncontested primacy."

As a result, what we see through the typical US or Chinese prism is not necessarily the entire picture but rather only some significant pieces of the puzzle or a few legs of a gigantic elephant. This seems to be a major reason why many international think tanks have started to focus more on diverse aspects of the world order or disorder. The NEAR Foundation also launched an inaugural Global Survey on the World Order titled "Quo Vadit Mundus?" last year and published a report that includes a list of "competing responses in a fragmenting world," going beyond the scope of just the United States and China, as well as their allies and partners.

That report was intended to complement and reinforce other major annual global reports, such as those published by the World Economic Forum (WEF) and the Munich Security Conference, with a greater focus on the Indo-Pacific region.

Diverse Diagnoses and Prognoses on the World Order/Disorder

This endeavor was inspired by several schools of thought in the policy community and academia across key regions that highlight a serious and fundamental question about the risks posed by the current transition and ways to prevent the ongoing crises and looming dangers in a fragmenting world from escalating into larger and more widespread problems and conflicts in the coming decade of peril.

At one end of the spectrum, we encounter a warning from former secretary of state Dr. Henry Kissinger, who cautions that the United States and China are in a "classic pre–World War I situation" that could lead to conflict. To a lesser extent, Dr. Richard Haass, president emeritus of the Council on Foreign Relations (CFR), suggests that a G2 conflict no longer seems like a remote possibility. He further stresses that "the frightening gap between global challenges and the world's responses, the increased prospects for major–power wars in Europe and the Indo–Pacific, and the growing potential for Iran to cause instability in the Middle East have come together to produce the most dangerous moment since World War II. Call it a perfect—or, more accurately, an imperfect—storm."

In fact, President Putin echoed this assessment in October 2022 when he addressed the Valdai Discussion Club, a conference of international policy experts, stating, "We are standing at a historical frontier: Ahead is probably the most dangerous, unpredictable, and, at the same time, important decade since the end of World War II." Professor Hal Brands joined the ranks by warning that today's regional conflicts resemble those that precipitated World War II.

In terms of the Indo-Pacific order, it is not yet on the brink of hot war or armed conflicts like in Ukraine and the Middle East, but there are a growing number of warning signs and strategic signals indicating that this region could become entangled in consequential challenges in the foreseeable future. Pacific waters are no longer pacific.

Like a black hole, the ongoing strategic competition between the United States and China is exerting such a powerful influence that it impacts nearly every aspect of interstate relations in the region. This influence transcends domains—not only geopolitical but also geoeconomic and geotechnological—adding to the already existing ideological and historical divides. Both sides are now fiercely competing to expand their coalitions, blocs, or like-minded groups. The regional landscape is further complicated by the Sino-Russia "no-limits strategic partnership" and emerging Russia-DPRK strategic coordination, unseen in the last twenty years. Whether these developments will lead to another axis of revisionists remains to be seen, but formal or informal trilateral coordination among the three cannot be ruled out.

At the other end of the spectrum, we are witnessing a noticeable pattern of indifference or hedging in response to geopolitical or geoeconomic competition or conflicts among major powers or their blocs.

This kind of response has been clearly demonstrated by a series of recent behaviors among geopolitical swing states, or fence–sitters, in the Global South. Ambassador Shivshankar Menon, former National Security Advisor to Indian prime minister Manmohan Singh, elaborated on this uncomfortable and harsh reality: "For them, the war in Ukraine is about the future of Europe, not the future of the world order, and the war has become a distraction from the more pressing global issues of our time. In this sense, for many parts of the globe, a year of war in Ukraine has done less to redefine the world order than to set it further adrift, raising new questions about how urgent transnational challenges can be met."

The "2023 Munich Security Conference Report[1]," also pointing to the fact that a considerable number of actors have not condemned Russia's aggression, stressed that "it is not enough for us to simply defend the status quo. If we do not address the resentment that countries in Africa, Latin America, and Asia feel toward the international order, which has not always served their interests, we will struggle to win the fence–sitters as allies in the defense of key rules and principles."

The NEAR Global Survey Report[2] echoes the MSC report's call for a vision of the international order that garners broader support, as well as a larger coalition of responsible stakeholders if we want to preserve the core principles of this order. Initiatives like the G7's Build Back Better (BBB) World Initiative, the EU's Global Gateway Strategy, and other similar initiatives, including several Indo-Pacific strategies, represent timely or belated efforts to address this weak link.

Somewhere between these two ends of the spectrum, we encounter more subdued or over-the-long-haul diagnoses regarding the nature of competition among states. For Ambassador Bilahari Kausikan, former permanent secretary of state of Singapore, competition is the more historically normal state of relations, and even the US-China strategic competition is not an existential threat. He stresses that "the war in Ukraine and U.S.–Chinese rivalry conform to established patterns of state behavior. The uncertainties and risks they pose—the possibility of accidents getting out of hand and nuclear escalation, among others—are what former US secretary of defense Donald Rumsfeld termed 'known unknowns.' Most countries successfully navigated previous phases of great–power competition, and many of them even grew and prospered under those harsh conditions. If they remain calm and exercise reasonable prudence, there is no reason they cannot do so again."

Professor Li Cheng at the University of Hong Kong[3] is also more straightforward in his projection of the future. He stated, "It will be naive to believe that the ongoing Russia-Ukraine war and the Middle East conflict are the last wars to reshape the international order or to think that [these] sort of bloody wars will be limited to Continental Europe or the Middle East."

Last but not least, it has become increasingly important to factor the impact of domestic politics and the leadership roles of key stakeholders like the United States and China into the cause of the ongoing fragmentation of the world.

Many in the United States regard China under President Xi Jinping as a revisionist power in terms of assertiveness and its stance on the rules-based international order. For instance, the original United States Innovation and Competition Act of 2021 (USICA) and "The Longer Telegram," written by an anonymous conservative author, reflect this perspective. Coercive wolf warrior diplomacy and the Belt and Road Initiative (BRI) are viewed as tools for changing the status quo that was previously well maintained by Xi's predecessors.

In a similar vein, incoherence, discontinuity, and reversals in the US's China-policy are criticized as key factors accelerating that fragmentation. Dr. Kissinger echoed this sentiment in his interview with *The Economist* in May 2023.[4] He argued that "the understanding forged between Nixon and Mao was overturned after only 50 of those 100 years by Donald Trump. He wanted to inflate his tough image by wringing concessions out of China over trade. In policy, the Biden administration has followed Mr. Trump's lead, but with liberal rhetoric."

Dr. Ivo Daalder, CEO and former president of the Chicago Council on Global Affairs, strongly criticized the Trumpian "America First" foreign policy as "the abdication of American global leadership" and called for "the roles of U.S. friends and allies to save the fracturing international order by leveraging their collective might to take on greater global responsibility." He further warned at the NEAR Global Conference in December 2023,[5] "The world order that was underpinned by a strong, democratic, outward-looking, alliance-sustaining United States, we may not have come January 2025, because we may have a president who doesn't believe in any of those things. The world that America made is also a world that America can unmake—not China, not Russia, not India. The U.S. election in November will be a contest about the nature of America's role in the world for the first time since 1940, actually 1936."

This concern was shared seven years ago by many US partners in the Indo-Pacific, such as ASEAN. Ambassador Tommy Koh of Singapore, one of the most senior and wise men in the region, expressed his thoughts upon hearing the inaugural speech of President Trump, stating, "we live in a very confusing world. It is confusing because the U.S., which has historically championed free trade and globalization, has abandoned both in favor of protectionism. The 45th president of the United States, Donald Trump, declared in his inaugural address that protection will lead to great prosperity and strength."

Dr. Richard Haass, president emeritus of the US Council on Foreign Relations, elaborated on what we should do and why. In his book *Foreign Policy Begins at Home,*[6] he submits that "the biggest threat to the United States comes not from abroad but from within—how well the nation continues to fare on the global stage will depend largely on whether the United States puts its own house in order."

The reality is that the phenomenon of "my country-first" parochial nationalism is now contagious, and even several US partners tend to resort to populism-oriented politics. It no longer stops at the water's edge.

INDO-PACIFIC CHALLENGES/CONTINGENCIES AND THE DECADE OF LIVING DANGEROUSLY

Implications of the Fragmenting World Order On the Indo-Pacific and vice versa

Despite the Russia-Ukraine and Israel-Hamas wars, the United States regards the Indo-Pacific as the epicenter of twenty-first-century geopolitics and places US-China strategic competition at the top of its agenda.

Fierce competition is now in full swing in the Indo-Pacific—on both geoeconomic and geotechnological fronts—between the United States and China, as well as their respective coalitions.

Flashpoints are once again in the limelight, with the potential to ignite big, medium, and small fires. Economic security has emerged as a new focal point in this post–post–Cold War era. Technology is now rapidly driving geopolitics, as emphasized by former Google chairman Eric Schmidt. Artificial Intelligence (AI) is expected to fundamentally alter the landscape of future warfare unless properly controlled.

On a geopolitical plane, as the USINDOPACOM commander regularly reports, the United States is focused on addressing key threats while managing lesser concerns with due attention. The 2022 US National Security Strategy elaborates on why this should be the case.

Among other things, regarding a possible conflict between the United States and China, former prime minister of Australia Kevin Rudd, a longtime China hand and incumbent ambassador to the United States, has long advocated for managing strategic competition between the two countries in a responsible manner. He has also suggested ways to avoid a war between them.

The Biden administration seems to have echoed such a strategy through its 2022 National Security Strategy and Indo-Pacific Strategy. At the US-China summit in San Francisco, California in November 2023, President Biden stressed the importance of ensuring that the strategic competition between the United States and China "does not veer into conflicts." This sentiment was preceded by months of diplomacy.

As a result, President Biden and President Xi were able to agree on some form of modus vivendi, including the resumption of military dialogue. The outcome is a modest yet meaningful arrangement consisting of security guardrails and some areas of cooperation, such as climate change.

The White House claimed that the outcome in California represents the US commitment to "manage strategic competition responsibly."

Big and Small Fires Over the Geopolitical Horizon

Similar to poly-crises on the global level, the various flashpoints in the Indo-Pacific, including the Korean Peninsula, Taiwan, and the East and South China Seas, appear to be competing for attention. Which flashpoint will be the first to face the fall of the sword of Damocles? In other words, which contingency should be given top priority for deterrence and prevention? Will these actions be simultaneous or sequential? Moreover, will the contingencies affect only key stakeholders or virtually drag in all stakeholders?

These questions are pertinent to the success or failure of integrated deterrence or collective defense, as well as the combined capability of allies and partners to deal with multiple wars or conflicts of similar or different natures—conventional, nuclear, or gray-zone.

The 2018 National Defense Strategy shifted the US Department of Defense's (DoD) focus toward the challenges to US security interests posed primarily by China, followed by Russia. It emphasized the importance of restoring the Joint Force's warfighting edge against these major power competitors and stressed the necessity of clearly prioritizing these objectives over lesser interests.

Taiwan Contingency

The United States has its eyes on multiple fronts, but the Taiwan contingency tends to take precedence over others, despite the absence of a bilateral defense treaty. This is likely due to its long-standing political commitment and the implications of the Taiwan contingency on the possible first hot war between two great powers since the end of World War II, as well as on the potential collapse of the world order.

All the public commitments and actions by the US administration, Congress, and the military in recent years substantiate this tendency. According to a Carnegie Endowment for International Peace (CEIP) report of 2023, the congressional groundswell of debate and action on China is reminiscent of the period from 2001 to 2004 when Congress responded to the al-Qaeda terrorist threat. The sheer number of legislative proposals on China, and the legislative proposals that continue to be introduced as of fall 2023 all suggest that Congress will continue to seek ways to push back hard against China, strengthen military deterrence, cut off China's access to US resources, and perhaps even alter US policy on Taiwan.

Some sense of Congress's current military priorities can be gleaned from the 2023 report of the select committee. For example, Congress passed the CHIPS and Science Act (H.R. 4346) with bipartisan support in 2023 despite simultaneous high levels of partisan rancor. It also established the Select Committee on the Strategic Competition between the United States and the Chinese Communist Party (CCP).

From a standpoint of deterrence and defense, US Indo-Pacific Command's (USINDOPACOM) reports and activities are eloquent testimony to where their focus lies. For example, Admiral John C. Aquilino, commander of the USINDOPACOM, testified on March 21, 2024, stating that "all indications point to the PLA meeting President Xi Jinping's directive to be ready to invade Taiwan by 2027. Furthermore, the PLA's actions indicate their ability to meet Xi's preferred timeline to unify Taiwan with mainland China by force if directed." He further mentioned the increasing interconnectedness of the threats posed by three adversarial regimes—the People's Republic of China

(PRC), Russia, and the Democratic People's Republic of Korea (DPRK)—implying synchronization of threats to the United States and its allies.

One recent projection of a grim scenario came from Professor Li Cheng, a longtime Brookings Thornton Center director and current director of the Center on Contemporary China and the World (CCCW) at the University of Hong Kong. At the NEAR Global Conference on World Order in December of last year, he warned of a potential war in Asia and the Pacific. He stated, "If there is a war between the U.S. and China over Taiwan, it will be the first AI war in human history, and it is imperative for the international community to address the highly consequential challenges relating to AI."

Most of the 2023 NEAR Global Survey participants across the globe identified this contingency as a top priority among others.

DPRK Threat and a New Axis with Its Patrons

South Koreans regard North Korea's nuclear and missile capabilities and its preemptive use doctrine as existential threats and prioritize these aspects accordingly. In response, the United States and South Korea reached a landmark agreement in 2023 to establish the Nuclear Consultative Group (NCG) and started engaging in joint nuclear and strategic planning, as well as the implementation of US extended deterrence. Additionally, three Camp David Summit joint statements in 2023 provided a new framework to counter the North Korean threat more efficiently among Korea, the United States, and Japan.

Nevertheless, given the DPRK's diversified means of threatening the Republic of Korea-United States alliance, lesser contingencies also draw attention due to their interconnectedness and the nature of multidomain warfare. Such contingencies could arise from premeditated actions or escalate from smaller conflicts into larger ones, by either miscalculation or mistake.

Kim Jong-un, the North Korean leader, likely believes that this is the most favorable external environment since he took power in 2012. In an increasingly fragmenting world, he finds himself in high demand from Russia and China, who see more value in North Korea vis-a-vis their confrontations with the United States. It is no wonder that Kim has joined the chorus of calls characterizing the current international order as a "New Cold War."

Amid the prolonged Ukraine-Russia war, Russia has once again tilted toward North Korea after more than two decades of maintaining a balancing policy toward both Koreas. Last October, Russian foreign minister Sergey Lavrov made it clear during his visit to Pyongyang that their bilateral relationship has "reached a qualitatively new and strategic level."

In response to Kim Jong Un's meeting with President Putin of Russia last September, North Korea is known to have begun shipping munitions to

Russia in support of the conflict with Ukraine in exchange for diplomatic, economic, and military concessions.

President Putin's visit to Pyongyang in June, this year become a crowning moment in upgrading their relations to unprecedented heights. As Kim dubbed this relationship a foremost one, Putin's visit is likely to not only expand the scope of their agenda but also institutionalize such bonds, perhaps in strategic and other dimensions, as their new treaty on comprehensive strategic partnership stipulates.

The arms transactions and multipronged collaboration between Russia and North Korea have tended to reinforce real or perceived concerns about on-again, off-again triangular coordination among Korea's three northern neighbors. It could manifest as a division of labor concerning the "triple storms" coming from North Korea, Ukraine, and the Taiwan Strait. Alternatively, it could take the form of intervention by Russia and China in a DPRK-provoked crisis.

USFK commander Paul LaCamera testified on the latter point at the Senate Armed Services Committee on March 21, 2024, stating, "Due to geographic proximity, there is significant potential for third-party intervention and influence on the Korean Peninsula should a crisis occur, specifically from the PRC (Korea lies within the PRC's Anti-Access/Area Denial defensive layers) and Russia."

This seems to be the context in which Kim Jong-un redefined the inter-Korean relationship as "two belligerent states at war," marking a significant departure from the decades-long principle of unity of the Korean nation. Defining South Korea as "enemy number one," Kim announced that North Korea "will accelerate preparations for a major upheaval to secure the entire territory of the South by mobilizing all physical means and capabilities, including nuclear forces."

Various follow-up measures are now underway on military, diplomatic, and inter-Korean fronts to materialize his new declaration, alongside destabilizing actions such as missile launches, nuclear tests, support for Russia, and sanctions evasion.

The recent 2024 Annual Threat Assessment report by the US intelligence community accurately dissected the motives behind the DPRK's investment in military might. It stated, "North Korea's military will pose a serious threat to the United States and its allies by its investment in niche capabilities designed to provide Kim with options to deter outside intervention, offset enduring deficiencies in the country's conventional forces, and advance his political objectives through coercion."

The DPRK's latest move represents Kim's multifaceted game plan to fully exploit the ongoing global poly-crises, including the prolonged Ukraine-Russia War, intensifying US-China strategic competition, the Israel-Hamas war, tensions around the Taiwan Strait, and the forthcoming US presidential election.

For Kim, the US presidential election could be another opportunity to tilt the balance to his advantage and deal with the United States directly. Regardless of the election outcome, Kim will attempt to shut out South Korea and pursue nuclear weapon state status, leveraging the DPRK's nuclear and missile capabilities as bargaining chips. A nuclear arms reduction deal will be advantageous for Kim. No deal or no negotiation will deter him, as long as he can continue to bolster his nuclear arsenal and rely on renewed solidarity with his two big saviors to counter ROK-US-Japan security ties. Recently, Kim has also sought to play Japan against South Korea, hinting at the possibility of a DPRK-Japan summit.

Whether such a move will escalate into a full-fledged war, trigger lesser conflicts like those in 2010, or result in another round of summitry or interim steps, the ROK-US alliance will face a critical juncture and a new, complex geopolitical environment reminiscent of the Cold War era.

East and South China Seas

In the South and East China Seas, Beijing's maritime presence near contested areas and its military bases in the Spratly Islands have been sources of persistently high tensions for many years between the PRC and its neighboring competing claimants. These tensions increase opportunities for miscalculation, even though stakeholders likely prefer to avoid direct conflict.

A series of coercive collisions with Filipino supply ships by the PRC near the Second Thomas Shoal in the South China Sea raises the prospect of inadvertent escalation by either side. This could thrust the United States and China into an unwanted but escalating spiral of retaliation.

The decades-old tension between China and Japan over the Senkaku/Diaoyu Islands occasionally shows signs of aggravation due to actions and counteractions between Chinese ships in the proximity of the islands and Japan's Self-Defense Force ships monitoring their activities. The United States has affirmed that they are covered by the US-Japan alliance. A Chinese move against them would threaten a major escalation.

Some South Pacific states are becoming acute targets for co-option by China and the United States due to their military value for Chinese ships.

India-China

According to the 2024 Annual Threat Assessment report, the shared disputed border between India and China will remain a strain on their bilateral relationship. While the two sides have not engaged in significant cross-border clashes since 2020, they maintain large troop deployments, and sporadic encounters between opposing forces risk miscalculation and escalation into armed conflict.

Growing Chinese, DPRK Nuclear Arsenal and a
New Nuclear Age in the Indo-Pacific

In November 2021, the Pentagon's annual China Military Power Report (CMPR) to Congress projected that China could possess 700 deliverable warheads by 2027, and possibly as many as 1,000 by 2030 (US Department of Defense 2021, 90). The 2022 Pentagon Report increased the projection even further, claiming that China's stockpile of "operational" nuclear warheads had surpassed 400 and will likely reach about 1,500 warheads by 2035 (US DoD 2022b, 94). The rapid growth of the arsenal underscores the urgent need for trilateral nuclear arms reduction talks, which China opposes.

The United States and the USSR came to accept arms control efforts by the late 1960s/early 1970s. Both grasped that missile and nuclear warhead arms racing was unwinnable and costly. This model could be applied to a Sino-US confrontation too, but not in the near future due to strong Chinese objections.

The Indo-Pacific is entering a new nuclear age. This is fueled by the Chinese arms buildup, the threat of Russia and North Korea to use nuclear weapons in conventional military contingencies, and North Korea's development of tactical nuclear weapons, among other reasons.

Steady Evolution Toward Regional Contingency
Planning and Collective Defense

The persistence of ongoing and emerging or potential conflicts has triggered a new debate in the United States and among its allies and partners regarding their capacity and readiness to cope with multifront wars or conflicts. President Biden's oft-repeated assertion that the United States would defend Taiwan in the event of a Chinese invasion has intensified the debate about whether the alliance should broaden its scope to include regional contingency planning.

Notably, former United States and South Korean military leaders have highlighted the need to consider how an armed conflict in the Taiwan Strait would impact the alliance. For instance, former US secretary of defense Mark Esper cautioned that South Korea is unlikely to be able to avoid being drawn into such a conflict. Additionally, some retired Korean military leaders have argued that the alliance should consider the possibility of simultaneous contingencies arising in both the Taiwan Strait and on the Korean Peninsula.

In this context, General Paul LaCamera, commander of US Forces Korea (USFK) and South Korea-US Combined Forces Command, testified in a confirmation hearing in May 2021, remarking that "USFK forces are uniquely positioned to provide the commander of [the U.S. Indo-Pacific Command] a range of capabilities that create options for supporting out-of-area

contingencies and responses to regional threats." He reiterated similar sentiments on several other occasions.

It is also noteworthy that in his testimony to the US Senate Armed Services
Committee in March 2024, he emphasized the rationale behind having over
28,500 American service members forward deployed to the ROK, stating that
"our presence within Korea is advantageous; it is better to be prepared *from
within Korea* rather than to fight our way in."

As the commander rightly pointed out in the same testimony, the Washington Declaration and the Camp David Summit of 2023 helped to expand
alliance cooperation and reinforce US extended deterrence commitments.
Particularly, the three joint statements from the Camp David Summit provided a comprehensive framework to "consult expeditiously" among the
United States, Japan, and Korea in response to "challenges, provocations
and threats in the Indo-Pacific region." Despite disclaimer provisions, this is
a remarkable development when compared with the final language adopted
by the United States, Japan, and NATO in their respective national security strategies and New Security Concept documents. While stopping short
of using the term "threat," the United States, NATO, and Japan identified
China as "America's most consequential geopolitical challenge," a "systemic
challenge to Euro–Atlantic security," and the "greatest strategic challenge,"
respectively.

But in a world of poly-crises with finite resources, policymakers must
grapple with painful trade-offs between their priorities. For example, these
trade-offs have already impacted the annual joint military exercises between
United States and ROK Marines this spring. Additionally, US support for
Ukraine is known to have diverted some weapons away from Taiwan.

In this regard, RAND made a valid recommendation that the USAF should
prepare to cooperate with allies and partners in defending against a wider
range of contingencies, rightly recognizing that US allies and partners are
concerned about a broader set of security issues and may interpret a narrow
US focus on Taiwan as an indication that the United States is not committed
to their security more broadly.

There are divergent views on the sequencing of two contingencies. While
some experts typically envision a scenario where a Taiwan Strait contingency
occurs first, leading to North Korea carrying out some sort of provocation,
others believe that the reverse could occur (i.e., a conflict on the Korean Peninsula could prompt Beijing to attack Taiwan).

After all, the scenario of "simultaneous conflicts" in the Taiwan Strait and
on the Korean Peninsula dates back to the Korean War in the 1950s. Today,
a growing number of experts are emphasizing the likelihood of a two-front
conflict—regardless of who initiates it.

Though there are some calls for an Asian NATO, we still have a very long way to go due to different views on the conditions and environment for collective defense arrangements. Instead, the 2023 NEAR Global Survey suggested the expansion of several US-led minilateral groupings in the Indo-Pacific, such as AUKUS and the Quad, and possibly the Five Eyes alliance as well.

Economic Security and Technology Competition Between the United States and China

Great power rivalry and concerns about economic security are changing the economic landscape that policymakers face. Adjusting to a world where national security interests are more prominent in economic issues than they have been in the past decades will be key for stakeholders to successfully navigate the changing economic environment.

The structural nature of the tech competition between China and the United States may not be reversible at this point as it is too intricately tied to their views of national security. Nevertheless, full decoupling is neither feasible nor the objective of the United States, as seen in its "small yard, high fence" approach.

The real question is how far and how willing the United States and China are in separating their technology ecosystems. This raises a question for other states too, that is, whether there may be scope for other states with interests in the technology field to work together to mitigate or persuade the United States and China to scale back their competition.

Even the small window of possible cooperation will be fragile as long as it is held hostage to the broader relationship between the two countries.

Against this backdrop, it is noteworthy that Professor Li Cheng projected at the NEAR conference last December a long list of ten areas that could be related to economic and tech war between the two great powers in the coming years:

- Trade and investment
- Industrial chains and supply chains
- Oil, natural gas, and the new energy lines
- Two credit card payment systems
- Financial and currency systems
- 5G and internet system
- Satellite navigation systems
- Outer space exploration programs
- Military and ideological blocs
- A possible hot war in the AR era

He said that this dark scenario, of course, is not inevitable and it may not result in full-fledged decoupling, but some of these decoupling or decoupled blocs have already emerged, some even completed, and others may accelerate in the years to come.

STRATEGIC RAMIFICATIONS OF CONTRASTING APPROACHES BY TWO GREAT POWERS ON THE GLOBAL AND REGIONAL ORDER

Much to the relief of the United States, China, and the rest of the world, the US-China Summit in San Francisco provided a timely opportunity to reduce tensions stemming from the two countries' strategic competition across various domains. During the summit, some agreements were reached on implementing guardrails and enhancing global governance, including the resumption of military dialogue and commitments to address climate change.

Despite the modest agreement on a modus vivendi to responsibly manage the competition for the time being, it would be unrealistic to expect this summitry to pave the way toward a strategic compromise or bargain anytime soon considering the two countries' complex strategic rivalry over the regional and global order. Strategic distrust remains, and the potential re-election of Donald Trump could upend any legacy left behind by President Biden, including his China policy on managed competition or some aspects of the Indo-Pacific strategy.

The hard truth is that regardless of the outcome of the upcoming US presidential election, the leadership roles of the two great powers will greatly impact the global and Indo-Pacific order. Their respective visions and strategies will shape the geopolitical and geoeconomic landscape, as well as the configuration of forces among the Global West, Global East, and Global South, each representing pieces of the fragmented world.

Therefore, it is essential for the United States, China, and their partners to understand how each other's vision and approach will fare in terms of garnering support from the rest of the world and reshaping the global and Indo-Pacific orders.

Chinese Vision and Strategy

"Planet Earth is big enough for the two countries to succeed, and one country's success is an opportunity for the other." President Xi Jinping made this statement to President Joe Biden during the summit held on the sidelines of the APEC summit in California in November of last year.

What is often overlooked in Xi's remarks, however, is the strong and renewed message couched in his oft-used metaphor, which carries significant implications for the emerging new world order/disorder and the evolving nature of US-China relations in terms of the competition for global leadership.

Let's first contrast Xi's remarks above with his previously frequently used metaphor that "the vast Pacific Ocean has enough space for the two large countries of China and the United States." This phrase was widely recognized as Xi's proposal for what is termed "a new type of great power relationship," and he repeated this phrase on several occasions, including during the Obama-Xi summit in Palm Springs, California, in 2013. Xi has been advocating for this concept since he formally assumed power in 2012, and even earlier during his time as vice president.

Xi's expansion of China's *lebensraum* from the Pacific to the entire globe serves as a symbolic declaration to the United States and the rest of the world that China now considers itself a great power on par with the United States. His specific five-pillar proposal to President Biden includes an enhanced role for the two great powers in world affairs, rather than confining their mutual interests solely to the Indo-Pacific. During a press briefing in San Francisco, Foreign Minister Wang Yi made it clear that "building a community of common destiny for all mankind is in line with the mainstreams of history and a move in the right direction to strengthen global governance."

Paradoxically, as the United States pivots and rebalances to Asia and the Pacific and advocates for an Indo-Pacific strategy regardless of changes in government, China is now highlighting its global vision and ambition to extend beyond the Pacific more than ever. It appears that President Xi is paraphrasing President Biden's "360-degree strategy" outlined in the 2022 National Security Strategy and reconceiving Wilsonian globalism in a Chinese way.

As a matter of fact, China's twin strategies of "a new type of great power relations" and a "community of common destiny for all mankind" have progressed in tandem since 2013. These concepts were formally endorsed as two key goals of Chinese foreign policy by the CCP's 19th NPC in 2017. Furthermore, the latter was formally incorporated into the preamble of the Chinese constitution in 2018.

Now, these concepts are being coherently translated into more specific policy formulas across three domains: the Global Security Initiative (GSI), the Global Development Initiative (GDI), and the Global Human Community/Civilization Initiative (GHCI/GCI). These policies are supported by the Belt and Road Initiative, which celebrated its tenth anniversary in 2023, and the strategy of a "new type of international relations" targeting the rest of the world.

President Xi appears to emulate Chinese military strategist-cum-philosopher *Sun Tzu* to justify his Chinese Dream or official vision of the "Great Rejuvenation of the Chinese Nation" not just on a regional level but also on a global stage. He seems to employ both out-boxing and infighting tactics to gain an advantage over the US Indo-Pacific strategy, benchmarking his founding predecessor Mao Zedong. To support this approach, China emphasizes global multilateralism to contrast with the United States' emphasis on alliances and minilateralism or sub-regionalism.

Whether these concepts or initiatives are nothing but slogan politics is of little consequence, as China tends to justify them through tangible actions. Similarly, the ongoing debate over whether China is still a rising power or a risen power does little to enhance our understanding of the ongoing reconfiguration of forces amid the poly-crises at this historical inflection point, or *Zeitenwende*. What truly matters is that China is taking full advantage of the end of Pax Americana and the emergence of multipolarity to outcompete and outmaneuver the United States in its quest for the Chinese Dream across all domains.

China's Global Overreach versus US Minilateralism and MAGA

One recent notable example is China's leading role in expanding BRICS from five countries to eleven countries in 2023, only thirteen years after its formation. As of now, more than two dozen countries are known to have applied for either formal membership or some kind of association. Current and prospective members include close strategic partners of the Global West, such as India, Saudi Arabia, and the UAE. In the midst of global poly-crises, the geopolitical and geoeconomic implications of this coalition of the Global East and key members of the Global South cannot be underestimated.

The voting patterns of the UN General Assembly on resolutions concerning Russia's aggression against Ukraine in recent years serve as another disappointing reminder of how fence-sitters or geopolitical swing states are likely to behave now and in the future on matters involving a fundamental breach of the UN Charter by a major power. This was a key factor prompting both the MSC annual report and the NEAR Global Survey Report of 2023 to alert the Global West to adopt a more proactive approach and stronger role vis-à-vis the Global South in addition to strengthening and expanding like-minded groups and coalitions.

US Vision and Strategy

Inward-looking MAGA Runs the Risk of Being Overshadowed by MCGA on the World Stage

If the call for "Make America Great Again" (MAGA) is not coupled with a coherent regional and global strategy, it could be an invitation for China to further expand its strategic space. It could unintentionally help "Make China Great Again" (MCGA). China would lose no time in filling any leadership vacuum left by a US retreat to Fortress America. This concern has been raised by many US think tankers and policymakers, especially globalists.

In this regard, a series of US strategy reports published in 2022, including the National Security Strategy, National Defense Strategy, and Indo-Pacific Strategy, are timely responses to growing criticism, such as "The Longer Telegram" of 2021, which argued that the United States lacks an overall comprehensive China strategy.

The 2022 National Security Strategy highlights that "the PRC presents America's most consequential geopolitical challenge. Although the Indo-Pacific is where its outcomes will be most acutely shaped, there are significant global dimensions to this challenge." The report goes on to state, "Competition with the PRC is most pronounced *in the Indo-Pacific*, but it is also *increasingly global*. Around the world, the contest to write the rules of the road and shape the relationships that govern global affairs is playing out in every region and across economics, technology, diplomacy, development, security, and global governance."

In fact, the World Economic Forum (WEF) and Munich Security Conference, two major global forums, in addition to international institutions like the UN and G20, spent much of their time in 2024 discussing ever-worsening global challenges. With more than two dozen topics on the agenda, US-China competition and the Russia-Ukraine war accounted for only a fraction of their concerns. During his WEF speech, the Chinese new premier, Li Qiang, seized an opportunity to advocate for globalism and multilateralism.

In this context, the 2022 NSS aptly pointed out that "while this competition is underway, people all over the world are struggling to cope with the effects of shared challenges that cross borders—whether it is climate change, food insecurity, communicable diseases, terrorism, energy shortages, or inflation. These shared challenges are not marginal issues that are secondary to geopolitics."

This perception is in line with the original intent of the US Innovation and Competition Act, which defined the nature of the US policy of strategic competition with China as part of a broader strategic approach to the Indo-Pacific and the world.

The question remains whether both sides can place common interests on the same table and how to broaden that common ground. In the wake of the San Francisco summit, the meeting in Thailand in January between National Security Advisor Jake Sullivan and State Councilor Wang Yi appeared to be intended to initiate a journey toward a more cooperative, albeit long and rocky, road.

THE WAY FORWARD

As discussed in previous chapters, the strategic competition between the United States and China across various domains is at the top of our agenda, impacting numerous stakeholders in the emerging international order, including South Korea. Nevertheless, it is not the only defining factor in our universe. There are several other driving factors, along with a new configuration of forces, shaping our environment in a world facing multiple simultaneous challenges.

The Need for a Comprehensive Examination of the Whole Matrix

The nature and complexity of the poly-crises we face demand a holistic and diversified perspective, spanning various issues, domains, regions, and time frames. Such a comprehensive examination of the entire matrix or gamut of the international order, encompassing the US-China competition, will enable us to differentiate between small and big fires, tectonic shifts, and short-lived shocks, and discern our immediate, medium, and long-term priorities.

Standing at a historic inflection point, we must brace ourselves for the emergence of a new regional and global order over the long haul. A top priority at present is to navigate the dangerous transition over the next decade without triggering catastrophic consequences all the while expanding the scope of common interests.

Navigating the Dangerous Transition

To effectively navigate this transition, key stakeholders in the Indo-Pacific and Euro-Atlantic regions must exercise leadership by implementing a far-sighted strategy that balances competition, confrontation, and cooperation.

While maintaining strong deterrence is essential, every effort should be made to minimize the negative effects emanating from the collision of visions and strategic interests.

The strategic competition between the United States and China seems unavoidable. However, it must not escalate into a direct military clash over regional flashpoints such as the Taiwan Strait, the Korean Peninsula, or the East and South China Seas, whether by miscalculation, escalation, or accident. The same is true for other stakeholders involved.

In this context, it is at least reassuring that both President Biden and President Xi appear to recognize the need for a competitive symbiosis. President Biden has pledged to manage the relationship responsibly so as "not to veer into conflict." Additionally, President Xi publicly stated on several occasions, including as recently as this March, that *"the 'Thucydides Trap' is not inevitable."* Such messages serve as impactful strategic signals and should be echoed by the next president of the United States, who will take office early next year.

Recommitment to a Rules-based International Order

As an overarching guidepost, the international community should not only restore but also revitalize a rules-based international order on all fronts. It should respond firmly to rule-breakers, particularly those who resort to the use of force in violation of the UN Charter and international law, including maritime regulations. The damage done to the UN Charter and the UN Security Council following Russia's aggression against Ukraine and the DPRK's habitual breaches of international law is only the tip of the iceberg.

In an era marked by the multifaceted nature of global confrontations, it is crucial to share the vision of a liberal international order with as many countries as possible, especially those in the Global South, to garner support from a broader coalition of responsible stakeholders who can commit to the core principles of this order.

The roles of key stakeholders are crucial in fostering an international environment that facilitates the provision of global public goods while simultaneously maintaining their leadership in such an endeavor. Middle powers, in particular, have demonstrated their tact in navigating these turbulent waters. Additionally, more focus should be placed on the confrontation between status quo and revisionist powers.

In this regard, existing international multilateral institutions such as the UN may need to adapt through reforms, but there is no reason to abandon them altogether.

It Is Cooperative Global Agendas, Stupid

Despite the ongoing fragmentation in the world order, there remains a shared recognition of the potential for cooperation on global challenges of common interest, such as climate change, pandemics, natural disasters, nuclear nonproliferation, environmental sustainability, energy transition, and food security.

Strategic competition and bloc-to-bloc rivalry can be mitigated through efforts to provide such regional and global public goods.

As such, it is in everybody's interest to maintain the relevance of global governance by expanding its scope to encompass global challenges that affect every country and every generation.

Economic Security and Supply Chain Resilience

The intertwining of national security with economics and technology is becoming the new reality in the emerging techno-polar order or tech-driven geopolitical landscape.

Nevertheless, there is also widespread recognition that close economic ties, particularly between the United States and China, as well as between China and the Global West, make complete decoupling impossible. In this regard, the shift from decoupling to de-risking and diversification at the unilateral (US), bilateral, and multilateral (G7) levels serves as an important strategic signal.

It is also vital to continue refining the "rules of the road," which should accurately reflect the changing dynamics within the economic and technological orders. Failure to do so could lead to the breakdown of these guidelines. The weaponization of economic interdependence and over-securitization both run the risk of triggering a Mutually Assured Destruction (MAD) trap in a world of complex economic interdependence. Any use of coercion must be met with a firm and collective response.

Toward a Synchronized Indo-Pacific Strategy

The United States and other Indo-Pacific states have offered a convincing rationale ("free, open, and inclusive") for the new Indo-Pacific order. However, the challenge now lies in implementing this vision through tangible actions. In this regard, both the Quad and AUKUS statements, followed by the three joint statements released after the Camp David Summit in August 2023, can serve as valuable cornerstones in fostering solidarity and cooperation among like-minded states in the Indo-Pacific. These initiatives should be implemented in sync, reinforcing each other in a way that preserves regional peace and prosperity.

However, it is also true that China and some other countries in the region have different rationales and approach to the regional order.

Therefore, the United States and China must continue efforts to foster stability in the region and build strategic trust. This applies not only to United States and Chinese allies and partners but also to the new US administration set to take office after the presidential election in November.

The potential negative impact on US-China relations stemming from the domestic politics of major powers, whether related to government, party, legislation, leadership style, ideology, or public opinion, must be carefully managed to avoid upending the entire relationship.

Among other measures, it is essential to bilaterally enhance deterrence systems, including nuclear deterrence and assurance. In addition, minilateral security cooperation (e.g., the Quad, AUKUS, ROK/US/Japan trilateral mechanism), organized flexibly with a small number of like-minded states, should be bolstered. These groupings should be prepared to address multiple, sometimes interlinked, contingencies that could arise in Northeast Asia and the East and South China Seas, either simultaneously or sequentially alongside crises in other regions.

The steady expansion of measures aimed at establishing a modus vivendi/operandi (i.e., guardrails, firewalls, or crisis management mechanisms) is essential for stabilizing efforts to address matters related to colliding visions and strategic interests.

In this endeavor, both regional mechanisms and inclusive plurilateral coalitions (e.g., Asia Pacific Economic Cooperation, East Asia Summit, Association of Southeast Asian Nations dialogue partnership, Regional Comprehensive Economic Partnership, Comprehensive and Progressive Agreement for Trans-Pacific Partnership) could serve to broaden the scope of common interests.

Rebuilding Multilateralism for a New Era

Existing multilateral economic and security systems are imperfect and sometimes dysfunctional, as evidenced by the decline of the UN system, yet they are still considered valuable.

It is noteworthy that different countries have different perceptions regarding the meaning of multilateralism.

While traditionalists regard global multilateral institutions such as the UN and WTO as the primary drivers of the international order, the United States and other like-minded states are increasingly relying on minilateral and plurilateral arrangements as the basis of the current international order.

Therefore, it would be beneficial to align minilateral frameworks with subregional, regional, and global cooperative frameworks, such as the G7 and G20, as well as existing global institutions like the UN. This would allow these arrangements to complement and reinforce each other during the shaky transition period of weakening multilateralism.

Many stakeholders believe that regional institutions and/or minilateral groupings are necessary to supplement, rather than replace, multilateral institutions. However, these stakeholders also believe that multilateralism and multilateral institutions are in need of reform.

Role of Middle Powers and South Korea's Place in the World

Key stakeholders in the international system, including middle powers, may converge or diverge in their views and approaches on various issues of common concern and interest, even when they share common objectives like peace and prosperity, a rules-based international order, or multilateralism.

Regarding the possible roles of the region's middle powers, opinions vary on the degree of influence that these countries have over shaping and managing poly-crises, including the US-China rivalry. There does seem to be a notable distinction between US allies and partners on the one hand and nonaligned or independent middle powers on the other.

The former group tends to think that America needs strong partners in the Indo-Pacific to serve as security, economic, and diplomatic force multipliers when confronting regional challenges, and that middle powers could play a pragmatic facilitating role.

The latter group, primarily comprising countries in Southeast and South Asia, leans more toward a dialogue-oriented approach and tends to encourage compromises between major powers and contesting claimants. Some of these nations opt for fence-sitting or hedging roles in an attempt to maintain favorable relations with all major powers.

As for South Korea, in 2022, the new government under President Yoon adopted an ambitious and future-oriented global strategy dubbed the Global Pivotal State (GPS) initiative, alongside an Indo-Pacific Strategy. Both strategies aim to expand Korea's diplomatic horizon beyond the Korean Peninsula and Northeast Asia, encompassing the entire region and the world across various domains.

They are well aligned with the regional and global strategies of the United States and its partners across the world. At the current stage, these strategies do not necessarily conflict with China's regional and global strategies.

The ROK-US relationship has matured into a "global, comprehensive, and strategic alliance" and is now stronger than ever. However, South Korea and China have also maintained a strategic cooperative partnership for more than the last two decades, despite experiencing several ups and downs in recent years.

In an era marked by poly-crises and the ever-deepening strategic competition between the United States and China, South Korea is called upon to assume a more significant role in the region and the world, in line with its enhanced stature and capability.

Navigating the turbulent waters of the Indo-Pacific and the world presents a daunting task not only for the current Yoon government but also for future Korean administrations. However, as former British prime minister Winston Churchill admonished, "Kites rise highest against the wind—not with it." South Korea, no longer a shrimp between whales, has the responsibility and the potential to be a rule-shaper, not just a rule-taker.

Part I

WILL IT BE SMOOTH SAILING FOR THE XI JINPING REGIME?

Chapter 1

Xi Jinping's Third Term and Updates in China's Inner Politics

Yang Gabyong

Xi Jinping's third term has begun. His priority in 2023 was the reform of the CCP and government institutions, and in 2024, policy adjustments to support economic recovery and a renewed open-door policy. At the center is the authoritarian leader, Xi Jinping. The Xi Jinping regime is centered on such stated precepts as *Community of Common Destiny* and socialism with Chinese characteristics, and Chinese nationalism. These precepts manifest themselves in the form of expansionism and interventionism. Coupled with his domestic integration policies, Xi Jinping's regime poses an unprecedented challenge to Korea. It is in this complex and precarious strategic environment *vis-a-vis* China that Korea is struggling to protect its sovereignty, right to life, and identity. Thus, Korea is forced to redefine its national objectives in the short term, despite its wish to coexist peacefully with China in the long run, and yet, the Xi Jinping regime is finite, while China is permanent; therefore, we must analyze the new aspects of Xi's third term on this premise.

CONTINUATION AND EVOLUTION IN CHINESE POLITICS

Procedurally, the 20th Party Congress did not deviate much from the past ones. However, the 20th Party Congress was imbued with special meaning in two ways. First, it was to be the starting point of nation-building based on "modernization of socialism." Second, it was to be an auspicious commencement of the countdown toward the Centennial of the People's Republic of China (中华人民共和国成立一百周年), expected to fall on October 1, 2049.

This means a number of substantive changes. The 20th Party Congress Report amended the party guideline based on the changing state of affairs and reflected what the CCP considered the recent accomplishment of Marxism in China. This was a logical step beyond the mandate contained in the 19th Party Congress Report for the sinicization, popularization, and modernization of Marxism. In addition, the 20th Congress included the new political concept of the Governance of China with rational principles (治國理政), calling for a *Chinese style* of governance with a focus on the continuing fight against corruption and establishment of the exemplary model (作风建设). To bolster the ideological foundation for these lofty objectives, the 20th Congress added provisions for the education of the Party History, New Chinese History, History of Reform and Openness, and History of the Development of Socialism in the History of the Chinese Nation (中華民族史). But the reinforced assessment and enforcement regime will also mean a more rigid bureaucracy.

The emphasis on the History of the Chinese Nation (中華民族史) is closely related to Xi's focus on Chinese unification. His objective is to unify Hong Kong, Macau, and Taiwan with China by highlighting the nationhood of the Chinese people and suppressing ethnic separatist movements, as represented by his new banner slogan, Community of Chinese Nation (中華民族共同體).[1] In his Chinese New Year greetings delivered during his inspection tour of Tianjin in February 2024, he made a conspicuous point of addressing the ethnic Chinese of Hong Kong, Macau, Taiwan, and other Chinese diaspora. He is attempting to embrace all ethnic Chinese in what he considers Chinese nationhood and use the same in his drive for the unification of China. Nationhood itself has become an ideology.

Another important reason behind emphasizing the History of the Chinese Nation (中華民族史) is to evoke nationalism and patriotism in the Chinese youth, thereby strengthening the statism of his rule. Indoctrination of nationalism and patriotism has been a focus of Chinese education since previous administrations. What Xi Jinping added was what he considers "Chinese culture." When his concept of Chinese culture is added to nationalism and patriotism, the result is a potent mix, a very useful tool for Xi Jinping to legitimize his rule and achieve his objectives. The downside of this explosive cocktail is that Xi Jinping's China may alienate the rest of the world with its obtrusive Chinese Exceptionalism.

DECISION-MAKING IN THE CCP

The 20th Party Congress reintroduced the term *Chinese-style modernization.* This concept is not significantly different from the idea of "growth" and "development" during the earlier reform and openness era. It is a concept for domestic consumption, meant to distinguish the Xi Jinping era from those that came before. As such, it is not to be understood in the international context. Nevertheless, the key aspects of "Chinese-style modernization" must be understood before one can understand how the Chinese government operates under Xi Jinping.

All checks-and-balance mechanisms relating to Xi's policy directions have been all but eliminated. Nothing stands in the way of implementing Xi's decisions any longer. Since the reorganization of the Politburo of the Central Committee and the Politburo Standing Committee at the 20th Party Congress, any vestiges of a debate culture or collective deliberation have disappeared. The Politburo, once a policymaking institution, has now become a ratification machine. All decisions are being made in committees where Xi Jinping is the chair. It has become institutionally impossible, for all intents and purposes, to counter Xi's thoughts and decisions.

The theoretical advantage of such extreme centralization of power is, of course, efficiency. The obvious disadvantage is that without deliberation among wise statesmen, one man, for better or worse, makes all decisions. This centralization of power in Xi Jinping is, in fact, accompanied by a state-sponsored personality cult, reminiscent of the Cultural Revolution under Mao Zedong.

Experimental policies will have no place in such a policymaking structure. Fear of retribution in case of failure makes the CCP bureaucrats and technocrats extremely reluctant to propose any new or creative plan of action. This, of course, is leading to the atrophy of the CCP institutions and the degeneration of the bureaucrat class.

The flip side of the coin is that with no one daring to speak up with any creative policy ideas, it is only the execution of policies that matters, not the propriety of policymaking processes. Even here, however, the ossification of the policymaking body is likely to lead to rigidity in the implementation of policies as well. Everyone fears retribution in case of a failure in implementing a policy, rather than the failure of the policy itself. With nobody willing to step up to the plate or voice independent opinions, China's policies and guiding ideologies are now determined solely by Xi's personal preferences and propensities.

People Relationship over Factionalism within CCP

The composition of the Politburo Standing Committee under the 20th Party Congress reflects the domination of Xi Jinping's acolytes rather than factional accommodation. Personal loyalty to Xi is what matters now. This spells the end of meritocracy (賢能政治) and the relevance of factionalism in Chinese politics. This in turn gives rise to speculation that any future political changes in China will occur along the fault line between the CCP and the people, rather than factional lines within the CCP.

The schism between the People's expectations and what the CCP can deliver is widening. For instance, the CCP announced in April 2023 that China had fully emerged from COVID-19, and the economy would soon rebound. The reality was, of course, much more stark; the economic growth rate fell during the second quarter of 2023. After announcing the youth unemployment rate of 21.3 percent for the same quarter,[2] the government has stopped reporting the youth unemployment rate altogether since then. The CCP clearly feared the widening chasm between what it can deliver and the people's trust.

The relationship between the CCP and the people can be summed up by an aphorism trending in China: government positions are inherited, wealth is inherited, and poverty is inherited (官二代, 富二代, 穷二代). The impact of the draconian lockdown measures under the zero-COVID policy on people's lives has exacerbated the decoupling between the party and the people, imposing a serious political risk on the Xi administration. This, of course, does not bode well for the Xi regime when many economists are projecting a hard landing for the Chinese economy. The Chinese populace is full of discontent, bemoaning the severe polarization along the socioeconomic fault line in particular. Adoption of a people-first policy would be advisable at a time like this.

Xi needs above all to secure legitimacy in the eyes of the people. Otherwise, the crisis of trust between the CCP and the people may lead to social unrest, threatening Xi's rule itself. If people's mounting discontent is not assuaged or managed, Xi is liable to lose control over China's populace. With deteriorating economic conditions, Xi Jinping's Orwellian social surveillance and control are losing support among the people, if not its very relevance. Social unrest bubbling up from deep discontent is all the more critical to a one-party state like China that has no election mechanism to confer legitimacy on the administration people have chosen. The only way for Xi Jinping to avoid a political catastrophe is to facilitate economic recovery, giving people some degree of affluence. The key words are, therefore, economy, public sentiment, and people's trust in the CCP. The relationship between the CCP and the people has supplanted the traditional factional politics in the CCP as the determinant of Chinese politics.

COMPOSITION OF THE NEW LEADERSHIP AND POLICY DIRECTIONS

Leadership Formation

On the surface, the technical procedures for the appointment of leadership in the 20th Party Congress did not significantly deviate from those of the previous congresses. Traditionally, the composition of the Politburo of the Central Committee and the Politburo Standing Committee used to be determined through factional balancing among the party elders, including the current and former Politburo Standing Committee members. However, the 20th Party Congress took place while all power was concentrated in Xi himself. The final appointments are likely to have been decided by Xi himself, despite titular collective feedback procedures. It was a brazen exercise in the *New Zhijiang Army* (習家軍) (aka Xi Jinping Faction) political appointment.

This change in the political landscape means that Deng Xiaoping's political legacy of factionalism among the Shanghai Clique (上海幫), Communist Youth League of China (共青团), and Crown Prince Party (太子黨) (aka Children of the Communist Aristocracy Party) is no longer relevant. The Politburo seats have been filled with those technocrats who are willing to carry out Xi's agendas faithfully and unquestioningly.

The number of Politburo members was reduced by one compared to that of the 19th Congress. The Politburo now consists of seventeen members, excluding the seven Politburo Standing Committee members. Among them, only Li Hongzhong (李鴻忠), Zhang Youxia (張又俠), Chen Min Er (陳敏爾), and Huang Kunming (黃坤明) kept their offices. All four of them are personally acquainted with Xi Jinping. The remaining thirteen members are new appointees. In particular, four former Politburo members from the 19th Party Congress, party secretary of Shanghai Li Qiang (李强), mayor of Beijing Cai Qi (蔡奇), party secretary of Guangdong Li Xi (李希), and Manager of the General Office of the Central Committee Ding Xuexiang (丁薛祥) were all promoted to Politburo Standing Committee members. Shi Taifeng (石泰峰) was promoted to Politburo member and became head of the United Front Work Department of the Chinese Communist Party, infamous for repressing religious freedom and ethnic minorities.

On the other hand, at the 14th National People's Congress in 2023, the new premier Li Qiang failed in his appointment of the ministers for the State Council of the PRC. Of the twenty-six ministerial positions, all but National Development and Reform Commission chair Zheng Shanjie were appointees from the tenure of his predecessor, Premier Li Keqiang, including Minister of Foreign Affairs Qin Gang and Minister of Justice He Rong. As a result, Premier Li Qiang is said to have even less power than fifth-ranking member of the Politburo Standing Committee, Cai Qi. This, of course, does not bode well for his implementation of China's economic policies.

Policy Direction and Focus

Xi Jinping's third term policy directions are included in the 20th Party Congress Report, consisting of fifteen sections. First, the report identifies the core missions of the CCP as required under Xi Jinping's third term policy directives. Second, it calls for Chinese-style modernization. Third, it calls for a drive toward a higher level of qualitative growth. Qualitative growth refers to the conditions necessary for realizing "common prosperity," for which the government is expected to make a concerted effort.

The year 2023 marked the tenth anniversary of the Belt and Road Initiative. The Belt and Road Initiative being Xi Jinping's signature project, a strong push from the government to accomplish the goals of the project is expected to continue. China hosted the third Belt and Road Forum for International Cooperation in October 2023 in Beijing. Unlike the first and second Belt and Road Forums, Western governments declined to participate for political reasons, including Italy, which had participated in both of the previous forums. Deputy Minister of Foreign Affairs Ma Zhaoxu said, "Together with our partners, we will advance high-quality Belt and Road cooperation on a broader scale, at greater depths and on higher levels, to make continued advances toward the goal of common development and prosperity," but this lofty declaration only amounted to a soliloquy in an echo-chamber filled with a Sino-friendly or Sino-dependent audience.

As to the eastern destination of the Belt and Road Initiative, the three northeastern provinces of China have been persistently asking the central government to extend the Belt and Road into North Korea. If this happens, in view of the unique China-North Korea relations, China and North Korea will enter into much tighter cooperation in an effort to leverage the Belt and Road Initiative for maximum return. That eventuality will drastically alter the geopolitical parameters for South Korea and require deep and multifaceted revisions in its strategic posture.

The 20th Party Congress Report also emphasizes innovation and growth in capabilities in science and technology. Increasing scientific and technological capabilities are linked to the emphasis the report places on what it calls the "Indigenization of Science and Technology." This represents a shift in strategy in the face of intensifying strategic competition with the United States It can be understood as China's strategic countermeasure, premised on the actual decoupling between the United States and China.

Xi Jinping's Third Term Compared to His Two Previous Terms

The 20th Party Congress marked the end of the so-called Deng Xiaoping-style balanced personnel appointments that had been the norm for the past forty years. Xi Jinping has established an environment in which he is no longer a mediator and balancer, but someone who wields final authority with veto power in setting policy directions and personnel appointments.

Through the personnel appointments at the 20th Party Congress, political power in China has been consolidated in the person of Xi Jinping. This move virtually disabled the preexisting policymaking system based on collective leadership. In its wake, efforts on revising, supplementing, and adjusting rules and regulations to institutionalize this new norm are sure to follow. In this historic transition to one-man autocratic rule, however, securing its legitimacy in the eyes of the CCP rank and file and the Chinese people at large still remains.

There were several surprises during the 20th Party Congress: the retirement of Premier Li Keqiang and chairman of the Chinese People's Political Consultative Conference Wang Yang. Some were dramatic: the "suspicious" exit of former president Hu Jintao (胡錦濤) and the demotion of Hu Chunhua (胡春华) to the Central Committee. These incidents ingrained the new reality that no one can challenge Xi Jinping's power into the memory of everyone present or witnessing the convention on the media. The system of checks and balances that existed during Xi's first and second terms vanished. Now, only the infallible Paramount Leader remains in the CCP. This is the most striking attribute of Xi Jinping's third term.

This dramatic development, however, also means that Socialism with Chinese characteristics is losing its autogenic ability. Chinese politics is an insular system that evolves from within. To wit, without a healthy internal checks-and-balance mechanism suppressing the formation of a monopoly of power, the stability of the system cannot be sustained. No outside factors like the transition of power through election cycles will come to the rescue. A case in point was the purge of Bo Xilai in 2013, when the checks-and-balance mechanism failed, and the scandal went public, displaying the cracks in the ruling elites of the CCP. Likewise, as the internal balancing mechanism no longer functions for all intents and purposes in Xi Jinping's third term, one sees the odd situation where Premier Li Qiang's prestige is sliding while that of fifth-ranking member of the Politburo Standing Committee Cai Qi is on the rise. This anomaly is indicative of the loss of the tradition of checks and balances in Chinese politics, as blind obedience to Xi Jinping has become the new norm in the CCP.

Death of Generational Change in Chinese Politics? A Revival?

As a result of the absolute power Xi Jinping amassed through the 20th Party Congress, the horizontal collective policymaking is being replaced by top-down decision-making even among the Politburo Standing Committee members. The title of "People's Leader" (人民領袖) for Xi Jinping, an extreme honorific title, is also proliferating in and outside the party. This atmosphere indicates the possibility of Xi's long-term rule as long as his health permits. However, the issue of generational change in political leadership still remains.

First, the Politburo Standing Committee is composed of Xi Jinping's personal acquaintances. This change had the effect of weakening the traditional practice of adjusting personnel appointments along the generational line. With no successor identified, either explicitly or implicitly, governance through generational leadership change lost its efficacy and the possibility of Xi's long-term rule increased.

Second, there were mixed instances of conventional career advancement and surprise appointments in the Politburo. The so-called rise of the 1960s (those born 1960~-1969) is not observed. There was no representation of women or minorities among the new Politburo members.

Third, there were wide-ranging changes in the Central Committee through the 20th Party Congress. The total number of full members of the Central Committee has not changed.

Among them, eleven are women and thirty-four have been promoted to full members from their alternate member status following the 19th Party Congress. The total number of new members increased dramatically to ninety-nine. Overall, any indication of generational change is not observed in the sixties category but is notable in the large number of seventies (those born after 1970) who became new alternate members.

These new faces will form the axis of the new generation of leaders. Li Yunze (李云澤) and Ah Dung (阿東) reached the ministerial level first among the seventies (those born after 1970). Another seventies Hu Haifeng, son of the former president Hu Jintao, entered the State Council of the PRC as the Deputy Minister of the Ministry of Civil Affairs (民政部) in January 2024. As of January 2024, twenty-seven 70s are working in the State Council, and among them, Chen Changsheng (陈昌盛), born in August 1976, is the youngest. Evaluated through the CCP's "step-by-step growth and unprecedented selection" mechanism, they are expected to form the core of the generational succession structure that will emerge, replacing the fifties and sixties generation leaders.

XI JINPING'S GLOBAL AND REGIONAL PERCEPTIONS

The 2012 18th Party Congress Report posited a new thesis in international affairs: *New Type of Great Power Relations.* China hoped to escape the Thucydides Trap by establishing a new paradigm in its relations with the United States. Xi Jinping attempted to formalize this relationship during his visit to the United States in April 2013 by stating that China would faithfully discharge its responsibilities in the great power relations.

The great power responsibilities Xi referred to are not as an adherent to the US-led liberal international order, but as a powerful member within the ambit of the UN. China has taken every opportunity to declare that it would adhere to the purpose and principles of the UN Charter and protect the UN-centered international system. Wang Huning, chairman of the Chinese People's Political Consultative and often referred to as the Emperor's Teacher (帝師), was the architect of this strategic ideology—an antithesis to the US-led liberal international order. At the 20th Party Congress, Wang Huning was reappointed as a member of the Politburo Standing Committee. Wang Huning's reappointment heralds no significant change in China's perception of the world during Xi's third term: China will continue its commitment to the UN-centered international system over the US-led liberal international order.

Former foreign minister Wang Yi's appointment to two positions during the 20th Party Congress was noteworthy. His appointment as the successor to Yang Jiechi as director of the Central Committee Foreign Affairs Commission signaled how Central China considers its relations with the United States to be, as has been the case since the 18th Party Congress. At a time when China faces structural constraints in achieving positive results *vis-a-vis* the United States due to the strategic competition between them, China was sending a strong signal. At the same time, Wang Yi's concurrent appointment as a member of the Politburo was a signal that China would work to strengthen its diplomatic ties with neighboring countries in response to the US effort to contain China on a broad front.

On the other hand, Qin Gang's surprise appointment could not be explained but for Xi Jinping's interposition of his personal preference. Born in 1966, Qin Gang was the youngest among the fellow ministers, and among the foreign ministers of the past. Qin Gang had been the poster child of China's Wolf Warrior Diplomacy. His appointment as the new foreign minister was a nuanced signal that Xi Jinping would continue with his hard-line diplomacy to secure what he considered China's national interests to be *vis-a-vis* the world, especially the United States.

Qin Gang's Fall and Xi Jinping's Political Responsibility

Then suddenly, Qin Gang disappeared from the public eye for nearly two months beginning in May 2023. His mysterious disappearance was followed by an announcement during the fourteenth meeting of the Standing Committee of the National People's Congress on July 25, 2023, that Wang Yi would replace Qin Gang as the foreign minister. Wang Yi was thus reinstated to his old post without so much as a word explaining the sacking of Qin Gang.

It has been widely speculated that the Central Commission for Disciplinary Inspection plenary session held in January 2024 would have dealt with the Qin Gang incident, but no official announcement has been made to date. Curiously, however, Qin Gang's name is still on the roster of the State Council of the PRC.

Scandalous personnel debacles are not limited to Qin Gang. Li Shang Fu was suddenly removed from his office of defense minister, soon followed by the purge of the top commanders of the PLA Rocket Force. Speculations of corruption in military procurement are rife in the cases of these generals, but as in the case of Qin Gang, no official explanation has been forthcoming. Though putatively recommended by the premier of the State Council, it was Xi Jinping alone who made the decisions to appoint these men to their offices. All responsibilities for the failed appointments fall on Xi Jinping alone. And yet, no one is discussing the political or moral responsibilities for these failed appointments.

These spectacular personnel appointment failures indicate a rather elementary personnel vetting process by the Organization Department of the CCP and the Central Military Commission. The real problem, however, is that Xi Jinping is the sole and ultimate authority behind official appointments, rendering even the rudimentary vetting processes moot. These systemic failures raise a critical question: Is the Xi Jinping regime stable? In this regard, the Qin Gang scandal is particularly onerous to Xi Jinping in that he now has to scramble to send a more credible message to the United States about the strength and stability of his regime.

China's Position on Russia-Ukraine War

On the other hand, China believes that it has more space to maneuver in its relations with neighboring countries. China-Russia relations are at the front and center of China's relations with neighboring countries. Russia has become a pariah in the international community since its invasion of Ukraine in February 2022. From its perspective, Russia saw the need to invade Ukraine to forestall the eastern expansion of NATO. That strategic need, however, does not excuse Putin's decision to wage war to achieve it, and on this account, China is maintaining a certain distance from Russia. Chinese official rhetoric is that wars and the resulting humanitarian crises must be avoided. Nevertheless, China is one of the few friendly nations remaining for Russia and a strategic partner.

China and Russia are members of the Shanghai Cooperation Organization (SCO) and BRICS. The role of China and Russia is expanding in the governance of BRICS since South Africa joined in August, 2023.[3] China and Russia apparently find it important to act in concert as much as practicable, as India, a member of BRICS, is cooperating with the United States and Japan in their Indo-Pacific strategy and is in the process of expanding its influence as a regional power. This need is well reflected in Xi Jinping's visit to Russia in March 2023, where he upgraded China-Russia relations to that of a "comprehensive strategic partnership of coordination." Xi Jinping is wont to introduce Vladimir Putin as his "old friend," and this apparent trust at a personal level between the two men is deepening China-Russia relations.

On the other hand, China also considers Ukraine an important country strategically. Since the outbreak of the Russo-Ukrainian War, China has been trying to maintain its relations with Ukraine, not by direct diplomatic involvement, but through indirect means like providing humanitarian aid. Behind this ambivalent attitude is China's perception that Ukraine brought the war on itself by trying to join NATO and the EU. For example, China's UN ambassador Zhang Jun continues to intimate the inevitability of the Russo-Ukrainian War in his speeches at the UN. Nevertheless, China still maintains its embassy in Ukraine and is intent on finding ways to play a role regarding the war short of getting directly involved.

China's Relations with the Korean Peninsula

As to North Korea, while adhering to the nonresponse principle to escalating provocations on the one hand, China is actively pursuing across-the-board closer ties with North Korea on the other. For example, in January 2024, immediately following his visit to the United States., External Liaison Department Chief Liu Jianchao met with North Korean ambassador to China Ri Ryong-nam to brief him on the result of his US visit. Vice Foreign Minister Sun Weidong recently visited North Korea, as did the Liaoning Province Cultural Delegation's visit, and the North Korean minister of physical culture and sports visited China and signed the Mutual Exchange and Cooperation Agreement, just to name a few. China's effort to improve ties with North Korea is underpinned by the following strategic calculations: China needs to guard against close North Korea-Russia relations, China considers North Korea an important leverage in its dealings with the United States, and China is a stakeholder in the Korean Peninsula. In his New Year's greeting to Kim Jong Un of North Korea, Xi stated ebulliently "both sides have maintained close strategic communication, intensified working-level cooperation, and strengthened coordination and cooperation in multilateral international issues, saying such efforts have promoted the continuous development of relations, defending the common interests of the two countries and regional peace and stability." The point of this message was that China considers North Korea a partner in strategic considerations.

By contrast, Korea-China relations remain strained. Changes in the balance of power and diversification of the actors in the international situation limit Korea's strategic flexibility. Broadly, China is making two demands on Korea. First, Korea should remain true to the spirit of the Joint Communique agreed upon during the diplomatic normalization in 1992. Second, Korea should behave in ways befitting the "strategic cooperative partner" relationship the two nations entered into during the Lee Myung-bak administration in 2008. From China's perspective, Korea is shirking its responsibility to act in strategic cooperation with China. If the current state of affairs continues, room for strategic cooperation between the two nations is bound to shrink, and China's outlook toward Korea will inevitably cool. At times like this, it is vital for the two nations to maintain Track II or backchannel diplomatic connections, as exemplified by the ceremonial transfer of the remains of fallen Chinese soldiers of the Korean War that took place in November 2023.

China, Taiwan, and Global South

Taiwan, of course, has been and will continue to be the centerpiece of Xi Jinping's domestic and global outlook. He declared in his New Year's address for 2024, "China's reunification with Taiwan is inevitable." During the San Francisco summit with President Joe Biden, Xi Jinping officially denied the conjecture popular in the West that China would invade Taiwan in 2027, but that does not mean he renounced military invasion of Taiwan altogether. Xi Jinping continues to stand firm on the notion of "one China," as he emphasized the message during the diplomatic normalization with the Republic of Nauru, potentially a key strategic island in the South Pacific. The message is sure to be repeated in establishing diplomatic relations with Tuvalu, another potentially strategic island nation in Oceania.

For the moment, China's approach toward Taiwan reunification is to isolate Taiwan diplomatically from the international community, rather than initiate an armed invasion. As of the beginning of 2024, the Republic of Nauru severed diplomatic ties with Taiwan, leaving only twelve nations with diplomatic relations with Taiwan. In Tuvalu as well, the pro-Taiwan candidate lost the presidential election, making future diplomatic relations with Taiwan doubtful. Ten countries severed diplomatic ties with Taiwan since Tsai Ing-wen became president in 2016, and the number is expected to grow after the inauguration of president Lai Ching-te. Interestingly, diplomatic normalization between China and the Vatican also plays an important role in furthering China's strategy of diplomatically isolating Taiwan.

China is expected to increasingly focus on its relations with neighboring countries during Xi's third term, to wit the China-Central Asia relations, China-Korea relations, China-Japan relations, China-Korean Peninsula relations, and China-ASEAN relations. Added to this list will be China's focus on the China-Global South relations with renewed urgency. When the Russo-Ukrainian War broke out, the United States called for international solidarity in implementing economic sanctions on Russia, but much of the Global South did not stir. Now, the United States and China are locked in a heated diplomatic competition to win the hearts of the Global South, with China utilizing such platforms as the Global Development Initiative (GDI), Global Security Initiative (GSI), and Global Cultural Initiative (GCI), all under the rubric of "Community of Common Destiny for Mankind."

POLITICAL SIGNIFICANCE AND EVALUATION OF XI JINPING'S THIRD CONSECUTIVE TERM

Is the Third Consecutive Term the Start of a New Norm or a Dictatorship?

While President Xi Jinping has not explicitly or publicly repudiated China's earlier era of economic reform and openness, he has consistently emphasized the "New Era" during his last two terms. Quietly downplaying the legacy of the reform and openness appears to have been his way of breaking with the past.

During the Deng Xiaoping era, productivity was one of the most important indicators of growth and development. Productivity was the means of validating Chinese socialism. However, the Xi Jinping regime has moved on from the paradigm of economic productivity to one of China's place in the history of civilizations. Xi does not see China's recent history in two stages—that is, revolution and construction on the one hand and reform on the other—but rather in three stages: revolution, construction, and reform. As such, a quiet but clean break from the earlier era of reform and openness is a necessary part of this paradigm shift. Xi Jinping wants the world to acknowledge China's prestige in the new G2 international order, essentially different from China's place during the former reform and openness era.

Above all, going beyond realizing socialism at a national level, Xi Jinping's China is determined to fulfill its destined duties in realizing Marxism for all mankind. In order to set this aspiration on a concrete footing, the 20th Party Congress signaled the need to break with or go beyond Deng Xiaoping's reform and openness paradigm. Regardless of whether this break leads to a new mode of governance or an outright dictatorship, it appears clear that Xi Jinping will roll out a new path for China, distinguishable from Deng's legacy.

Does Xi Jinping Have the Support of the Party Members and the Public for His Three Consecutive Terms in Office?

President Xi Jinping was the ultimate authority behind all reports from the 18th, 19th, and 20th Party Congress which encapsulated Xi Jinping's governing principles and aspirations. In form, the customary practices and procedural aspects relating to all three Party Congresses remained by and large unchanged. In substance, however, the 20th Party Congress Report represented a fundamental departure: it signaled a break with the political legacy of the Deng Xiaoping period.

Since a third consecutive term went against the party's existing practices, finding a justification was paramount. The CCP led the effort to establish the legitimacy of Xi Jinping's continued rule by inculcating ideological correctness in its grassroots bureaucrats (基層一線) and the Chinese public. Political education focusing on the "spirit of the 20th Party Congress" was carried out for some two months following the 20th Party Congress. The so-called lecture group (宣講團) activities became a daily occurrence. Collection of quotes and guidelines from Xi Jinping became required reading. Ironically, however, these frenetic activities meant that he still lacked the trust and support of the CCP rank and file and the Chinese public.

The fact of the matter is that trust and loyalty of the CCP members and the public can only be won by maintaining a robust economy, thus the standard of living. The realities on the ground have remained far from this expectation since the end of the COVID-19 pandemic, and the trust of the CCP rank and file and the public in the Xi Jinping administration is faltering.

Since the 2023 Two Sessions (兩會), China has expected a gradual economic recovery. However, the economic indicators remained dismal, with domestic demand and inflationary pressure being of particular concern. With the current account balance foundering, the Politburo of the Central Committee announced in July 2023 a policy turn toward domestic consumption to pull the Chinese economy out of the morass. This, however, had an opposite effect: the personal saving rate increased. This indicated the public's unease about the continuing economic uncertainty; people wanted to protect themselves through hoarding liquid assets. Meanwhile, the CCP's propaganda efforts to calm the nerves of the public are not showing any appreciable effect. The widespread fear of market failure and policy failure remains too strong, which may, in turn lead to a leadership crisis for Xi Jinping.

"Common Prosperity," A New Driving Force in Xi Jinping's Third Term

Xi Jinping's signature campaign during his first term in office was a campaign against corruption, and during his second term, construction of a

"Prosperous Society." In the third term, his motto may be "Common Prosperity" (aka "collective prosperity"). For Xi, who promised the "great rejuvenation" of the Chinese race, Common Prosperity is a useful catchphrase to unite the rank and file CCP members and the people. The Chinese authorities have designated Zhèjiāng Province as a pilot district to showcase common prosperity. According to Xi Jinping, common prosperity is the ultimate goal of modern socialism. The CCP propaganda machine has promulgated the common prosperity policy far and wide, forming the central theme of Xi Jinping's third term.

Xi's common prosperity is not wealth redistribution in the sense of downward equalization, where everyone is equally poor—an equality of the unfortunate. To quote Chinese authorities, common prosperity can be realized only after achieving a high level of development. As such, it is not a policy amenable to five-year plans as in the case of the anti-corruption drive or the prosperous society initiative. It is the kind of grand objective that requires continuous effort until, say, 2049, the 100th year anniversary of the founding of the People's Republic of China, which has been earmarked as the target year for the realization of a "strong, democratic, civilized, harmonious, and modern socialist country." Common prosperity is thus a mid to long-term project that will begin in earnest during Xi Jinping's third term and is expected to bear fruit by 2050.

Xi Jinping's obsession with common prosperity stems from his concern that socioeconomic inequality may engender a sense of estrangement in people, threatening the legitimacy of CCP rule. Despite the rapid economic progress during the Deng era, his development model produced urban-rural divergence, income inequality, and regional disparities. The Xi Jinping administration fears that it will be difficult to achieve its objectives during his "New Era" without first alleviating such inequalities. Failure to do so will make it impossible for China to become a great "modern socialist power." Stated differently, common prosperity without inequalities is the prerequisite for his great modern socialist power. Common prosperity, Xi's flagship policy, will continue as long as his regime stands.

POLITICAL MOBILIZATION FOR XI JINPING'S "NEW ERA"

As seen above, the fact that the current Politburo Standing Committee consists entirely of Xi Jinping's acolytes means the emasculation of the collective leadership system, a political legacy from the Deng Xiaoping era. Although the rules and regulations on collective leadership have not been officially abolished, it does not mean that the institution is still standing. This change in the governing system has all but announced the arrival of Xi's one-man authoritarian rule.

On the other hand, the means and procedures relating to the constitution of the Politburo members or the Central Committee members have remained generally unchanged. Although the Politburo Standing Committee was largely filled with Xi's close associates, the Politburo itself was generally constituted in conformity with precedents. In a sense, Xi Jinping did not see the need to completely upend the existing personnel practices, reflecting his plan to implement gradual changes.

Similarly, personnel appointments for the Central Committee followed the pattern observed in previous Party Congresses. Approximately 100 Central Committee members were replaced, representing a substantially similar ratio of replacements compared to those of the 18th and 19th Party Congress. This reflects Xi's need not to stir up negative public opinion, having completely occupied the Politburo Standing Committee with his cronies.

However, the inevitable generational change in politics presages the question of succession regarding the Paramount Leader. Any hint on this all-important question remains hidden behind the veil, if there is one to begin with, as none of the 1960s (those born after 1960) managed to make himself conspicuous as a possible heir to Xi Jinping during or after the 20th Party Congress. Xi Jinping himself certainly has made a point of not hinting at who might succeed him.

However, the seniority track with respect to the ministerial positions (正職) and deputy ministerial positions (副職) is generally observed: retirement age of sixty-five for the former, and sixty-two for the latter. Appointments for Politburo membership are limited to those who have risen to the level of ministerial positions (正職). Any potential candidate to succeed Xi Jinping will be found among them when the time comes for them to let themselves emerge out of the fog.

So far at least, who that successor might be is solely at Xi Jinping's discretion. During the times of Deng Xiaoping, Jiang Zemin, and Hu Jintao, the collective leadership paradigm was still in operation, where the consensus among the *elder statesmen* resulted in a chosen successor. With that system no longer in operation, one can speculate that a consensus among the former and incumbent members of the Politburo Standing Committee may decide upon the successor—until one is reminded that Xi Jinping holds the veto power. It will be Xi Jinping, and Xi Jinping alone, who will designate his successor.

In declaring the national objective for the 100th anniversary of the founding of the PRC in 2049, namely becoming a "strong, democratic, civilized, harmonious, and modern socialist country," Xi Jinping proposed 2035 as an interim checkpoint to achieve a "moderately developed" economy. This may be a hint that he has given himself time up to 2035 to achieve his goals in what he sees as his historic role in today's China. Conversely, that also means that he plans to stay in power at least until 2035. By that time, those in ministerial positions (正職) and deputy ministerial positions (副職) will all be in their seventies (those born after 1970). Logically, therefore, Xi Jinping's successor will likely be someone of the seventies generation alive among us now.

Chapter 2

A Question of Political Stability and Sustainability

Yang Gabyong

STRENGTHENING XI'S RULE AND GARNERING PUBLIC OPINION

The 20th Party Congress Report and the Amendment of the Party Constitution heralded the arrival of Xi Jinping's undisputed one-man rule. He was dubbed the "People's Leader" (人民领袖), an extreme form of honorific title in Chinese. This, however, conjures up the image of an infallible leader, reminiscent of the excesses of Mao Zedong during the Cultural Revolution. China had officially recognized the danger of the concentration of power in one man in the "second Historical Resolution" convened under Deng Xiaoping, and the subject of the rebuke was none other than Mao Zedong himself.

As the People's Leader, Xi Jinping is invoking patriotism, nationalism, and culturalism as tools for corralling public opinion in support of his one-man rule. The problem is that patriotism and nationalism are a double-edged sword. Additionally, culturalism, emphasizing the superiority of Chinese culture, smacks of the unwanted imposition of Chinese exceptionalism on other peoples. These three ideologies have merged into what might properly be called "patriotic culturalism."

On October 7, 2023, the National Propaganda, Ideological and Cultural Work Conference (全国宣传思想文化工作会议) was convened in Beijing.[1] At this conference, Xi Jinping delivered an important mandate, which Chinese media began to call "Xi Jinping Cultural Thoughts." Here, a careful rhetorical analysis is in order. Note that the phrase does not say, "Xi Jinping's Cultural Thoughts" but "Xi Jinping Cultural Thoughts." Just as in the case of the phrase "Xi Jinping Diplomatic Thoughts," this represents an attempt to exalt Xi Jinping as the original creator of a new concept. Also note that what used to be National Propaganda and Ideological Conference (全国宣传思

71

想工作会议) became National Propaganda, Ideological and Cultural Work Conference (全国宣传思想文化工作会议) by adding the word "culture" (文化). Culture (文化) has become of equal importance with Ideology and Propaganda thereof.

Why culture? An answer to this question can be traced to the philosophy of Wang Huning (王沪宁), chairman of the Chinese People's Political Consultative Conference, who is popularly referred to as the "Emperor's Teacher" (帝師). Wang Huning stresses that governance must be based on a keen understanding of Chinese history, philosophy, society, and culture. Among them, culture in particular is the determinant factor in international affairs, and as such cannot be subsumed under political, economic, or military factors.[2] At a Cultural Heritage Advancement Conference that took place on June 2, 2023, Xi Jinping said that "culture is the fundamental principle (國本) in administering China, and is part of China's national destiny (國運)." He went on, "We must create a modern civilization for the Chinese race through creative transformation and innovative development of China's superior traditional culture."[3]

He was reinventing culture from the perspective of nationalism, patriotism, and statism toward greater Chinese unity in building a modern Chinese socialist civilization.

The fact of the matter is that ideologies like patriotism and nationalism, which can inflame guttural emotions in people, can be useful tools in garnering public support for a regime. However, if patriotism and nationalism are allowed to boil over, they can yield opposite results, especially today when China faces myriad difficulties brought on by the COVID-19 pandemic. That makes patriotism and nationalism 鷄肋 (chicken ribs—In the Chinese classic *The Romance of Three Kingdoms*, a king likens a region he is struggling to subdue to chicken ribs; it looks scrumptious but, in reality, there's nothing much to bite on) in Xi Jinping's eyes. In fact, the CCP is aware that mobilizing patriotism and nationalism is showing diminishing returns. This is where Xi Jinping Cultural Thoughts come in. All indications are that the technique of inflaming nationalism and patriotism will take a backseat behind the glorification of Chinese culture. The objective, however, remains the same: unify public support behind Xi Jinping's one-man authoritarian rule and its policies.

VERTICAL CENTRALIZATION OR HORIZONTAL DECENTRALIZATION

As Xi Jinping's personal power grows, the former decentralized decision-making model known as the "collective leadership" is giving way to a hierarchical model of centralization. China is also using international issues in domestic politics with increasing frequency. However, it would be a mistake to construe this trend solely as an effort to cement Xi Jinping's power. In the face of myriad intractable challenges both domestic and international, China has seen a need to reinvent its concept of power. This need has resulted in the revival of the concept of 班長 (squad leader), once expounded upon by Mao himself for the position of general secretary of the CCP. It appears Xi Jinping is the beneficiary of this development.

Nothing stands in the way of his unquestioned leadership in the Politburo Standing Committee anymore. Xi Jinping has eliminated all competitors and opponents among the Chinese ruling elite. The traditional 元老政治 (elder statesmen leadership) has become titular only. Xi Jinping no longer needs to expend time and energy to suppress opposing factions. However, all this does not mean calcified centralization. On the contrary, now that internal factional conflicts have been all but swept away, there may be more exchange of opinions in policymaking. For this reason, Xi Jinping's third term is expected to display remarkable efficiency in policymaking, which, in turn, may lead to a certain degree of flexibility in governance.

Xi Jinping sees no need to display more rigidity because his opinions automatically become the party's decisions. There is nobody who would dare disagree or dissent, or who can form an opposing faction. The leader of the Chinese Youth League, Hu Jintao was practically dragged away from the stage of the 20th Party Congress for the whole world to see. Premier Li Keqiang suddenly passed away from a heart attack on October 27, 2023. Former vice premier Hu Chunhua was demoted to the Central Committee of the CCP, without even a privilege to attend the Politburo meetings. Former minister of natural resources Lu Hao has been relegated to the State Council Research Office. Former general secretaries of the Chinese Youth League have all been deprived of offices or demoted through the 20th Party Congress. Figures like Li Keqiang, who checked and balanced Xi Jinping, are no longer to be found. That no such figures exist anymore is certainly a cause for concern, as it diminishes the flexibility in policymaking under Xi Jinping's one-man authoritarian rule.

Under Xi Jinping, the traditional 元老政治 (elder statesmen leadership) collective leadership ("elder statesmen collective leadership") has been all but eliminated. Elder statesmen collective leadership had provided the function of checks and balances in Chinese politics in two ways. First, there used to exist a tradition of seeking consent or consensus from elder statesmen about a proposed policy or course of action through free deliberations and fierce debates away from the prying eyes of the public. This process promoted circumspection and imbued credibility in the resulting policy. Second, the mere presence of respected and experienced elder statesmen often facilitated compromises and fine-tuning necessary for arriving at policy decisions. Now, that tradition is gone, leaving one-man totalitarian rule.

Xi Jinping has also rolled out an across-the-board anti-corruption campaign since he came to power in the 18th Party Congress, purging many high-ranking politicians and officials. He even broke the unwritten rule that retired Politburo Standing Committee members were off-limits. Even those who had retired years before were arrested and punished. People were elated, and Xi Jinping enjoyed great popularity during the early years of the anti-corruption campaign. The inevitable side effect began to surface; however, continuing inspection and investigation fostered a new trend where no government official would bother to carry out his duties with creativity and enthusiasm, preferring to lay low so as not to be seen. The Chinese proverb 過猶不及 says too much is no better than too little.

However, the anti-corruption drive continues unabated in Xi Jinping's third term in office. Xi Jinping has been using it adroitly, providing catharsis to the people and eliciting loyalty from his subordinates, thus keeping both firmly under his control. The anti-corruption drive has been a very useful tool in securing the efficacy and legitimacy of his rule.

And the anti-corruption initiative has not translated into ossification of CCP governance. Rather, it can be said to have eliminated internal conflicts, making room for a freer exchange of ideas in policymaking. Some even argue that now that Xi Jinping's ideas automatically become policy, he feels no need to calcify the workings of the CCP.

As seen above, no one dares to offer opposing arguments or factions. In fact, the CCP may roll out propaganda portraying his authority in a soft pastel light, putting him on a pedestal as a capable and benevolent ruler. That, of course, may strictly be for domestic consumption. As Xi Jinping becomes less likely to entertain different views when it comes to foreign affairs, China's already rigid foreign policy posture may become sclerotic.

INNER PARTY STRUGGLE: GONE OR LATENT?

The nature of power is that once you taste it, you cannot put it down. Xi Jinping is the happy recipient of two powerful ideological support: 兩個維護 (two maintenance—of himself as the supreme leader and the dictatorial authority he carries) and Socialism with Chinese characteristics. So long as he is physically able and willing, it appears he will stay in power indefinitely. One indication of this projection is that he has refused to name a successor through the 19th and 20th Party Congress.

In particular, the membership of the Politburo Standing Committee constituted in the 20th Party Congress shows no hint of a possible successor.

The 12th Party Congress in 1982 abolished the institution of party chairman, replacing it with one of general secretary. Its rationale of preventing excessive concentration of power in one person still rings true in the minds of some. For this reason, reviving the institution of party chairman requires careful calibration even for Xi Jinping, as it is for all intents and purposes synonymous with staying in power indefinitely. Therefore, one possible interpretation of his refusal to name a successor is that Xi Jinping is looking ahead toward naming himself "party chairman," thus laying the groundwork for an indefinite stay in power.

Xi Jinping may designate his successor at the 22nd Party Congress in 2032 and can retire at the 23rd Party Congress in 2037, having satisfied himself with the coming-of-age of said successor. Having designated 2035 as the interim checkpoint for the roadmap toward building a "Modern Socialist Power" by 2049, the 100th anniversary of the founding of the PRC, Xi Jinping likely feels that he must see to it personally that the foundations are properly laid for achieving said goal. Having done so, he may gracefully come down from his throne at the 23rd Party Congress in 2037. He will be eighty-four years old then, not too old when compared to President Joe Biden who, if he wins the 2024 election, will begin his second term at the age of eighty-three and remain president until the age of eighty-seven. Xi Jinping's health is the only remaining variable in his quest for long-term rule.

In this scenario, the seventy 後 (those born after 1970) who are in their mid-forties and fifties as of 2024 will be in their mid-fifties or sixties at the time of the 23rd Party Congress in 2027. Assuming that their careers advance generally following the Public Official Advancement Regulations with retirement age set at sixty-five for the ministerial positions (正職) and sixty-two for the deputy ministerial positions (副職), they will be the generation of public officials who can be named the successor to Xi Jinping. At present, thirty odd number of such seventy後 (those born after 1970) are visible in the CCP. The big question is who, among them, will be appointed to the Central Committee of the CCP at the 21st Party Congress in 2027.

In short, the future successor to Xi Jinping is now among the 20th Party Congress Central Committee Alternate Members, or 21st Party Congress Central Committee Full Members in 2027. As the appointment of the 20th Politburo Standing Committee members was, in fact based on loyalty to Xi Jinping, it is obvious that loyalty will be the determining factor in shaping the future succession structure as well.

Power struggle around a successor, however, is an ember that can never be extinguished. In that regard, the formation of young acolytes around Xi may sow the seeds of China's future political instability. First, internal conflicts and confrontations may emerge. Structures where disagreements cannot exist demand conformity, and power struggles may intensify in the process.

Second, a power disparity may emerge due to institutional and procedural irregularities. For example, neither the premier nor the four deputy premiers of the State Council have been nominated as members of the Central Committee during the 20th Party Congress. Third, the succession structure is by nature uncertain, and the generational transition ultimately depends on the will of the supreme leader. The successor, whoever it may be, lies latent somewhere in the pyramid of the CCP. Discussions on potential successors will be a burning issue at the 21st Party Congress in 2027.

Naturally, Xi Jinping is not getting any younger, and his health will become an issue sooner or later. Unless he resolves the succession structure at an appropriate time, the risk of catastrophic confusion in Chinese politics cannot be ruled out. However, the moment the succession discussion commences, it will suck in all other issues like a black hole, making it difficult for the CCP to address them competently and timely. This is a risk Xi Jinping is loath to let burst. Although the issue of succession will be broached at the time of Xi Jinping's choosing, how it will be received will depend on the cobweb of multiple variables that constitute Chinese politics. For one thing, how the issue should be broached is itself a difficult question. In a single-party authoritarian society, it makes little sense to discuss succession out in the open on a public forum. Converse is equally difficult: dealing with succession behind closed doors runs the risk of alienating the CCP rank and file and the Chinese people. How China deals with the upcoming succession process will determine the stability and continuity of China's politics for generations to come.[4]

STABILITY OF THE XI JINPING REGIME

Superficially, the extension of Xi's rule into the third term has followed the existing institutions and procedures. Underneath, however, there are signs that the stability of the system as a whole is being eroded. The recent wave of blank paper protests is a case in point. Of course, it is unlikely that protests like these will lead to a countrywide popular uprising any time soon. It is nevertheless noteworthy that a protest like it took place anyway in a totalitarian state like China. Participating in such a protest in China means exposing one's ideological leanings—a very dangerous thing to do indeed. Many Chinese chose to bear this risk and participate in mass protests during and beyond the COVID-19 lockdowns. This fact has deep ramifications for the CCP and Xi Jinping's rule.

As much as the CCP encountered severe difficulties in dealing with the COVID-19 pandemic, the Chinese public suffered horrendously under its draconian lockdown measures. Unlike in the West, the CCP's totalitarian quarantine measures were compulsory and ubiquitous, and people had no outlet to voice their grievances. It was with this unprecedented backdrop that residents and students began protesting, sporadically in some places and collectively in others. What was remarkable was that such collective protests began taking place at all.

However, lacking grassroots organization, centralization, and direction, these protests dissipated on their own, allowing the CCP to gain an upper hand in suppressing them. In this process, the CCP's strategy of bringing people's grievances into its own orbit in addressing them contributed to its successful control over the situation. In fact, the CCP's display of eagerness to aggressively accommodate people's needs and expectations often resulted in people rallying around the state, the CCP, and Xi Jinping himself.

Nevertheless, the lessons learned and confidence gained from such collective actions will manifest themselves in future protests, and in that sense, the stability and authority of CCP rule may be eroding away. One thing absolutely clear, however, is that concentrating power in one individual does not guarantee stability. Despite the outward appearance of a monolithic authoritarian government apparatus in full control, the recent stir in public opinion implies a chink in the armor of Xi's political legitimacy. In a single-party totalitarian state like China, the stability of its government comes solely from the support of the party members and the people; there is no other built-in mechanism like the peaceful transition of power through elections. If public support leaves Xi Jinping, the very existence of his regime comes under threat.

Well then, will Xi Jinping's third term be able to continue in existence despite the eroding stability? What is needed is a homeostasis of sustainable economic growth, sustainable social control, and trust between Xi Jinping and the people, including the CCP rank and file. However, the regime is facing numerous challenges both at home and abroad.

First of all, the economic indicators fall far below people's expectations. The COVID-19 pandemic, the Ukrainian War, the Israel-Hamas War, and the US containment of China are stunting China's economic growth. This unfortunate situation is unlikely to be resolved any time soon. China's economic growth rate for 2023 is said to have been 5.5 percent according to official figures, but the wide quarterly differences make it difficult to say that the economy grew steadily. Second, the growing economic disparity is threatening social stability. The authorities are confronting this problem with political education stressing the legitimacy of CCP rule, but such measures can only bring temporary relief. The lessons learned and confidence gained from the protests during the COVID-19 years may very well embolden the masses going forward. It behooves the CCP to find permanent solutions for these problems fast.

However, all indications are that the Xi regime is employing increasingly stifling Digital Legalism —intensified social control utilizing high-tech surveillance and censorship mechanisms—in dealing with people's discontent. While Digital Legalism may artificially keep Chinese society under control, it may also push people's pent-up grievances to congeal into a unified and organized popular uprising, and this spectacle has traditionally been the greatest fear of the CCP.

FACTORS THAT MAY WEAKEN THE XI JINPING REGIME

Conflict between Nationalism and People's Needs

Xi Jinping has relentlessly emphasized ideology and inflamed patriotism to legitimize his rule over the past decade. This conflicts with the evolution of the Chinese people. As China has achieved economic growth through reform and openness, people's fundamental needs have progressed from visceral physical survival to liberty, as witnessed in the blank paper movement. This transition is especially pronounced among the younger generations.

This demand for freedom transcends politics. It is a demand for fundamental human rights. The theory of political development tells us that a society which successfully pulls itself out of subsistence begins to demand political freedom, notably the election of its leaders. China has yet to reach this stage. China has only just overcome the subsistence level of existence by adopting a reform and openness policy starting in the Deng Xiaoping era. The Xi Jinping regime, however, framed the questions of survival and needs for livelihood in an Ideology Trap and turned the Chinese people into Idealtypus (Ideal Type). Xi Jinping has chosen to turn the Chinese people into automatons operating pursuant to his teachings. This reversion to the Mao Era is the inherent limitation of the Xi Jinping regime, and difficult times may lie ahead during his third term.

Abraham Maslow's *Hierarchy of Needs* identifies the most fundamental human need as the "physiological needs." China is facing criticism that the government's draconian COVID-19 measures, including nationwide lockdowns, have turned the clock back to the past when China had to worry about meeting people's physiological needs. At least until the end of Hu Jintao's time in office, such physiological needs were accommodated. But, as seen above, things have not improved economically since the pandemic, and Xi Jinping still persists in suppressing people's freedom to pursue survival and life in his attempt to artificially maintain social stability. When people satisfy their physiological needs, they pursue what Maslow's calls "self-actualization." Xi Jinping, however, has locked the Chinese people in the neo-Maoist ideological framework at a time when people's physiological needs cannot be met.

Another factor that is corroding the regime is that "reverence" for Xi Jinping as "People's Leader" is not taking place spontaneously, but is instead forced upon people through state-sponsored personality-cult propaganda. Add to this the fastidious enforcement of Digital Legalism by the Ministry of Public Security forces, and you have an Orwellian nightmare playing itself out in real life in the twenty-first century. If this approach becomes more rabid, Xi Jinping will lose the "reverence" of the CCP rank and file and the Chinese people. The Chinese people of the Xi Jinping era are qualitatively different from those of the Mao Zedong era. They have already experienced affluence and freedom; they will not stand for the claustrophobic, ideology-driven personality cult of the Mao Zedong era.

Misjudgment of the Younger Generation

Xi Jinping's failure to appreciate the changes in the younger generation is also accelerating the erosion of the legitimacy of his regime. The thoughts and lifestyle of the younger generation of Chinese are no longer those of the earlier generations. They were born in a China of material abundance and are intimately familiar with a dizzying array of social media. They have tasted liberalism and are adept at navigating the cyberspace of communication with the outside world.

Xi Jinping has been steadily intensifying control over people during his first and second terms. This approach is no longer acceptable to the younger generations. The CCP's inculcation of nationalism and patriotism in them may very well be a mistake with those who have already evolved past Maslow's physiological needs phase. Internationally, Chinese youth have deep pride in China's status as a G2 nation, but at the same time, feel deeply disconcerted by the low opinion the rest of the world has on China and the Chinese. This, of course, goes against their expectation of a global display of respect for China commensurate with its economic status. The Chinese youth are not willing to accept this skewed reality. They may hold Xi Jinping accountable for this vitiated global image of their country.

Young Chinese crave wider freedom. This explains the fact that protests are increasingly taking place on college campuses. Despite the CCP's efforts to unify Chinese youth in patriotism and nationalism, the youth themselves are looking to the West with starry eyes full of yearning for freedom.

Xi Jinping and the CCP may temporarily control the young people, but they can never completely suppress their desire for freedom. One can only wonder whether Xi and the CCP are committing a fundamental error by misreading their own people. Meanwhile, Xi Jinping has populated the political elite around him with his closest aides, emphasizing vertical hierarchy rather than horizontal cooperation. This raises concerns that China's political heritage, the "ecosystem of planned cultivation of future leaders," is no longer functioning. The disappearance of this practice robs hope from the young people of China, leaving them feeling disenfranchised and decoupled from their own future. This state of affairs can only destroy any affinity and trust that may have existed between the Xi Jinping regime and the CCP rank-and-file and Chinese people.

People's Desire for a New Value System

The Soviet Union collapsed because it had chosen the survival of the party over that of the people. Locked in an arms race, the Soviets ignored the people's physiological needs, and as a result, Mikhail Gorbachev had no choice but to commence a far-reaching reform across society.

Likewise, Mao Zedong imposed sacrifices on the Chinese people in an effort to prop up CCP rule. This policy brought about unforeseen catastrophes, and the people's lives were devastated. It was inevitable that a leader like Deng Xiaoping would emerge following the deprivation of physiological needs during the Mao period. Since then, as China came through the Jiang Zemin and Hu Jintao periods, the Chinese people have achieved some degree of satisfaction of their physiological needs, that is, those of survival and life. Now, the Chinese people are at a stage where they are beginning to demand the luxury of freedom and self-actualization. Unlike Gorbachev, however, Xi Jinping has chosen to suppress individual freedom, especially freedom of speech, instead forcing CCP ideology upon the Chinese people.

To make matters worse, the quality of life in China has deteriorated. The Xi regime may dangle inducements to divert people's discontent temporarily, but it will find it difficult to hold off the swelling anger of the Chinese people if the Chinese economy continues its downward spiral. In such a state of affairs, repressing freedom with ideology cannot be maintained for long, as the people who have already tasted affluence would not tolerate it. Using an antiquated style of rule on modern Chinese through suffocating control can only hasten the demise of the Xi Jinping regime.

Experience of Affluence and Changing Zeitgeist

In the midst of the world in turmoil, complete with dismal economic growth, the Russo-Ukrainian War, the Israel-Hamas war, and the intensifying US-China competition, it would behoove Xi Jinping to realize that people's lives are what matters most. If not, as the water flowing under a sheet of ice can eventually melt the ice, his regime may meet an untimely end. Gorbachev's Perestroika and Deng Xiaoping's reform and openness were all possible because they saw this wisdom in time. Now, it is up to Xi Jinping to see this wisdom.

The blank paper protest was an eruption of people's demand for basic needs. In essence, it was a demand for fundamental rights to existence, not political freedom. The protesters were demanding adequate distribution of medical supplies and daily necessities. However, the CCP chose to see this public demand as a challenge to its rule.

If the CCP continues on this path, what will next be written on the blank papers of the protester may in fact become demands for freedom, equality, and democracy, not innocent demands for survival. To ensure the future stability of his rule, Xi Jinping will have to realize that demanding a return to the Maoist past is impossible. He is dealing with a nation of people far evolved from those of the Mao era.

The path Xi Jinping should choose in the new era is to meet the basic needs of the people and to promote reconciliation within the entire Chinese society. Xi Jinping himself and his cronies may want to roll out Maoism 2.0, but cannot impose anachronistic ideologies on the Chinese people anymore. Having already experienced affluence during the reform and openness era, they cannot be herded back to the Maoist past. They have simply come too far. There is no alternative but for Xi Jinping and the current ruling elite to read the current of change and offer a new vision of China's future acceptable to the Chinese people.

Blind Nationalism and Monolithic Foreign Policy

China borders fourteen countries and faces Korea and Japan across the sea. China's relations with neighboring countries will be an important variable for the continuation and stability of Xi Jinping's regime. Xi Jinping's foreign policy strategy for his third term is to balance its diplomacy vis-a-vis major powers through strengthening its relations with neighboring and developing countries. If China fails to secure a favorable reception from its neighbors, it will face an uphill struggle in realizing its stated aspiration of building a Community of Common Destiny—with itself at the center of course.

As to its relations with neighboring countries, however, China's external image has deteriorated considerably. According to the US Pew Research survey and Korean domestic surveys, nearly 80 percent of Koreans view China in a negative light. As such, China's new diplomatic initiative is of utmost interest to Korea—or rather, concern.

Korea is a dynamic country that has already entered the ranks of developed countries. However, given China's attitude toward Korea, it appears it still has not shed its traditional view of Korea as one of its vassal states. It is regrettable that China still holds on to its historical perceptions and attitudes in dealing with Korea today. Knowing that Korea-China relations are vital to both Korea and China, China should instead view Korea as an opportunity to improve its reputation among neighboring countries by recognizing what Korea is: an economically and culturally developed regional power.

If China were to develop into a responsible member of the global community of nations, it should evaluate its national identity carefully and seek to coexist with other nations based on the concept of equality of sovereign states. If not, China will not be acknowledged as a responsible and respectable country in return. If China wants respect for its leadership role as a major power, it will have to earn it.

As to its relations with developing countries, China's new diplomatic focus is on the Global South. China does not perceive the concept of "Global South" as having arisen through the efforts of major powers to help solve various problems faced by developing countries, but rather their efforts to exploit the developing countries to the exclusion of competitors. China's message to the developing countries is monolithic: peace, development, fairness, and justice can be achieved only through their cooperation and solidarity among themselves with China in the middle. To bring the developing countries into its sphere of influence, China has focused on multilateral institutions and formed large-scale funds to support the economic growth of the Global South. China has also established GDI, GSI, and GCI, claiming that "[they], along with the Belt & Road initiative, generate endogenous energy for the development of the Global South, provide cooperative platforms, and generate actual economic benefits."[5]

Xi Jinping's ultimate error during his terms in office has been to destroy the framework for US-China coexistence. If China reverts to its Maoist legacy, it is highly possible that the legitimacy of Xi's regime will be weakened even if it achieves the magical $20,000 per capita GNI. The Chinese people may not be willing to tolerate Xi Jinping style of nationalism, patriotism, and police state. This state of affairs will accelerate if Xi adopts a closed-door policy, including the so-called Dual Circulation Strategy. The only way out for Xi is to repudiate isolationism and seek a path of coexistence with the international community.

Until now, China has used external threats as a pretext to solidify internal unity with some success. However, with modern Chinese who have experienced affluence, heavy-handed top-down rule a la Mao Zedong no longer works. What China needs then is the opportunity for the younger generation of Chinese to interact with the outside world, sharing the global standards.

As China is about to enter the era of $20,000 GNI per capita, it is no longer feasible to continue its ascendency with antiquated oppressive top-down command systems. China must learn quickly why the international community does not afford it the due respect befitting its economic size. Toward that end, China should transition toward a more open and inclusive form of nationalism from the closed form of nationalism anchored by vociferous patriotism. Such a transformation will help dispel the image of China as an unpleasant gargantuan bully on the world stage. China should realize that this would be in its own interest, as well as that of the world.

For instance, China should realize sooner rather than later that it is against its image as a responsible stakeholder on the global stage to continue coddling North Korea which continues to threaten the global community with its nuclear brinkmanship. China should display its neutrality stance when it comes to the North Korean nuclear threat. Only then will the international community begin to trust China's credibility, and China's prestige will be secured.

Unilateralism can work for small countries, but not a major power. China should realize that the bigger a country, the more flexibility it should be willing to exercise. Only then will China deserve the respect it so craves. Otherwise, China will spiral into a myopic and ideologically micro-managed country, with the chasm between it and the global community only growing wider.

TEETERING XI JINPING REGIME

Surprisingly, blank paper protests continued sporadically in China despite the strong surveillance and control system. This means widespread collective opposition from the public, an important barometer of public sentiment. The world is watching to see if this changing public sentiment will bring changes to the way China is governed.

Are Blank Paper Protests a Sign of Changing Public Sentiment?

The blank paper protests can be analyzed as an instance of the CCP's accommodation of the citizen's right to resist. Or it may be a telltale indicator of the CCP's unique stance where, while it would show flexibility in regard to issues about people's lives, it would not waver from its uncompromising position in regard to ideology or the authority of the CCP rule. Nevertheless, the mere fact that the blank paper protests happened at all portends the possibility of further and widening public protests.

However, it is unreasonable to expect explosive protests any time soon. In order for civil unrest to reach the level of a revolution, a recognizable opposition leader and a supporting organizational structure are prerequisites. None can be observed at the moment. Or, rather, it would be more accurate to say that none exist. Nevertheless, the explosive potential is very real, in that protests observed in China today are demands for survival and minimum well-being.

The Xi Jinping regime's response to the blank paper protests has been a learning experience for Chinese authorities. In the end, the outbursts of public sentiment and the regime's response thereto will determine whether the regime can continue in existence.

CAN INTERNAL POWER STRUGGLE ARISE?

The China Leadership Monitor reported on August 29, 2023, that the power rankings of secretary of the Secretariat of the Central Committee Cai Qi (蔡奇) and Premier of the State Council Li Qiang were in a flux.[6] Currently, Cai Qi is fifth ranked, and Li Qiang second ranked after Xi Jinping. However, since Xi Jinping's third term began, their respective rankings have flipped with Cai Qi now leading in power ranking.

Cai Qi is the current secretary of the Secretariat of the Central Committee and the director of the General Office of the Central Committee. The General Office is in charge of providing support for the Central Committee and its Politburo, including record-keeping of high-level meetings, editing the resulting documents, codifying and executing the instructions of the Central Committee and the general secretary, and providing security services for the high-level leaders and the general secretary himself. The men who guided Hu Jintao from the stage of the 20th Party Congress were operatives from the Security Bureau of the General Office. As director of the General Office, Cai Qi acting as the chief secretary (akin to the chief of staff in the White House) in the closest vicinity of Xi Jinping. He is widely considered to be at the very center of power. Cai Qi is also the secretary of the Secretariat of the Central Committee. The Secretariat is responsible for controlling the flow of documents and agendas in and out of the Politburo of the Central Committee—a very powerful post indeed.

At a personal level, Cai Qi is closer to Xi Jinping than Li Qiang. Although both men became members of the Politburo through the 19th Party Congress, Cai Qi's promotion to Beijing party secretary would not have been possible but for Xi Jinping's direct intervention. Until the 19th Party Congress, Cai Qi was a mere representative of the National People's Representative Meeting. To become the Beijing party secretary and a Politburo Standing Committee member, he had to jump three levels of ranking in one bound: those of Central Committee reserve member, Central Committee full member, and Politburo member. Cai Qi's rise, then, was no small feat; it could not have been done without Xi Jinping's trust at a personal level.

In contrast, as the premier of the State Council, Li Qiang's hold on power is inextricably tied to the performance of China's economy. As the reopening policy designed to pull China out of the economic debacle in the wake of the COVID-19 pandemic has failed to demonstrate any positive movement, it appears Li Qiang is being set up as the fall guy. Although the Politburo Standing Committee is said to be a horizontal decision-making body, Cai Qi's power in it is based not only on his standing among his peers but more importantly on the trust of General Secretary Xi Jinping himself founded upon Cai Qi's boundless loyalty.

If the fifth ranked is known to overpower the second ranked in the Politburo Standing Committee, all resources, intelligence, and personal allegiances are bound to converge on the fifth ranked. Whether to wield such power in a power struggle is, of course, a matter of personal decision. Nevertheless, both Cai Qi and Li Qiang have risen as Xi Jinping's subordinates; a power struggle between them is not yet conceivable. In view of the general wisdom that current power is better positioned to secure future power, Cai Qi can be said to have an upper hand in a future power competition. If so, it is entirely conceivable that Cai Qi's intentions about the power succession are being secretly reported to Xi Jinping himself in real time. Again, in view of the general wisdom that an imbalance of power within a power group begets discontent and fissures, the current situation merits close attention to whether Cai Qi's ascendency will eventually light the fuse of an internal power struggle of historic consequences.

Ever since his appointment as the premier during the two sessions in March 2023, Li Qiang has not had the pleasure of exercising what was supposed to be his power. It was his prerogative to recommend ministerial appointments, but apart from appointing Zheng Shanjie to the post of the National Development and Reform Commission (NDRC), Li Qiang could not influence any other ministerial-level appointments as the candidates had all been officials of the State Council. Logically, it would behoove Li Qiang to seize control of the State Council and procure stellar economic recovery during his tenure. Neither, however, is looking good for Li Qiang. Worse yet, any exercise of his prerogative relating to official appointments must go through the Secretariat and the General Office of the Central Committee, and that's where his nemesis Cai Qi is standing tall. In the end, the post-Xi succession will wholly depend upon which power block can bring the seventy後 (born after 1970) into its folds. In this sense, the internal power struggle is already underway; it is just not yet visible to the public.

HOW LONG WILL XI JINPING STAY IN POWER?

With the conspicuous absence of a designated successor, it appears Xi Jinping plans to remain in power even after the third term. It appears unlikely that he would have engaged in such risky and dramatic machinations leading up to the 20th Party Congress just to stay in power for five more years. Simple math tells us that if he designates a successor at the 21st Party Congress in 2027, Xi Jinping will stay in power until 2032. If he designates a successor at the 22nd Party Congress in 2032, he can theoretically remain in power for twenty-five years until 2037, just 1 year shy of Mao Zedong's stay in power from 1949 to 1976. For now, Xi Jinping's health appears to be the only unknown variable.

Paradoxically, the longer Xi Jinping stays in power, the greater the risks to the survival of his regime may become as a result of continuing repression, intensifying nationalism, and tightening isolation in the international community. This risk can be magnified if more public protests like the blank paper movement arise and coalesce into full-blown social unrest. If and when the Chinese people rise to demand freedom and democracy amenable for self-actualization beyond mere survival or livelihood, such an event will be an existential challenge to Xi Jinping. If so, just what people will demand and how long such demand will persist will determine whether the Xi Jinping regime will survive or be toppled over.

At the US-China summit in Bali on November 13, 2022, US president Biden emphasized "competition without confrontation," "conflict management," and "maintaining communication" with China. Nevertheless, the United States has made it clear that it will continue economic containment of or pressure on China. In response, China may embark on extreme behaviors under the pretext of stabilizing the regime. This is another variable we must pay close attention to in evaluating the stability of Xi's regime.

THE FUTURE OF THE XI JINPING REGIME

China does not want a clash with the United States; it wants its share of the globe. For now, it is not showing a clear intent to pursue hegemony over that of the United States, but rather seeking a way to coexist with it.

Xi Jinping and Joe Biden met for over four hours during the APEC gathering in November 2023. That was one year after the summit between the two in Bali in November 2022. These were followed on January 26, 2024, by a meeting between Foreign Minister Wang Yi and National Security Advisor Jake Sullivan in Bangkok. These meetings show that China and the United States are working together to quell the fears of a military clash between them and to find a way forward through dialogue and negotiation. Both nations are intent on continuing with restrained dialogue between them.

China proffers that it is dealing with the United States in good faith, as it recognizes the United States as a major player and a superpower regionally and globally. Both nations are adhering to the notion of competing but not destroying their relationship. China does not yet consider itself a superpower, but certainly a great power. As a G2 nation, China considers it natural that it discusses global issues with the United States, such as military dialogue between the two, AI governance, the fight against drug trafficking, Middle East conflicts, Russo-Ukrainian War, the Uzbekistan issue, the Korean Peninsula issue, the Myanmar issue, the South China Sea dispute, and the Taiwan issue.

Following their Bangkok meeting, Jake Sullivan said, "[t]he two sides held candid, substantive and constructive discussions on global and regional issues." On his part, Wang Yi posted on the Chinese Ministry of Foreign Affairs website homepage, "The two sides had candid, substantive and productive strategic communication on implementing the common understandings reached between the two heads of state at the summit meeting in San Francisco and properly handling important and sensitive issues in China-U.S. relations."

China maintains that the Taiwan issue is an extremely sensitive matter that relates to its core national interests, but is not beyond discussion between China and the United States. The US posture vis-a-vis China is that of managing their relationship while acknowledging the US-China competition. China focuses on finding a way to coexist through mutual respect, peaceful coexistence, and cooperation. The key concept in China's posture is maintaining the "status quo."

Militarily, the two sides agreed to the resumption of military-to-military dialogue at the San Francisco summit to avoid accidental military conflict, and the follow-up Bangkok meeting made a provision for US-China Military Maritime Consultative Agreement (MMCA) talks, in early 2024. These developments indicate the two sides' determination to maintain the momentum of dialogue, despite the continuing US pressure on China through its Indo-Pacific strategy and participation in AUKUS.

The United States and China don't always see things eye to eye. For instance, the sides diverge significantly on such issues as the Russo-Ukrainian War, Middle East conflicts, and even the attacks on the Red Sea shipping by the Houthis. Nevertheless, China appears to prefer to ensure its long-term growth while maintaining the status quo, even if it has to acknowledge the superior power of the United States in the interim. China apparently feels that time is on its side.

The Taiwan issue is, of course, the central problem in US-China relations, and China takes every chance to emphasize to the United States and the world that China has sovereignty over Taiwan. At the Bangkok meeting, Wang Yi stressed that "the Taiwan question is China's internal affair, and the election in the Taiwan region cannot change the basic fact that Taiwan is part of China." He added, "Taiwan independence" poses the biggest risk to cross-Strait peace and stability and the biggest challenge to China-U.S. relations."

Wang Yi's statements reveal China's perception of the Taiwan issue in the context of US-China relations. On the other hand, Jake Sullivan made clear that the United States is approaching the Taiwan issue from the perspective of protecting Taiwan's peace and stability.

To some, these fundamental differences in perspective make the Taiwan issue ultimately irresolvable. Does the United States then support China's Taiwan reunification?

To Xi Jinping, the question of Taiwan reunification is fundamentally ineluctable. The United States, on the other hand, avoids indicating its support of reunification by maintaining that it "[does] not support Taiwanese independence" instead. This strategic ambiguity on the part of the United States is not satisfactory to Xi Jinping. During the San Francisco summit, he told Biden to "stop arming Taiwan, stop interfering in China's internal affairs, and support China's peaceful reunification." As diplomatic language goes, Xi's statement is as blunt as it gets.

The United States and China are in a relationship where they compete while cooperating, and cooperate while competing. In recognition of this state of affairs, both sides appear to be hard at work trying to arrive at a mutually acceptable stewardship arrangement in US-China relations and global governance.

How will the indefinite duration of Xi Jinping's rule affect the relationship between Korea and China?

For China, Korea is a very important partner in establishing and maintaining stable relationships with its neighboring countries, and yet at the same time, it is one of the pillars of the Korea-US alliance. On December 28, 2022, the Korean government announced its Indo-Pacific Strategy, in which Korea made clear that unlike the United States and Japan, it does not regard China as a potential enemy but as an essential partner for cooperation. This was a signal from the Korean government that it would suppress external variables to the maximum extent possible in its bilateral relations with China.

However, Korea-China relations are at a low point at the moment. China is being forced to reevaluate its perception of Korea's place in the world, in the swirling midst of the containment policy of the US Indo-Pacific strategy, the establishment of Korea's own Indo-Pacific strategy, and the agreement on military cooperation among Korea, the United States, and Japan. As such, it behooves China to reassess Korea's core national interests that conflict with those of China, and carefully identify the potential causes of conflict between the two nations.

Korea and China have experienced several unforeseen conflicts in recent years. In the process, conflicting national interests have been laid bare, and in some instances, China has resorted to applying actual pressure on Korea. Conflicts over the deployment of THAAD and human rights issues in the Xinjiang Uyghur Autonomous Region have become familiar issues between the two nations and are not expected to see many changes during Xi Jinping's time in office.

From Korea's perspective, it is vital to identify possible future points of contention in its relations with China and prepare the responses. The sociocultural conflicts between Korea and China will intensify. The Xi Jinping regime, with its emphasis on nationalism and patriotism, will lean toward sociocultural policies and behaviors designed to stoke Chinese people's national pride. From the Korean perspective, this will have all the markings of sociocultural aggression. Future conflict between Korea and China will probably involve territorial issues, especially on territorial waters. In particular, we anticipate that how the peoples of each country perceive each other will have a decisive impact on the changing Korea-China relations in the future. As to those issues already established between the two nations, Korea may be able to persuade China to agree to disagree or to ignore them, having already seen each other's hands.

However, the North Korean nuclear issue will continue to be a bone of contention. China is extremely touchy when it comes to the US suppression strategy on North Korea. In response, South Korea is seeking a breakthrough with a South Korean version of the Indo-Pacific strategy, which emphasizes the importance of communication and cooperation with China. On the other hand, a strategic decision is also required as to whether the North Korean issue should be framed within the purview of South Korea-China relations or the preservation of the liberal international order. We need to limit it to a regional issue involving South Korea, North Korea, and China, and demand that China adopt a more forward-looking stance on the North Korean issue. We need to hasten the development of the rationale with which to persuade China to step up to the plate and help denuclearize North Korea and stop its provocations.

Coming into 2024, North Korea has declared South Korea as its main enemy, currently engaged in continuing military conflict, and accelerated its provocations, including missile tests. In a Ministry of Foreign Affairs press conference on February 5, 2024, spokesperson Wang Wenbin issued the familiar platitude that China supports efforts to improve the relations with North Korea, but did state that the North Korean declaration of its new policy is a matter of North Korean sovereignty[7]. In short, China is refusing to exert effort to diffuse the situation and is instead offering a thinly veiled support to North Korea. As the only nation that can influence North Korean behavior, however, China has the responsibility to try to bring North Korea into the international community if China wishes to be taken seriously as a responsible major power on the global stage.

In addition, only when China takes up its role as a responsible major power in the international and regional order and actively participates in the effort to resolve the North Korean issue can South Korea persuade the United States to ease its aggressive Pivot to Asia stance. South Korea needs to engage in in-depth analytical thinking to secure strategic room for maneuver vis-a-vis China.

Chapter 3

Xi Jinping's Brand of Social Control Work?

Nam Suk Ha

OUTLOOK FOR SOCIETAL CONTROL DURING XI JINPING'S THIRD TERM

The word "safety" (安全) appeared ninety-one times in the 20th Party Congress Report. The keywords "safety" (安全) and "risk" (風險) nearly doubled in frequency over their appearance in the 19th Party Congress Report. This increase can be interpreted to reflect the increased tension in international relations. However, they may also be referring to domestic safety and risk factors. In particular, the so-called blank paper protests that swept across the country in the heels of the 20th Party Congress are raising many eyebrows about the stability of Xi's third term in office. After all, people's expression of widespread frustration with zero-COVID lockdown policies and even the CCP and Xi Jinping himself is in stark contrast to Xi's emphasis on social stability in the report.

Sociopolitical Background and Dilemma for Three Consecutive Terms

On October 31, 2017, shortly after the 19th Party Congress, seven new Politburo Standing Committee members visited the venue of the 1st Party Congress in Shanghai—the birthplace of the CCP. From the perspective of the party, a certain degree of concentration of power complements the weakness of the collective leadership system, that is, dissipation of power among the Politburo Standing Committee members. The emergence of a strong leader concentrated power in the CCP and by extension in said person. The issue that presents itself then is the legitimacy of the CCP rule of this type.

Political authority and legitimacy to rule for the CCP do not come from popular elections. The CCP seized power through a revolution and has claimed legitimacy to rule based on the notion that it is the protector of equality among the people of China. As China embarked upon reform and openness and its socialist identity began to dilute, the Chinese leaders turned to the so-called performance legitimacy. As economic growth slowed during Xi Jinping's time in office, the CCP began to bank on nationalism and patriotism to buttress its political legitimacy.

This shift comes with a set of problems: interpretation of history becoming Sino-centric, diplomatic communications becoming increasingly combative and vociferous and voices of the grassroots people being stifled in the name of reaching the national objectives. Despite the CCP's slogan "common prosperity," it is not clear whether it plans to resolve the problem of income polarization through a more aggressive redistribution of wealth.

In order to achieve "common prosperity" through sustainable and stable redistribution of wealth, the introduction of progressive tax and direct tax is a prerequisite. However, Xi's common prosperity does not mention any plan to implement such tax reform. One reality peculiar to Chinese politics is that the rank-and-file CCP members and their families form the core of Xi's political base. Whether the new middle class formed around them would submit to such tax levies or increase is questionable. Rather, such measures may trigger a backlash among his own power base. Broad grassroots support requires broad redistribution of wealth. But such redistribution may cause his own power base to turn against him, and therein lies one of Xi Jinping's deepest dilemmas.

Xi Jinping's Approach to Social Control

It was no exaggeration to say that China was caught in a triple trap: the *middle-income trap, authoritarian trap, and Thucydides trap.* It appeared that China was on this course through the Jiang Zemin and Hu Jintao administrations, sociopolitically and economically. However, the path China chose under Xi Jinping was systematic social control founded on an authoritarian state system. This shift spawned the concept of *top-level design for full control (頂層設計).*

Social conflict arose through the course of economic growth following the introduction of reform and openness policies, as existing social relations were dismantled, and the gap between the rich and the poor widened. This, of course, rocked the foundation of social stability. In response, the CCP has consistently put forth the slogans of Moderately Prosperous Society (小康社会) and Social Management (社会管理) as its central policy goals throughout the

2000s. The goal of maintaining stability (維穩) has remained unchanged, but great differences in approach are observed in its implementation.

Under the slogan of Harmonious Society (和諧社會), the Hu Jintao administration rolled out programs to redress the adverse impact sudden nationwide marketization and commercialization inflicted on society in the latter part of the 1990s. Faced with a tsunami of petitions from frustrated masses and mass incidents, the government attempted to protect the people's rights and to ameliorate societal conflicts through compromises and regulatory improvements. In contrast, the Xi Jinping administration has attempted to resolve social conflict by applying Orwellian surveillance and control. Toward this end, the Xi Jinping administration has vastly increased the power of the domestic security apparatus and tightened CCP's control thereof.

The state control over public opinion and censorship of the media has been vastly reinforced compared to the Hu Jintao era. The Xi administration began to mobilize powerful means of surveillance and control, including new regulations and digital technology. VPNs, for instance, are now heavily regulated compared to the Hu Jintao era, as part of a vastly intensified cyber control. In addition, the CCP operates troll farms like the Fifty Cent Party (五毛黨) and Navy (水軍) to control online public opinion.

China's online censorship and public opinion control engender resistance in those with liberal tendencies or experience of living abroad. Those engaged in labor movements or human rights movements in China are conducting perilous cat-and-mouse games with the authorities online, struggling to carry on with their movements under the watchful eyes of the Orwellian *big brother*. It appears that this deadly hide-and-seek game on the internet and social media will continue unabated for the foreseeable future.

The People's Acquiescence to State Social Control

Although adverse public opinion does exist, the Xi Jinping regime has maintained a level of popular support through a wide-ranging anti-corruption drive and *people-first policy* (親民 policy). It is not unusual in the Chinese context to see popular support for highly centralized power. This does not, however, automatically legitimize Xi's extended rule. Clearly, demands for liberal democracy are not strong in China. Nevertheless, voices for democracy within the socialist framework have been heard intermittently, but consistently. There has been a steady stream of strikes and protests demanding the protection of workers' rights and farmers' rights. Such movements and protests are now facing powerful oppression at the hands of the Xi administration.

The situation in China evokes the fable of the *Sword of Damocles*. Xi Jinping uses this metaphor mainly to describe external threats, but one wonders whether it more aptly points to the will of the people. Although Xi Jinping has often emphasized the people, pushing forward his moderately prosperous society (小康社會) and people-first (親民) policies, the CCP's oppressive social control measures continue. His extended rule and concentration of power in one man may help with the efficiency of policy implementation, but make the accountability for any policy failure that much more stark and grave. If he fails to create institutional channels through which grassroots voices can be heard, and his policies fail to produce results tolerable to the people, public opinion will not remain merely satirical.

DIGITAL TECHNOLOGY AND SOCIETAL CONTROL

Xi Jinping's stated political philosophies of rule by law (依法治國) and strict governing of the party (從嚴治黨) are reminiscent of the legalism (法家) tradition from ancient Chinese history. He wants to add transparency and efficiency to it by leveraging digital technology—a *Digital Legalism*, if you will.

The Origin and Methods of Social Control

An infamous security surveillance system called Tian Wang (天網), comprising twenty million plus high-performance security cameras with built-in facial recognition technology, is ubiquitous in all urban areas of China. There is also the Xueliang (雪亮) system, a public surveillance network that connects security cameras installed nearly everywhere, including quiet rural roads, to people's TVs and smartphones so that the public and security authorities can conduct surveillance together in real time. Meanwhile, in 2014, China announced its *Establishment of Compulsory Social Credit System 2014-2020.* The plan is for China to award certain points, that is, a social credit score, to individuals by using all personal information collected in the national database, including personal credit and financial information, criminal history, and social activity records. Said score, then, is used in financial transactions, education, and the medical coverage of the social safety net.

China's Social Credit System is unique: first, it is designed to derive a comprehensive evaluation of an individual citizen by aggregating various personal information such as credit ratings and legal infraction records into one system; second, it uses the resulting aggregate score in the state's reward or punishment system *vis-a-vis* the individual citizen; and third, it collects data in the realm of "big data" using advanced ICT technology and ubiquitous surveillance systems. China is testing this system in various pilot cities and regions. The Social Credit System can and is likely to mutate into a more powerful surveillance and punishment system.

Why Has Xi Jinping Chosen the Path of Digital Legalism?

Despite China's reputation as a rising power, it has been subjected to endless speculations about its collapse. Whenever a color revolution emerged in another authoritarian country, the world's media spotlighted Tiananmen Square. Until just a few years ago, many China experts warned of the China risks and the "middle-income trap." Many also voiced dire concerns over China's debt crisis, financial instability, sluggish export and domestic demand, and ecological and environmental devastations.

The solutions offered by major Western media outlets and analysts were democratization and marketization. The rationale was elegantly simple: as authoritarian one-party rule and market economy are innately antithetical, democratization and free-marketization were the only ways out. Xi Jinping's choice, however, was the concentration of power in one paramount leader—himself. China was to plow through the myriad risks and colossal difficulties with powerful centralized leadership. Although many have criticized this choice as a surefire path toward authoritarian dictatorship, simple dichotomous democracy-versus-dictatorship analysis has its limits. We must look into what China is trying to accomplish through its seemingly retrogressive choice.

For instance, China's seemingly draconian social control utilizing cutting-edge digital technology can be used to monitor corruption among party officials and businesses, thereby increasing transparency in policy implementation and business transactions. It can also increase transparency in implementing tax regulations and policies and reduce administration costs. Unsurprisingly, there still remains a strong public opinion in China that a certain loss of individual liberties should be tolerated for the public good. Nevertheless, there is a stronger tendency among Chinese to view the marriage of social control and cutting-edge technology not as a price to pay to realize a utopia under China's traditional legalism (法家) but as a path toward a dreaded dystopia.

Future of the Digital Legalism

While it cannot match other platform providers (Google, Facebook, YouTube, etc.) in terms of the diversity of data, Chinese platform providers have an advantage in terms of the depth of data. In the big data model like the Chinese platforms, their value and utility increase when the data are centralized rather than distributed or partitioned. In that regard, China's Social Credit System features the following: first, it collects all sensitive personal information such as credit ratings and legal infraction inquiries in one data storage and renders a comprehensive social credit score for each subject individual; second, it uses this social credit score as a criterion for reward and punishment in various aspects of said citizen's life; third, the system collects big data by utilizing advanced ICT technologies and surveillance systems.

As of yet, the CCP appears to use the Social Credit System as a monitoring mechanism on citizens' moral behaviors rather than as a mechanism for strict reward and punishment. In other words, the high-tech system is being used to extol the virtues of the traditional ideologies of the nation under Confucian and legalist political philosophies (儒法國家). Of course, the technology behind this system makes it possible to upgrade it to a more powerful and all-encompassing mechanism for surveillance or punishment at any time. This is the expected result when China's one-party rule and centralized power structure meet big data technology. With low social awareness of the concept of private property or the right to privacy, China maintains a centralized one-party rule a la Orwellian "Big Brother." This makes the CCP more willing to apply digital surveillance technology to the everyday lives of ordinary citizens much more aggressively than other countries can. If this is meant to be the attractiveness of China's soft power, the Chinese solution that China has been offering the world cannot be the new global alternative. If Xi Jinping's *"New Era"* were to avoid becoming Huxleyan "Brave New World," China would have to be able to assuage the fears of many around the globe.

WILL XI JINPING'S SOCIETAL CONTROLS WORK?

Blank Paper Protests in the Heels of the 20th Party Congress

Chinese society appears to be responding rather passively to the heightened surveillance and control systems under Xi Jinping. Protests of various kinds have taken place sporadically over the years, but nationwide protests have not materialized since the Tiananmen Incident of 1989. Instead, expressions of public discontent have been in the form of petitions. In the absence of an alternative to the CCP, multiparty system, or electoral system, people are petitioning the central government for the punishment of municipal officials or local capitalists for their infractions or abuse of power, such as arrearages in payroll, corruption, or administrative restrictions unfairly imposed. This can be said to reflect the perception of the Chinese people that there must be a strong central government in order to keep local municipal authorities and people of influence in check. However, civil discontent about the Xi regime is on the rise as the concentration of power in one man solidifies, the real estate market stagnates, and the zero-COVID restrictions intensify. Although not national in scope, graffiti protests took place in a number of areas not only overseas but also in China.

From the Foxconn factory protests in Zhengzhou, the Urumqi apartment fire protest, the destruction of the Lanzhou PCR testing facility, physical clashes in Guangzhou, memorial protests in Shanghai about the Urumqi fire, to the Liangma River blank paper protests in Beijing, protesters even demanded Xi Jinping to step down, going beyond mere expression of discontent against the CCP rule. A case in point was the famous hanging banner protest on Sitong Bridge (四通橋) in Beijing days leading up to the 20th Party Congress. The banner declared: We the people want food, not the PCR test, liberty not lockdowns and control, dignity not lies, reform not Cultural Revolution, and elections not dictators. Let's not be slaves, but citizens. Boycott classes! Strike! Bring down the traitorous dictator Xi Jinping! ("不要核酸要吃饭，不要封控要自由，不要谎言要尊严，不要文革要改革，不要领袖要选票，不做奴才做公民罢课罢工罢免独裁国贼习近平.")

With the increased intensity of social control, the breadth of Chinese people's antipathy has also increased compared to five years ago. It was the first time since the Tiananmen Square massacre in 1989 that demonstrations with the same slogans arose simultaneously in major cities and universities across China. Although China has seen over the past three decades numerous protests like workers' protests, farmers' protests, resistance from intellectuals, environmental movements, and ethnic minority movements, they had by and large remained localized, isolated incidents.

Now, however, discontent spanning across the spectrum of issues such as the economic slowdown, youth unemployment, oppression of freedom of speech, and coercive policies appear to have converged on a unified demand: the anti-zero-COVID slogan. Above all, the fire at the Urumqi apartment was a catalyst. This incident, like many disasters in other countries, seems to have become a focal point that broached the accumulated grief of the Chinese people over their government's handling of domestic affairs. The central authorities had been touting the zero-COVID policy as the most conspicuous achievement of the CCP in protecting the lives and safety of the people better than those of other countries. However, the tragic paradox where innocent citizens perished in a high-rise fire precisely because the zero-COVID quarantine regulations prevented the firefighters from reaching them incensed the Chinese people and breached the dam that had been holding back the accumulated discontent about their government.

How Will China's Popular Resistance and Government's Social Control Play Out?

The recent waves of protest call to mind the trauma of the 1989 Tiananmen Square massacre. However, the possibility of a full-scale violent crackdown was low. At the time of the Tiananmen Square Incident, the authorities had been able to target the protesters and organizers gathered in the square. By contrast, the recent protests were, like those of other countries in the twenty-first century, dispersed and lacking centralized organization. For this reason, it was not feasible for the CCP to characterize the current waves of protest as the works of domestic enemy or foreign infiltrators.

As such, the most expedient direction of the Chinese authorities' response was to prevent the spread of protests through low-intensity suppression and silence the protesters' demands by adjusting quarantine policies. While accommodating the public's demand for easing the quarantine measures to a certain extent, the CCP would label and suppress the demand for freedom of speech or any criticism of the government as "foreign intervention." In fact, Chinese authorities are known to have been using various digital surveillance techniques, which were used during the protests in the Xinjiang Uyghur region or Hong Kong to weed out, arrest, and repress current protest leaders. The fact that the protests have entered a lull due to the drastic easing of the zero-COVID policies attests to this strategy on the part of the central government.

However, the ember still remains. In the absence of an alternative to the CCP, it is difficult for the majority of the Chinese people to oppose CCP rule itself. However, the enmity toward Xi Jinping is growing. The blank paper protests forced the authorities to do an about-face and abolish the zero-COVID measures overnight, but in return, many people have been helplessly exposed to the virus and perished. If this situation continues, leading to the collapse of the healthcare system and the economy, people's anger will find another outlet to vent itself. Realistically, it will be difficult for people to organize large-scale resistance movements, but sporadic resistance is expected to continue.

In order to foreclose such resistance, what the CCP chose was the strengthening of the security apparatus and the revision of counter-espionage laws. In particular, the amended Counter-Espionage Law ("CEL") that went into effect on July 1, 2023, expanded the scope of espionage activity from *steal (ing), spy (ing) for, purchas (ing), or illegally provid (ing) any state secrets or intelligence* to *steal (ing), spy (ing) for, purchas (ing), or illegally provid (ing) any state secrets or intelligence, or other documents, data, materials, or items of concern to national security.* This new definition is so expansive and abstract that it immediately raised the concern that the CCP can arbitrarily apply it to activities hitherto not considered espionage activities. In fact, the accusation of collusion with foreign elements has been the go-to technique for the Chinese security apparatus in silencing or rounding up domestic resistance groups. It is a legitimate concern that the newly expanded CEL will be utilized indiscriminately to further suppress and crack down on any criticism of the CCP. This concern has already been borne out in many instances where the Chinese security apparatus has applied the expanded CEL to conduct intrusive investigations on or arrest not only domestic anti-government voices but also foreign businessmen in China.

CHINA'S SOCIAL ISSUES AND POLICY CHALLENGES

Zero COVID-19 Policy and Changes in Public Sentiment

A review of China's quarantine policy prior to the zero-COVID policy is in order. In the early days of the COVID-19 outbreak in Wuhan, from late December 2019 to January 2020, Xi Jinping faced the biggest threat since taking power. People's dissatisfaction with Xi's regime skyrocketed as a result of the bungled initial response to this mysterious illness, the collapse of the medical system in Wuhan and Hubei, and the panicky draconian quarantine measures, only to be followed by mass deaths. In particular, the crisis was likened to "China's Chernobyl Moment," as the situation went out of control in the midst of the government's imposition of total information control and censorship. This macabre analogy was, of course, referring to the behavior of the former Soviet Union in clamping down on information, leading to greater deaths and damage to itself and neighboring countries.

However, as the West's more lenient COVID-19 responses led to many deaths, while China's merciless zero-COVID policy armed with repressive quarantines and digital surveillance technologies managed to keep the death toll relatively low, this accomplishment became a matter of nationalistic pride. This swell of patriotic feeling became equated with the confidence that China's governing system is more efficient and stable than those of the democracies. However, 2022 saw the reversal of this breathless patriotism. The West gradually transitioned to with-Corona mode, thanks to the effective vaccines and the mutation of the Corona virus to less virulent strains. China, on the other hand, stuck to its zero-COVID policy with its unrelenting quarantine measures, especially in large cities across the country like Shanghai, resulting in a chorus of criticism. Many in China's private sector and other nations hoped for the easing of the zero-COVID policy following the 20th Party Congress, but to no avail.

In particular, the appointment at the 20th Party Congress of new Politburo Standing Committee members Li Qiang, Shanghai party secretary who led the strict quarantine policy in 2022, and Cai Qi, Beijing party secretary who persisted with equally repressive lockdown measures for over two years, exacerbated public anxiety. People's anger manifested itself in the form of the blank paper protests. Added to the protest was the failure of China's healthcare system to cope with the avalanche of infections, making it infeasible for the central authorities to continue with the suffocating quarantine measures. The CCP abruptly tore down the zero-COVID policy in December 2022 and entered the with-Corona mode like the rest of the world.

Transition to Living with COVID-19 and China's Dilemma

Having plunged into the with-Corona mode, China is in the midst of a massive chaos. Unlike in Korea, the vaccination rate of the elderly, especially those in rural areas who are most vulnerable to the Omicron variant, is low. Chinese vaccines themselves are not very effective, and China lacks sufficient healthcare facilities. These factors have created a perfect storm in the spread of Coronavirus, necessarily triggering massive nationwide confusion and misery. Although the lockdowns have eased, the spread of infection has prevented the Chinese people from going back to their normal lives. In addition, there is a dearth of medicine and medical support, and the stockpiling of daily necessities in preparation for self-isolation after infection is prevalent. The authorities are in a panic-stricken damage control mode, refusing to count asymptomatic infections in their announcement of infection data, and even resorting to falsifying the number of deaths.

Ahead of the 20th National Congress, when the central government ordered flexible zero-COVID quarantine measures tailored to local situations, provincial governments could not easily ease their local quarantine policies. Rather, they imposed even stricter quarantine measures in a desperate effort to evade future reprimands from above. In fact, during the SARS crisis twenty years ago, the central government sacked the minister of health and the mayor of Beijing as scapegoats. Their crimes were concealing information and inappropriate handling. And even in the early days of the outbreak of COVID-19 in 2020, Xi dismissed the municipal health policy officers as well as the party secretaries of Hubei Province and Wuhan City, the most immediate targets of people's rage, in an effort to create a buffer between the unfolding debacle and himself. This hierarchical relationship between the central government and local governments is unique to China and is the main reason behind China's failure to transition smoothly from the zero-COVID policy to the with-COVID policy. In negotiating this bottleneck of a transition, local governments displayed their all-too-obvious inability to respond effectively to the challenges at hand, intensifying people's frustration and anger.

People's frustration with the government, as manifested in the blank paper movement, was not the sole reason behind the sudden about-face with the zero-COVID policy. Above all, the fiscal burden that local governments had been forced to bear in executing the zero-COVID policy was no longer sustainable. According to media reports, for instance, the financial outlay of Guangdong Province in relation to COVID-19 exceeded 146.8 billion yuan over a three-year period, equivalent to 27 trillion Korean won. This figure includes only the costs of PCR tests, vaccinations, and administrative expenses. With the costs of patient care included, the actual figure far exceeds 146.8 billion yuan. To make matters worse, the real estate sector, the biggest source of revenue for local governments, plunged into an abysmal slump, and the fiscal solvency of local governments emerged as an urgent problem. To borrow a Korean proverb, the blank paper protest was like a slap in the face of the Chinese authorities as they were about to break out in tears. Or, a more cynical observation would be that the blank paper protest served as an excuse for the authorities' abrupt transition to the with-COVID policy—the *will of the people.*

Actually, China had about a year around 2022 to sufficiently prepare for the transition to with-COVID. However, busy singing the laurels of the zero-COVID policy and cementing Xi Jinping's third term in office, the CCP simply missed the "golden time." Many in and outside of China voiced criticism that China should have adopted the relatively more successful policies of its East Asian neighbors, including limited social distancing, revamping of healthcare systems, and importing and administering mRNA vaccines and treatment drugs, instead of insisting upon the zero-COVID policy.

Youth Unemployment and Policy Challenges

Today in China, a cynical epigram about young people is in wide circulation: literally "Four No Youth" (四不青年). They don't love (不戀愛), don't marry (不結婚), don't buy homes (不買樓), and don't have children (不生子). There is another one: literally "Full-time Children (全職兒女)." This epithet refers to college grads who cannot find employment and thus work for their parents or grandparents as household helpers, drawing salary for their services. This phenomenon reflects the official May 2023 youth unemployment rate of 20.8 percent, the lowest ever. The "Full-time Children" are known to enter into a written employment contract with their parents or grandparents, and as such may not be said to be totally dependent on them. In reality, however, there is scant difference between China's "Full-time Children" and Korea's "Kangaroo Tribe." Korean Kangaroo children, of course, don't go independent as they grow into adulthood, but remain dependent on their parents for livelihood.

As to buying a house at stratospheric prices in urban areas, there's the aphorism "Generational Mortgage Payment (愚公還貸)." This is a clever modification of an old four-character idiom 愚公移山, which means trying to move a mountain through unending toil lasting through generations. Chinese youth call such phenomena "involution (內卷)." "Involution" used to refer to the failure of China's economy to transition to mature capitalism, as it could achieve only quantitative development, never qualitative development. This meaning of "involution" morphed in the 2020s into the expression of exhaustion and hopelessness resulting from the extreme intensification of societal competition.

Many Chinese youth have adopted Tang Ping (躺平) as a way of coping with their despair in the face of "involution (內卷)." Tang Ping is a slang term that means "lying down and doing nothing." It is a statement of protest against "involution (內卷)" through noncooperation. One reason behind this slang word's going viral online was the intensification of the CCP's suppression of resistance movements from any age segment of the population. The CCP is trying to crack down on Tang Ping (躺平) movement on the one hand and to turn the public opinion around through its Common Prosperity (共同富裕) policy on the other. Unfortunately, the call for Common Prosperity has remained a mere slogan, and worse yet, the CCP has been taking advantage of it as a pretext to repress and regulate private enterprises.

China is currently facing a crisis at the confluence of deteriorating fiscal health of local governments resulting from a deep real estate slump, a falling economic growth rate resulting from declining exports, and loss of growth potential resulting from population decline and population aging. According to the official census announced on January 17, 2023, the population of China was at 1.41175 billion, a year-on-year decline of 850,000. This population decline is the first since 1961, when millions of Chinese perished of starvation during the Great Leap Forward campaign. According to the official figures announced on January 17, 2023, China's 2022 economic growth rate stood at 3 percent, far below the target growth rate of 5.5 percent. This shortfall is the result of the lockdown measures of the zero-COVID policy through 2022, the real estate slump, and weakening export. In the middle of the intensifying US-China strategic competition and worldwide economic recession, China is likely to find it difficult to reverse the falling growth rate.

Over the past decades, the CCP's political legitimacy has stood on continuing economic growth. If economic growth halts, public discontent is sure to increase. Above all, the CCP needs to turn the public opinion around by improving China's healthcare system and social safety network. Regulatory reform alone is unlikely to achieve these critical objectives. Unless the CCP adopts a pro-people approach and succeeds in establishing sufficient social security and welfare systems instead of insisting on a repressive social control approach, Xi Jinping's third term is likely to experience mounting pushback from the disgruntled populace.

Chapter 4

Has China Peaked?

Status of the Chinese Economy

Pyeong Seob Yang

PEAK CHINA DEBATE AND GROWTH POTENTIAL

Peak China Debate

China's economic growth rate has fallen by 1 percent every three years since reaching the high of 14.2 percent in 2007. In *The World Ahead 2023* published in May, the *Economist* asserted the "Peak China theory." According to this argument, China's economic development had reached its apogee. Joseph S. Nye also argues in an article that China has reached the pinnacle of its development, the United States has taken the lead, and, in concert with its allies, should leave China behind. In *The Danger Zone: The Coming Conflict with China*, Michael Beckley of Tufts University and Hal Brands of Johns Hopkins portray China as a major power that has reached its peak as well. In the face of population collapse, checks from the West, ills of one-man authoritarian rule, and property sector collapse, China is in precipitous decline, making it dangerous. The demographic collapse will reduce the productive population, pursuit by other developing countries has put an end to China's latecomer advantage, real estate sector collapse, and accumulation of corporate debt have rendered investment-led growth no longer viable, and increasing international isolation, due in part to the US-China competition, has imposed a severe limitation on innovation-led growth.

Chinese scholars object, decrying that it is too early to talk of Peak China. China is meeting the declining population bonus with a vigorous talent bonus. A recent Renmin University of China report, *Absurd Narratives: An Examination of Recent "Peak China,"* argues that the Chinese economy still possesses ample growth and recovery potential based on continuing science and technology development, structural upgrades, urbanization, and renewed reforms and openness policies. All the talk of China's economic woes, like the housing market collapse, are exaggerations by the West.

Economic Growth Potential

The *14th Five-Year Plan for Economic and Social Development and Long-term Objectives Through the Year 2035* announced in October 2020 set out an objective of doubling the size of China's economy by 2035. That goal would require a 4.7 percent+ economic growth rate per annum until 2035. Chinese economists anticipate that China will be able to sustain a 4 percent+ economic growth potential through 2035, as a result of an increase in the talent pool with higher education and total factor productivity (TFP) despite the decreasing productive population. However, an eminent economist Zhang Xiaojing (张晓晶) and former state councilor Wang Yong (王勇) did express a caveat that, if the US-China decoupling actually becomes a reality, China's growth rate may fall below 3 percent.

International institutions outside of China, however, all predict a much faster economic slowdown in China than those offered by the Chinese government or research outfits. August 2024 study by the IMF projected that China's growth rate would fall to 3.4 percent by 2028. A December 2022 study by the Asian Development Bank projected that China's growth rate would fall below 3 percent after 2026 and below 2 percent after 2031. A November 2022 study by the Japan Center for Economic Research projected that China's growth rate would temporarily rise as China recovers from the effects of the COVID-19 pandemic, but sink to 3 percent after 2031 and 2.2 percent after 2035.

Table 4.1   China's Mid- to Long-Term Potential Growth Rate Projection

YEAR	2021–2025	2026–2030	2031–2035
Chinese Academy of Social Sciences (2020)	5.42	4.92	4.48
David Li, Tsinghua University (2023)	5.9	5.8	5.2
Bank of China (2024)	5.0	4.3	3.8
Zhang Xiaojing & Wang Yong (2023) (Assuming total US-China decoupling)	5.27 (4.83)	4.83 (4.53)	4.35 (3.81)
ADB (2022)	5.3	3.5	2.7

Source: by the author based on compilation of various sources.

CHALLENGES TO CHINA'S ECONOMY

Loss of Growth Potential

Peak China debates point to the demographic collapse, property sector crisis, corporate and regional government debt, and de-risking driven by the United States and the West as factors that may slow China's economic growth in the long run.

First, as the "growing old before getting rich" (未富先老) phenomenon becomes a reality, China's population bonus is being supplanted by a population burden. According to a 2022 study by the Asian Development Bank, whereas China's strong labor market had contributed to the increase in its potential growth rate by 0.3 percent up until the 2006–2010 period, said rate turned to minus territory starting in 2011 as the population bonus began to lose steam. China's worsening demographics is projected to pull down its potential growth rate by –0.5 percent during the 2026–2035 period.

China's active labor population (ages 15–64) reached its peak in 2015 at 998 million and has been declining since. After 2027, when the second baby boomers begin to retire, the rate of decline will accelerate. When China entered the era of an aged society in 2022 with people sixty-five years and over comprising 14 percent of the overall population, China's dependency ratio had risen sharply to 46.6 percent, having hit a low of 34.2 percent in 2010. China is expected to enter the era of a super-aged society by 2035, with people sixty-five years and over comprising over 20 percent+ of the overall population. By then, population aging will impose a significant drag on economic growth and national finance. China, meanwhile, is hoping that qualitative improvement in human resources will offset the declining population in absolute terms, and that an infusion of labor from rural areas and an increase in the retirement age will alleviate the negative impact of population decline to a certain extent.

Second, China's economy is floundering in a real estate trap, and as a result, China's real estate sector-driven economy has reached its limit. In the mid-1990s, China embarked on the commercialization of homes—a seismic departure from the previous communist practice of free distribution. For the next thirty-some years, China's real estate sector has been the main pillar of China's economic growth, accounting for as high as 29 percent of China's GDP. During its heyday, the real estate sector accounted for 30 percent of all investments, and proceeds from the sale of long-term land leases accounted for 20 percent of the revenue of the central government and 50 percent of the municipal governments. As such, a contraction by 20 percent of the real estate sector can lead to 5–10 percent decline in GDP.

Ominously, over-investment in real estate has led to an untenable accumulation of debt and inefficiency in resource allocation since 2000, putting a significant strain on China's economy. Recognizing that the demand for real estate had peaked, Beijing began a number of initiatives to facilitate a soft landing. In the late 2010s, the central government initiated a de-leveraging campaign in the real estate sector. As part of this effort, the central government revamped China's property laws and regulations in 2018 to improve the financial health of real estate firms, and in 2020, instituted the "three red lines" rules relating to mortgage lending. These measures, however, severely curtailed real estate sector investments and led to the cash flow crises and outright bankruptcies among giant real estate developers such as the Evergrand in 2021 and Country Garden in 2023. This crisis in turn led to instability in the financial system, capital markets, and overall economy.

A more fundamental problem is that the Chinese real estate market has reached a monumental level of excess supply and is thus burdened with a colossal housing bubble. Official statistics place the total area of unsold homes at 312 million m^2 and state that it will take a minimum of two years for the market to absorb the inventory. However, unofficial statistics place the number at much higher values, especially in rural cities and northeastern provinces. Loss of demand due to high prices, a declining number of potential buyers, high home ownership, and stagnant urbanization all point to the conclusion that China's real estate sector has passed its peak. Market capitalization of the real estate sector is at 476 trillion Yuan (2021 figure)—1.5 times that of the United States and more than ten times that of Japan. China's home ownership rate is at 90 percent (compared to a 60 percent rate in both the United States and Japan), with multiple home ownership rates at 20 percent, and as such, the demand for homes has weakened. The Price to Income Ratio (PIR) in major cities is at the highest level in the world, at 49.1 in the case of Shanghai and 49.7 in the case of Beijing, pushing average Chinese workers out of the market. China's real estate trap appears slated to slow down China's economic growth.

Third, China is also ensnared in a debt trap of its own making. As China pursued investment-driven rapid economic growth, it incurred a debt to GDP ratio of 280 percent (nonfinancial sector). In addition to the massive pressure on all levels of economic players to repay the debt, the de-leveraging process is expected to slow China's economic growth. Government debt and household debt at 50 percent and 60 percent of GDP, respectively, cannot be said to be high compared to the international average, but corporate debt (nonfinancial sector) stands at 160 percent, the world's highest debt to GDP ratio. Since the Economy Working Group Meeting of December 2015 announced the "supply-side reform," the government has focused on managing corporate debt. In this effort, the government's concentrated effort on de-leveraging the real estate sector has led to the slowing of the real estate market.

In particular, the de-leveraging effort regarding China's distinctive "local government financing vehicles" (LGFVs) is expected to dampen the nation's economic growth momentum by stifling local governments' investment capacity. Despite the central government's efforts to reduce LGFVs' debt and restrain their modus operandi involving debt since 2014, the scale of their enterprises and debt size continued to balloon. According to the IMF, the size of the LGFV industry is approximately 66 trillion Yuan, comprising 53 percent of the GDP. The debt reorganization of the LGFVs is expected to be a protracted one, as their collective debt size is immense, the question of responsibility between local governments and LGFVs is opaque, and the debts resemble a conflation of corporate debt and government debt. The recent economic slowdown and real estate market crisis has also led to aggravating profitability of LGFVs. Further, they led to a precipitous drop in revenue from the sale of long-term leases of lands for the local governments, casting doubt on their ability to make good on their guarantees on LGFV debts. In short, the chain reaction from the property crisis will propagate out starting with the collapse of profitability of LGFVs, to reduction in fiscal revenue for local governments, to distressed transfer of LGFV debt, to deterioration of local governments' fiscal soundness, and to loss of growth momentum at local levels, eventually leading to economic instability and a falling economic growth rate at the national level.

Fourth, the environmental trap has begun to strangle China's economy, as deep-rooted environmental, resource, and energy problems have surfaced. According to official statistics, the average surface temperature has been going up by 0.26°C every ten years, and the sea level by 3.4 mm every ten years. China imports 72.1 percent of its crude oil needs and 66.4 percent of LNG. China accounts for 80 percent of the global production of gallium, magnesium, and tungsten, and 15 percent of cobalt, nickel, and lithium. China spends $500 billion to import crude oil and $380 billion to import other natural resources. These costs translate to ⅓ of all revenue generated by exporting finished products. The constraints imposed by environmental, resource, and energy problems can eventually lead to catastrophic consequences for the Chinese economy.

Market Distrust and Liquidity Trap

As China emerged from three years of COVID-19, it had high hopes of its economy rebounding strongly. However, the economic indicators from 2023 remained significantly below expectations. The economic growth rate exceeded the 5.2 percent target, but the economy revealed deep and widespread instability. Private economy and consumption, the foundation of the Chinese economy, are not showing signs of recovery. In the process of recovering from COVID-19, China lowered interest rates in stark contrast to the global trend and implemented an expansionary monetary policy of massive scale. China's total currency ratio (M2/GDP) rose to 232 percent in 2023 from 199 percent in 2018. Unfortunately, these efforts did not lead to corporate investment and consumption but instead plunged China into a liquidity trap, as people chose to save, fearful of the uncertain future of the economy. This phenomenon can be attributed to domestic traps the Chinese economy finds itself in: the "birdcage trap" and "distrust trap."

First, the private economy, the core of China's economic growth momentum, is caught in a birdcage trap. Chen Yun (陳雲) had introduced what he dubbed a "bird cage economic theory," to wit "a bird (economy, market) can be controlled only if it remains in a birdcage (government, planning)." This was meant as a theoretical underpinning for the limited incorporation of the market economy into China's socialist planned economy. This was followed up by Jiang Zemin's Theory of Three Represents (三個代表論) that laid the foundation for the development of the private economy in China. Over the past thirty years, China's economic reforms have been built upon marketization and a private economy that included nonpublic ownership. The result has been the "56789" phenomenon of the private economy, where private activities account for 50 percent of fiscal revenues, 60 percent of GDP and investment, 70 percent of industrial upgrades and innovation, 80 percent of jobs, and 90 percent of enterprises. In particular, the private economy has been the central pillar of China's growth momentum, as witnessed in such areas as the internet and real estate. In short, without the revival of the private economy, a resurgence of the Chinese economy may not be feasible.

Since Xi Jinping's second term in office, however, China has been cracking down on private enterprises under the banners of "suppression of barbaric growth of private capital," "common prosperity," and "strengthening of national security." It is in essence a counter-privatization. Loss of vibrancy and energy in private enterprises is inevitable. In fact, the share of private investments in total investment fell from 90 percent in 2015 to 54 percent in 2022. Under the "pivot to state" policy, state capital is now overtaking private enterprises.

Second, as China's economy became caught in the birdcage trap, market players withdrew their trust in the government's policies—distrust trap. In the four decades that followed the reform and openness, China's economy has developed as the market players consumed and invested, trusting in the government policies. Wen Jiabao called this "confidence economy" (信心經濟). This trust in the government and its policies is eroding. This erosion began to accelerate since the government began rolling out overtly socialist policies during Xi Jinping's second term in office. As seen in the government crackdowns on Alibaba, the gaming industry, and the online-education industry, trusting in, let alone following, the government's policies has become a huge risk factor. Xi Jinping's call for "common prosperity" only increased the suspicion in the market.

This deterioration of trust in the government has led to massive youth unemployment, well beyond the mere cooling of entrepreneurial spirit in the marketplace. This loss of trust in the government is coming to the fore in the real estate sector as well. Despite the government's real estate market recovery measures, the market players are refusing to heed the government's lead. Everyone harbors a suspicion that if and when the market recovers, the government will crack down on it again. Without regaining the trust and confidence of the people and market, the new economic growth engine, that is, private economy and entrepreneurial energy, will not function.

New Economic Growth Engine and Checks from Outside

Since the mid-2010s, China has pursued a transition from real estate-led investment to consumption and high-tech industry development as its new growth engine. Through this "rebalancing," China wanted to transform itself into a manufacturing and technology powerhouse. Toward this end, China has rolled out various measures to modernize its economic sectors, like the "Made in China 2025" initiative. The fourteenth "5-Year Plan" announced the "Dual Circulation" strategy to dramatically improve the self-sufficiency rate in China's domestic supply chain. These initiatives have been met with some success. While traditional textile, clothing, and computer industries have been downsized, new electric vehicles (EV), secondary cell, and solar energy industries have seen explosive growth. China's global share in the production of secondary cells and solar panels has been exemplary. China has emerged as the biggest exporter of EVs in the world. Further, at the beginning of 2024, China promulgated the "Six Pillars of Promoting the High-quality Development of China's Future Industries" strategy. Its stated objective is to build an ecosystem where competitive future industries and traditional industries can harmoniously coexist by developing core technologies for future industries and making new technology, new products, and new business models universally available. The six future industrial categories include manufacturing, information, material, energy, space, and health.

However, this is where China has been snared in a "major-power check trap" of its own making; it lost the trust of the West. Based on the "international cycle theory" (国际大循环论), Deng Xiaoping chose his signature policy of reform and openness. Under this umbrella policy, he embraced foreign capital and markets, thus incorporating the market economy into China's socialist economy. In the process, he secured the hitherto absent growth engine for China's backward economy. In Deng Xiaoping's footsteps, Jiang

Zemin saw China's successful accession to the World Trade Organization (WTO) in 2010, and Hu Jintao used the WTO to drive sweeping domestic institutional reforms. In particular, the cooperative relations with the United States that followed China's accession to the WTO made immeasurable contributions to China's spectacular rise.

Entering the Xi Jinping era, however, this heady atmosphere has been replaced by China's coercive foreign policy postures. Weaponizing its newfound economic might and the neighboring countries' reliance on it, China began asserting its power on the global economic order. Xi Jinping's coercive, at times belligerent, leadership sowed the seed of distrust in the West and China's neighboring countries. This distrust is now manifesting itself in the US-China strategic competition, including trade war, technology war, and competition of economic systems. The United States' check on China's threatening rise has now evolved into cooperation among many other Western nations in "de-risking" vis-a-vis China. As a result, China's supply chain has now come under threat. The United States and the West have revived explicitly competitive industrial policies designed to foster domestic industries, including paying subsidies to those companies investing within their borders. Some cases in point are the US Chips and Science Act and Inflation Reduction Act and the EU's Net Zero Industry Act and Critical Raw Materials Act. The revival of protectionist policies like these has had a great impact on the supply chain of China, whose economy had seen such a spectacular rise through the work breakdown structure within the open international economic system. These checks by major powers will constrain the growth of the manufacturing sector of the Chinese economy and ultimately limit its growth momentum.

The conflict with the United States surrounding cutting-edge technology and the de-risking posture of the West in general will curtail China's access to advanced technologies. The share of the four core commodities in China's supply chain—critical raw materials, energy transition, information and communication technology, and public healthcare—in overall imports rose to 65.8 percent in 2023 from 58.6 percent in 2018. This represents a critical vulnerability in China's supply chain in the event the United States severs technology transfer to China. China's 2022 share of the global import value of semiconductor devices (commodity code HS 8542) reached 34 percent. The United States' check on the largest importer of semiconductor devices in the world is leading to a crisis in China's high-technology supply chain.

Further, China is witnessing an exodus of multinationals. Many multinationals have adopted the "China+1" strategy, whereby they relocate manufacturing operations to countries other than China. This trend has reduced foreign direct investments and strained the importation of semiconductor cutting-edge technology and associated equipment. In response, Chinese companies are expanding their direct investment into neighboring countries, such as the ASEAN member countries.

CHINA'S AMBITION TO OVERTAKE THE US ECONOMY WILL BE DELAYED

China was able to maintain political stability during the period of rapid economic growth because of the increased income and improved quality of life the reform and openness policy brought about. China maintained cooperative relations in the international community during this period and saw an average annual economic growth rate of 9.4 percent during the Deng Xiaoping period, 8.1 percent during the Zhang Zemin period, and 8.7 percent during the Hu Jintao period. Entering the Xi Jinping era, however, the era of large-scale investment-driven growth is ending due to population decline and a sharp drop in marginal productivity on investment. With the end of hyper-globalization, China is also losing access to overseas markets, technology, and capital. Furthermore, US-Chinese friction has limited the total factor productivity through technological innovation, raising a red flag for the Chinese economy.

First, in the Xi Jinping era, the Chinese economy is moving from an era of "medium to high speed" growth to an era of "medium to low speed" growth. Since 2007, China's economic growth rate has been on a long-term downward slope, falling by one percentage point every three years. It recorded 6.1 percent on average during the first 10 years of Xi Jinping's rule (2013–2023). During his second term (2018–2022) in particular, it fell to 5.2 percent as the US-Chinese conflict and the COVID-19 pandemic coincided with the already slowing Chinese economy. This period saw a conflation of a contracting labor force, falling marginal productivity of capital, and intensifying US-China competition, made worse by a socialist economic development strategy strangling innovation, all conspiring to constrict China's potential growth rate.

During Xi Jinping's third term, all these factors are expected to become compounded by energy and resource problems, conflict with the international community at large, and a controlled economy under the socialist development model. The result is likely to be a "medium speed growth" mode for China, where the average annual growth rate languishes at 4–5 percent. In order to achieve Xi Jinping's target set for 2035, China must maintain an annual growth rate of more than 4.7 percent. To do so, the transition toward a consumption-based growth model must succeed. If delayed, even the medium-speed growth may not be achieved, which in turn may cause social unrest threatening the legitimacy of the Xi Jinping regime.

Second, as the Chinese economy enters an era of moderate growth, the projected time at which China will become the world's largest economy may have to be postponed. China has already surpassed the United States in terms of purchasing power parity (PPP), but its GDP remains at 77 percent that of the United States. So far, China has been projected to become the world's largest economy, surpassing the United States by about the 2030s, as it maintains an average growth rate of about 5 percent compared to 2 percent for the United States. However, a number of internal and external factors make this projection increasingly untenable. China's total factor productivity is falling due to disappearing demographic bonuses, shrinking marginal productivity on investment, and worsening environmental and resource constraints. Socialist development strategies emphasizing "Common Prosperity" are stifling technological innovation in the IT and platform industries. US regulations limiting export to China of cutting-edge semiconductor technologies have placed a stranglehold on China's ambition to increase productivity through digitalization. Add to this the intensifying US-China competition and China's loss of soft power resulting from its stance on the Taiwan strait issue, many theorize that China has thrown away its opportunity to overtake the United States for good.

As the Chinese economy has already reached its peak, the argument that the Chinese economy has lost its chance to overtake the US economy for good sounds increasingly persuasive. Australia's Lowy Institute predicts that it will be impossible for China to significantly overtake the United States into the mid-twenty-first century. The Economist predicts that after China's GDP reaches 90 percent of that of the United States's in 2030, the gap will widen again. The Japan Economic Research Institute predicts that China's nominal GDP will not be able to overtake the United States' even into 2035. In 2020, the same institute had predicted that China's GDP would surpass the United States' by 2029, and in 2021 by 2033. Now, however, the institute holds that it may have become impossible for China to overtake the United States, taking into consideration such factors as China's weakening growth potential, the decrease in GDP adjusted for depreciating Yuan, and the reversal of the growth rate between the United States and China after 2030. China's economy is expected to recover temporarily into 2025 as the impact of COVID-19 dissipates, but is expected to fall to 3 percent in the ensuing five years, and 2.2 percent over the five-year period following that. Moreover, if Xi Jinping's hold on power continues indefinitely, China's economy may descend to 1 percent economic growth, as the CCP's continued restriction on the IT sector delays the transition to a digital economy, and as geopolitical factors such as the Taiwan issue and the US-China competition constrict trading volumes and accelerate the exodus of foreign investment.

Third, there is a possibility that the Chinese economy will not be able to escape from the "middle-income trap" for an indefinite period of time as a result of its slowing economic growth rate. Under Xi Jinping, China became a middle-income country by building a *Xiǎokāng* society (moderately well-off society). By defeating absolute poverty, China achieved its first mid- to long-term strategic goal. In February 2021, the Chinese government declared that absolute poverty had been eradicated in rural areas. This was a colossal achievement when one considers the historical data that, in 1978, China's population living in absolute poverty reached 770 million, 97.5 percent of the total population. In a speech on the 100th anniversary of the founding of the CCP in July 2021, Xi Jinping declared, "We have realized the first goal in our 100-year struggle and have built a full-scale *Xiǎokāng.*" China had escaped the low-income country designation with a per capita GDP of $1,053 in 2001, and became a middle-income country in 2010 with a per capita GDP of $4,550. In 2021, China was on its way toward becoming a high-income country at $12,500. China's path of surpassing the $10,000 mark is more reminiscent of the paths of Korea, Japan, and Taiwan, rather than those of the Latin American countries that fell into the middle-income trap. At the fifth plenary session of the 19th Meeting of the Central Committee of the CCP in October 2020, Xi Jinping proposed a vision whereby China would double the size of its economy and per capita GDP by 2035 to become a developed country. Assuming steady growth, it is expected that China could comfortably reach this goal with its manufacturing competitiveness, human capital potential, and domestic market potential. If so, it is relatively unlikely that China will fall into the middle-income trap. However, many economists now argue that China has entered a period of growth stagnation and is unlikely to become a developed country because of such structural problems as a decrease in the working-age population, aging population, and state-controlled economy.

CHALLENGES OF XI JINPING'S THIRD TERM: PREVENTING GROWTH SLOWDOWN

If China's economy fails to reestablish a virtuous cycle within three years and falls into a middle-income trap, Chinese politics may face a tumultuous period around 2027 when Xi Jinping's fourth term is slated to commence. It follows, therefore, that the primary focus of the CCP will be economic recovery between now and then. In order to achieve it, however, the CCP must return to its former flexibility with regard to the market system. If Xi Jinping persists with his current ideology-driven "socialist market economy with Chinese characteristics" policies, the Chinese economy will remain mired in recessionary pressures, and the chasm between the economy and politics will grow wider.

Xi Jinping will be forced to make some hard choices and his political dream may become unattainable. The all-important public sentiment will turn favorable only with the recovery of the Chinese economy. People's lives, livelihoods, and survival will be the fundamental elements that will sustain Xi Jinping's hold on power. China's economic recovery will also be the pre-requisite for the continuation of its bold foreign policy posture. For the next three years, Xi Jinping and the CCP will have to go all out to stabilize China's economy above all other considerations.

KOREA-US-CHINA TRIANGULAR ECONOMIC RELATIONS

Korea and the United States are allies under the 1953 Mutual Defense Treaty. Beyond the formal military alliance, however, the two nations are de-facto allies in terms of economy and, especially, shared values like democracy and human rights. At the same time, Korea, a powerful exporter of manufactured goods located in East Asia, maintains close economic ties with China. As such, the geopolitical shifts brought on by the US-China strategic competition pose significant risks to the Korean economy.

US-China Competition versus Korea-US-China Triangular Relations

China's accession to the WTO and the resulting cooperative economic relations between the United States and China have been a major driving force behind globalization and the growth of the global economy. This state of affairs began to undergo a fundamental change with the advent of the Trump administration. The "de-risking" strategy of the Biden admin-istration and the allies of the United States is reshuffling the international economic order.

First, with the arrival of the Trump administration, the United States began imposing various restrictions on Chinese companies and products. The United States accused China of shunning fair competition within the global value chain, for example, stealing the United States' cutting-edge technology, and flouting the universal values of the existing global economic order. Instead of "decoupling," an outright severance of relations, however, the United States focused on decoupling from China within the global value chain, thereby increasing the price China had to pay in accessing the global value chain. Over the past decade, the United States has imposed a 25 percent punitive tariff on Chinese high-tech products. The United States has also imposed bans and limitations on export, investment, and financing related to semiconductor devices and related equipment, 5G technology, battery technology, AI technology, and drone technology in order to foreclose China's rise as a new global leader in high-tech industries.

The Biden administration has formed a de-facto alliance among like-minded advanced countries around the idea of "de-risking" from China's menace. Having determined that the existing WTO regime is no longer capable of containing China's challenge to the international economic order, the United States is building a new international economic order with itself at the middle. Indo-Pacific Economic Framework for Prosperity (IPEF) is a case in point. The United States is also scrambling to bolster its economic security by strengthening its domestic supply chain, thereby protecting its economy from overreliance on China. The United States has passed the US Chips and Science Act of 2022 and the US Inflation Reduction Act (IRA) of 2022 in order to attract foreign investment, thereby stifling China's technological influence in the semiconductor and battery industries. The United States has also placed limitations on IPOs by Chinese companies in the US stock market and prohibited transactions with Chinese communication and defense industries. The Biden administration's "de-risking" quasi-alliance became apparent at the Hiroshima G7 summit meeting in May 2023.

Second, China perceives these moves by the United States as decoupling-China (脫中國), and in response, has instituted various policies to protect its supply chain. Domestically, China has invoked national mobilization on a path toward indigenization of its supply chain and technology under such initiatives as Made in China 2025 (MIC 2025), strategic emerging industries, and "Zhuanjingtexin (專精特新), which is underpinned the specialized, sophisticated, and innovative small giant companies, aka "Small Giants" or "Hidden Champions." Internationally, China has adopted the Dual Circulation (双循环) strategy, which prioritizes domestic consumption while remaining engaged in international trade and investment.

In response to the de-risking strategy of the G7 countries, China is expanding its influence vis-a-vis the Global South through such institutions as the Belt and Road Initiative, Regional Comprehensive Economic Partnership (RCEP), BRICs, and Shanghai Cooperation Organization (SCO). The objective is, of course, to secure its access to the international supply chain, especially for raw materials and energy. In response to US pressure, China has restricted the export of rare earth minerals, graphite, manganese, and magnesium, for which China enjoys a dominant global market share. As to all nations which may turn unfriendly against it, China has also enacted the Anti-Foreign Sanctions Law and Anti-espionage Law, and adopted Provisions on the Unreliable Entities List, as potential economic weapons.

Third, Korea has shifted its strategic posture from "U.S. for Security, China for Economy" to "U.S. for Security, World for Economy." Meanwhile, Korea is in the process of building a "comprehensive alliance relationship" with the United States, through such vehicles as the FAB 4, Indo-Pacific Economic Framework for Prosperity (IPEF), Mineral Security Partnership (MSP), and Korea-US High-Level Talks on Economic Security. Korea attended the 2021 and 2023 G7 summits, that is, participated in the talks that formulated the de-risking postures of the G7 countries. Korea also proclaimed its own Indo-Pacific Strategy in 2022 and entered into the American-Japanese-Korean trilateral pact based on the Camp David Principles (JAROKUS). These diplomatic and military arrangements Korea has opted to enter into indicate that Korea is participating in the US-led value alliance and the broader containment effort by the West arrayed against China. These US-leaning choices Korea has made may give the impression that Korea is an active participant in the US containment of China, and as such may lead to strained and possibly conflict-ridden Korea-China relations.

The Yoon Suk Yeol administration has proffered "cooperation based on mutual trust, compliance with international order, and mutual prosperity" as the new keynote for Korea-China relations. The gravamen of this statement has its roots in Korea's perception of China's high-handed and coercive economic and diplomatic behaviors and the previous Moon Jae In administration's submissive diplomatic response thereto. This explains Korea's shift from "US for Security, China for Economy" to "US for Security, World for Economy." What has changed is that Korea is committed to diversifying its export market, thereby reducing its reliance on the Chinese market. China is Korea's single largest trading partner, both in import and export. A clear and present threat to the Korean economy is inevitable in the event the US-China strategic competition escalates into a higher level of conflict. This keenly felt vulnerability is driving wide-ranging debates in Korea regarding the extent of 脫中國 (break away from China) Korea should contemplate.

Breaking Away from US-China Interdependence

The US-China strategic competition is leading to a gradual break from mutual dependence between the United States and China. In the midst of this tectonic shift, Korea is struggling to reduce its overreliance on the Chinese economy.

First, the United States is attempting to break away from China by increasing imports from friendly nations. China's share of US. exports has remained steady at 7 percent since 2018, but its share of US imports fell to 13.9 percent in 2023 from 21.2 percent. Meanwhile, the friendly IPEF countries' share of US imports rose from 18.7 percent to 21.7 percent during the same period. Particularly, the ASEAN countries' share in US imports rose from 7.3 percent to 10.6 percent. No meaningful change was observed in the case of Canada and Mexico, two countries that share borders with the United States.

America's breakaway from China is in full swing. China's share in US imports of four items subject to US "supply chain management"—critical minerals, ICT products, energy, and healthcare products and equipment—fell from 22.9 percent in 2017 to 19.1 percent in 2022. Especially as the US-China technological hegemony competition heats up, China's share in US import of ICT products fell from 42.8 percent to 31.8 percent during the same period. The United States is diverting its import of critical minerals to Canada and Australia, and ICT products to Vietnam, Korea, and Taiwan. Nevertheless, the United States' overall reliance on Chinese ICT products still remains high.

Second, China meanwhile is also accelerating its break away from America. The US share in China's exports fell from 19.2 percent in 2018 to 14.8 percent in 2023, and in imports from 7.3 percent to 6.5 percent. China is expanding its trade with ASEAN and BRI countries, and SCO and other Global South countries in place of countries friendly to the United States. The share of the non-Asian participants of IPEF in China's exports fell from 31.7 percent in 2018 to 26.4 percent in 2023 and in imports from 34.7 percent to 29.7 percent.

China's reliance on Korea and the United States for intermediate components has been decreasing steadily as the US-China competition continues. Korea and the United States' share in China's import of parts and components fell from 23.9 percent in 2018 to 20.1 percent in 2023. Most notably, Korea and the United States' share in China's import of semiconductors (HS 8542) fell sharply from 30.1 percent in 2018 to 21.2 percent in 2023, as the US-China semiconductor competition continues. The United States' share in China's import of nonenergy minerals also fell sharply from 9.5 percent in 2018 to 2.1 percent in 2023.

Reality: Korea's Continuing Reliance on Chinese Economy

Although Korea's overreliance on China in terms of export and investment is on the decline, its reliance on Chinese intermediate goods and raw materials has increased. First, Korea's overall reliance on the Chinese economy is decreasing, while Korean exports to ASEAN and EU nations are increasing. China's share of Korean exports fell sharply from 26.8 percent in 2018 to 22.8 percent in 2022, and 19.7 percent in 2023. In contrast, the United States' share of Korean exports has rebounded to 18.0 percent as of July 2023, having dropped from 21.8 percent in 2000 to 10.1 percent in 2011. China's share of Korea's intermediate goods exports also dropped sharply from 29.8 percent in 2018 to 23.9 percent in 2023. These are positive trends toward reducing Korea's overreliance on the Chinese market.

Second, Korea's 脱中國 (break away from China) phenomenon is more conspicuous in overseas investments. China's share of Korean overseas investment fell sharply from 22.6 percent in 2018 to 11.6 percent as of September 2023 (balance basis). The number of new Korean investments in China is falling fast, and the repatriation of investments is steadily increasing. In fact, the number of repatriations has outpaced new investments since 2020. China's share in Korean manufacturers' overseas investments fell from 32.3 percent to 29.6 percent during the same period (balance basis). Korean manufacturers' overseas investments are being diverted from China to Southeast Asia. Especially in the high-tech sector—semiconductors, batteries, and EVs—their investments in the United States have seen a marked increase.

Third, Korea's reliance on China in terms of intermediate goods and critical minerals has in fact risen. China's share of Korean imports of these items generally increased from 19.9 percent in 2018 to 22.2 percent in 2023. China's share of Korean imports of intermediate goods, in particular rose from 24.6 percent to 28.8 percent during the same period. China's share of Korean imports of the four items of supply chain management (SCM)—critical materials, energy, ICT, and public healthcare—has steadily risen steadily from 16.5 percent to 19.5 percent, and that of critical minerals from 14.0 percent to 21.6 percent during the same period. These trends indicate a continuing Chinese influence on Korea's economic security.

KOREA'S CHOICE: "US FOR SECURITY, WORLD FOR ECONOMY" AND PARETO OPTIMUM

Decline of Korea-China Complementary Relationship

For three decades following the diplomatic normalization between Korea and China, the two nations have expanded trade between them based on a mutually complementary economic framework. However, this symbiotic relationship is changing. Although Korea has aided China's rise as a supplier of intermediate goods, the synergistic industrial framework is fast declining as China has achieved domestic sourcing capability and surpassed Korea in certain new technology industries.

First, the "bottleneck phenomenon," which has been the source of great opportunities for Korea in its trade with China, is disappearing as China enters a medium-low speed economic growth era. During its high-speed growth era, China often encountered unequal developments across its industrial activities. Because of the break-neck changes in China's economy, industry, and society, different industries advanced at different speeds, resulting in widespread bottleneck phenomena where certain industrial sectors could not support other sectors. This presented lucrative opportunities for Korea, Japan, and Taiwan, especially in the intermediate goods sector.

Second, the recent transformation of China's economic growth model increased indigenization of intermediate goods supply, reducing the need for their imports. From 2017 to 2020, China's rate of dependence on imports (amount of imports/gross output) fell from 5.0 percent to 4.4 percent, its import rate (amount of imports/aggregate supply amount) fell from 6.2 percent to 5.7 percent, and its intermediate goods localization rate rose from 92.1 percent to 92.9 percent. This transformation of China's economic growth structure, in turn, reduced the effect China's economic growth has had on the economic growth of neighboring countries. While the rate at which China's final demand drove value added rose from the mid-2000s onward, that of the neighboring countries fell—in the case of Korea from 1.2 percent in 2018 to 1.0 percent in 2020. These trends indicate the weakening of the Korea-China work breakdown structure (Korea ⇒ domestic fabrication in China ⇒ export to third destinations). The reasons are increasing domestic consumption in China, rising wages in China reducing the need for economic dependence between the two nations, and changing the structure of the intermediate goods market resulting from China's advancement in technology. For example, the correlation coefficient between Chinese imports and Korean exports fell from 0.63 percent in 2015 to 0.21 percent in 2023. These data indicate that Korea's export industry structure is not keeping up with the changes in China's import demand structure. ASEAN countries and Taiwan are filling China's intermediate goods needs where Korea is falling behind, and advanced economies like Japan and Germany are claiming a lion's share of China's needs for semiconductor equipment and EV parts.

Third, Korea no longer enjoys a trade surplus with China. Korea's trade surplus with China plunged from $62.8 billion in 2013 to $1.2 billion in 2022. In 2023, the trade balance with China turned into an $18 billion deficit. If the export of semiconductors (HS 8542) is excluded, Korea already recorded a trade deficit with China in 2021, expanding the deficit to $34.4 billion in 2023. It is very likely that Korea's trade deficit with China will continue, especially as Korea shifts from surplus to deficit in intermediate goods trade. Korea had seen a trade deficit with China in consumer goods already in 1994, in capital goods in 2020, and now sees a trade deficit in intermediate goods excluding semiconductors as of 2023. As China's self-sufficiency grows in new materials and parts industries (other than semiconductors), the falling revenues of Korean companies operating in China are forcing them to buy back their own shares, exacerbating the trade imbalance.

Fourth, the sluggish performance of Korean companies operating in China reflects their falling competitiveness in an era of low growth. The profit ratio of the Korean companies in China fell from 7.3 percent in 2013 to 1.0 percent in 2022, and the Sales-Investment Ratio also dipped from 4.90 percent to 2.60 percent over the same period. The market share of Korean passenger car manufacturers in China plunged from 9.0 percent in 2014 to 1.6 percent in 2023, leading to business restructuring. In traditional manufacturing, Korean companies have no choice but to relinquish market share, undercut by indigenous manufacturers in pricing. In emerging industries, China's demand for materials, parts, and equipment continues to grow, but Korea lacks the ability to supply them effectively. Meanwhile, China's hope of indigenization will be slowed by the US-China competition for technological hegemony. Korea must turn the current difficulties into a springboard to improve its technology and supply capacity in cutting-edge materials and parts sectors where China's demand is expected to continue.

US for Security, World for Economy

The heady Korea-China economic relations Korea once experienced since the Korea-China Diplomatic Normalization of 1992 are fading into history. The past "bandwagoning" strategy is no longer feasible. Nevertheless, the Chinese market is not disappearing either. Amid growing asymmetry, Korea-China economic relations are falling into the vortex of the US-China strategic competition. Korea needs a "rebalancing strategy" in its relations with China: we must find the Pareto optimum where Korea can secure economic security and stability in the Korea-China economic relations.

First, Korea needs to diversify its export markets while managing the Korea-China economic relations for stability. Declining reliance on the Chinese market is a common phenomenon found in all countries friendly to the United States that are maintaining the de-risking posture. From 2020 to 2023, China's share of US exports fell from 8.7 percent to 7.3 percent, of EU exports from 4.2 percent to 3.3 percent, and of Japan's exports from 22.0 percent to 17.6 percent. China's share of Korean exports fell sharply from 26.8 percent in 2018 to 19.7 percent in 2023. Some argue that this figure will fall to as low as 15 percent. Such projections, however, are taking into consideration political factors like the US-China conflict and China's market entry barriers in their analysis, as well as the change in the industrial structures between the two countries.

The slowing growth of its economy does not mean an economic crisis or geopolitical decline for China. The singular importance of the Chinese market remains. Even if China's economic growth rate drops to 2 percent beyond 2031 as projected by the Asian Development Bank, it means that the Chinese economy will be growing at a rate commensurate with those of the United States and EU. The sheer scale of China's imports (China + Hong

Kong) reached $3.8 trillion in 2022, having previously surpassed that of the United States in 2018. Among all nations, China wields the greatest influence on the global economy not only as the world's factory but as a market. As of 2022, China accounted for 17.7 percent of the world's GDP (second largest) (*the* largest at 18.4 percent per Purchasing Power Parity), 30.1 percent of the global manufacturing value-added, 13.3 percent of the global consumption (second largest), and 21.8 percent of the global industrial product exports (*the* largest). If China retains its status as the world's factory and the largest exporter despite the slowing economic growth rate, Korea, which earns its keep by exporting intermediate goods, should maintain its economic cooperation with China. Moreover, as a global manufacturing base, China remains the most important destination for Korean overseas investments. When one considers the characteristics of the Korean export sector—intermediate goods import and export structure, concentration in ICT industries, and ties between export and overseas investment—it needs to maintain an appropriate level of dependency on the world's largest market for export. The Chinese market accounts for 24 percent of Korea's intermediate goods exports and 33.8 percent of its ICT exports. China is also the core manufacturing base for Korean firms, accounting for 32.3 percent of manufacturing-related overseas investments, and 50 percent of ICT-related overseas investments.

At a more fundamental level, a key consideration is that declining exports to China leads to the decline in Korea's competitiveness and sensitivity to the changing product composition of China's imports. In 2023, 30 percent of the decline in Korean exports to China was attributable to the fall in Chinese demands, 32 percent to the decline in Korean competitiveness, and 38 percent to the failure to anticipate the product composition of China's imports. Before contemplating lowering its reliance on China, Korea needs first to diversify its export product composition and improve its overall competitiveness.

Second, as a pivotal middle power on the global stage, Korea must establish an arm's-length Korea-China diplomatic relationship. Korea needs to explore a more nuanced Korea-China relationship amid the US-China competition in technology, supply chains, and economic systems. As the US-China competition shows little sign of abating, Korea's former strategy of "US for security, China for economy" has been supplanted of late by "US for security, world for economy." This new strategy implies pursuing a stronger comprehensive alliance with the United States on the one hand and distancing from the Chinese economy on the other.

In this context, however, the Korean government is currently taking a stance excessively inclined toward the United States. It has even decided to partake in the Korea-US-Japan trilateral pact. These strategic inclinations may be detrimental to Korea's national and economic interests. Their damaging effects can already be observed in the semiconductor and battery industries, as the US-China strategic competition is fundamentally disturbing the cooperation and work breakdown structure between Korea and China. This is why Korea urgently needs to bolster the cooperative framework with China as a counterweight to the strengthened relations with the United States. In addition, it is necessary to rethink our strategies built on the assumption that the US-China conflict will continue indefinitely. It is eminently possible that China may opt for a more friendly and forward-looking relationship with the United States. If so, Korea needs an exit plan for such a contingency. It is time for Korea to make urgent efforts and find the elusive Pareto optimum.

Chapter 5

Global CHIP War and Korea-US-China Relations

Heungchong Kim

It was Deng Xiaoping's reform and opening-up policy of 1978 that propelled China onto the global economic order, and it was China's joining the WTO that earned her the moniker "world's factory." Successfully weathering the Global Financial Crisis in 2008, China emerged as the world's second-largest economy.

Throughout this process, the character of US-China relations shifted from cooperation and mutual benefits to competition and, eventually, conflict. Although this conflict became apparent after President Trump took office, the "Pivot to Asia" policy initiated during the Obama administration had presaged this historic development. The US perception of China was changing from that of an eager new member of the US-led liberal international order to that of a disruptor. It was a challenge the United States felt it could not ignore. The trade war began in earnest during the Trump administration, which imposed high tariffs on cheap imports of Chinese steel and aluminum to address trade imbalances. However, at the core of the conflict was the semiconductor industry.

With the advent of the digital age, semiconductors have evolved into a critical component that influences all human life and future industries. As such, they have become a critical strategic asset directly linked to national security. Their importance continues to grow. A case in point was the US sanctions against Huawei that brought the semiconductor competition between the two countries to the forefront in 2019. China had made significant strides in semiconductor technology and manufacturing leading up to it, as it had in other industries. The semiconductor competition between the two nations has grown so intense that it is now dubbed the "Chip War."

The development of the modern semiconductor industry went through a period when a few American companies held a virtual monopoly in technology, design, and production. Since then, it has spread to countries such as Japan, Europe, Taiwan, Korea, and China that were positioned to handle the unique characteristics of the semiconductor industry, to wit: functional differentiation into memory semiconductors and logic semiconductors, separation of semiconductor design and manufacturing, and the huge high-risk capital investment required by the rapid integration and short product cycle. These characteristics have also meant that semiconductor industries developed in countries where governments played an integral part in it. Even in the United States, where the private sector is said to be the driving force of the economy, the role of the Pentagon in the early development of the semiconductor industry cannot be ignored.[1] Cases in point are the rise of the Japanese semiconductor industry in the 1980s and the chip war being waged between the United States and China. Other countries have attempted to follow suit by supporting R&D through massive subsidies and working to build stable semiconductor ecosystems in their own countries.

Korea, along with Taiwan, is the largest producer of memory semiconductors, such as DRAM and NAND flash. Korea is squarely in the middle of a complex global supply chain where it produces semiconductors using US source technology and materials/equipment from US, Japanese, and European companies, and supplies them mainly to mainly China and elsewhere.

China, of course, is the largest consumer of semiconductors in this supply chain. Korea will inevitably be one of the countries hit hardest if the US-China competition intensifies, leading to sanctions and boycotts, disrupting the global supply chain. Korea is thus facing a dire challenge to find a strategic solution in the semiconductor war.

This chapter analyzes the global semiconductor industry landscape by country and the market position held by each and evaluates the likely trajectory of future competition and cooperation in it. This chapter also offers a few possible ways forward for the embattled Korean semiconductor industry caught in the middle of the US-China chip war.

OVERVIEW OF THE GLOBAL
SEMICONDUCTOR INDUSTRY

The semiconductor phenomenon was first theorized by William Shockley of Bell Laboratories in 1945. It was followed in a few years by the development of the first working transistor, which quickly replaced vacuum tubes, by the Bell team composed of William Shockley, Walter Brattain, and John Bardeen. Soon, the transistor evolved into the form of an integrated circuit (IC) through the efforts of scientists like Jack Kilby of Texas Instruments in 1958 and Robert Noyce[2] of Fairchild Semiconductor. IC technology would continue to evolve in ways that put ever more transistors onto ever smaller silicon wafers.

Since then, semiconductor manufacturing technology has developed at a blinding pace—Moore's law posits that the number of transistors embedded in an integrated circuit doubles every eighteen months. Prices also fell exponentially as a result of continuing innovations in manufacturing technology and the increasing scale of mass production.

Having outgrown its origin as a mere radio component, the semiconductor has become the most important core element in modern technology-driven devices, including all automated home appliances, automobiles, advanced military weapons including missiles and aircraft, robots, all devices needed for space exploration, and mobile phones. As of 2022, the use of semiconductors is divided into Communications (30 percent), PC/Computer (26 percent), Automotive (14 percent), Consumer (14 percent), Industrial (14 percent), and Government (2 percent), including Military end-use.[3] In emerging advanced technology industries such as AI, autonomous driving, and supercomputers, the performance of semiconductors decides the competitiveness of products. Semiconductors have become the very foundation of future industries, where it is difficult to imagine instances where they are not needed.

Currently, semiconductors are categorized into memory semiconductors and nonmemory semiconductors. Memory semiconductors are divided into short-term memory chips such as Dynamic Random Access Memory (DRAM) and Static Random Access Memory (SRAM), and long-term memory chips such as flash memory. Flash memory is further divided into NAND flash memory and NOR flash memory. Nonmemory semiconductors, also known as logic semiconductors or system semiconductors, are chips that do not store data but calculate and process it. Central Processing Unit (CPU), GPU (Graphics Processing Unit), SRAM, System-on-Chip (SoC), and Application Processor (AP) are those of the typical examples.

In 2022, the global semiconductor sales reached $600 billion, having grown by an average of 6.67 percent annually since 2001. Of these, the United States has a market share of 48 percent of the total market, followed by Korea (19 percent), Japan (9 percent), Europe (9 percent), Taiwan (8 percent), and China (7 percent).[4] The global semiconductor market is expected to reach $1 trillion by 2030, with computing and data storage (35 percent), wireless communications (28 percent), automotive electronics (15 percent), industrial electronics (13 percent), and consumer electronics (9.5 percent) expected to be the main uses.[5]

Let's look at the current structure of the global semiconductor market. DRAM, which accounts for most of the memory semiconductors, is a three-way system of Samsung Electronics, SK Hynix, and Micron. For example, in the fourth quarter of 2023, Samsung Electronics had a 45.7 percent share,

SK Hynix 31.7 percent, and Micron 19.1 percent, for a total of percent of the global market. In the case of NAND Flash, which accounts for most of the flash memory, Samsung Electronics, SK Hynix, WDC, Kioxia, and Micron collectively hold the majority market share. In the fourth quarter of 2023, Samsung Electronics had a 36.6 percent share, SK Hynix 21.6 percent, WDC 14.5 percent, Kioxia 12.6 percent and Micron 9.9 percent, for a total of 95 percent of the global market.[6]

Memory semiconductors are general-purpose semiconductors that require an extremely large-scale investment for production, as well as technological and manufacturing know-how. It is not easy for new companies to enter this market. Memory chip properties are short-cycle and highly volatile, while astronomical investment is required to build production lines to produce new generations of memory chips. Companies with production experience have a decisive advantage. The manufacturer must also be capable of a very agile sales strategy to recover the investment in a short period of time.[7]

The nonmemory chip market is about three times larger and growing faster than the memory chip market. In 2022, the memory chip market accounted for 23.9 percent of the total semiconductor market of about $600 billion, while the nonmemory chip market accounted for 76.1 percent. The nonmemory chip sector also does not involve as much price volatility as the memory chip sector.

However, the nonmemory chip sector is very diverse, and production varieties are frequently created and withdrawn depending on market demand. In 2022, Intel (12.7 percent), Qualcomm (7.6 percent), Broadcom (5.2 percent), AMD (5.2 percent), and T.I. (4.2 percent) led the industry, with Samsung Electronics at just below 3 percent.

However, we can see that the ranking in the top group varies greatly depending on the type of semiconductors. For example, in the AP sector which comprises 17 percent of the nonmemory chip market, Qualcomm currently enjoys the largest market share at 27.9 percent, followed by Apple at 21.7 percent, MediaTek at 14.2 percent, AMD at 5.6 percent, and Samsung Electronics at 4.0 percent. In the CPU sector, which comprises 14.2 percent of the nonmemory chip market, Intel at 73.8 percent and AMD at 19.1 percent together occupy 93 percent of the market. As can be gauged from these sets of data, the names of the top companies in the two fields do not overlap at all[8]; it is that diverse. In fact, there is a hidden nonmemory chip colossus: Taiwan Semiconductor Manufacturing Company Ltd. (TSMC) of Taiwan. As a company that only manufactures semiconductors by the orders of many fabless companies, TSMC is not even included in these semiconductor production statistics, but it supplies most of maden chips to the orders by the fabless companies.[9]

In fact, since 2009, TSMC has specialized in the production and supply of nonmemory chips according to the designs of the aforementioned companies.

For example, by producing the APs for Apple and Android phones, TSMC has experienced explosive revenue growth. Currently, TSMC and other Taiwanese companies supply more than 90 percent of the nonmemory semiconductor demands of such giant digital platform companies as Amazon, Google, and NVIDIA, and myriad fabless manufacturers.

Established in 1987 with investments from the Taiwanese government, Philips, and an assortment of Taiwanese enterprises, TSMC has grown into the first foundry specialist under the guidance of its visionary founder Morris Chang, specializing exclusively in semiconductor manufacturing and production. TSMC is currently focused on nonmemory chip production, while maintaining a very close collaborative relationship with US-based fabless companies which specialize in semiconductor designs.

By way of comparison, Samsung Electronics, an Integrated Device Manufacturer (IDM) like Intel, entered the foundry business only in 2005 when it established Samsung Foundry internally. In the third quarter of 2023, TSMC dominated the global foundry market with 59 percent market share, followed by Samsung Foundry at 13 percent, Taiwanese UMC at 6 percent, multinational company Global Foundries with Middle Eastern capital at 6 percent, and Chinese SMIC at 6 percent.[10]

The following is the overall picture of the global semiconductor market share by country (based on 2022 data).

(1) memory semiconductors: South Korea (58 percent), United States (28 percent), Japan (8 percent), and Taiwan (4 percent).
(2) nonmemory semiconductors: United States (67 percent), Taiwan (9 percent), EU (8 percent), China (6 percent), and tied for fourth place are South Korea and Japan (4 percent).
(3) semiconductor equipment: United States (42 percent), Japan (27 percent), EU (21 percent), and South Korea (3 percent).
(4) materials: Taiwan (23 percent), China (19 percent), South Korea (17 percent), Japan (14 percent), United States (10 percent), and EU (6 percent).[11]

However, the most striking feature of the global semiconductor industry is that there exists "bottlenecks" where the global supply chain relies totally on a particular country or a manufacturer for certain products. For example, China supplies over 80 percent of the global demand for gallium and germanium, which are used in chip manufacturing. The United States holds a virtual monopoly in the supply of ion implanters, while the Dutch company ASML enjoys a similar dominance with respect to EUV lithography equipment. Meanwhile, only TSMC and Samsung Electronics have the capability to produce sub-5-nanometer advanced semiconductor chips.

THE CHIP WAR

Semiconductor Industry Development Policies by Country

United States

All pioneers of the semiconductor industry were American companies: Bell Labs, Texas Instruments, Fairchild Semiconductor, Intel, and others. America not only developed the semiconductor transistor but also pioneered the development of the integrated circuit and photolithography technologies. America has developed numerous other proprietary technologies and now leads the world in basic research, where China has emulated America.

In the process of checking the rise of the Japanese semiconductor industry in the 1980s, the United States allowed countries such as Taiwan, South Korea, and Singapore to establish themselves in the front-end process of semiconductor manufacturing and in the back-end process of Outsourced Semiconductor Assembly and Test (OSAT), including packaging and testing. These East Asian countries have been very successful in establishing their own semiconductor industries, such that they stand in the top rankings of the fields. Nevertheless, the United States still leads the world in semiconductor design and nonmemory chip manufacturing, as well as proprietary technology.

The Biden administration' semiconductor strategy can be seen in the CHIPS and Science Act of 2022. The act makes a provision for the allocation of a $78.2 billion budget for the support of R&D, human resources development, and fabrication facilities in the form of subsidies and tax credits. It also incorporates guardrail clauses targeting China, including export controls and secondary boycott measures. Through the enactment of this and other semiconductor support laws, the United States aims to check the progress of the Chinese semiconductor industry and reestablish America's semiconductor ecosystem by vastly strengthening US domestic production capabilities. While some materials and equipment in the front-end process may require cooperation with friends and allies, the ultimate aim is to become self-sufficient in all steps of semiconductor development and manufacturing.

It does appear that the United States will permit outsourcing of some of the back-end processes to Southeast Asian countries like Singapore and Malaysia. However, the overall scheme does not appear to align with the interests of the Korean and Taiwanese semiconductor industries, which rely heavily on the Chinese market despite their dominant positions in the memory front-end process. Conversely, however, TSMC's plan to establish a semiconductor supply chain and ecosystem linking the United States, Japan, Taiwan, and Singapore by building fabrication facilities in Japan and the United States probably aligns with the US strategy. Unfortunately, Korea is nowhere to be found in this picture.

Japan

In the mid-1980s and for about a decade afterward, Japan outperformed the United States in semiconductor manufacturing. At one point, six out of the top ten semiconductor companies in the world were Japanese. Since the 2000s, however, Japan has experienced a significant decline in competitiveness in semiconductor production, although it still maintains strengths in semiconductor equipment and some parts of wafer production.

Under the Kishida administration, Japan announced its semiconductor and digital industry revitalization strategy in June 2021. According to this strategy, Japan's focus is particularly on fostering the development of and securing production capabilities for advanced sub-2-nanometer semiconductor technology in both front-end and back-end processes, for such applications as AI chips, data center technology chips, and next-generation logic chips for automotive applications.

Recently announced semiconductor factory plans attest to this effort. Rapidus, a semiconductor company, jointly established by eight Japanese firms, plans to set up a ¥500 billion factory in Hokkaido by 2027. TSMC also intends to establish a ¥1.1 trillion logic semiconductor factory in Kumamoto by 2024. Micron plans to build a ¥50 billion High Bandwidth Memory (HBM) semiconductor production plant by 2026, with 20–40 percent of the investment coming from the government.

Japan's new semiconductor strategy aims to leverage Japan's geopolitical advantage highlighted during the US-China semiconductor rivalry. By attracting next-generation memory and logic semiconductor manufacturing facilities in Japan above and beyond the existing manufacturing equipment industries, the strategy seeks to vastly expand the front-end processes and establish a self-sufficient domestic semiconductor ecosystem.

Once these plans come to fruition, it would be possible for Japan to establish a stable domestic semiconductor ecosystem largely independent of China, in close collaboration with the United States in the design stage and with Singapore or Malaysia in the back-end processes. Just as it supported Japan during the Cold War era to reinforce its line of economic power against the Soviet Union in the Pacific, the United States appears to have decided to support Japan's plan to revitalize its semiconductor industry as part of the US containment policy against China.

However, there is no guarantee that this US strategy will pan out as the United States hopes. Supporting Japan's semiconductor strategy may not necessarily lead to a successful blocking of China's access to semiconductors, and if it does, the United States may then be left with powerful Japanese semiconductor industries to contend with, as in the 1980s–1990s.

EU

In August 2022, the EU and its member states agreed on the European Chips Act (ECA) to strengthen the European semiconductor ecosystem by investing a total of 430 billion euros in the semiconductor industry. This investment aims to expand fabrication facilities, establish semiconductor hubs for developing next-generation semiconductor technologies, and improve capital accessibility for semiconductor companies. Furthermore, in May 2023, they initiated the Chips for Europe Initiative (CEI), focusing not only on expanding fabrication facilities but also on enhancing design capabilities, investing in next-generation semiconductor technologies including quantum chips, establishing competence center networks, and implementing projects to enhance semiconductor funding for startups and SMEs.

With respect to China, the EU lacks precise guidelines akin to those of the United States but aims to enhance semiconductor supply monitoring and crisis response capabilities. Additionally, the EU plans to establish semiconductor alliances with like-minded countries to enhance information exchange, intellectual property protection, and monitoring and restrictions on trade and investments.

The EU aims to increase its global semiconductor market share from its current level of around 10 percent to 20 percent through a series of legislations. Currently, Intel and TSMC have revealed plans to invest in Germany, Ireland, Poland, and other countries. However, challenges such as the scale of investments, differing requirements among member states, expanding regional demands, garnering support from competitor nations like the United States, securing talent, and other hurdles need to be addressed for their semiconductor ecosystem-building plan to be fully realized. It seems that the EU will need to act more boldly and expeditiously if it were to achieve its goal.

Nevertheless, if visible successes in the front-end manufacturing process can be achieved, a significant level of the semiconductor industry may be established. This progress will require help from overseas, particularly in the back-end processes. It is anticipated that the EU's plan to boost its semiconductor industry will draw further demand for overseas procurement, albeit steady increases.

Taiwan

With such dominant semiconductor foundries as TSMC and United Microelectronics Corporation (UMI), Taiwan boasts strength in both front-end and back-end processes and excels in logic semiconductor manufacturing.

Moreover, such companies as MediaTek are also leading the industry in semiconductor design, fabless business, materials, and back-end processes.

Taiwan possesses both strengths and weaknesses in the global semiconductor sector. Looking at its strengths first, Taiwan has a close relationship with the United States due to its history of active personnel exchanges with Silicon Valley, together with its formidable human resources. This has resulted in the enviable position Taiwan now enjoys in semiconductor manufacturing and design. On the other hand, TSMC started out with an investment from the Dutch company Philips in its early days of the 1980s when early US semiconductor companies only gave it cold shoulders. This unique beginning has led to distinct relationships with Dutch semiconductor industries. Through these experiences, TSMC has built long-standing cooperative relationships with US companies like Intel and T.I., and the Dutch company ASML.

The most glaring weakness of Taiwan when it comes to semiconductors is the fact that many Taiwanese semiconductor facilities, including TSMC and UMC, are located in the Hsinchu Science Park, situated in the northwestern coastline of Taiwan, squarely facing mainland China. This location vividly illustrates the vulnerability of the Taiwanese semiconductor industry in the face of physical threats from China. Additionally, Taiwan relies almost entirely on overseas suppliers for semiconductor manufacturing equipment, and there are uncertainties as to whether Taiwan can remain at the forefront of next-generation semiconductor technology development.

Southeast Asia

Singapore and Malaysia have achieved substantial advancements in both front-end manufacturing and back-end processes due to close collaborations with United States and Taiwanese companies. If Taiwanese semiconductor companies were to move out of Taiwan due to security concerns, many forecast Japan or Southeast Asia as the most likely destination. As such, at least in the area of manufacturing and OSAT back-end processes, these nations are uniquely positioned to play an important part in the international division of labor despite their hot and humid climate. It remains uncertain, however, whether Southeast Asia has the capacity to independently cultivate global semiconductor companies.

US Sanctions and China's Response

In May 2015, China's State Council declared the "Made in China 2025" initiative. It called for China's becoming the global leader in the top ten strategic industries. Based on this plan, China has significantly expanded R&D

budgets and launched an aggressive campaign to recruit overseas talent and secure in-bound technology transfer.

Between 2015 and 2017, many Chinese private companies and state-owned enterprises went on an aggressive merger and acquisition spree of "small giant" tech companies in Europe, the United States, Japan, and Korea. A case in point was the series of successful or attempted M&As of US, Taiwanese, and European tech companies by Tsinghua Unigroup in this timeframe. Belatedly realizing the seriousness of the situation, Western countries began restricting foreign investments from China starting around in 2017. This trend continued into the early 2020s with a series of legislations implementing foreign investment review mechanisms.

China's Made in China 2025 initiative aimed to increase self-sufficiency in semiconductors to 70 percent by 2025. To achieve this ambitious target starting from below 15 percent, all within a decade, would have required various means beyond what was domestically available. Suffice it to say that the self-sufficiency rate currently remains still in the 20 percent range. Some attribute this lackluster pace to US sanctions against China.

US sanctions targeting China's high-tech industries began with the 2019 prohibition on US companies from supplying semiconductors to Huawei. This action was taken due to concerns that "backdoors" installed in Huawei's 5G communication equipment would enable China to access sensitive information from various countries' communication networks. Subsequently, following a 100-day investigation, the Biden administration expanded the sanctions in 2021 to include export controls, import controls, investment restrictions, and financial sanctions. The Biden administration also implemented a secondary boycott, restricting technology exports to Chinese companies not only by US companies but also by European, Japanese, Taiwanese, and Korean companies that utilize US proprietary technologies.

The US sanctions on China in the semiconductor sector are fundamentally rooted in American confidence in its dominant position in the semiconductor industry. In terms of value-added in semiconductor manufacturing processes, the United States exhibits a high level of competitiveness globally, ranging from 23 percent to 96 percent market share in design (IP and EDA), front-end equipment and manufacturing, and back-end equipment and manufacturing, even though it does not manufacture wafers.

This stands in stark contrast to other nations in the global semiconductor supply chain: South Korea holds 20 percent market share only in design and front-end and back-end manufacturing processes. Japan excels in wafer production and front-end equipment but lags behind in other areas. Europe is dominant only in IP and front-end equipment. Taiwan is specialized in front-end manufacturing and only recently has had notable advancements in design; and China shows a significant presence only in back-end packaging.[12]

The US sanctions against China increasingly give the impression of precision strikes targeting critical points. Hot on the heels of the CHIPS and Science Act of 2022, the US government announced in October 2022 restrictions on the export to China of DRAM below 18 nanometers, NAND flash with 128 layers or more, and equipment for manufacturing system semiconductors below 14 nanometers.

However, as China's YMTC started mass-producing 128-layer NAND flash in the first half of 2023 and Huawei 7nm mobile phone chips in August 2023, breaching the US guardrails, the US Department of Commerce announced in December 2023 further strengthening of sanctions against China even in the legacy chip field.

This additional sanction appears to be in response to China's recent moves. In response to US sanctions, China achieved an overwhelming market presence and competitiveness in manufacturing in the field of legacy chips, which was not subject to US sanctions. This appears to have been China's strategic move to increase dependence by foreign advanced chip producers on China, thereby buying time to catch up with US technology. Needless to say, the United States is monitoring this development closely.

Points of Clash

Enhancing Foundry Production Capacity

But for back-end packaging, China lacks significant competitiveness in most of the semiconductor industrial stages. Only in design does China display an improving competitiveness. China recently focuses on enlarging capacity in foundry, that is, semiconductor manufacturing only, although it remains at the level of producing legacy chips in manufacturing. This structural characteristic stems from China's historical reliance on Taiwan's TSMC in the foundry sector.

As the US-China competition intensifies and TSMC finds it increasingly difficult to accommodate Chinese fabless companies, China is attempting to replace TSMC with its own partially state-owned pure-play foundry company, Semiconductor Manufacturing International Corporation (SMIC). The result has been far from satisfactory so far. Building up China's own foundry capability is expected to be a long-haul project, as it will take much time to narrow the technology gap. A case in point is the bottleneck involving lithography equipment: Netherlands-based ASML, a major producer of EUV equipment, can no longer supply its products to China due to US sanctions. Huawei's much-touted 7nm mobile phone chips appear to have been produced using the DUV equipment previously supplied by ASML.

China's strength lies in its vast market and demand. Recently, over 50 percent of Korea's semiconductor exports worldwide are directed toward China, and Samsung and SK Hynix operate large-scale factories at five different locations in China, including Xi'an and Wuxi, for Chinese domestic use. As such, China is the "biggest customer" for the Korean semiconductor industry. Given that China will find it difficult to meet semiconductor demand internally for the time being, it will continue to act like a black hole sucking in semiconductors from around the globe. From Korea's perspective, semiconductors are its top export, with a global market share reaching 20 percent. Korea simply does not have the luxury of missing out on the Chinese market.

The US government designated Samsung Electronics and SK Hynix as Verified End Users (VEUs), thereby approving the import of equipment for their factories operating in China. It was apparently a last-minute "creative" measure to accommodate Korea's precarious position in the global semiconductor landscape. However, Korean semiconductor companies are facing mounting challenges going forward. For one thing, Korean companies are competing fiercely to secure EUV equipment. Samsung Electronics had recently been competing with Intel and TSMC for ASML equipment supply. As it was decided that ASML equipment would go to Intel first, there is much hand-wringing as to whether the Korean semiconductor industry is being relegated to the background. Worse yet, the competition with TSMC for equipment still remains. The new fab plants being constructed in Japan or Southeast Asia are not cutting-edge players, and as such, do not pose an immediate threat to Korea. Production of legacy chips is a different matter altogether, however: the United States, Taiwan, and Korea are now locked in an existential competition.

Semiconductors typically have short cycles of two to three years, requiring colossal investments within each cycle. Semiconductor companies must bear this cost upfront and also secure funds for the development of next-generation semiconductors within each cycle. Naturally, the companies must also sell their products in a timely manner to make all this possible. This reality makes the idea of foregoing investments in China to explore other markets for a few years simply unrealistic. As to government subsidies, no government provides support in excess of 10 percent of an enterprise's investment. Actually, the average is at 1–2 percent. The global semiconductor sector has evolved into an autonomous, market-driven industry.

Combine the facts that the United States owns most of the proprietary technology and is imposing sanctions on China; it is clear that semiconductor trade with China will only become more difficult with time. However, trade with China in legacy semiconductors should continue, as is the case with the United States or Japan.

Developing New Semiconductor Technologies

SK Hynix entered High Bandwidth Memory (HBM) manufacturing early, and the resulting first-mover advantage has put SK Hynix in a very advantageous position in the HBM market. While HBM currently holds a small market share in the memory market, the huge growth potential of the HBM market bodes well for SK Hynix and Samsung Electronics, which practically divides the market between them. However, as HBM does not represent such a highly advanced level of technology, both companies face the added challenge of maintaining a sliver of technological advantage over competitors, above and beyond expanding their market share. The memory chip sector is a fiercely competitive field, where US, Japanese, Korean, and European firms must engage in battle for sheer survival. This is also where the policies of their respective governments will clash.

In the nonmemory sector, understanding the overall landscape can be challenging due to the immense variety of semiconductor types being developed for different purposes. Success or failure of a firm engaged in the nonmemory sector often hinges on the success or failure of the industries and products its nonmemory chips are intended for. AI chips, currently gaining prominence, represent a field with immense growth potential. Governments and companies worldwide are in a mad dash to develop high-performance AI chips. The AI chip sector, however, is also likely to see a gradual separation between general-purpose and specialized chips, and as such, success and failure will be determined by the strategies adopted by the competing countries and companies.

China's Semiconductor Policies

Assuming continued US sanctions on China, one can anticipate two main strategic directions from the Chinese government. The first is to dominate the universal semiconductor sector with 10-nanometer or higher chips as an unrivaled importer and supplier. This strategy would allow China to exert ongoing influence on competing nations like Korea and the United States, while focusing all its resources on upgrading its semiconductor technologies. This strategy would also allow Chinese companies to dominate the global universal semiconductor market. In that case, Korean, Japanese, Taiwanese, European, and American firms would be forced to engage in intense competition over the export of materials and equipment to the Chinese market. This state of affairs may inadvertently contribute to the rise of the Chinese semiconductor industry.

In the second scenario, China could opt to bifurcate the world into two camps and dominate one with its own rules and standards. That camp will consist of China, Russia, and the Global South countries tethered to the Belt

& Road initiative. Should this happen, the Korean semiconductor industry would lose access to the Chinese market, resulting in significant economic repercussions for Korea. Of course, pursuing this scenario comes with significant risks and uncertainties about its potential success. And, it may also have the effect of rendering any further strategic competition among the US, Japanese, Taiwan, and Korean companies vis-a-vis the Chinese market moot.

Human Resources and Electricity[13]

The semiconductor industry requires a vast array of talents, energy consumption equivalent to that of a city, and large quantities of ultrapure water. Talent recruitment in the semiconductor industry is in essence a zero-sum game in the short term, and for this reason, it is a point of clash among competing countries. The business leaders and high-level technical talents are inherently highly mobile, making talent recruitment a decisive factor in the future success of the semiconductor industry of each competing country.

Though not as often discussed, well-trained field engineers and general semiconductor workers are another critical factor. Field engineers possess crucial on-site skills that contribute to increasing yield, and they also play a significant role in developing new technologies. Although they generally do not move internationally as frequently as top-level talent, recruiting field engineers and keeping them is another point of clash among competing countries.

In the case of electricity, the challenges are twofold. The first issue is whether there is a sufficient and stable supply of electricity. One of the peculiarities of semiconductor production is that, if there is a power outage, all the wafers being worked on become useless, leading to significant losses. In fact, the power outages that occurred in Taiwan and Korea caused damage amounting to billions of won. The second challenge involves Environmental, Social, and Governance (ESG) considerations. Using electricity produced through processes with lower carbon emissions can help mitigate the risk of indirect carbon indirect emissions, making it possible to comply with increasingly stringent international environmental regulations.

Whether a country can provide a stable and sufficient supply of electricity generated from renewable energy sources such as wind, solar, and nuclear power varies from country to country. Depending on the timing and extent of international regulation on clean electricity, the fortunes of semiconductor industries, which consume vast amounts of electricity, in different countries may change. This aspect will be yet another point of clash where it will be determined whether the semiconductor industry of a given country can maintain international competitiveness.

SOUTH KOREA'S POSITION AND RECOMMENDATIONS

The Impact of the Chip War

South Korea is perched on the most challenging and exposed position in the semiconductor war. Let's compare Korea to other countries in the global semiconductor playing field.

Only partial impacts are felt in Europe. There is currently chronic excess demand for advanced chip manufacturing equipment like EUV from countries outside of China, such as the European countries, the United States, Taiwan, and Korea. So, there is no impact of the US sanction on the advanced equipment market at all. However, the US sanctions include a secondary export ban on equipment for legacy chip production as well, such as DUV equipment that used to be exported to China. Also, although it is essential for equipment exporters to maintain on-site presence at local fabs even after delivering the equipment, the majority of European equipment exporters have had to pull out their on-site personnel from China in compliance with the US demand. This is a huge problem for China and has marginal impacts on ASML. The overall impact of the US-China chip war on Europe is limited.

In Japan's case, material and equipment companies, the mainstay of the Japanese semiconductor industry, are currently facing some temporary difficulties as a result of the chip war. However, many semiconductor fabs under construction in Japan and the Unites States are expected to come online soon, driving up demands for the Japanese material and equipment companies. The overall outlook remains very positive.

The impact of the US sanctions on China's semiconductor industry is most pronounced in the case of Korea and Taiwan, both of which manufacture and supply advanced chips. Furthermore, for the advanced chip market to thrive globally and justify the astronomical investments involved, it needs unhindered and uninterrupted access to the global market. Blocking Chinese demand poses an immediate threat to this market and could impact future advancements in semiconductor chip technology as well.

In the case of Taiwan, its semiconductor industry has thrived through a well-established division of labor with Chinese semiconductor companies. However, US sanctions on China have resulted in short-term losses for Taiwanese semiconductor companies like TSMC. Nevertheless, Taiwan's situation is comparatively better than Korea's, as the overall size of TSMC fabs in China is minimal, accounting for less than 10 percent of the total volume. Taiwan can also mitigate this minor loss through close cooperation with Japan, local investments in the United States, and strong ties with the United States.

By contrast, Korea's semiconductor industry currently operates factories in China that produce DRAM and NAND flash memory, with Samsung Electronics accounting for one-third of the total production and SK Hynix for over 20 percent, with demand mainly coming from China itself. Although these factories do not produce advanced chips below 5 nanometers, they have been negotiating with the United States to import equipment for legacy chips. While continued equipment imports are currently possible under the VEU program, the long-term survival of these factories is highly uncertain.

Ultimately, the Korean semiconductor industry is most at risk from the impact of the US sanctions on China due to several factors. First, Korea's semiconductor industry is heavily specialized; its main focus is on the front-end process of memory chip manufacturing. Second, the price of memory chips is inherently volatile. Third, Korea's semiconductor industry is heavily focused on cutting-edge chips that require astronomical up-front cyclic investments. Last, Korea maintains an extensive portfolio of investments in fabs operations in China, as well as in the United States in the near future. These factors, individually or combined, amplify the challenges posed by US sanctions on China, with a very real possibility of a perfect storm lurking beyond the horizon.

Recommendations

Due to this unique positioning, the Korean semiconductor industry finds itself starkly exposed at the following points of clash in the chip war:

First is the expansion and diversification of manufacturing and production capacities. Countries like Korea that specialize in fabs are likely to face severe headwinds from China's efforts to enhance its domestic production capabilities, even as they are in hot pursuit of Taiwan or being pursued by the United States and Japan. To counter this, exploring new markets such as Europe, India, Southeast Asia, and Australia could be a potential solution. However, the limited growth potential of these markets and their increasing interest in their own fabs could pose limitations. It particularly behooves Korea to keep a close eye on India's ambitions in this regard.

Second is the competition for cutting-edge semiconductor technologies. Korea should actively participate in international networks, for example, for nonsilicon-based semiconductor production methods like quantum IT, and establish a niche leadership position in the field of emerging semiconductor production technology. Korea needs to actively engage in joint research with participating countries and acquire the capability to participate and lead in all processes of semiconductor production.

Third concerns Korea's relationship with China. Even if China's relations with Korea and its allies weaken as China pursues self-sufficiency in semiconductors, it does not appear that Taiwan and Japan will sever their ties with China. In particular, Taiwan's cultural affinity with China is expected to keep Taiwan and China in a close orbit one way or the other. It will be unwise for Korea to sever its ties with the Chinese market in plain view of these realities.

Fourth involves talent development. The competition for talent will intensify with no distinction between friends and foes. In cultivating a rich pool of specialized professionals, simply establishing and expanding semiconductor departments at educational institutions is not enough. Advancements in all fields of engineering, such as electrical and electronic, chemical, mechanical, and materials, are imperative, as are concurrent developments in physics, mathematics, and even biology. This is because semiconductor technology has already transcended the realm of electronic engineering. Korea, therefore, must maintain close exchanges with friends and allies to be able to recruit top talents internationally. Once recruited, Korea must be able to keep them by providing quality living arrangements and a well-structured semiconductor research ecosystem.

Fifth, it is essential to clearly articulate demands and strive to achieve the goals with the United States and China, the two combatants in the semiconductor war. The United States should acknowledge Korea's unique and vulnerable position and advanced chip manufacturing capabilities and afford Korean semiconductor companies sufficient time to make adjustments to their operations in China. In addition, the United States, having begun the semiconductor war, should continue to ask itself whether its reshoring policy of bringing all processes back onto its shores is indeed wise in view of the international division of labor so widely established in the global semiconductor industry. Intellectual explorations in many regions and countries have brought the global semiconductor industry to where it is today. All stakeholders in this field should view one another not as foes to overcome but as partners in cooperation. And, these words are also applied to China.

Chapter 6

Xi Jinping, the Man

Impact of Xi Jinping's Personality Traits on Decision-Making

Yang Gabyong

Whether democratically elected or authoritarian, the top leader of a country exerts great influence on its policies. In dealing with a country like China where the ultimate political power rests in one man, however, understanding the leader's personality traits is all the more critical. How Xi Jinping sees domestic and international issues and renders political responses thereon determine China's policies and behaviors to a degree far beyond that of a democratically elected leader.

"Personality" refers to the discernible patterns in thoughts, perceptions, emotional responses, and behaviors that manifest themselves in interpersonal relationships. In analyzing someone's personality, consistently recurring patterns in these areas form the core of the inquiry. In this sense, personality, once formed, does not change easily; it is deeply embedded in a person's psyche, largely subliminal and multifaceted.

President Xi Jinping himself said during his 2015 visit to the Shaanbei region, "Everything I learned in my youth was all from my experiences in Liangjiahe village. My 下放 (to demote a party cadre to work in the countryside) stay there left deep impressions on me. It taught me the virtue of 自强不息 (self-improvement)."[1] He was referring to what had happened to him in 1969: the fifteen-year-old Xi Jinping had been sent down to the Liangjiahe village as a 知青 (young intellectual) and spent the next seven years there.

Xi had a political awakening during his enforced stay at Liangjiahe. His perspectives on the party and state, formed during his exile in Liangjiahe, still influence his thoughts today as China's president and general secretary. Xi reminisced, "I was devastated and did not know what to do when I came to this deep countryside at the age of fifteen, but by the time I left at twenty-two, I was a confident young man with clearly defined life goals."[2]

Theodore Millon provides the theoretical basis for personality analysis based on eight attributions. They are expressive behavior, interpersonal conduct, cognitive style, mood/temperament, self-image, regulatory mechanisms, object representations, and morphologic organization.[3] Applying this theoretical framework, Aubrey Immelman and Yunyiyi Chen analyzed Xi Jinping's personality based on five observable elements: expressive behavior, interpersonal behavior, cognitive style, mood/temperament, and self-image.[4] According to the study, Xi Jinping's personality manifests itself primarily in his expressive behaviors.

XI JINPING'S PERSONALITY TRAITS

According to this study, Xi Jinping's personality can be described as follows, in the order of prevalence: dominant/controlling, conscientious/respectful-dutiful, and ambitious/confident/self-serving. To elaborate,

- His dominant/controlling side manifests itself in forceful, aggressive, tough, and unsentimental behavior.
- His conscientious/respectful-dutiful trait manifests itself in more technocratic than visionary tendencies, lending him to be diligent and attentive to details.
- Last, his confidence/self-serving side finds its expression in his bold, competitive, optimistic, and self-assured bearing.

Xi Jinping's dominant/controlling personality is evident in his dominant, aggressive behavior pattern, where he enjoys leading others and has the power to influence them. This trait is seen in his strong-willed, outspoken, unsentimental, and unyielding behavioral patterns. This personality type is dominant, controlling, and inflexible, leading at times to uncompromising and power-hungry behaviors. However, these traits can also result in effective leadership qualities. The ruthlessness he displayed in eliminating his political enemies is a good example of his domineering and aggressive personality, along with his decisive and combative leadership style.

Xi Jinping's conscientious/respectful-dutiful side finds its expression in respectfulness and obedience, anchored in earnestness. A person of this personality displays earnestness, diligence, strong vocational ethics, and detail-orientedness. Strong moral principles and conviction underpin these qualities. Xi Jinping himself is deeply loyal to his party and its cause, and is formal, proper, and dignified. Xi's demands to others of loyalty to the state, the CCP, and the Paramount Leader can also be understood as a manifestation of this personality. This personality type deals with traitors and deserters decisively and severely, as it has no tolerance for apostasy. This explains Xi's ruthless punishment of the party officials found to be corrupt by the Central Commission for Discipline Inspection.

Xi Jinping's ambitious/confident/self-serving personality trait manifests boldness, competitiveness, optimism, and self-assuredness. This personality type likes to reveal ambitions and is achievement-oriented. It is also adept at persuading others through its charm. For example, Xi Jinping's grand vision of China Rise is an expression of his ambitious nature. His Belt and Road Initiative and its corollary objective of bringing the countries along the Belt and Road under Chinese influence reflect his achievement-oriented personality trait. A person of this type also expects others to recognize him as a man of special qualities. That he acquired the title of "Leading Core" at the Sixth Plenary Session of the Eighteenth Central Committee in 2016 speaks volumes of this trait. Internationally, this personality trait of Xi Jinping has become conflated with the CCP's policies that demand recognition of China's exalted status among nations. A man of ambition exudes confidence, assumes leadership roles, and even considers himself unassailable. However, a man with these qualities is liable to perceive himself infallible. If China fails to guard against this possibility, it might find a second Mao Zedong in its hands.

XI JINPING'S MULTIFACETED NATURE

President Xi Jinping also displays a cooperative and kind side toward those whom he deems to be on the same wavelength as him. This is consistent with his behavior of promoting loyal aides and confidants to the Politburo Standing Committee.

Of course, alarmed by his fervent call for transforming the PLA into a strong modern military and reclaiming China's rightful place on the world stage, the international community frets over impending military adventurism by China. True, this personality type tends to ignore tradition, disdain mundane matters, and at times be impulsive. However, China has displayed caution so as not to cross the red line in its standoff with the United States over the Taiwan Strait. It appears that Xi is instead using thorny international issues to bolster internal unity. This policy orientation can be understood as a complex blend of Xi's strong will and pragmatism. Xi knows full well that China needs to strike a balance it can live with in international affairs. Xi's seemingly indomitable will for the China Rise, which to him will be consummated only with the reunification of Taiwan, appears to be tempered by his appreciation of a complex web of factors facing China, both domestic and international.

On the other hand, an introvert with a strong autocratic trait is obstinate and tenacious. Xi Jinping's childhood experiences attest to this. Absolute trust and infinite loyalty to the party and the state are deeply instilled in him. This personality trait makes Xi Jinping's leadership intolerant of any opposition, unwilling to heed new ideas but achievement-oriented. As such, this personality trait covets control and influence. The protagonist is, of course, Xi Jinping himself.

In so doing, this personality tends to view the world dualistically in terms of good and evil; to wit, those countries that cooperate with China are friends, and those that do not are enemies. This quality in Xi Jinping tends to manifest itself in China's behavior of trying to maximize its interests by reorganizing the international system—a revisionist tendency. As specious as it may seem, China's call to restore the international order with the UN at the center may very well reflect this dualistic tendency. Conflicts are inherent in international order, and therefore the world needs to be divided into us and them. The resulting good camp and bad camp will then engage in perpetual conflicts and confrontations. And yet, leadership based on this type of personality tends to focus on security and status and to favor low-commitment action for immediate short-term changes internationally. Not a very comforting thought.

PROS AND CONS OF XI JINPING'S PERSONALITY

On the positive side, Xi Jinping is a powerful authoritarian leader who can author detailed policies and execute them down to the details. He is confident and ambitious. He has a pronounced tendency to trust himself and his abilities. This confidence manifests itself as his loyalty to the CCP and the government, just as his experience during his 下放 (demotion of a party cadre to work in the countryside) in Liangjiahe Village turned him into a confident, loyal young communist.

It is meaningless to hope that Xi Jinping's thoughts may change as they are inextricably embedded in his psyche. It is also difficult to expect any accommodation of public opinions or consensus-building from this type of leadership. This type of leadership is solely founded upon the leader's personal judgment and decision and is insensitive to the need to mobilize support from the public or the CCP cadres. Instead, this type of leadership tends to be more confrontational and insensitive to public, legal, or international disapproval. This is the reason behind the impasse surrounding certain of China's policies approved by Xi Jinping despite strong objections from the Korean government. A case in point is the failure to hold working-level negotiations to resolve the issues surrounding the deployment of THAAD on the Korean Peninsula.

These aspects of Xi Jinping's personality are fundamentally changing China's policy decision mechanism. Xi considers himself infallible. Essentially, he does not consider other people's opinions to be very important. As such, the checks-and-balances mechanism that once governed the decision-making by the Politburo Standing Committee, widely recognized as the legacy of the Deng Xiaoping era, is unlikely to be seen at least during Xi's third term. This is a natural result of Xi's personality traits. The cooperation-based horizontal decision-making mechanism will be replaced by a vertical hierarchical system. Technically, the collective decision-making system has not entirely disappeared since the Party Constitution has not been amended to that effect. For all intents and purposes, however, Xi Jinping will be the sole decision-maker.

Of course, one-man rule does have an advantage: decisions can be made efficiently and in real time in response to the ever-changing domestic and international situations. This advantage, of course, holds true only if one assumes the infallibility of such a leader. In reality, policymaking is a rational process and a collective effort to arrive at the best possible course of action. If all decisions by the Paramount Leader are unquestioningly obeyed and perfunctorily executed without any input from opposing voices, the responsibility for all consequences, intended or otherwise, will fall on Xi Jinping himself. It is a situation where no one will be foolish enough to volunteer to tie the proverbial bell on the neck of the tiger. There is a historical precedent for this unfortunate state of affairs: the Cultural Revolution, where nobody took responsibility for the devastating consequences of Mao's policies but instead agitated and mobilized ideologically brainwashed young Red Guards to justify them.

You Sangchul[5]

Xi Jinping is, for better or worse, a colossus in the modern history of China, and by extension, the world. What follows is a discussion on six idiosyncratic aspects of Xi Jinping's complex persona, discussed more in depth in my book *Into the Mind of Xi Jinping*,[6] published in October 2023. I hope the insights offered here would serve as a valuable "other angle" in understanding the trajectory China has been and will be in our times. Please understand that I am not at liberty to disclose my sources; it is my duty to protect their identity.[7] China's Anti-Espionage Law (rev. 2023) is watching.

XI JINPING'S IDIOSYNCRASIES

"To understand today's China, one must focus on de-facto emperor Xi Jinping's idiosyncrasies. For all of China's policies are determined by the will of this absolute Paramount Leader notwithstanding their outward appearance of systemic or institutional propriety."

History teaches us that a leader of a nation often exerts outsized influence on its history. For China, which existed under the rule of emperors (皇帝) for over 2,000 years, the power its modern-day ruler wields is nearly absolute. The one-party rule under the CCP does not alter this phenomenon. That American journalist Harrison E. Salisbury called Mao Zedong and Deng Xiaoping "new emperors" is probably on the mark.[8]

"Emperor" is a befitting title for Xi Jinping as well. He wields absolute power and shows no hint of stepping down from the throne. There's no such thing as retirement for an emperor of China. By definition, an emperor relinquishes his power only upon death. In the case of Xi, he amended the PRC Constitution that used to limit the number of presidential terms in March 2018, clearing a path for him to be president for life.

In March 2023, Xi Jinping started his third term, and his rule continues with no hint of succession of power observed. Under these circumstances, it is no exaggeration to say that he wants to stay in power indefinitely like an emperor of old. If so, it behooves anyone trying to analyze China's place in today's world to first understand Xi Jinping, the person. For his thoughts exert absolute influence on all of China's policies.

Xi Jinping is "the destined one" (定于一尊) among 1.4 billion Chinese today. Therefore, the rest of the world has no choice but to try to decipher what Xi Jinping thinks as to his place in history, and the future of China and the world. But, reading Chinese leaders is a notoriously difficult thing to do. British sinologist Kerry Brown observed that Jiang Zemin's clowning was a carefully constructed facade to hide his true capabilities, and Hu Jintao's silence represented uncomfortable moments for his counterparts to fill in.[9] Xi Jinping is also a notorious poker face. He rarely, if ever, shows his emotions—a true master of masking one's true thoughts or feelings (厚黑).

Since Xi Jinping came to power, rule of law has become less important in China. Xi Jinping is fond of quoting ancient sages from 2,500 years ago: "If they no longer benefit the people, old laws do not have to be obeyed, and if another way is better, old customs do not have to be adhered to (苟利於民 不必法古 苟周於事 不必循俗)." He refuses to be bound by conventions (慣例) and unspoken rules (潛規則). If so, understanding Xi's characteristics takes on even more urgency.

However, even after ten years in power, the question of what thoughts reside in his head remains opaque. According to those who have known him, Xi Jinping can mingle with a variety of people, but never reveals his thoughts. One recalls a drinking bout where five friends including Xi Jinping drank ten bottles of 120 proof baijiu (Chinese distilled liquor), where Xi was the only one left in control—or, rather, did not blurt out any personal thoughts out of drunkenness. In fact, Xi always appeared "on guard" even when meeting his friends. Now, why was that?

SIX IDIOSYNCRASIES FORMED DURING XI JINPING'S FORMATIVE YEARS

It is December 1966. Xi Jinping is thirteen years old. He makes a fateful acquaintance with 中央黨校 (Central Party School), for which he becomes principal forty years later. Young Xi made a fatal mistake of speaking lightly of the Cultural Revolution that had just started. The consequence was cruel. He was arrested as a "counter-revolutionary" and incarcerated at the Central Party School. The "school" held a criticism rally against six 走資派 ("Capitalist Roader"). Xi was the only minor among them. The accused were all forced to wear pointed metal hats as part of the humiliation punishment, with Xi alone holding his up above his head because his neck couldn't bear its weight. The rabid spectators chanted "Beat him to death! Xi Jinping!" with clenched fists raised in the air over and over again. Among the crazed chanting mob was Qixin, Jinping's mother. She had to.

The sight of one's own mother chanting "Beat him to death! Xi Jinping!" is beyond the imagination of most of those who have not lived through it. Even after the criticism rally, Jinping's mother could not visit him. This was the time when young Bo Xilai, later to be deemed Xi Jinping's political rival, publicly struck his father to survive by demonstrating his loyalty to the CCP—a truly epic time of a whole population gone mad. One night, it rained mercilessly. While the guards were slacking off, young Jinping escaped the Central Party School prison and ran away home. As his alarmed mother interrogated him as to how he had come home, all shivering Jinping could gasp out was, "Ma, I am hungry. Ma, I am hungry." His mother turned her back on him, and promptly left to report to the local communist commissar that her son had escaped.

Jinping's mother, of course, was terrified of the rest of the family facing execution because of what her boy Jinping had done. Jinping collapsed and wept out loud in front of his sister An'an (安安) and brother Yuanping (遠平). He ran off into the stormy night, starved and despairing. How can any young man who experiences such terror grow up to be a carefree person, let alone a chatty one?

Born with a silver spoon in his mouth, Xi Jinping fell to the level of 賤民 (despised low social status). Only when one understands how his early life shaped his persona, the trajectory of today's China will reveal itself. In South Korea, it looks as though anti-China sentiment has become a zeitgeist.

Various polls show that South Koreans' contempt for China hovers above 70 percent and for Xi Jinping himself still higher.

China used to be called a land of opportunity; now, it is called a land of debacles. And yet, turning our heads away from China without more only does us a disservice; for whether we like it or not, China influences us all. What is called for, therefore, is not anti-China but know-China. If Mao Zedong's life had been one of ideological revolution, Deng Xiaoping's was a pragmatic revolution. How about Xi Jinping's? Many believe he wants both.

The Xi Jinping era will stretch forward for at least another ten years, perhaps twenty. During this era, to know Xi Jinping is to know China. What makes him tick? What does he think? The answers to these critical questions can be found in how he grew up, and in his unique, peculiar even, personality traits.

OBSESSION WITH POWER

"To Xi Jinping, power is the only ultimate truth. All he has done through the last ten years of power has been to wrest power away from competing political factions, and to focus and refocus power on himself alone."

A close acquaintance of Xi Jinping confided, "Xi never allowed himself to trust anyone. To him, only power was the ultimate truth." The most deeply entrenched personality trait in Xi Jinping is his obsession with power. Power is a double-edged sword: if used wisely, it benefits the country and the people, but if abused, it destroys others and the holder himself. This ancient wisdom never stopped Xi Jinping in his single-minded quest for power.

While serving as vice president, Joe Biden met the then vice president of China Xi Jinping several times, and gauged his potential as a leader. Biden said, "Xi Jinping was deeply interested in learning how the U.S. political system worked. He was curious about what powers state governors had in our federal system, and above all how much power the president could exercise over the military and intelligence apparatus." What Xi Jinping most wanted to know was how power worked in America.

Some sinologists observe that Xi's reign over the last ten years has been a series of seizing power (脫權), centralizing power (集權), and re-centralizing power (再集權), and little else. All he has accomplished is to take away power from Jiang Zemin's Shanghai Bang (上海幫, Shanghai Clique, aka Shanghai Yao) and Hu Jintao's Communist Youth League (共青團) and concentrate the power on himself, and himself alone. Professor Wang Hsin-Hsien of National Chengchi University of Taiwan divides Xi's drive to concentrate power on himself into three categories: (i) from market and society to state; (ii) from municipalities to the central government; and (iii) from the CCP to himself. What explains this extreme obsession on power? He understands better than anyone the abject realities of being sidelined from the center of power. As a youngster, he witnessed his father branded a counter-revolutionary, and his family fall from communist aristocracy to despised outcasts. "Execution by a firing squad hundred times over is too good for him," he heard over and over again. This painful coming-of-age calcified his deadly serious rapaciousness for power. For him, loss of power does not merely mean a loss of job; it can cost him life, property, family, and place in history—a total erasure from history.

Xi Jinping was born on June 15, 1953, the day of the Dragon Boat Festival (端午節). Xi's father Xi Zhongxun (習仲勳) was the head of the Propaganda Department of the Central Committee of the CCP, and in 1959, became the vice premier. His household had security guards, chefs, nannies, and other household helpers. Every summer, his family would vacation at Beidaihe (北戴河), an exclusive beach resort, and on national holidays, attend cultural events in Zhongnanhai (中南海), an enclave in Beijing for the CCP elites. Xi Jinping's older sister Qiqiaoqiao (齊橋橋) fondly remembers the time as the family's belle epoch.

Xi Jinping attended the most exclusive kindergarten of them all, Beihai (北海). He then attended an prestigious elementary school, the August 1st School (八一), reserved for the children of the communist aristocracy. The glorious time came crashing down when his father became embroiled in a scandal surrounding the novel *Liu Zhidan* (劉志丹) that rocked the entire power structure of the CCP in 1962. "Dad committed a grave error within the party, and I have been criticized. Do not play with other children in Zhong-nanhai (中南海) from now on." Xi Jinping was nine years old.

This nine-year-old watched as security personnel ransacked his house and took everything away. His family was forced out from Zhongnanhai (中南海), and had to move to a small house in a decrepit alley. Still, up until the beginning of the Cultural Revolution, he was allowed to attend the August 1st School. The Cultural Revolution, however, turned everything upside down yet once more. Young Jinping wasn't sure if he would be allowed to live.

To Xi Jinping, Loss of Power Equates Annihilation

He had become the despised son of a counter-revolutionary (黑幫子女), from the son of a hero of the communist revolution. Then, following his stint at the Central Party School, he was sent to a juvenile detention center and subjected to Laogai (劳改) (reform through labor) for many years. These were terrible times. Xi Jinping's half-sister Xi Heping (習和平) committed suicide. Deng Xiaoping's eldest son Deng Pufang (鄧樸方) became a paraplegic when he attempted suicide by jumping off a building.

Xi Jinping chose 上山下鄉 (educated youth being sent to deep country to re-learn the values of Maoism) in 1969. It was a move to stay alive somehow. Even this did not turn out the way he and his mother imagined. His plan was to go down to his father's hometown in Shaanxi (陝西) province and subsist by farming with the help of their relatives. This was a naive miscalculation. None of the relatives dared to help 黑幫家族 (literally "black pioneer family," meaning the family of a counter-revolutionary) like Xi Jinping. Still an impressionable teen, Xi Jinping was drenched with the cold terrifying realities of life in communist China. He had to find a different way to survive.

Xi Jinping would later say, "To those who have not been close to power, power perhaps appears mysterious or exciting. But, I have seen the dark side of power. It's not just glory and accolades, but also the concentration camps and 炎涼世態 (when in power, people flock to you, but when out of power, they discard you). I grew to learn that politics is a coldhearted terrifying game." Swords sharpen on sharpening stones, and men toughen through adversities.

His next escape to Yanchuan (延川) in the northeast of the Shaanxi Province proved to be just as unwelcoming. He ran away again, this time back to Beijing, where he was promptly arrested and committed to hard labor as part of a plumbing crew. Xi Jinping would later say with some irony, "We laid all of the plumbing pipelines in the Haidian (海淀) district of Beijing."

This young fugitive, however, experiences a great awakening. He owes it to his maternal uncle Wei Zhenwu (魏震五) who advised young Xi Jinping, "Go into the people. Only among the masses, do you have any future. When I was a college student in the northeast, and later in Taihang Shan (太行山), I was able to grow as a man because I was in the middle of the masses. Your father was able to participate in the revolution because he was among the masses; you need to be a part of it too."

Determined to make something of himself out of the ashes, Xi Jinping voluntarily went back to Yanchuan (延川). There, he reinvents himself. He plowed the field, carried coal, and transported human manure buckets slung over his shoulders. He injured his back and leg while building dikes. He would go three months without seeing a drop of oil in his diet, and when a few grams of pork was finally distributed, he wolfed it down in an instant.

There's an old Chinese proverb, "Struggle maketh man. One should even pay to buy struggles in youth." Having paid his dues, Xi Jinping finally rises to the top: he becomes general secretary of the CCP in 2012. In 2018, he eliminates the Constitutional limit on the number of terms of the president. Now, nobody knows when, or if, he will descend from the throne.

American journalist Harrison E. Salisbury called Mao Zedong and Deng Xiaoping "new emperors."[10] Emperors don't have terms. Having risen to the top of the CCP at the Zunyi Conference in 1935, Mao Zedong stayed in power until his death in 1976. Deng Xiaoping who took power in 1978 stayed in power until 1997 when he passed away at the age of ninety-three. Deng shared his power with Jaing Zemin by making him the chairman of the Central Military Commission, but the CCP continued to operate on the unwritten rule that "Deng Xioping decides all important matters."

Since the Dual Sessions (兩會) of March 2023 that confirmed Xi Jinping's third term, all of China has been learning the "Xi Jinping Thoughts." The CCP proclaims that Xi Jinping Thoughts stand side by side with those of Mao Zedong. Naturally, the objective is to place Xi Jinping on the same pedestal as Mao Zedong. Underpinning this propaganda drive is, of course, the logic of rule for life. Xi Jinping is living the destiny of an emperor.

BULLHEADED IN ANTI-WESTERN AND PRO-CHINESE SLANT

"Xi Jinping appears innately anti-all-things-Western. This personal outlook is related to his failed 1st marriage. Obdurately traditional, he deliberately uses traditional Chinese motifs to secure advantages in his dealings with the Western leaders."

One day during his first term in office, Xi Jinping made an inspection visit at a reputable university in Beijing. An economics professor later spoke of the meeting between Xi and the faculty where Xi asked, "Wouldn't it be possible for you to steer China's economy from a traditional Chinese perspective, rather than Keynes' or such other western economists' theories?" Disconcerting as it may sound, this episode bespeaks Xi Jinping's wish to find solutions to all problems in Chinese tradition.

This explains what happened during the COVID-19 pandemic. While Western medicine was frantically developing mRNA vaccines and such, Xi Jinping wanted to look in the direction of traditional Chinese medicine. This is where the Honorary Principal Zhang Boli (張伯禮) of the Tianjin University of Traditional Chinese Medicine rose to prominence. With a mandate from none other than Xi Jinping himself, the good doctor rushed to Woohan and began treating patients using traditional Chinese medicine. The CCP had a propaganda coup claiming that China presented the world with China's unique solution to the deadly disease and bestowed on him the title of "Hero of the People" (人民英雄),

This somewhat odd propensity in his understanding of the world is not unrelated to his tumultuous childhood and family upbringing. He grew up deeply steeped in Chinese traditions. As his father Xi Zhongxun (習仲勳) was the head of the Propaganda Department of the Central Committee of the CCP and vice chair of the Government Affairs Council Culture and Education Committee, Xi Jinping grew up in close proximity to the who-is-who of Chinese culture, tradition, and arts. His family also frequented the performances of Chinese Operas (唱劇) or the timeless Chinese classic *Journey to the West* (西遊記) taking place in Zhongnanhai.

Xi's father used to line up his children against a wall in the house when they came home from school and repeated time and again, "You must remember how I participated in our historic communist revolution, and you too must participate in the communist revolutions of your generation." Xi Jinping became thoroughly indoctrinated as his father told and retold the trials and tribulations of the ragtag CCP forces in their desperate fight against the forces of the Western and Japanese imperialists. When Bo Xilai, four years older than Xi Jinping, was riding around on an imported British bicycle, Xi's elder sister used to wear canvas shoes dyed black. Xi Jinping's childhood had little exposure to anything Western.

Xi Jinping's distaste toward things Western also has its roots in his first failed marriage. Understandably, details of this marriage do not appear in any official documents. He married about 1979 when he was working as a secretary to the secretary of the Central Military Commission Geng Biao (耿飈) and divorced in about 1982. His young wife Ke Lingling (柯玲玲) was the daughter of Ke Hua (柯華), Chinese ambassador to the UK. Xi Jinping's father's family and Ambassador Ke's family went back many years as close acquaintants. Ke Hua's original name was Lin Dechang (林德常). He had studied at the Yanjing University (燕京), until he joined the communist Eighth Route Army (八路軍) of the National Revolutionary Army in 1937 when the Second Sino-Japanese War erupted. It was Xi Jinping's father who recommended Ke Hua to Zhou Enlai, helping Ke embark on a diplomatic career. Ke was serving as Chinese ambassador to the UK at the time of Xi Jinping's marriage to Ke Lingling.

Xi Jinping's Childhood Immersed in Chinese Tradition

Ke Lingling was two years senior to Xi Jinping, and they had known each other since childhood. Ke Lingling was tall and pretty, and plain-spoken. Ke Lingling graduated from the 101 Middle School, famous for its Soviet Union style curriculum and large number of children of the CCP aristocracy. It is said that the relationship of the young couple was good at first when they used to live in the Xi Cheng (西城) of Beijing. Trouble started brewing when Ke Lingling expressed her desire to study abroad in England. It made perfect sense to Ke Lingling in that her English was already good, and her father was the ambassador to the UK.

Ke Lingling suggested that they both go study in England for a couple of years and start a new life abroad or come back to China to pursue high-end careers. Xi Jinping adamantly opposed any such thought. They fought day and night. Neither would relent. Eventually, Ke Lingling left for England by herself, and the marriage dissolved. Some speculate, perhaps not without reason, that the pain of this failed marriage contributed to his decision to move to distant Zhengding (正定) in Hubei Province. Before leaving Beijing, now alone, Xi Jinping borrows a few lines from the poem *Bamboo Rock* (竹石) by a Qing poet and artist Zheng Banqiao (鄭板橋) to express his resolve:

Biting onto the mountains, never loosening its hold
Its firm roots originating from within the fractured rocks
The thousands of hardship only bring about greater fortitude
Never relenting to winds from any direction[11]

Xi changed a few words of this poem to express his own emotions: from mountains to Loess Plateau (aka red clay plateau, i.e., the provincial place he was moving to) (黃土高原), and from fractured rock to the masses of people (as his maternal uncle had advised). Well, some Chinese scholars are somewhat more cynical regarding these interlineations: they argue (in private) that Xi Jinping never learned much growing up during the Cultural Revolution. Zhang Lifan (章立凡) of Second Red Generation (紅二代) quips he heard that Xi Jinping did read a lot, but only the Kung Fu novels.

But not everyone is that cynical. Yang Zhongmei (楊中美), the author of the sweeping biography of Xi Jinping, is of the opinion that Xi Jinping is relatively well-read. Japanese journalist Minemura Genji, who famously interviewed Xi Jinping's daughter at Harvard, also says citing Chinese sources that Xi Jinping has been a voracious reader since his youth and has read most of Chinese classics. Especially, he read through all twenty volumes of Xunzi (荀子) while he was self-exiled in the countryside, to the extent that he could quote any part of it at will.

Xi Jinping's literature teacher at August 1st School (八一) Chen Qiuying (陳秋影) said in 2015 that Xi Jinping had liked the tragic statesman-poet Du Fu (杜甫) and soccer. His literature grades were good, but not enough to become a poet or an author. A year earlier in 2014, something happened that enraged Xi Jinping. An elementary school in Shanghai deleted eight classic poems including *On the Stork Tower* By Wang Zhihuan (登鸛雀樓) and *River Snow* (江雪) by the Tang Dynasty Chinese poet Liu Zongyuan (柳宗元) from its literature textbook. Xi Jinping decried, "Removing Chinese classic literature from textbooks is to delete Chinese tradition from education, and I for one cannot agree to it."

Finding Solutions from Chinese rather than Western Tradition

An incident that took place at the 119th celebration of Mao Zedong's birth on December 26, 2012—about a month after becoming the most powerful man in China—speaks volumes of this side of Xi Jinping. He said he had heard from a respected elder statesman that the CCP officials must hold on three dictums at all times: you must not lose China's 5,000 year history; you must not destroy the political institutions your predecessors built; and you must never allow the territory of China bequeathed to you to be diminished in size. It appears that Chinese tradition is held deeper in Xi Jinping's heart than socialism.

In 2013, during a first visit in twenty-one years by a Paramount Leader to Confucius' birthplace Qufu (曲阜) in Shandong Province, Xi Jinping declared that "the Chinese people of glorious tradition from time immemorial will surely revive the glittering Chinese culture." In September 2014, at the 2,565th celebration of Confucius' birth, he said, "the CCP is the proud heir to China's glorious traditional culture."

Xi Jinping often tries to gain diplomatic advantage over Western counterparts by emphasizing Chinese tradition. During a state visit by President Barack Obama in November 2014, Xi Jinping invited him to a sumptuous banquet on Yingtai Island (瀛台) in Zhongnanhai and discussed the sad fate of Emperor Guangxu (光緒帝) who ruled China from 1875 to 1908, but under the near total domination by his aunt Empress Dowager Cixi. Xi Jinping even asked president Obama to study Chinese history, saying that "to understand China of today and its future, you must know her past. The genes of traditional Chinese culture runs through China's governing principles."

During Donald Trump's state visit in 2017, Xi Jinping invited him to the Forbidden City (故宮) and enjoyed the performance of a Peking Opera (京劇). Xi's use of Chinese culture and tradition was particularly profitable during the state visit by the French president Emmanuel Macron. To make a point of his affinity with President Macron, Xi invited him to the Songyuan Binguan in Guangdong Province.

The Songyuan Binguan is famous for the Lingnan Garden (嶺南園林). There, he had a 2,000-year-old musical piece *Running Water* (流水) performed on an ancient Guqin just for President Macron. One can venture a guess as to what they discussed together. This musical piece has a symbolic correlation with the tale of friendship between Bo Ya (伯牙), a quin master, and Zhong Ziqi (鍾子期), a humble woodcutter, during the Spring and Autumn Period in ancient China. When Bo Ya spontaneously composed and played a piece, say about unbroken mountain ranges or raging waters, it was only Zhong Ziqi who could instantly recognize what the music conveyed. They became fast friends and vowed to see each other again.

Later when Bo Ya learned of Zong Ziqi's death, lamenting over the passing of the only man who could truly appreciate his music, Bo Ya cut the strings of his guqin never to play again—thus leaving the four letter idiom 伯牙絕絃 (Bo Ya cuts his strings). Inviting President Macron to Songyuan Binguan then was suggestive of the special friendship Xi Jinping wanted to convey to Macron—to France. The theatrics worked apparently. Upon returning to France, Macron made many sino-friendly remarks like "Europe must resist pressure to become 'America's followers'," much to the chagrin of the United States. Whether Macron agrees or not, Xi Jinping in fact says China's path should be built solely on the bedrock of Chinese tradition and culture.

Xi Jinping's DNA then compels the assertion of Chinese culture and tradition, and its inevitable mirror image, anti-Western frame of mind.

RED JIANGSHAN THOUGHTS (江山思惟) OF THE RED SECOND GENERATION (紅二代), THE CHOSEN FEW

"The blood of the Red Second Generation (紅二代) flows through Xi Jinping's veins. As their fathers paid for the unified China with their blood and toil, the Red Second Generation feels the sacred duty to forever safeguard the red wave of communism in China."

"We are not the 5th generation. We are the 2nd generation of the revolution!" Xi Jinping is fond of saying. That's odd. Chinese people, and the world for that matter, call him the fifth-generation leader, following in the footsteps of Mao Zedong, Deng Xiaoping, Jiang Zemin, and Hu Jintao. But Xi Jinping insists that he is the second-generation leader.

What he means, of course, is that he is the successor to Mao Zedong, not Deng Xiaoping. According to Chinese sources, Xi Jinping is known to have said: "I will seize power in three stages. First, I will use Jiang Zemin's power to retire Hu Jintao. Then I will have Hu Jintao wreak revenge on Jiang Zemin. Then I will establish a new China with you, my comrades."

The "comrades" here refers to the Red Second Generation (紅二代), the children of the "revolutionary elders." This concept encompasses the children' spouses and sons-in-law. Xi Jinping himself is a Red Second Generation.

In his scheme to remove Jiang Zemin and Hu Jintao using the classic 以夷制夷 strategy (use barbarians to control barbarians), one can sense that Xi Jinping wanted to keep a distance from Deng Xiaoping, but outright regard Jiang Zemin and Hu Jintao as enemies. This stance reflects the perception and sentiment of the Red Second Generation.

Hu Muying (胡木英), daughter of Hu Qiaomu (胡喬木) who served as Mao Zedong's secretary and a member of the Politburo of the Central Committee of the CCP, founded and serves as the chairman of Yan'an Red Second Generation Society (延安兒女聯誼會) in Beijing. She bemoans, "Some call us 'Second Generation Officials' (官二代), but we are no such thing. We are Red Second Generation (紅二代). Our fathers fought and struggled for the people. The apparatchik today, however, work only for their own power, interest, and promotion, and their children reap untold wealth and special privileges." This is no mere lamentation; it drips with anger.

Red Second Generation (紅二代) calls the twenty-some years under Jiang Zemin and Hu Jintao the "Lost Twenty Years." They also fault Deng Xiaoping for choosing Jiang Zemin and Hu Jintao as his successors. It is now time for Red Second Generation (紅二代) to answer the call of history and restore the Red Homeland at the forefront of its struggle, and Xi Jinping, their great leader, is calling them to action.

Xi Jinping came to power with enthusiastic support from Red Second Generation (紅二代). They proclaimed, "We support Xi Jinping, and we will not interfere with the execution of his mission." Hu Muying (胡木英) exclaimed, "Now, at last, fresh air is rising, blowing away the clammy tepidness." They have faith in Xi Jinping that he will rid China of Deng Xiaoping's legacy, and the anti-corruption drive is but the first step.

Many Red Second Generation (紅二代) remain bitter in that they have been sidelined since the advent of Deng Xiaoping's Openness policy. They secured neither the riches nor political power during the openness era. Now, the table has turned and Red Second Generation (紅二代) is back in power. Several incidents highlight their rise in the CCP.

On October 15, 2013, a symposium commemorating the 100th anniversary of Xi Jinping's father Xi Zhongxun's birth was held at the Great Hall of People in Beijing. In front of a packed audience, the close comradeship between Mao Zedong and Xi Zhongxun was repeated no less than seven times. Some may question with genuine puzzlement why Red Second Generation (紅二代) venerate Mao Zedong when many of their parents were branded counter-revolutionary and suffered humiliation, incarceration, bodily harm, and even death during the Cultural Revolution. Historian Zhang Lifan (張立凡), a Red Second Generation (紅二代) himself, explains: "To Red Second Generation (紅二代), a parent is a parent, and a godfather is a godfather. Mao in their hearts is immovable and timeless. To question Mao is to question the legitimacy of the CCP."

Xi Jinping, the Successor to Mao Zedong—Not Deng Xiaoping

On July 1, 2021, a number of Red Second Generation (紅二代) were invited to the hallowed reviewing stand of the Tiananmen gate at the 100th anniversary of the founding of the CCP. The list of the invitees was literally the who-is-who of the highest communist aristocracy. According to freelance journalist Gao Yu (高瑜), the seating arrangement for the invitees conformed to the ranks of their fathers. Gao Yu also noted the six passengers of the limousine bus number 1. These were the second generation of the founding fathers of the People's Republic of China, including Mao Zedong's daughter Li Min (李敏), Zhou Enlai's niece Zhou Bingde (周秉德), and the like. According to this carefully orchestrated protocol, Deng Xiaoping only ranked fifth.

Gao Yu said, "Hu Jintao and Wen Jiabao are mere butlers, and their children are called the 'Second Generation Officials' (官二代)." Red Second Generation (紅二代) are the chosen ones, not the Second Generation Officials (官二代). Gao Yu's post on Twitter (Twitter is blocked in China but Chinese people use it through VPN) stated, "Following the ceremony, the elder Red Second Generation (紅二代) took a commemorative photograph with Li Min in the middle. They stood where Mao Zedong used to stand." The Red Second Generation (紅二代) now accounts for approximately five hundred families.

A legendary anecdote has come down over the last several decades. It pertains to the CCP's treatment of Li Ne (李訥), a daughter born between Mao Zedong and Jiang Qing (江青). After Mao's death, Li Ne fell from grace and was incarcerated. She was suffering from a kidney disease. Unable to obtain medical care, indeed afford, Li Ne wrote to the CCP, "If I could be allowed to inherit just a small portion of my father's estate, I would forever be grateful to the party."

Deng Xiaoping's response was cold: "What you refer to Mao Zedong's estate are all assets of the party and the state." Li Ne was thus denied the dialysis treatment. In contrast, Xi Jinping invited Li Ne, her half-sister Li Min, and Zhang Yufeng (張玉鳳), Mao's personal secretary who tended to him at his deathbed, to a special banquet held in their honor at the 120th commemoration of Mao's birth. In addition, upon hearing the aging Li Ne was frail and unable to feed herself properly, Xi Jinping assigned a chef, security personnel, a chauffeur, and a secretary to Li Ne and her family, official courtesy protocol befitting a deputy minister in the CCP hierarchy. Many aging Red Second Generation (紅二代) were moved to bitter tears.

What then is the core beliefs of Red Second Generation (紅二代) from which one can read the tenets of Xi Jinping's rule? It can be summarized as rule under the mandate of heaven (治國天命) based on the Jiangshan Thoughts (江山思惟)—their fathers shed blood to reunite the rivers and mountains of China (打江山) and, therefore, the Red Second Generation (紅二代) must ensure that Red China last through eternity (保江山).

In this line of thought, Red Second Generation (紅二代) is the one with the mandate of heaven. According to Professor Kou Chien-Wen of National Chengchi University of Taiwan, "Xi Jinping also thinks he was chosen to uphold the mandate." For instance, upon becoming the Shanghai party secretary in March 2007, Xi Jinping made well-publicized visits to the hallowed grounds of Shanghai's 1st Party Congress and the 2nd Party Congress. He was letting his countrymen know that he is a Red Second Generation (紅二代), and that he was loyal and committed to its Jiangshan cause (江山思惟). Professor Kou Chine-Wen states, "Xi Jinping is totally committed to the belief that he can remodel China, and indeed the world, based on the socialist ideals of the Mao Zedong era." The China Dream (中國夢) and Belt and Road Initiative are the manifestations of this belief in his destiny.

Emperor beyond Red Second Generation (紅二代)

Not everyone agrees. Professor Sun Liping (孫立平) of China's Tsinghua University criticizes Red Second Generation (紅二代) for harboring Jiangshan Thought (江山思惟), as it stands for the idea that because their ancestors reunified China, they inherit the 江山 (literally rivers and mountains) of China. This attitude presumes that China's 江山 are theirs to have, which is diametrically opposite of the fundamental communist political principle that it is the people who bestow power on the CCP (權爲民所賦). 江山 belong to the people, not to Red Second Generation (紅二代).

Another problem with Red Second Generation's (紅二代) Jiangshan Thought (江山思惟) is that Red Second Generation (紅二代) is fragmenting from within. It is all good and well that Xi Jinping's power base Xi Jiajun (習家軍) (aka, Xi Jinping clique) helped defeat Jiang Zemin's Shanghai Clique (上海幫) and Hu Jintao's Communist Youth League (共青團), but even Red Second Generation's (紅二代) are now the subject of political purges for speaking out their thoughts. A case in point is the sacking of Liu Yazhou (劉亞洲), once dubbed a "talented man in the army" (軍中才子), from his exalted post of the Political Commissar of the PLA National Defense University.

According to former Professor Cai Xia (蔡霞) of the Central Party School who defected to the United States, Liu Yazhou made the mistake of writing a letter to Xi Jinping in 2017 recommending the revision of the party's Xinjiang policy. He promptly disappeared, and his whereabouts remained unknown until 2023 when Hong Kong media reported that he "had been sentenced to death with two-year reprieve for engaging in grave economic corruption."

A Red Second Generation's (紅二代) industrialist Ren Zhiqiang, known for his penchant for speaking his mind, called Xi Jinping a "clown" in February 2020, criticizing Xi's bungling responses to COVID-19. He was sentenced to eighteen years in prison for this outburst. As Ren Zhiqiang is known to be a close associate of Wang Qishan (王岐山), once dubbed the right-hand man of Xi Jinping, deep rumbles are reverberating among the CCP cadres.

Xi Jinping is a Red Second Generation's (紅二代), rose to power thanks to Red Second Generation's (紅二代), and thinks he is carrying out the heavenly mandate of the Jiangshan Thought (江山思惟). The conspicuous problem now is that he no longer heeds Red Second Generation's (紅二代). Not all Red Second Generation's (紅二代) are born equal. Xi Jinping is perhaps an emperor, beyond Red Second Generation (紅二代) though born as one.

INSTINCT FOR STRUGGLE AND BOLD BETRAYAL

Xi Jinping considers conflict a natural state of politics. His instinct is to wrest power through struggle. This is a universal perception found in all Cultural Revolution generations. Such individuals are trapped in a time capsule where he is a righteous destined to do battle against the wicked."

"Not having factions in a political party would be a truly bizarre thing," said Chen Duxiu (陳獨秀), the founder of the CCP, in his writing *Four Character Classic* (四字經). Chen was mocking Kuomintang, fragmented by countless factions, but later Mao Zedong was fond of repeating this quote. Mao thought it human nature that strongmen would emerge in any groupings of people, and they would naturally vie for supremacy.

In fact, the CCP has been embroiled in internal power struggles under the guise of competition for policies ever since its foundation in 1921. "The victor gets to be a king, and the vanquished a traitor." is perhaps a timeless universal truth. As such, in the one-party rule of the CCP especially, rule of law is often ignored. The victor arbitrarily revises the rules to suit his needs, and the vanquished can only wait on his knees until the victor hands down the punishment.

Xi Jinping, a man who came of age through a precarious rite of passage in a suffocating communist state full of deadly intrigue, developed a fearsome instinct for struggle in the deep recesses of his soul. Professor Kou Chien-Wen of National Chengchi University of Taiwan sums up thus: "In Xi Jinping's world view, struggle is the natural state of politics, and cooperation is only ancillary. His instinct is to achieve victory through never-ending struggle."

According to Professor Kou Chien-Wen, this world view of Xi Jinping explains his fight against corruption. This flagship policy on his part is a battlefield of 敵我矛盾 (either you are for us or against us). In this sense, corruption in Chinese society is a useful enemy indeed for Xi Jinping—a venue and target for his continuing struggle.

In August 2014, Xi Jinping visited a gym in Nanjing to give talks of encouragement to Chinese boxing hopefuls. Xi Jinping says in a short video clip on CCTV, "I used to box as a young man myself. I just saw your uppercut, and I like it. Our boxers don't use uppercuts very much, but European boxers' uppercuts are very intimidating." It cannot be confirmed whether he formally trained as a boxer in his youth, but it is commonly accepted that he grew up embroiled in countless street brawls.

Add to this his daring belligerence, you see in Xi Jinping a glimpse of the notion of struggle commonly observed among the Cultural Revolution generation. As Red Second Generation's (紅二代) historian Zhang Lifan (張立凡) dubs it "Bold Betrayal." The targets of struggle during the Cultural Revolution evolved as the tragedy played itself out, starting with teachers and intellectuals, followed by "Breaking the Four Olds" (四舊打破), that is, old cultures, old customs, old habits, and old ideas. The Cultural Revolution generation then targeted classmates from families of questionable communist credentials and old party functionaries, leading eventually to Mao's mouthpiece Cultural Revolution Group (中央文化革命小組) and ideological party line itself. Xi Jinping's daring audacity in saying, acting, and taking charge was forged during his youth through the crucible of the Cultural Revolution.

A Chinese academic's explanation is on point: "In his youth, Xi Jinping firmly believed himself to be the righteous, undergoing hardships due to the oppression of the wicked. He had to develop himself through indomitable effort, and carry on the fight against the unrighteous." This is reminiscent of an old proverb Mao Zedong used to quite often: A Foolish Old Man Moves Mountains (愚公移山). The moral of the story is, of course, that righteousness will triumph in the end if you work at it tirelessly without end.

THE PARAMOUNT LEADER DEMANDING CEASELESS STRUGGLE FROM THE CCP RANK-AND-FILE

Xi Jinping's struggle instinct was on full display in a speech he delivered at a school entrance ceremony of the Central Party School of the CCP in September 2019.

"The CCP, the PRC, the Openness policy, the New Xi Jinping Era all were born through struggle, developed through struggle, and realized through struggle. . . . The Great Rejuvenation of the Chinese People cannot be achieved by striking gongs and beating drums; if you want to realize it, you must struggle for it . . .

This struggle we face is not one of short term, but of long term . . . the two pillars of communist struggle are the enlightened leadership by the party, and the jealous struggle for socialism . . .

Struggle is a form of art. You must be good at it, and have courage not to yield an inch when it comes to principles. Struggle instinct and ability are not born; you must develop it in you through relentless training.

If you have problems and obstacles, you must struggle . . . a CCP official is both a commander and fighter in all sectors of governance like domestic affairs, diplomacy, and defense. . . . You must struggle boldly and courageously, and be skilled fighters in it . . ."

This speech addressing CCP cadres in their mid-forties starts with struggle and ends with struggle. One can see why China has maintained such an abrasive and combative approach under Xi Jinping both internally and externally on the world stage.

Educating the CCP cadres and rank-and-file on the importance of struggle continues. The speech that opened the lectures for middle-level party officials at the Central Party School exhorted the students that "just as the brave come out victorious in an alley rumble, you must be bold and skilled in struggle . . . only then will you be able to secure the sovereignty and interests of our great nation."

To Xi Jinping, China is not at peace; it is a time for struggle. This perception pervades China's endless anti-corruption drive internally, and Wolf Warrior diplomacy it confronts the world with.

During the early years of the CCP, political power struggle was a deadly affair. This changed following the prosecution of the infamous Gang of Four in the aftermath of the Cultural Revolution. Many wanted the death penalty for Jiang Qing, Mao's wife. However, Chen Yun (陳雲), second in command after Deng Xiaoping, argued against a death penalty saying, "We must not set a precedent of death penalty in cases arising out of political struggles within the party. Otherwise, we will not be able to manage the future of the CCP." His argument carried the day, and Jiang Qing's death penalty was commuted to life imprisonment. She was later released for medical reasons, but died by suicide in 1991.

The Gang of Four chapter established a tradition of not handing out death penalties in political trials, but Xi Jinping's embrace of struggle is thought to have brought back the death penalty. The true problem lies elsewhere: Xi Jinping's philosophy of seeing struggle as a fundamental part of politics has pervaded China's diplomatic corps and its international behavior creating an irreversible enmity between socialism of China and democracy of the West. Professor Kou Chien-Wen of National Chengchi University of Taiwan explains, "Xi Jinping learned class struggle in his youth. He lacks stabilizing faculty. Fundamentally, he believes that political rivalry is a zero-sum game." What's truly regrettable, however, is that the South Korea-China relations and the US-China relations appear to be shaped by Xi Jinping's philosophy of endless truculent struggle.

CONSUMMATE PRAGMATISM

"Xi Jinping eludes easy understanding. He is like a fog that moves. If needed, he can discard pride and lower himself even to his subordinates. He is a consummate pragmatist."

"A clever man adapts to changing tides, and a wise man makes institutional changes when needed," said Xi Jinping in August 2013 at a Publicity Department of the Central Committee meeting. This quote is from *Yantie Lun* (鹽鐵論) (Discussions on salt and iron) by Huan Kuan (桓寬) during the Han dynasty. Xi Jinping repeated this quote at the Conference on Interaction and Confidence Building Measures in Asia (CICA) in 2014. Just what does he mean by this adage? Is he recommending shifting principles and courses of action for different circumstances ignoring established rules and institutions? This aspect of his belief system makes it extremely difficult to assess what Xi Jinping is really thinking. A case in point is his recent claim that he has "steadfastly supported private industries" when in fact he had been relentless in oppressing the private sector to bring it firmly under his control for all to see.

Here, we encounter the fifth element of Xi Jinping's personality: a consummate pragmatism. Among the many ancient Chinese wisdoms dear to Chinese heart is the idiom 屈臣制天下 (one rules all under heaven by bowing to one's subordinates). In pursuit of interests, Xi Jinping can apparently do things others, especially in the West, could imagine or would anticipate. He can confront the strong with aggression, but if circumstances turn disadvantageous, he can readily retreat too.

Professor Kou Chien-Wen of National Chengchi University of Taiwan observes, "When necessary, Xi Jinping is fully capable of exercising 韜光養晦 (Hide your capabilities, and bide for your time)." Xi Jinping has yet to mention publicly this classic dictum of Deng Xiaoping, but if he deems it necessary, he is fully capable of sacrificing his pride in pursuit of practical gains. 2007 was such a year.

Having assumed the post of Shanghai party secretary in March 2007, he received Hu Jintao in an "inspection tour" in October. In a one-on-one meeting that followed, Hu Jintao informed Xi that he had been selected as the next-generation leader of China. Indeed, at the 17th Party Congress held in mid-October, he was announced as a member of the Politburo Standing Committee. He became a Chu Jun (儲君, crown prince).

All he had to do was not make mistakes and win support—at least no outright opposition—for five years, and he would be the next emperor. A Second Red Generation (紅二代) himself, he had to win support of *all* factions of Second Red Generation (紅二代). There were four factions, the Deng faction led by Deng Xioping's son Deng Pufang (鄧樸方) being the most powerful. Xi Jinping had to win its support, and others would follow suit. But, there was a problem.

The beginning of the long running animosity between the Xi family and the Dng family can be traced back to the 1950s. The first clash between Xi Jinping's father Xi Zhongxun and Deng Xiaoping took place during the Gaogang (高崗) controversy of 1954. Gaogang was one of the founding fathers of the CCP along with such close personal friends and comrades as Xi Zhongxun and Liu Zhidan (劉志丹). Gaogang was arrested in 1954 accused of being counter-revolutionary; however, he ended his life by suicide. During this incident, Deng Xiaoping stood on the side of Zhou Enlai, and hurled accusations at Gaogang. As we have seen above, Xi Jinping's dreamy childhood would come crashing down when his father Xi Zhongxun was purged as a result of a political scandal surrounding the novel *Liu Zhidan* (劉志丹) in 1962. But this was not the end of the bad blood between the Xi family and the Deng family.

Xi Jinping Knows When to Be Strong, But Also When to Retreat

The second feud took place in 1987 surrounding the purge of Hu Yaobang (胡耀邦), the party general secretary at the time. Deng Xiaoping used to hold the Democratic Life Meeting (生活会) of the CCP at his home at this time. In one such meeting, Deng lays out a plan to purge Hu Yaobang accusing him of being lax in cracking down on "bourgeois liberalization" and their demand for privatization of property. This was only a pretext, however. In fact, Hu Yaobang and Xi Zhongxun were pushing for a reform of the Chinese economy and political structure, and toward this end, wanted to see Deng Xiaoping retire completely. Deng Xiaoping snapped at one point, "Let's be brutally honest, here. You just don't like my meddling in the CCP affairs, isn't that right?"

Finally, conservative elders of the Democratic Life Meeting demanded Hu Yaobang's resignation. The enraged Xi Zhongxun got up and shouted pounding the desk, "The Democratic Life Meeting cannot decide on matters such as this; it is against the CCP principle of process!" Xi Zhongxun was intimating that Deng Xioping was following the footsteps of Mao Zedong's totalitarian dictatorship. Through this outburst, Xi Zhongxun may have earned a glowing reputation among Chinese people, but certainly provoked the ire of aging Deng Xiaoping.

Xi Zhongxun appears to have been a man of principle. Xi Jinping, however, is a consummate pragmatist. It was Xi Jinping who desperately needed support from the Deng faction of the Red Second Generation (紅二代) group.

Xi Jinping turned to Yu Zheng Sheng (俞正聲) of the illustrious Yu (俞) family to effect a historic reconciliation between his family and the Deng family. Xi Jinping asked Yu Zheng Sheng to arrange a dinner meeting with Deng Pufang. After agonizing over the request, Deng Pufang sent his sister Deng Rong (鄧榕) and her husband to the dinner, himself feigning illness. Some claim that this was a reconciliation of sorts between the two families, but others argue that Deng Pufang made an unforgivable mistake of failing to recognize the would-be emperor.

Xi Jinping wouldn't hesitate to embrace an enemy if he feels the need. In October 2010, Xi Jinping delivered a speech praising the life and times of Liu Lantao (劉瀾濤) at the 100th anniversary of his birthday. Liu Lantao had been the vice chair of the Anti-party Activity Investigation Committee which investigated Xi Zhongxun during the *Liu Zhidan* (劉志丹) scandal. Recall that it was this investigation that had brought about the Xi family's fall from grace. He was now delivering a glowing tribute to a sworn enemy, because he needed support from Red Second Generation (紅二代).

In early July 2018, a young woman threw Chinese ink over Xi Jinping's portrait. It was a protest against the ever-intensifying personality cult of Xi Jinping. To the surprise of many, the CCP began removing portraits and posters bearing Xi Jinping's face. Instead of forcing the issue on disgruntled citizens, the CCP propaganda machine was shrewdly adjusting its pace.

In 2022, as Xi Jinping's draconian zero-COVID policy kept Shanghai under lockdown for over two months, the public opinion began to fester and the Chinese media began airing sympathetic views on Premier Li Keqiang. That fall, many Western media opined, "Li Keqiang is on the rise, and Xi Jinping is in decline." Nothing could have been further from the truth. Li Keqiang could remain in his position only to the extent permitted by Xi Jinping, but Xi Jinping did not strike him down this time. As he had done with the Chinese ink incident, Xi Jinping was shrewdly biding time for a more opportune moment to deal with Li Keqiang who dared to upstage him.

During the early days of Xi Jinping's rule, some pundits posited Xi was pursuing Deng Xiaoping's Openness policy economically, while simultaneously pursuing Mao Zedong's authoritarianism politically. Not necessarily. The consummate pragmatist Xi Jinping is more likely to adopt whatever is more expedient for the problems at hand, whether Deng's openness or Mao's authoritarianism. Xi Jinping is fond of saying, "An era has its unique problems, and the man of the era has his missions." The gist of this enigmatic statement is rather straightforward: different eras bring different challenges, and a person living in that era just needs to address them unbeholden to old rules and protocols. That's Xi Jinping, the consummate pragmatist.

COLLECTIVISM BUILT ON INDIVIDUAL SACRIFICES

"Xi Jinping reveres the value of collectivism, typical among the Cultural Revolution generation. He demands ceaseless public service from the CCP members and never-ending individual sacrifices from the people."

Chinese speak of Three Fundamental Views (三觀): world view, philosophy on life, and values. In forming these three fundamental values in an individual, the trend of thought (思潮) of an era plays a decisive role— the zeitgeist. What zeitgeist helped form Xi Jinping's fundamental views?

Writer and former journalist at *People's Daily* Ma Licheng (馬立誠) argues that some eight different zeitgeists swept through China over the last thirty years, some of which led to the formation of political power blocks. Ma Licheng lists the following waves of isms: Deng Xioping's socialism with unique Chinese characteristics; paleo-leftism (舊左派) representing Mao Zedong's thoughts from his later years; neo-leftism (新左派) influence by the West's leftists; democratic socialism influenced by Europe's democratic socialism; liberalism based on the Western notion of human rights; nationalism proclaiming the great rejuvenation of the Chinese people; populism; and, neo-Confucianism.

Meanwhile, historian Xiao Gongqin (蕭功秦) identifies six such waves. The first wave was liberalism, which arose in the wake of the implementation of the Openness policy. It represented a pushback against the excesses of Mao Zedong's extreme leftist ideologies. It called for the sanctity of human life, human values, freedom, and liberation from ideologies hitherto inculcated. The problem inherent in this wave was unviability: the hope of instilling this Western ideology in the backward agrarian society of China proved to be wholly illusory. A case in point was the backlash from the greater Chinese public to the ill-fated democracy movement, forever etched in the memory of the West as the images from the Tiananmen Square tragedy on June 4, 1989.

The pushback manifested itself in the form of neo-conservatism (aka neo-authoritarianism) starting in the latter half of the 1980s, calling for gradual, moderate, but progressive authoritarianism that promotes social order and stability. Only development under enlightened autocracy (開明專制) could lead China to democratization and modernization. Historian Xiao Gongqin considers himself an adherent to neo-conservatism, as does Wang Huning (王滬寧), current chairman of the Chinese People's Political Consultative Conference and a prominent political philosopher/theorist who has served under three Paramount Leaders from Jiang Zemin, Hu Jintao, to Xi Jinping.

Coming into the twenty-first century, however, the hitherto ubiquitous presence of neo-conservatism began to wane. One reason is that radical liberalism largely disappeared; neo-conservatism ran out of its targets. Another reason is that, by the early 1990s, China had successfully entered the era of neo-conservatism; there was no more need to advocate what had already been established.

Starting in the mid-1990s, however, neo-leftism began to emerge. Its tenet was a return to egalitarianism, as the Chinese society was sick with corruption and inequality brought on by its experimentation with capitalism. Neo-leftists claimed that they had re-discovered the values of the Cultural Revolution from Mao Zedong's later years. Neo-leftism had a strong appeal to many young Chinese, as they had not experienced the hardships and suffering of the Cultural Revolution.

China Dream, the Holy Grail of Collectivism

Neo-nationalism emerged at about the same time. It rubs the old wound in the Chinese psyche stirring up raw ultra-nationalism: the collective memory of the misery and utter helplessness against the West and Japan during the Century of Humiliation between the Opium Wars of the 1840s and the founding of the People's Republic of China in 1949.

Together with neo-nationalism arose cultural conservatism. Emerging from the shock of globalization and the end of the Cold War in the waning years of the twentieth century, China sought to liberate itself from the problems brought on by the secular culture of the West by re-affirming its own cultural identity. A movement to revive Confucianism, thus re-establishing the Chinese national spirit, gained momentum.

The last wave of the zeitgeist to hit China in early 2000s, according to historian Xiao Gongqin (蕭功秦), was democratic socialism. It focuses on what Marks and Engel said in their later years, namely that a transition from capitalism to socialism can be accomplished without a violent revolution. The idea is to achieve ideal socialism through democratization, while maintaining the CCP as the sole ruling party. Former vice chancellor Xie Tao (謝韜) of Renmin University of China argues that "only democratic socialism can save China."

Xi Jinping is adamantly opposed to two of these six thoughts: liberalism and democratic socialism. Xi Jinping has even mobilized scholars sympathetic to his rule to denounce Xie Tao's democratic socialism. On the other hand, Xi Jinping himself appears to have been strongly influenced by the intervening four zeitgeists: neo-conservatism, neo-leftism, neo-nationalism, and cultural conservatism. It is none other than Xi Jinping's China Dream (中國夢) where these four frames of thought have been adroitly melded into, all designed to achieve the Great Rejuvenation of the Chinese People.

The China Dream is not one of an individual, but is the aspiration of 1.4 billion Chinese. This is where one can discern the last of Xi Jinping's personality traits: belief in collectivism built on sacrifice of individuality. Professor Kou Chien-Wen of National Chengchi University of Taiwan argues that Xi Jinping has a very strong belief in collectivism, and his China Dream is in essence a rallying call for collectivism. His brand of collectivism demands tireless and self-less contribution from the rank and file members of the CCP, and from the people, demands sacrifice of individual rights for the attainment of objectives set by the CCP. Xi Jinping edifies his people thus: "There is no such thing as 'self-Perfection and self-Beauty' (至善至美) in this world. An individual's abilities are limited. One cannot achieve anything away from the people, and apart from the ruling party."

Xi Jinping's collectivism germinated through his early upbringing. He lived in dormitories as a child at the August 1st School (八一), a school for the children of the Chinese communist aristocracy. The motto of the dormitory life was "individual is subordinate to group." This creed was inculcated into the minds of the young students through rigorous daily militaristic regimen. His father Xi Zhongxun also constantly demanded the ideal of solidarity and collectivism from his children.

Call for Ceaseless Sacrifice for the China Dream

Xi Jinping recollects in his writing *Son of Red Clay*, "The ideal of collectivism was the only thing that sustained me in my exile in the deep countryside of Northern Shaanxi province (陝北)." This reverence for collectivism is a universal phenomenon among the generation that survived through the Cultural Revolution. It is also a timeless Chinese value.

Zhang Weiwei (張維爲), the chair of the Chinese Studies Department of Fudan University in Shanghai, reminds everyone an old four-character idiom: 國破家亡 (If the country is lost, the family is destroyed too). He argues that, therefore, "China Dream is an amalgamation of national dream and family dream." The Century of Humiliation was an all too painful case in point.

However, collectivism brings with it serious adverse reactions. Xi Jinping thinks that the sacrifice of the people is justified in the pursuit of state objectives like the China Dream. Naturally, such extreme collectivism necessarily entails irreversible damage to individual interests. One does not need to look far for an example. Just look at the monstrous collective misery the indiscriminate lockdown measures brought upon the Chinese masses during the COVID-19 pandemic. Despite the waves of zeitgeist discussed above, the overblown collectivism turned out to be a recipe for people's revolt in the form of the Blank Paper Movement.

"Whether a celebrity bought a winery chateau in France legally or illegally is secondary; it is the fact that she indulged in individualism instead of engaging in sacrifice for the party and the state that is unforgivable for Xi Jinping," notes Professor Wang Yun (王韻) of the National Chengchi University of Taiwan. The prohibition on young people's use of TikTok beyond forty minutes is also founded on the concept of collectivism. The rationale appears Orwellian: what matters is not that the youth are addicted to TikTok but that they are wasting valuable time on personal gratification that can be devoted to the collective good. By logical extension, spending too much time online is a de-facto challenge against collectivism.

This demand for draconian collectivism has its roots in Maoism, and Xi Jinping is its modern-day evangelist. Xi Jinping is demanding a total sacrifice of individuality at the altar of collectivism, which he dubbed China Dream.

Part II

IMPACT OF XI JINPING'S ERA ON THE WORLD ORDER AND KOREA-US-CHINA TRILATERAL RELATIONS

Chapter 7

China's View of World Civilization, Community with a Shared Future of Mankind

In-Hee Kim

WHY DO SO MANY COUNTRIES JOIN THE SHARED FUTURE OF MANKIND?

According to a Chinese study, "[t]he uniqueness of the [phrase] 'China-Korea Community with a Shared Future of Mankind' is that it was the Moon Jae-in administration of Korea that first proposed it, and China accepted it."[1] There are three people who mentioned the phrase "Community with a Shared Future of Mankind" in the Moon Jae-in administration.

In October 2017, South Korean ambassador to China, Young-min Roh, said in an interview, "Korea and China are a Community with a Shared Future of Mankind and have common interests."[2] In December of that year, Chu Mi-ae, chairman of the Democratic Party of Korea, said in a keynote speech at the World Political Parties Dialogue held in China, "Let's create a future with a Community with a Shared Future of Mankind and happiness through solidarity and cooperation between our political parties."[3]

President Moon Jae-in mentioned this Community with a Shared Future of Mankind twice. At the Korea-China summit on December 3, 2017, he said, "It is true that the relationship between Korea and China is one of competition, but in a bigger sense, I believe that the two countries are fated partners and a Community with a Shared Future of Mankind that prosper jointly through cooperation." At the Korea-China-Japan summit held in Chengdu, China, on December 24, 2019, Moon reiterated, "China is dreaming of developing as a Community with a Shared Future of Mankind together with its surrounding countries, and we are, economically, a Community with a Shared Future of Mankind."

President Moon Jae-in's remarks were criticized for his pro-Chinese orientation as the 2020 COVID-19 crisis began to unfold. On the other hand, some pointed out that President Moon Jae-in's remarks were "distorted or exaggerated"[4] and that it was "limited to the economy."

Actually, it was not just government officials who responded positively to Xi Jinping's proposal for the Community with a Shared Future of Mankind. The Korean media began to pay attention to this concept when Xi Jinping proposed it at the Nineteenth Party Congress in October 2017. At that time, Korea-China bilateral relations were at a low point because of the deployment of THAAD on the Korean Peninsula, and most Korean media took Xi's call for a Community with a Shared Future of Mankind as a conciliatory gesture. One media outlet reported, "Though abstract, the proposal for a Community with a Shared Future of Mankind does emphasize the recovery and deepening of community relations, so [Korea] should also make a concerted effort to find the justification for the inevitability of cooperation between Korea and China."[5] Another media report quoted an expert as saying, "Xi Jinping's declaration of Community with a Shared Future of Mankind was a deliberate indication of China's conciliatory policies going forward in order to facilitate smooth prosecution of its One Belt One Road strategy."[6]

At that time, the Moon Jae-in government of Korea was the first to announce its intention to participate in President Xi Jinping's proposed a Shared Future of Mankind. Not only South Korea, but many countries around the world have participated in various destiny communities proposed by China. In particular, there have been many positive responses from third world countries such as Africa and South America. So why have so many countries joined China's proposed destiny community?

What explains such widespread elation on the part of Koreans? According to Xi Jinping, the Community with a Shared Future of Mankind that China dreams of is referring to a global community of peace, safety, shared interests, shared values, and common responsibility, in which humans and nature coexist in harmony. It was perhaps difficult for anyone to say "NO" to this collection of noble platitudes. Another reason is the extreme ambiguity of the phrase. Although Xi repeated the message many times in his public engagements, his speeches were invariably populated with abstract expressions. The truth of the matter is that nobody really knows just what the Community with a Shared Future of Mankind is supposed to look like in real life.

PAX SINICA AND GLOBAL GOVERNANCE

Global Economic Governance and the One Belt One Road Initiative

China intuitively realized that the time had come for China to assert itself on the global stage, having witnessed the behaviors of the Western democracies in response to the 2008 international financial crisis. China's assessment was the following: "The 2008 financial crisis revealed significant flaws in global governance mechanisms and systems and the powerlessness of major Western powers. G7 countries were forced to relinquish control over the global economy to G20 nations."[7]

Additionally, China took its participation in the 2008 G20 meeting held in Washington to mean that it was now one of the key members of the decision-making group composed of elite nations. It felt that the newfound status among nations as a driver of global governance was only befitting China's stature as the greatest developing country, the world's second largest economy, and home to the celestial Chinese civilization.

The One Belt One Road Initiative is China's signature global economic governance system. To support the colossal project, China also established the Asian Infrastructure Investment Bank (AIIB), the BRICS Development Bank, and the Silk Road Fund. The objective of this ambitious project, proposed in 2013, is to form an economic "belt" connecting the three continents of Asia, Europe, and Africa. Currently, thirty-two international organizations and 149 countries, including Korea, have signed One Belt One Road agreements with China.

I once attended a One Belt One Road academic conference in Hangzhou, China, in 2017. A senior researcher at China's global think tank, the Center for China and Globalization (CCG), gave a keynote lecture. Since the conference was for a domestic audience, the speaker explained the goal of the One Belt One Road Initiative without equivocation or opacity. He said,[8]

"The reason for the One Belt One Road Initiative is not to 'revive ancient history' nor to 'accommodate domestic overcapacity.' The real reason is to achieve long-term development of the Chinese economy in the changing global economic structure, and the 'Great Revival of the Chinese Nation.'" Xi Jinping first uttered the "China Dream" at the Eighteenth Party Congress in 2012. It called for nothing less than the "Great Revival of the Chinese Nation." And China was seeking to achieve the following ambitions through its One Belt One Road Initiative.

First, the initiative would create an external growth environment for the long-term development of the Chinese economy. The only way out of China's slowing economic growth was through "economic integration." China would implement a strategy to expand from Asia to Europe and Africa, integrating Eurasia into the world's largest economic bloc.

Second, the Initiative would establish a new global value chain with China at the center. China would work with countries aligned with the One Belt One Road initiative and build the new global value chain, thereby enhancing China's international stature. Finally, the speaker urged a correct interpretation of the One Belt One Road initiative. He said, "One Belt One Road is not China's version of the Marshall Plan, the dumping ground of our overcapacity, nor a route for China's expansion. It is for building a Community with a Shared Future of Mankind among sixty some countries through cooperation, development, and joint prosperity as equals. Leaders of all levels, the media, and experts must clearly understand this. In particular, experts and the media must refrain from making irresponsible remarks."

The speaker's remark that "[the initiative] is not for China's expansion of power" was an example of rhetorical irony—a rhetorical device intended to warn the audience to use extreme caution when discussing One Belt One Road with foreigners. He was warning against the One Belt One Road initiative being perceived as a "Chinese threat." All Chinese scholarly articles on One Belt One Road unanimously employ the following cliche: "One Belt One Road initiative is not for China to secure hegemony, but to make contribution to world peace and prosperity." This is, of course, in conformity with the government's guidelines. However, no amount of high-minded platitudes will cover up the true intention behind the One Belt One Road initiative: as the speaker himself said, it is a global economic governance infrastructure intended to bring about "The Great Revival of the Chinese Nation."

Global Diplomatic Governance and Partnership

In order to expand its diplomatic influence, a country must garner as many friends as possible in the international community. China has entered into partnership protocols with a number of countries. Partnership is different from a coercive hierarchical relationship. In general, it refers to a relationship where the parties pursue co-prosperity and development through reciprocal and democratic cooperation. If an alliance is for mutual defense against a common enemy, partnerships mainly emphasize cooperation in the economic sector. Of course, partnerships can also include cooperation in political, military, and security sectors.

In Chinese, a partnership is called *"huo ban"* (火伴, partner). This word originated from the troop management system of the ancient Northern Wei dynasty. During the Northern Wei dynasty, ten soldiers constituted one *huo ban*. They not only fought together but also lived under the same roof during peacetime. Therefore, for Chinese, "partnership" means a relationship similar to the one among comrades in arms, who share military and economic security. China began to form partnerships with other countries in 1993. Since 2013, when Xi Jinping proposed at the Regional Foreign Affairs Working Group Symposium, "Let's make many friends across the world on the premise of non-alliance,"[9] the number of partners has risen sharply. That year, of course, was the year Xi Jinping promulgated the One Road One Belt initiative.

So far, China has established partnerships with 105 countries, fully 54 percent of the 193 member nations of the UN. This means that more than half of all countries have special diplomatic relations with China. The United States and Japan are important countries in China's foreign relations, but they are not partners, but rather they are competitors. Korea is an ally of the United States, but China entered into a partnership with Korea because Korea is important to China economically and geopolitically. North Korea has not formed a partnership with China because it is China's only ally.

Table 7.1 China's Current Established Partnerships

Types of the Partnership	Partner Nations
1 Comprehensive Strategic Partnership of Cooperation for a New Era (新时代全面战略协作伙伴关系)	Russia
2 All Weather Strategic Partnership of Cooperation (全天候战略合作伙伴关系)	Pakistan
3 Comprehensive Strategic Partnership of Cooperation(全面战略合作伙伴关系)	Vietnam, Thailand, Myanmar, Cambodia, Laos, Mozambique, Congo, Sierra Leone, Senegal, Namibia, Zimbabwe, Guinea, Ethiopia, Kenya (14 nations)
4 Strategic Cooperative Partnership (战略合作伙伴关系)	Korea, India, Sri Lanka, Afghanistan, Brunei, Bangladesh, Republic of Cyprus(7 nations)
5 Comprehensive Cooperative Partnership (全面合作伙伴关系)	Croatia, Nepal, the Netherlands, East Timor, Tanzania, Liberia, Equatorial Guinea, Gabon, Madagascar, Sao Tome, Principe, Uganda (13 countries)
6 Significant Cooperative Partnership (重要合作伙伴关系)	Fiji
7 New-type Cooperative Partnership(新型合作伙伴关系)	Finland
8 All-round Partnership of Friendship and Cooperation (全方位友好合作伙伴关系)	Belgium
9 All-round Partnership of Cooperation (全方位合作伙伴关系)	Singapore
10 Twenty-first Century Global Comprehensive and Strategic Partnership of Cooperation(面向21世纪全球全面战略伙伴关系)	United Kingdom
11 Permanent Comprehensive and Strategic Partnership of Cooperation (永久全面战略伙伴关系)	Kazakhstan

(Continued)

Table 7.1 (Continued)

Types of the Partnership	Partner Nations
12 Comprehensive Strategic Partnership (全面战略伙伴关系)	Italy, Peru, Malaysia, Spain, Denmark, Indonesia, Mexico, Mongolia, Argentina, Venezuela, Brazil, France, Algeria, Belarus, Greece, Australia, New Zealand, Egypt, Saudi Arabia, Iran, Serbia, Poland, Uzbekistan, Chile, Ecuador, Hungary, Tajikistan, South Africa, Kyrgyzstan, United Arab Emirates, Uzbekistan, Turkey (32 countries)
13 All-round Strategic Partnership (全方位战略伙伴关系)	Germany
14 Strategic Parternship (战略伙伴关系)	Czech Republic, Iraq, Turkmenistan, Tonga, Nigeria, Canada, Samoa, Micronesia, Vanuatu, Papua New Guinea, Ireland, Ukraine, Angola, Qatar, Costa Rica, Jordan, Sudan, Czech Republic, Morocco, Uruguay, Djibouti, Bolivia, Congo, Bulgaria (24 countries)
15 Innovative Strategic Parternship (创新战略伙伴关系)	Switzerland
16 Innovative Comprehensive Partnership (创新全面伙伴关系)	Israel
17 Comprehensive Friendly Partnership of Cooperation (全面友好合作伙伴关系)	Maldives, Romania
18 Friendly Partnership (友好伙伴关系)	Jamaica
19 Friendly Strategic Partnership (友好战略伙伴关系)	Austria
Total (105 nations)	

China identifies what the counterpart nation means to its interests and enters into a partnership using very complex and archaic diplomatic language. By deciphering the esoteric language used, one can read what China thinks of the particular partner nation. The most important partner for China is Russia. China has formed a "Comprehensive Strategic Partnership of Coordination for a New Era" with Russia. "New era" connotes the era of Xi Jinping. "Coordination," a term reserved for a situation where the partnership is most urgently needed regionally or globally, has been used only with Russia thus far.

China has entered into a "Strategic Cooperative Partnership," the next level of importance to China, with approximately thirty countries, including Korea and other countries in Southeast Asia, Africa, and Europe. Early on, those in Asia that entered into a Strategic Cooperative Partnership with China were countries sharing a border with China, and military security was the main purpose of such partnerships. The most important among them is Pakistan, and in 2017, Chinese chose Pakistan as their most favored country. China and Pakistan are acting in concert economically and militarily on the global stage, based on a long-standing political trust between them.

China entered into a "Strategic Partnership" with sixty-one countries in Central Asia, West Asia, Europe, and South America. This list includes a large number of countries along the route of the One Belt One Road projects, as well as some South American countries that have traditionally maintained friendly relations with China. Except for those in Europe, these countries are either developing or socialist countries, thus in a similar position to that of China.

Since China launched its One Belt One Road iIitiative, the Chinese government has formed partnerships with as many countries as possible to ensure economic and military security. The Chinese are concerned that China does not have many *"peng you"* (朋友, friends) around the globe. Forming partnerships is one way China feels it can create a *"peng you quan"* (朋友圈, circle of friends).

Governance of Global Ideology and Community with a Shared Future of Mankind

In order for China to lead global governance, strengthening solidarity among community members is essential. China proposes a variety of a Community with a Shared Future of Mankind and is striving to create a sense of *'we-feeling(*我们感*)'* a sense of community called "us" among the community supporters. The Chinese government is trying to do so by disseminating and popularizing its "Discourse on the Community with a Shared Future of Mankind'" among the community members.

The first person who popularized the term ""community" was the vice-principal of the Central Party School of the CCP, Zheng Bijian.[10] In 2004, he proposed the "construction of a community of interest." The 2011 white paper entitled "China's Peaceful Rise" stated that "Countries with different systems, types, and stages of development rely on each other and blend their interests, forming a community with a shared future."[11] That was the birth of the official Discourse on the Community with a Shared Future of Mankind.

Table 7.2   Types of China's Community with a Shared Future of Mankind

Coverage	Types of the Partnership	Partner Nations
Global	Community with a Shared Future of Mankind?	
	Community of a Shared Future in Cyberspace (网络空间命运共同体)	
	Community of Shared Future for Nuclear Safety	
Regional	China-Africa Community with a Shared Future	
	China-Central and Eastern Europe Community with a Shared Future	
	Asia Community with a Shared Future	
	Shanghai Cooperation Organization(SCO) Community with a Shared Future	China, Russia, Kyrgyzstan, Tajikistan, Uzbekistan, Pakistan, India, Kazakhstan, Iran
	Asia-Pacific Community with a Shared Future	
	China-Southeast Asia Community with a Shared Future	
	China-Latin America Community with a Shared Future	
	China-Arabia Community with a Shared Future	
	G20 Community with a Shared Future	G20 Member States
	Building a Community of Common Destiny (打造周边命运共同体)	20 countries bordering China and 26 countries that are not bordering China but are geographically closely related to China
	China-Pacific Island Countries Community with a Shared Future	
Nations	China-Pakistan Community with a Shared Future	
	China-Vietnam Community with a Shared Future	
	China-Uzbekistan Community with a Shared Future	
	China-Belarus Community with a Shared Future	
	China-Kazakhstan Community with a Shared Future	
	China-Laos Community with a Shared Future	

In Chinese, destiny means "'to share life and death, and joy and sorrow." Therefore, forming a Community with a Shared Future of Mankind among countries means that they share a collective rise and fall. According to one study, "Community with a Shared Future of Mankind is akin to an enhanced strategic partner, lower than alliance and higher than strategic partner, a de-facto political and security cooperative organization."[12] China's Community with a Shared Future of Mankind with various regions or countries overlaps with countries with which it has partnerships. [13]

Membership in China's Community with a Shared Future of Mankind comes with significant obligations. In the event of a political dispute or clash between China and other countries, the member must side with China. If impossible, at a minimum, they need to maintain neutrality. For example, Korea is an ally of the United States, but if a US-China conflict comes to a head, Korea is expected to at least remain neutral. Members of the Community with a Shared Future of Mankind must support each other's security needs. In the event of a military clash between members and countries outside the community, China must provide military support.

A Community with a Shared Future of Mankind may be classified geographically into global, regional, and national levels. A Community with a Shared Future of Mankind may also be classified into three categories according to its objectives. The first is the ideal Community with a Shared Future of Mankind. It is a worldwide Community with a Shared Future of Mankind, with cyberspace and nuclear safety included. The purpose of this community is to share responsibility and jointly respond to global problems.

The second is the Community with a Shared Future of Mankind of security. China borders fourteen countries. The regional Community with a Shared Future of Mankind encompassing these countries is for security purposes. Xi Jinping proposed the Asian Community with a Shared Future of Mankind at the Boao Forum for Asia (BFA) in 2015. To Xi Jinping, an Asian Community with a Shared Future of Mankind had to precede a Community with a Shared Future of Mankind.

In other words, Korea and other Asian countries must be rescued from the grips of the United States and be repatriated into the traditional Chinese order of Asia. This strategic thinking on the part of Xi Jinping is behind the recent intensification of historical and cultural disputes between Korea and China. In his speech at the Conference on Dialogue of Asian Civilization held in Beijing in May 2019, Xi Jinping once again stressed that the United States is indifferent to the clash between civilizations, and is trying to reshape or replace other traditions and civilizations, and therefore Asian Community with a Shared Future of Mankind must be established to fight off the cultural encroachment by Western civilization.[14]

The third is the economic Communit[ies] of Common Destiny. In view of China's economic capacity, this community constitutes China's second most important international strategic network. This community includes the Shanghai Cooperation Organization and the China-Arab Community with a Shared Future of Mankind. All members of the Shanghai Cooperation Organization are developing countries with authoritarian governments.

Recently, it was reported that Iran joined as a full member. The China-Arab Community with a Shared Future of Mankind was formed for the purpose of the One Belt One Road initiative. It was at the Boao Forum for Asia in 2015 that China began conflating the ideology of the Community with a Shared Future of Mankind on what was otherwise an economic project. In his opening speech, Xi Jinping presented the Belt and Road Initiative and the AIIB as the major means of building an Asian Community with a Shared Future of Mankind.

The fourth is the Community with a Shared Future of Mankind of friendship. The China-Africa Community with a Shared Future of Mankind and the China-Latin America Community with a Shared Future of Mankind belong to this category. China's effort to form a Community with a Shared Future of Mankind with African nations was aided by the shared historical memory of oppression and humiliation at the hands of the Western powers. It was a case of misery loves company, where fellow sufferers saw friendship in shared suffering of developing countries and negative perception of the West.

Country-level A Community with a Shared Future of Mankind overlaps with countries that have a Strategic Cooperative Partnership with China. The countries in this community support China vociferously. They are, therefore, China's most important international strategic asset. Most of these countries are or have been socialist countries with close ties with the CCP.

China seeks to strengthen its political, economic, and security cooperation by enhancing solidarity among the members of Communities of Common Destiny. In this respect, a Community with a Shared Future of Mankind are similar to partnerships. However, if a partnership emphasizes economic and military cooperation, the Community with a Shared Future of Mankind values common values, that is, ideology. In addition, if partnerships are based on a diplomatic agreement between two countries, a Community with a Shared Future of Mankind are unilaterally proposed by China. Therefore, many countries that belong to a worldwide or regional Community with a Shared Future of Mankind do not realize that they are sharing a common destiny with China with attendant risks, demands, and obligations—just as we Koreans are oblivious of it.

THE CHINA DREAM AND THE COMMUNITY WITH
A SHARED FUTURE OF MANKIND

The Highest Ideology of International Order: The Community with a Shared Future of Mankind

The first leader to mention the Community with a Shared Future of Mankind was Hu Jintao. At the Eighteenth Party Congress in 2012, he said, "Let's lead the world toward an awareness of the ideals of Community with a Shared Future of Mankind."[15] Thus emerged proselytization of the concept of Community with a Shared Future of Mankind as a major foreign policy weapon of the CCP.

From the time Xi Jinping took office until December 31, 2018, he publicly mentioned the Community with a Shared Future of Mankind 350 times. Xi Jinping's evangelizing of the Community with a Shared Future of Mankind intensified over time, as did their tone.[16]

Xi Jinping's first mention of the Community with a Shared Future of Mankind on the international stage was when he visited Russia in March 2013. In his speech at the Moscow State Institute of International Relations (MIGMO), he said, "Today, the interconnection between nations and the degree of interdependence have deepened immeasurably. Humans live in a global community, in time and space where history and reality intersect, and are united as an indivisible Community with a Shared Future of Mankind." In a speech at the UN Headquarters in September 2015, he declared, "We shall build a new type of international order and establish a Community with a Shared Future of Mankind"[17]. In a meeting at the UN Office in Geneva in January 2017, he gave a speech entitled "Let's Establish a Community with a Shared Future of Mankind Together." At the fifty-fifth meeting of the UN Commission for Social Development on February 10, 2017, a resolution on the "social dimensions for developing new partnerships in Africa" was unanimously adopted, and the "ideology of building a Community with a Shared Future of Mankind" was included in a UN resolution for the first time.[18]

In a report on the Nineteenth Party Congress held in October 2017, Xi Jinping once again stated, "The Chinese people will strive for the establishment of the Community with a Shared Future of Mankind with people of each country." At the Thirteenth National People's Representative Meeting in 2018, a high-minded proclamation, "We shall build a Community with a Shared Future of Mankind through the development of diplomatic relations, and economic and cultural exchanges with all nations,"[19] became part of China's constitution. Thus converged all objectives of China's diplomatic, economic, and cultural interactions with the rest of the world on the singular purpose of establishing the Community with a Shared Future of Mankind of all Mankind.

Xi Jinping avers that the ideology of Community with a Shared Future of Mankind is Chinese wisdom and a gift to the world. Specifically, Xi states that "the main ideology of the Community with a Shared Future of Mankind is to share, cooperate, coexist, and embrace each other by taking care of the rational interests of other countries when protecting and pursuing the national security and interests of one's own country. Mankind lives in the same global village, becoming a Community with a Shared Future of Mankind of 'You are among us, and I among you (我中有你, 你中有我).' In the face of serious changes in international politics and rational demands of all nations aboard the same boat, all nations shall collectively establish a new international order based on cooperation and coexistence toward world peace and collective development."[20]

Since it first proposed the ideology of Community with a Shared Future of Mankind at the Eighteenth Party Congress in 2012, China has been striving to win support from the international community for it. Various kinds of communities were proposed for the establishment of the Community with a Shared Future of Mankind. At the Nineteenth Party Congress in 2017, the concept of Community with a Shared Future of Mankind was once again affirmed, and it was officially made a part of the Chinese Constitution in 2018. The ideology of the Community with a Shared Future of Mankind has now become the loftiest creed for the international order the CCP envisions and its central diplomatic strategy.

China: Leader of the Community with a Shared Future of Mankind

Since Xi Jinping's inauguration, the hegemonic competition between the United States and China has become conspicuous, and in response, China has established an economic, financial, diplomatic, and ideological global governance system. As seen earlier, China has been building various precepts for global ideological governance, and the Community with a Shared Future of Mankind is the flagship ideology that emerged. The Chinese government claims that One Belt One Road is China's contribution to the purpose of building the Community with a Shared Future of Mankind. The reality is, in fact, the reverse: the ideology of the Community with a Shared Future of Mankind was proposed for the success of One Belt One Road. As noted in the Chinese speaker's lecture earlier, the purpose of establishing One Belt One Road is to realize the China Dream, the Great Revival of the Chinese Nation. It is rather plain, therefore, that the ideology of the Community with a Shared Future of Mankind is also an ideological strategy for the realization of the China Dream, not necessarily for world peace or the collective prosperity of all mankind.

China seeks to dispel the perception of a Chinese threat, and instead promote the prospect of Chinese opportunity through the Community with a Shared Future of Mankind. The Community with a Shared Future of Mankind centered on China is said to be salutary to all. China takes pains to argue, "China's development is an opportunity for the world and not a threat to anyone."[21] Like a parrot, Chinese officials relentlessly repeat the phrases "China's development is an opportunity for the world," and "We welcome any country to take a coat tail ride on China's high-speed economic growth relentlessly. It means, of course, that any country will enjoy economic boon just by cooperating with China economically. Stated differently, it means that since China is driving the world economy, China's economic development is not a threat but a benefaction to the world.

It was at the Boao Forum for Asia (BFA) in 2015 that Xi Jinping officially declared that China should lead the Community with a Shared Future of Mankind. His speech was entitled "Asia's New Future: Toward a Community with a Shared Future of Mankind." Although Xi talked of mutual respect for the ideologies and realities of one another and equal treatment for all participating nations, the core message was that China would fulfill its responsibilities as a great world power. Xi first asked a rhetorical question, "What will China do for the Community with a Shared Future of Mankind?" He answered it by saying, "China will maintain the 'three unwavering points (三个不动摇)' of peaceful development, co-development, and joint development of the Asia-Pacific, and China will take responsibility for and lead these points."

Hu Angang, an economics professor at Tsinghua University and the designer of One Belt One Road, chimed in, "China is already a great power at the center of the world stage, so it is only natural that China fully participates in the global governance. China, a world power growing stronger each day, must rightly take the full responsibility of a great power."[22] Xi Jinping and Professor Hu Angang both say that China will "take responsibility as a great power," which is another way of saying, "China will rule the world now."

Behind his pivotal assessment is his belief that the center of world power has already moved from the West to the East. Xi stressed that, "The world is experiencing a great transformation that has never been seen in the last 100 years. New powers are replacing the old in the international community, and China must play the role of a responsible great power." A "great transformation never seen in the last 100 years" refers to his world assessment of "East rises; West falls (东升西降)'. The East is naturally China itself, and as such, China should take control of world leadership.

When Xi Jinping was first proposing the Community with a Shared Future of Mankind in the early 2010s, the goal was to paint China as the source of opportunity. China did not reveal its true ambition, hiding behind the rhetoric of universal values and ideologies of mankind. Since joining G2 in 2015, however, the now supremely confident China saw no more reason to hide its belief that China should lead the Community with a Shared Future for Mankind. Xi Jinping finally revealed the answer to the question, "What kind of world does China want and how will we [Chinese] build it?"[23]

The Community with a Shared Future of Mankind as the World Order under Chinese-style Socialism

In a 2021 speech marking the one hundredth anniversary of the establishment of the CCP, Xi Jinping said, We have created the 'Chinese path to modernization' and 'a new form of human civilization,'[24] by maintaining and developing 'socialism with Chinese characteristics,' thereby leading the harmonious development of material civilization, political civilization, spiritual civilization, social civilization, and ecological civilization." Put one and two together, the logic becomes obvious: the Community with a Shared Future of Mankind equals the world domination of Socialism with Chinese Characteristics.

The burning question then becomes just what "Socialism with Chinese Characteristics" is. Socialism with Chinese Characteristics refers to a culture in which "China's superior traditional culture" and Marxism are conflated into one whole. The main ethos of "China's superior traditional culture" is Confucianism. Since the Community with a Shared Future of Mankind is the ultimate realization of Socialism with Chinese Characteristics, it follows therefore that the Community with a Shared Future of Mankind will be built upon the same ideology. In the Community with a Shared Future of Mankind, mankind will live under 'Tianxia-ism(天下思想) and 'Great Unity-ism (大同思想)' drawn from "China's superior traditional culture," and the notions of Socialist Internationalism and Ideal Society drawn from Marxism.

This ideology can be read in Xi Jinping's remark, "Let's build the Community with a Shared Future of Mankind based on our traditional ideology of 'All under Tianxia are of one family(天下一家).'"[25] Tianxia-ism was the underlying ideology and political doctrine among the ancient Chinese Confucian elites in dealing with China's domestic and foreign affairs. The underlying philosophy of Tianxia-ism is also referred to as "Tianxia political philosophy(天下观), while the operating system thereunder is called Tianxia political system. According to Tianxia-ism or Tianxia political philosophy, all under heaven is organized in a hierarchical concentric circles with Tianxia in 'Zhongyuan (中原, central plains of ancient China)' at the center, surrounded by 'four barbarians(夷蛮戎狄)' referred to as East, South, West, and North respectively." The system is interlaced with a tributary system with China as the suzerain.

The ideal Tianxia world is embodied in the Great Unity system Confucius dreamt of, as seen in the chapter "The Evolution of Ritual" of his book The Book of Rites:

> When the great principle is carried out, the world becomes fair, talented people are used, loyalty is respected, and the world is harmonious. One does not only consider one's own parents as their parents and one does not only consider one's own children as their children. Older people end their lives peacefully, young people have no worries about jobs, and children grow up safely. Single fathers and single mothers, children without parents and elderly without children, people without anyone to turn to, and people with illness all get help. Men have a place to work and women have a person to marry. Even if money is left on the ground, no one takes it. One is wary of one's own authority, and does not use it only for himself. Therefore, people do not slander one another, and the country is free of thieves or vassals disturbing state affairs. Thus, there is no need to lock one's house door. This is called "Great Unity(大同)."[26]

In the world of Great Unity, fairness is realized, and the community guarantees an individual's life, so there is no worry. In the discourse of the Community with a Shared Future of Mankind, internationalism matches Marx's Socialist Internationalism. Marx famously said, "There is no motherland for the proletariat." Marx had earlier claimed, "Let the proletariat from all over the world unite to liberate themselves from the exploitation [by the bourgeoisie]." According to this argument, a nation-state is meaningless; what matters is the solidarity of all workers across national boundaries.

Marx's Ideal Society is one that becomes viable when the human community enters the communism stage. According to Marx, when productivity reaches a certain level, there will be abundant material and wealth allowing communism, and the free men everywhere will unite to form the Ideal Society. Marx's conceptualization of the Ideal Society has great similarities with Xi Jinping's Great Unity.

> No one is locked into a particular scope of activity, and anyone can develop in any field. Since the society itself controls the overall production, one can do this work today, and do another work tomorrow, depending on one's interest. One can hunt in the morning, and fish in the afternoon. One can take care of livestock in the evening, and engage in political criticism after dinner.[27]

In this ideal society, there is no exploitation or oppression. There is friendly and equal harmonious coexistence among people. People become their own masters, free from dependence on material things.[28]

International order based on Tianxia-ism and Great Unity is from ancient China, and Marxist Socialist Internationalism and Ideal Society are from modern Western political struggles. However, these two strands of ideologies from afar in time and civilizations have a set of curious similarities. Tianxia-ism is similar to Marx's Socialist Internationalism, and Great Unity is similar to Marx's Ideal Society. These ideologies all value cross-border integration of all people under one ideology, and the interests of the community over an individual. They also share the aspiration to be the guiding ideology for the ideal existence for all mankind. However, there is one glaring difference: while Marx's Socialist Internationalism stood for equality among all proletariat across the world,

> Tianxia-ism insists on a hierarchical international order with China at the top with everyone else as subordinates. In sum, the Community with a Shared Future of Mankind China dreams of is a realized state of Great Unity or the Ideal Society that values communal unity over individual interests. Considering that China is to be the leader of Great Unity, what Xi Jinping envisions appears to be something closer to a traditional Tianxia world order, than to Marx' Socialist Internationalism. The Community with a Shared Future of Mankind then is perhaps an expanded version of Xi Jinping's New Age of Socialism with Chinese Characteristics.

"Story of China"" Dissemination Project

China sees the cause behind the division and conflict of the modern world in the Western world order. The Chinese thinkers argue, "The prevailing Western world order includes such attributes and claims as balance of power, hegemonic order, clash of civilizations, world governance system, and democratic peace. The problem is that, because the fundamental premise underpinning these attributes is the belief that humans are innately evil, the Western world order is inherently an order of conflict.[29]" As a replacement, China is trying to proselytize its discourse on the Community with a Shared Future of Mankind across the world as the new "standard of civilization," thus uniting the world under a Great Unity world order with China at the center of Tianxia.

Xi Jinping emphasizes, "We need to build a Community With a Shared Future of Mankind by disseminating China's voice far and wide, thereby strengthening China's influence and creating a favorable global environment of public opinion."[30] To build a "favorable global environment of public opinion," the Chinese government has been systematically conducting "cultural diffusion project(传播工程)." The core objective of the project is to spread awareness of the Community with a Shared Future of Mankind to the entire world.

As seen earlier, the discourse on the Community with a Shared Future of Mankind is a combination of Tianxia-ism and Marxism. It was alarming enough to the West that it drew criticism for "trying to export the Chinese regime."

New Zealand academic Jonathan Keir advised the Chinese government as follows: "The biggest obstacle China faces is the 'Leninism' of Chinese studies. In the atmosphere of the New Cold War, Western countries are suspicious of China's 'studies of ancient Chinese civilization and culture(国学)' that it is instrumentalizing or weaponizing Leninism. The world could converse with Confucius, but not Lenin; there is only distrust. If China wants to establish a new standard of "universal ethics,' it should make efforts to solve global problems by disseminating its traditional Confucianism wisdom."[31]

In fact, China is putting its traditional culture at the forefront in promoting the idea of Community with a Shared Future of Mankind. The Confucius Institute, officially ratified in 2004 by the State Council of China, provides Chinese language and cultural education across the globe. It is in fact the signature project of cultural diffusion project. The first Confucius Institute in Korea was established in Seoul in November 2004. By December 2019, 548 Confucius Institutes in 154 countries (regions) and 1,193 Confucius Classrooms had been established across the globe.[32] As of August 2021, there were a total of 24 Confucius Classrooms in Korea.

Chinese leaders spared no support for this cultural offensive. Visiting a Confucius Institute became a compulsory item in the itinerary of any Chinese dignitary during their overseas trips. In June 2004, Hu Jintao attended the agreement ceremony for the establishment of a Confucius Institute in Uzbekistan. In December 2009, Xi Jinping, who was vice president at the time, attended the signboard hanging ceremony of the Confucius Institute in Cambodia. In 2015, when Xi became president, he attended the opening ceremony of the All-England Confucius Institute and Academy.

Chinese language education is at the forefront of the cultural diffusion project that the Confucius Institute engages in. One researcher pointed out, "Cultural exchanges through the Chinese language are needed to establish the Community with a Shared Future of Mankind."[33] There are two reasons for this. One is that the process of learning the Chinese language is a vehicle to spread Chinese thought. According to an analysis of educational materials used by the Confucius Institute in Korea, some of the textbooks include content praising the Chinese regime. For example, the song "Waves of Honghu Lake(洪湖水浪打浪)" praises the greatness of the Chinese Communist Party.[34] The second reason is to make Chinese the world's *lingua franca,* replacing English. If this happens, the world will be one step closer to living in the Community with a Shared Future of Mankind.

Recently, Korea has seen a wave of public criticism of Confucius Institutes in Korea, and some are running campaigns to expel them altogether. Many Western countries recognize Confucius Institutes as a mouthpiece of Chinese communism and are in the process of expelling their Confucius Institutes. In the United Kingdom, for instance, with the appointment of Rishi Sunak as the new British prime minister, a proposed legal ban on Confucius Institutes is gaining wide support. Mr. Sunak, as the leader of the Tory Party, had identified Confucius Institutes as the "biggest threat to the security and prosperity of the U.K. and the world this century" and pledged to "close them down." Sweden has already banned Confucius Institutes, and the United States has stopped federal funding to those universities that have Confucius Institutes.[35]

Publishing books promoting Chinese classical works or the CCP and donating related materials to libraries in foreign countries is an important part of a cultural diffusion project. Between January and December 2014, 46,359 Chinese books from 521 publishers were stored in 20,000 libraries around the world. This is an increase of 23 percent compared to 2013.[36]

Korea is no exception. On the back of these books is marked "supported by the Chinese ○○○ Fund." Or, one can see media reports stating that "Chinese Ambassador Xing Haiming has donated more than 300 Chinese classical works to the Korean local government." Recently, a media outlet reported, "China is manipulating [Korean] public opinion in its favor using its 'sharp power' designed to scare influential figures such as politicians, academics, bureaucrats, and journalists, and have them engage in "'self-censorship' lest they may offend China." In support of this claim, the report cited the "Xi Jinping Donated Archives" at the Central Library of Seoul National University's Gwanak Campus and the Yonsei Charhar Center at Yonsei University as examples.[37]

Those who make remarks in support of the Community with a Shared Future of Mankind in Chinese media are mostly from socialist or developing countries like China. However, some Koreans also make similarly admiring remarks in Chinese media. "China practiced the Community with a Shared Future of Mankind ideology and supplied 2 billion doses of the COVID-19 vaccine to the world, setting an example of international quarantine cooperation and displaying responsible behavior befitting a great power."[38] "I believe that under the guidance of the CCP, China will surely contribute greatly to the development of humanity through the development of traditional Chinese culture."[39] Recently, there was even an article titled "Korean Scholar: Chinese Diplomatic Wisdom Will Contribute Greatly to Global Governance."[40]

The reason behind China's stepped-up cultural diffusion project targeting Korea appears to be the same as the reason for proposing Asian Community with a Shared Future of Mankind in 2015. China proposed the Asian Community with a Shared Future of Mankind to pull Asian countries away from the United States. The Asian Community with a Shared Future of Mankind is based on the Tianxia world order. Japan, however, has already chosen the United States and the Ryukyu Islands belong to Japan. Vietnam, a socialist state, appears to be on China's side despite the disputes regarding the Spratly Islands in the South China Sea. This leaves Korea as a prized target for China. China's historical and cultural infringement on Korea through its cultural diffusion project, which has become more frequent and blatant since Xi Jinping took office, reflects this strategic imperative on the part of China.

LIMITATIONS OF THE COMMUNITY WITH A SHARED FUTURE OF MANKIND IDEOLOGY AND THE OUTLOOK ON XI JINPING'S THIRD TERM

Limitations of the Community with a Shared Future of Mankind Ideology

China has experience in running an empire. As such, China's global strategies are detailed, interrelated, and dynamic. The One Belt One Road initiative, Asian Infrastructure Investment Bank (AIIB), partnerships, and A Community with a Shared Future of Mankind all play their respective roles in the economy, finance, diplomacy, and ideology, creating an enormous synergy among them.

It is not all smooth sailing for China, however. In the case of the Community with a Shared Future of Mankind, many around the world understand it as a "declaration of Chinese hegemony."[41] A Chinese researcher said, "The limitation of cultural diffusion project is that the content of cultural dissemination is superficial, so it cannot convey the depth of Chinese culture. The international community is not only unsympathetic, but even shows resistance."[42] However, the failure of the Community with a Shared Future of Mankind to win support is probably not solely because the message was not delivered "properly."

The limitations of the Community with a Shared Future of Mankind drive are found in many aspects. First, its strategic ambiguity has become poison. The Community with a Shared Future of Mankind concept seems bloated—an empty shell. Its meaning cannot be deciphered, and it does not evoke a sympathetic response. Naturally, no one with a discerning mind would care to join it. Strategic ambiguity, China's favorite diplomatic tool, is not earning trust from anyone.

The second limitation is the vulgarization of the Community with a Shared Future of Mankind. China has proposed and instituted so many Communities with a Shared Future of Mankind globally and regionally that it is difficult to find any country in the world that is not already in a Community with a Shared Future of Mankind of one kind or another. Some countries even belong to multiple overlapping Communities of Common Destiny. Naturally, it is difficult for members to take it seriously, let alone have a sense of belonging.

Third, China does not seem to care how the counterpart countries perceive the concept of Community with a Shared Future of Mankind. Chinese scholars proffer that the concept of Tianxia world order is innocuous. " Tianxia world order is different from that of Western imperialism in that the relationship between the suzerain and the tributary is one of "Confucian etiquette(礼), not one of dominion and subjugation. In Chinese history, China was never a conqueror, but the barbarians themselves desired to be sinicized, having been overwhelmed by the superior Chinese culture. Tianxia world order is different from that of Western hegemonic culture, and pursues the interests of all nations."[43] This line of thinking may make perfect sense for the Chinese, but from the perspectives of foreigners, it is threatening, not inviting.

Last but not least, there is the gaping discrepancy between China's rhetoric and deeds. China's actual actions do not match what it professes in the discourse of the Community with a Shared Future of Mankind. Xi Jinping said, "Of course, all countries must treat one another as equals, and respect one another. Each country has chosen its own governing system and path of development. Therefore, a country must respect others' core interests, deal with their growth and governing ideology objectively and rationally, and exercise 'qiutongcunyi(求同存异)' and 'jutonghuayi(聚同化异)'." qiutongcunyi means "seek common ground while reserving differences," and jutonghuayi "adopt common interests and adjust differences." In the realm of reality, however, China is confronting the world with Wolf Warrior Diplomacy, yielding no concessions to its core interests.

In short, the global impact of China's "A Community with a Shared Future of Mankind" drive is minimal. One Chinese researcher even says, "The Community with a Shared Future of Mankind may never happen, unless there is a huge threat from outer space."[44]

Changes and Bloc-ization of Value in Xi Jinping's Third Term

Entering his third term in office, Xi Jinping has all but admitted to the failure of his "Community with a Shared Future of Mankind" initiative, and has begun to offer an alternative. In the 20th Party Congress Report, he outlined the specific values to be shared among the members of the Community with a Shared Future of Mankind: namely, the 'Common Value of All Mankind' (全人类共同价值). This slogan includes 'Peace,' 'Development,' 'equity,' 'justice,' 'democracy,' and 'freedom.' The Common Value of All Mankind undergirds China's foreign policy strategy. There are two aspects of the Common Value of All Mankind that must be understood.

First, the Common Value of All Mankind is meant to be an ideological foundation for the "Peace Diplomacy" of Xi Jinping's third term. It contains six "values," but the foremost among them for Xi is "Peace." Xi Jinping's China had pursued Wolf Warrior Diplomacy, but it only succeeded in alienating most nations globally. Admitting the failure of the Wolf Warrior Diplomacy, he is now promulgating "Peace Diplomacy." The inclusion of "Peace" in the Common Value of All Mankind is to support this new "Peace Diplomacy" initiative. Second, the trend toward bloc-ization of values is conspicuous. The Chinese government posits that "the Common Value of All Mankind' tears down the inherent selfishness in the West's 'Universal Value.'"

"The 'Universal Value' of the West is based on capitalism, and as such only represents the interests of the bourgeois class and the West led by the United States. In contrast, the 'Common Value of All Mankind' is premised on Marxism, and as such represents the true universal interests of all mankind. Therefore, the 'Common Value of All Mankind" should supplant the Universal Value in the future of mankind. The 'Common Value of All Mankind' is particularly meaningful in that it represents the interests of China and the developing world."

The Universal Value of the West equates to the ideology of liberal democracy. Liberal democracy is premised on the value system of capitalism, which inevitably fuels competition and conflict in the world. Xi Jinping's bugle call proclaims that, from here on, the world should unite under the umbrella of the Common Value of All Mankind.

On the surface, the Common Value of All Mankind appears to argue for a sort of civilizational reconciliation that rejects civilizational conflicts and affirms civilizational diversity. In reality, however, the concept of Community with a Shared Future of Mankind is but a Sino-centric Marxist world order that combines Marxism and Chinese Tianxia political philosophy discussed above. Xi Jinping's China purports to "oppose Cold War thinking," and China "will never pursue hegemony." In reality, however, China's foreign policy is heavily laced with the bloc-ization of values. In other words, Xi Jinping's promulgation of the Common Value of All Mankind is tantamount to a declaration of war for a full-blown competition with the West not only in the realm of military and economy but also of ideology. Xi Jinping's China means to expand its influence as the "norm entrepreneur" of new rules, and indeed bring the world under a "Sinocentric World Order."

Last but not least, we must note the striking parallel between the choices Mao Zedong made and those Xi Jinping is making during his third term following the failure of their respective peace diplomacy. In fact, the concept of Community with a Shared Future of Mankind is essentially a continuation of Mao's "Overseas United Front." In his speech at a ceremony on June 28, 2014, commemorating the sixtieth year of the declaration of Mao's "Five Principles of Peace," Xi Jinping stated that "the 'Five Principles of Peace' are not a concept from a bygone era; they will be realized through China's continuing diplomatic efforts." Thereafter, the Nineteenth and Twentieth Party Congress Reports reaffirmed it stating, "China shall promote global partnership with the nations of the world based on the 'Five Principles of Peace.'"

In the wake of the failure of his peace diplomacy strategy, Mao Zedong unfurled the "Maoism-Third Worldism" whereby China would be the leader of the third world, setting up an anti-US, anti-Soviet Union Overseas Unified Front. Heavily influenced by the radicalization of China's leftist ideology at the time, China's foreign policy leaned toward "exporting (communist) revolution." China's leftist elites felt that the center of gravity of the global communist revolution was China, and only China had the ideological purity and credentials to lead communist revolution in the third world. Of course, considering how different today's world is compared to that of Mao, it is difficult to believe that Xi Jinping would adopt an identical course of action as Mao. However, all indications are that Xi's China is also becoming increasingly leftist and focused on the third world in the wake of its own diplomatic setbacks. This strongly indicates that the ideological bloc-ization will become increasingly prominent in the ROK-China relations and the US-China relations, and the world is likely to witness intensifying standoffs based on values and ideologies.

Chapter 8

US-China Conflict and Korea's Dilemma

Heungkyu Kim

CHAOS: THE US-CHINA STRATEGIC COMPETITION

This chapter addresses how US-China relations may evolve during Xi Jinping's third term and how it may affect Korea by analyzing the history of the US-China relations and key geopolitical variables. On the question of the evolution of the US-China relations, the focus will be on the US side; as it stands now, China's US policy appears to be static in the sense that it finds itself constantly responding to the shifting US policies on China. Ultimately, the changes in the United States's China policy dictated by the US domestic politics appear to determine the countenance of the US-China relations.

Modern US-China relations have gone through four distinct phases: era of enmity post-Korean War, era of engagement in the 1960s–1970s, the era of cooperation during China's reform and openness decades, and the era of strategic competition since 2018. The US-China strategic competition is expected to be a prolonged struggle. For neither the United States nor China has the power to bring the other to its knees. It is at this juncture that the world is spiraling into chaos, even as the world order is fragmenting.

A 2022 study conducted by the Center for the Future of Democracy at Cambridge University[1] observed that the world had divided into two camps along the value system and civilizational lines: West versus Non-West, that is, liberal versus illiberal. The majority of the people in the Western sphere held negative views of China and Russia. Meanwhile, the picture was the opposite in the Non-Western sphere: the majority held positive views of China and Russia over that of the United States. According to this study, the United States and the West were in fact on the losing side in this contest. The US-led liberal hegemonic order was in decline, if not on its way toward disintegration. It appeared unlikely that this unipolar world order could be revived.

The world order had already entered a multipolar paradigm. This diagnosis was mirrored in the 2022 US National Security Strategy Report and National Defense Strategy Report.[2] As the United States lacks the power or the means to arrest this paradigm shift, the Biden administration has rallied its friends and allies in a broad coalition arrayed against China.

The process of building a new world order will not be a genteel affair. No one knows how long it may take, or what the ride may be like. In modern history, a war between great powers always preceded a shift in world order. Few great powers ever relinquished their place in the world without a fight, as is evident in the history of the United States' defeat over Nazi Germany, Empire of Japan, and the Soviet Union. Likewise, two titans, the United States and China, are now locked in a Thucydides trap.

During the Cold War, the Mutually Assured Destruction (MAD) doctrine dominated the strategic thinking of the time. Ironic as it may be, the belief that no nuclear power could win a nuclear exchange with another nuclear power undergirded an uneasy stability between the United States and the Soviet Union. Now, however, the Russo-Ukrainian War is casting doubt on this time-honored belief. Beyond using a tactical theater nuclear weapon, Vladimir Putin appears willing to risk a full-scale conventional war or even a strategic nuclear exchange with another major nuclear power. Nothing appears sacrosanct anymore; the optimism of the US-led liberal international order no longer appears a given. That period may fade into history as a once ideal epoch.

Some argue that the possibility of a war between the United States and China is low.[3] In a nutshell, both the United States and China are too big to engage in a war against each other; neither has the power to overwhelm the other. Neither side would take the inherent unpredictability of the outcome of a war between them lightly. On the other hand, other contingencies like an accidental outbreak of a war cannot be ruled out, with incalculable consequences for the world.

These frayed times are particularly challenging for a country like Korea. To understand why, a brief history of Korea is in order. Since the mid-Goryeo dynasty (circa tenth to twelfth century ACE), Korea grew accustomed to securing political stability and security from foreign invasions as a vassal state to a suzerain. This had not always been the case; Korea had been a feisty nation that fought for its independence and unique culture. In the eleventh century, Korea fought a series of successful wars against the Liao dynasty (遼) covering what is present-day north and northeast of China, and in the thirteenth century, against the Mongols in a series of six wars over thirty years. Eventually, however, Goryeo succumbed to the might of the Yuan dynasty established by Kublai Khan, a grandson of Genghis Khan, and had to acquiesce to the subservient status and responsibilities of a 駙馬國

Table 8.1   Characteristics of International Order by Period[i]

Period	Cold War	End of Cold War	New Cold War (Cold War 2.0)
Ideology	Liberalism vs. Communism	Neoliberalism	Technological nationalism/Digital protectionism
Politics	Market vs. state	Market	State
Economy	Regional globalization (by blocs)	Full-scale globalization	Antiglobalization and border protection
Economy/Security link	Strong	Weak	Strong
Economy/Security Prioritization	Security over economy	Economy over security	Security over economy
Theory	Econo-Realism	Liberalism (Capitalist/ Commercial peace theory)	Realism (Geoeconomics)
International Political Structure	Polarization	US hegemony	Multipolarization

[i]This chart was inspired by a conversation with my colleague Professor Lee Wang-hui at Ajou University.

(son-in-law state), a humiliating moniker. By the time Yuan fell and the Ming dynasty took over, however, Chosun, a new Korean dynasty, had become acclimatized to being a vassal state, and readily acquiesced to Ming as its suzerain. Being a vassal had its advantages, after all; it didn't have to risk annihilation. This psychology persisted well into modern times. Upon liberation from the Japanese occupation in 1945, Korea again continued its precarious existence as a client state of the United States. Despite the fact that Korea transformed itself from one of the world's poorest nations to the tenth largest economy while under the US patronage, the fact remains that Korea has not been privy to formulating its own independent foreign policy—*until now*.

Many historians argue that this aspect of Korea's history represents the optimum survival strategy for a small peninsula nation wedged in between powerful neighbors. The problem starts, however, when the patron state becomes weak, forcing a client state to make hard choices of its own. Just when Korea must carve out an independent survival strategy, the force of habit from its history keeps it dangerously passive. Domestic politics splinters along which a powerful country has to sidle to, and the survival of the nation is laid bare.

Xi Jinping's third term is unprecedented even in communist China. No leader has served a third term since China chose the reform and openness policy in 1978. So long as Xi Jinping persists with his authoritarian rule during his third term, the economy and people's lives will not see stability. Nevertheless, his rule appears slated to continue unabated, with his policies from his second term becoming hardened and entrenched. By all accounts, it appears that this version of China will continue to assert itself on the global community.

Meanwhile, the United States' China policy will be heavily influenced by the deepening anti-China public sentiment among Americans. The 2022 US Congressional elections disclosed the deepening polarization in American politics, including with respect to China policy. The 2024 presidential election will be a watershed moment to see where the US-China policy may be headed. The result may affect the US relations with its allies, including Korea, thereby rewriting the playbook for the international order.

In the midst of this tumult, Korea faces the daunting task of formulating its own policies for survival and prosperity while wedged between the United States and China. Here, it is critical for Korea to realize that the answer will not lie in either a pro-US or pro-China stance, but in the compound multipolar dynamics of a newly emerging international order. Any such deliberation must begin with a clear understanding of how the United States' China policy has evolved to what it is today.

DONALD TRUMP: PARADIGM SHIFT IN THE US-CHINA RELATIONS

After thirty-odd years of a honeymoon following the 1979 diplomatic normalization, US-China relations plunged into an era of strategic competition in the late 2010s. Before the Trump presidency, the policy of engagement based on strategic cooperation used to form the mainstream approach.[4] China was perceived not as a challenger to the US hegemony, but as an aspirant for a regional power status. Before Trump, hostile relations with China could hardly be imagined. But now, China had grown into an economic colossus and was the most important supplier in the global supply chain. This new reality was an inadvertent result of the US policy for global capitalism of the previous years. While the economic power of the Soviet Union at its peak during the Cold War, and Germany and Japan in the 1970s–1980s, never exceeded 60 percent of the US economic power of the corresponding periods,[5] China reached this level in early 2014 and even surpassed 70 percent in 2020. According to a 2020 report by the Pew Research Institute, all European countries surveyed perceived China as the leader of the global economy over the United States.[6] In terms of purchasing power, the IMF announced that China had already surpassed the United States in 2014, and as of 2022, had 23 percent greater purchasing power than that of the United States.[7] Now, the United States and the West faced a behemoth, one that was not content being a model member of the US-led liberal international order, standing at their doorstep.

As soon as President Trump took power in 2017, he took steps for a complete overhaul of the US-China policy. Confident in the United States' hegemonic power, President Trump began applying an unprecedented level of pressure on China. The United States and China were now in a "strategic competition" according to the National Security Strategy Report published in December 2017.[8] It was followed in quick succession by the National Defense Strategy in January 2018, the Nuclear Posture Review in February 2018, the National Defense Authorization Act in 2018, 2019, and 2020, the Indo-Pacific Strategy Report in June 2019, A Free and Open Indo-Pacific: Advancing a Shared Vision in November 2019, and in May 2020, the US Strategic Approach to the People's Republic of China.

These publications show the evolution of the US strategic thinking on China during Trump's tenure in office. The strategic competition became all-consuming. Having begun with the US-China trade dispute in early 2018, by the end of the Trump administration in 2020, the strategic competition ran the gamut from trade, diplomacy, science, technology, finance, and eventually, international norms and institutions, and ideology. All the while, loathing of all things China continued to swell in the United States.

The main thrust of Trump's China policy was containment and was underpinned by a willingness to meet confrontation head-on. The familiar refrain of geopolitics, power politics, and unilateral foreign policy proliferated, along with the new concept of convergence of security with economy, science, and technology. US policymakers and experts perceived the US-China trade dispute as part of a long-term hegemonic competition. They premised that China was on a course to usurp the United States as the global hegemon based on careful strategic calculations. China's new multilateralist efforts, including the Asian Infrastructure Investment Bank, Regional Comprehensive Economic Partnership, and One Belt One Road initiative, were all evidence of this design. This made the US-China competition a zero-sum game, and it was necessary to apply maximum effort to contain China.

The speech Vice President Mike Pence delivered at the Hudson Institute on October 4, 2018, was tantamount to an across-the-board declaration of war against China.[9] The Trump administration's assertion that Xi Jinping should be addressed not as president but as general secretary signaled their hard-line stance. They also intimated that the United States might not honor China's sacrosanct One China Principle, which China had asserted as a prerequisite for continued US-China relations. Policy planners surrounding Trump, such as Mike Pompeo, Peter Navarro, Matt Pottinger, and Michael Pillsbury, all showed unfettered contempt toward China. The atmosphere toward the end of the Trump administration made one wonder if the world had entered a new Cold War era.

China was pushed off balance, but as the initial shock wore off, China surmised that the Trump administration's China policy lacked depth and nuance. China began devising countermeasures, and in the process of executing them, its foreign policy became increasingly belligerent.[10] The Chinese leadership understood the new US-China conflict as a de-facto state of war. In a speech at the Central Party School of the CCP in September 2019, Xi Jinping promulgated his historical perception that the world had now entered an era of grand transition. Chinese dialectical tradition posits that "[i]n the midst of chaos, there is also opportunity." In other words, Xi Jinping saw the then-current state of the US-China relations as a historic opportunity to overtake the United States.[11]

This hard-turn in US foreign policy, however, did not lead to desired ends. Trump and his strategists' somewhat obtuse China policy was the result of a convergence of many factors, to wit, China's rapid rise beyond expectations, China's belligerent conduct around the world, relative decline of the United States, isolationism in the US domestic politics, and failure of the prior US China strategy. It only led to China's growing confidence at the expense of US influence and prestige internationally. It succeeded in making a large swathe of the world view America as a selfish hegemon, while even failing to resolve the trade imbalance issue.[12]

BIDEN ADMINISTRATION: STRUGGLE TO RECALIBRATE THE CHINA POLICY

In the Biden administration, younger but more experienced and pragmatic strategists led the recalibration effort of the US-China policy.[13] The Trump administration's experience had shown that unilateral actions by the United States could not control or solicit changes from China's global conduct. As the COVID-19 pandemic spread and as China persevered under the US pressure through 2020, the biggest gain for China was perhaps confidence in dealing with the United States. Recognizing this reality, the Biden administration opted for a more nuanced long-term competition with China, in concert with friends and allies.

A Foreign Affairs article authored by Jake Sullivan and Kurt Campbell in 2019 provides a window into the mindset of the China policy team in the Biden White House.[14] Sullivan and Campbell did not agree with the Obama administration's assessment that strong and prosperous China would become a responsible member of the liberal international community. At the same time, however, they did not approve of the Trump administration's impetuous

China policy either, for it lacked sound analysis and nuanced reasoning. Such a monolithic approach, they reasoned, was unwise in dealing with China that was stronger than the Soviet Union had been, and already integrated into the interdependent globalized world. Their conclusion was that the United States had no choice but to coexist with China. The United States should accept all forms of competition with China but avoid military confrontation. A war between the United States and China would be too costly to bear for either side.

Moreover, the Biden administration's conception of foreign affairs no longer saw the United States as the sole leader of the international order. The Interim National Security Strategic Guidance report published by the White House in March 2021 detailed this view.[15] The United States acknowledged the growing gap between its aspiration to lead global politics and its ability to meet the burden.[16] Jake Sullivan and Kurt Campbell agreed.[17] The US hegemony based on liberal democracy was no longer feasible. The United States and China were locked in a struggle for supremacy in a bipolar world, each representing democracy and authoritarianism, respectively. As such, the United States should rally the friends and allies that share the liberal democratic values and stand up to the unwanted embrace of Chinese authoritarianism.[18]

Table 8.2 Four Principal Components of the US-China Strategy as Outlined by Jake Sullivan

Competition for governing values	Need to guard against the spread of the Chinese authoritarian political model in order to safeguard the liberal democratic values and the political models built thereon.
	Need to resolve the US domestic political dissonance on the values that underpin the liberal international order.
Consolidation of allies and friendly nations	Need to strengthen the coalition among European and Asian allies and friendly nations that share the market-based liberal democratic values.
	Need to check the spread of China's influence in order to establish a free, prosperous, and rules-based international order.
	Need to leverage the fact that the US accounts for 25 percent of the global economy, 50 percent when combined with its allies, in pursuing this goal.
Technology competition	The United States and its allies and friendly nations need to secure and maintain superiority over China in AI, biotechnology, quantum computers, and renewable energy.
	Need aggressive investment to achieve this aim.
Ready and willing to act	The US administration and its embassies need to send out clear and consistent messages to China and the world.
	Need to be ready and willing to make China "pay the price" for its actions on Xinjiang, Hong Kong, Tibet, and the Taiwan strait.

Source: Lee Chang-ju, 2021."China's Belt and Road Strategy and US-China Competition," "US-China Strategic Competition and Korea's Choice Study in the Biden Administration" (Seoul: KIEP).

CHINA POLICY OF THE BIDEN ADMINISTRATION

The development of the Biden administration's China policy has been an evolutionary process. Initially, there existed differing opinions on China within the Biden administration. Some, like Rush Doshi, emphasized China's hegemonic intentions and advocated stronger containment policies. Others, such as Jake Sullivan, Anthony Blinken, and Kurt Campbell, supported a more nuanced approach. Biden's early China policy appeared just as inimical as Trump's had been, leading many to feel that conflict and confrontation were the order of the day. Cases in point were such initiatives as strengthening G7, D10, and Quad Plus, establishing AUKUS, holding the NATO expansion summit, establishing the EU-US Trade and Technology Council, and above all defining the battleline as a confrontation between democracy and authoritarianism—all designed to surround and isolate China.

As the Biden administration's China policy evolved, however, it became clearly differentiated from that of the Trump administration in that it now pursued a managed long-term strategic competition in concert with friends and allies, rather than overt confrontation. Toward that end, the Biden administration has pursued a policy of building domestic consensus on the US-China policy, strengthening alliances and coalitions, and increasing domestic manufacturing capacity.[19] In an article published in the *Financial Times* on October 19, 2020, Anne-Marie Slaughter, chairman of the liberal-leaning think tank New America, characterized the Biden administration's China policies with "3Ds"—Domestic, Deterrence, and Democracy.[20] Stated differently, the Biden administration's focus has been on strengthening the US economy and industrial competitiveness, curbing China's expansionism, and enhancing democratic values and institutions.

It is clear that the Biden administration shared the sense of alarm at China's global behavior as had the Trump administration. In fact, it has doubled down on the efforts to prevent China from acquiring the core technologies for the Fourth Industrial Revolution or the strategic technologies that can fuel China's rapid growth in military power. Still, the Biden administration's pursuit of a nuanced, managed, long-term strategic competition has allowed more room for its China policy to evolve than was the case with Trump's one-dimensional approach. Logically, barring transactions involving strategically vital industry or technology, it should be possible to cooperate with China in necessary areas, rather than single-mindedly insisting on trade restrictions that force China into a corner. The world got a glimpse of this strategy during Jake Sullivan's speech on April 27, 2023, at the Brookings Institute, where he alluded to the "small yard, high fence" strategy in maintaining the US global economic leadership. It was no longer possible to separate diplomacy and security from trade, science, and technology. In fact, trade, science, and technology had become the primary battleground in the US-Chinese strategic competition.

In terms of coalition building with friends and allies, the Biden administration has been reticent about free trade agreements. Joining one will invoke the ire of the working and middle-class voters, something the Biden administration is loath to do. Instead, the administration proposed the Indo-Pacific Economic Framework for Prosperity (IPEF) as part of its Indo-Pacific strategic plan. IPEF is a multilateral economic cooperation framework among those countries that support democracy. In addition, the Biden administration convened a meeting among the world's top chip manufacturing nations—dubbed the Chip 4 alliance, composed of the United States, Korea, Taiwan, and Japan—in March 2022 to stabilize the global semiconductor supply chain. On the other side of the fence, China is also pushing hard for multilateralist free trade agreements and multilateral regional cooperation frameworks in a game of one-upmanship with the United States. The United States and China will undoubtedly compete fiercely for supremacy in multilateral economic cooperation frameworks. In this arena of strategic competition, Biden's approach is clearly distinguishable from that of Trump. Biden does not advocate Trump's "America First" foreign policy, a blatant manifestation of US unilateralism. The Biden administration is hard at work trying to restore the faith in America as a responsible superpower. Biden offers to engage in "responsible competition" with China for the world to see.

Militarily, Biden appears determined to maintain US military advantage over potential foes, suggesting he is a traditional internationalist in the Democratic Party. However, Biden remains cautious when it comes to overseas military intervention, which is in line with the domestic public opinion and the policy that has been pursued since the Obama administration. A case in point was the US-China talk held in Alaska in March 2021, where the Biden administration agreed to continue to acknowledge China's One China Principle and pledged not to attempt to change the status quo regarding the Taiwan issue.[21] Of course, the United States demanded that China reciprocate with a similar pledge to preserve the status quo. The meeting was a vital opportunity for the two sides to confirm each other's red lines in their continuing strategic competition.

To sum up, it appears clear that long-term competition, rather than direct confrontation, is the main theme of the US-China policy under the Biden administration. Biden's China policy takes pains to make clear that the US-China competition is not a zero-sum confrontation, that is, not a new Cold War. Kurt Campbell and Jake Sullivan have pointed out that China is a powerful and ideologically threatening challenger but reiterates that the US- China policy is not directly aimed at China.[22] The US-China relations are defined as a competitive relationship, but not a hostile relationship. The Chinese, on their part, have surmised that while the Biden administration does not see China as a "partner" as in the Obama era, it does not see China as an "adversary" of the Trump era either.[23]

US-CHINA RELATIONS DURING XI JINPING'S THIRD TERM: BETWEEN NEW COLD WAR AND MANAGED COMPETITION

The China Dream versus the International Order

Xi Jinping's third term began at the 20th Party Congress on October 23, 2022. There were more surprises for the world than the unprecedented third term: collective leadership was no more, replaced by one-man authoritarian rule under Xi Jinping. With this epoch-making change also came a categorical turn toward Xi Jinping's communist ideology reminiscent of that of Mao Zedong. These changes may have been thought useful for domestic control by the CCP leadership, but bode ill for the future of China's foreign relations.

A reading of the 20th Party Congress Report[24] reveals it is highly unlikely that China's global strategy and perception carried over from Xi's previous terms will change any time soon. The report repeatedly emphasizes security and reaffirms the CCP's commitment to realizing the China Dream. Together, these two concepts reflect Xi Jinping's perception that the world is at a pivotal moment in history: a once-in-a-century upheaval full of tumult, peril, and seismic shifts in world order. This "perception of history" underpins the legitimacy of Xi Jinping's one-man authoritarian rule. His one-man authoritarian rule is to guide China into the future toward "socialist modernization" by 2035 and "great modern socialist power" by the mid-century, and, this grand vision will continue to drive and color the foreign policy of China during Xi Jinping's third term. China will continue to reject the US-led Western liberal international order. In its place, China will insist on a multilateral international order under the principles of the UN Charter—naturally, with China at its center. It is only fitting, then, that China will continue to demand "the new type of great power relations" with the United States as well, the putative principles of which are to shun enmity between the two but to build a mutually respectful and reciprocal relationship as equals. In this grand design is firmly wedged the thorny issue of the reunification of Taiwan, which Xi Jinping has characterized as a prerequisite to achieving the China Dream by 2049, the 100th anniversary of the establishment of the PRC.

However, Xi Jinping appears to appreciate the challenges he will face in pursuit of these goals. During a speech at the 100th anniversary of the foundation of the CCP in 2021, he issued an undiplomatically explicit warning to outside powers: foreign powers hostile to China will "have their heads cracked on the steel walls of the Great Wall and bleed." This graphic metaphor is, of course, a jingoistic reiteration of the national security principle that China stands ready to make any foreign power, that is, principally the United States, pay a steep price for any hostile actions against China. But, this rhetoric is a telltale sign of how much Xi Jinping is feeling the heat from the US containment of China. He sees the US-China strategic competition as a "state of war."

Traditionally, China reacts to deteriorating relations with another major power by strengthening its relations with neighboring countries. Especially now, as the global supply chain is undergoing a fundamental restructuring, China all the more needs the support of friendly neighboring nations. Russia is China's "comprehensive strategic partnership of coordination for a new era," a step higher than the "strategic cooperative partner" that Western countries are to China. The two countries declared a "no limits partnership" during Vladimir Putin's visit to Beijing in February 2022. However, while this display of friendship may have given rhetorical support for Russia's invasion of Ukraine, China has carefully maintained a neutral stance in its actual foreign policy executions. As the *New York Times* noted in 2022, China appeared more interested in realizing practical economic advantages in its trade with Russia.[25] In fact, as China putatively pursues a multipolar world centered around the UN as an alternative to the US-led liberal international order, the invasion poses an uncomfortable problem for China. The Russian invasion of Ukraine violates the principle of territorial integrity of the UN Charter. China does not want to see Russia overly weakened, but it certainly does not want to see a Russian resurgence in power and influence. Also, remembering how it suffered catastrophic losses by getting involved in the Korean War in the 1950s, China remains wary of the Russia-North Korea rapprochement and Russia's expansion of influence in the Asia-Pacific region in general.

Japan has traditionally adhered to a two-track strategy where it upholds the US-Japan Alliance but leaves room for cooperation with China. It is expected that the two nations will keep the backchannel diplomacy open whatever the current contingency. It is the relations with Korea that may prove to be trickier. Korea is likely to be one of the most important strategic cogs in China's foreign affairs strategy. China will continue to adhere to the Sino-North Korean Alliance, but simultaneously seek to balance its relations with North Korea and Korea, respectively. China cannot afford to lean toward North Korea too much, as losing Korea would be extremely costly to China's geopolitical and geoeconomic calculations. These dynamics make the North Korean nuclear provocations a very awkward issue for China. True enough that the geopolitical value of North Korea has increased because of the US-China competition, but China certainly does not want the tail to wag the dog. As such, China is not likely to actively pursue Cold War-style alliances in and around the Korean Peninsula as some have brooded over. In fact, China's headache regarding North Korea can be seen in the fact that China's leverage vis-a-vis North Korea has substantially diminished since it obtained nuclear weapon capability.

On the other hand, it is highly probable that Chinese diplomacy will focus its energy on the Global South and the Middle East during Xi's third term. For these are the regions where the United States is fast losing influence, opening opportunities for China. China will also continue to establish a network of friendly nations along its Belt and Road Initiative which extends through Central Eurasia to the fringes of Europe itself, in a classic competition for the middle zone of the tripolar system. Ultimately, Western Europe is also in its crosshair.

China has been issuing a steady stream of bellicose rhetoric that it would never submit to external provocations, vastly strengthen and modernize its military power, and even unify Taiwan by force. However, China's US policy is basically reactive. China reminds its diplomatic corps of the discipline of 赶考的清醒和坚定 [be lucid of mind, but careful and strong in approach like a man entering the site of an imperial examination (to become a Mandarin, i.e., scholar bureaucrat)].[26] This circumspect approach stems from China's continuing, albeit reluctant, appreciation of the might of the liberal international order and the West's military power.

As such, China's priority is its continued development and local limited war capabilities, rather than projecting power abroad. Toward this end, China will focus more on fostering regional economic cooperation, thereby establishing an alternate, or at least supplemental, supply chain, over overseas military adventurism. China makes it clear that it does not want a new Cold War. In terms of diplomacy and security, China insists that it means to pursue a peaceful China Rise.

In the same breath, however, China also speaks of Maoist 人民战争 (People's War) and 局部战争 (local war). In a sense, Xi Jinping may be applying Mao's guerrilla warfare to the current international landscape. This means that China's international behavior may not turn out to be particularly peaceful or passive. Moreover, in view of the certainty that Xi Jinping's China Dream will continue to fuel the US-China strategic competition, Xi Jinping is likely to respond aggressively to any outside challenge to these historic objectives—the most sensitive being the reunification of Taiwan. It is thus that the discord between the provocative elements inherent in the very concept of the China Dream and the hard realities of diplomacy with major powers that feel threatened by such provocations characterizes China's place in the world today.

Evolution of United States' China Policy through Joe Biden's First Term as President

The year 2022 was a pivotal year in US-China relations. China announced Xi Jinping's third successive term in October, and the United States had the mid-term elections in November. It was also a time for the United States to update its playbook on China now that Xi Jinping had shown his true colors and all but announced that he was to be an authoritarian dictator for life. America's new direction, which the White House began to unveil in mid-2022, however, was not a headlong dash toward confrontation.

The US government strategy publications and Secretary of State Anthony Blinken's May 26th speech at George Washington University in 2022 made official the unsettling observations of our epoch: the post–Cold War era was over, and a new world order was in the making, and, a great power was challenging the values that had underpinned the world order for the past seventy years. Although Russia "pose[d] a clear and present threat," China was "the most serious long-term challenge to the international order."[27] And, China was "the only country with both the intent to reshape the international order and, increasingly, the economic, diplomatic, military, and technological power to do it."[28] The United States was facing the paramount task of helping establish a new international order rooted in liberal democratic values against authoritarian, dictatorial revisionist challenges posed by China. Although it fell short of calling China an enemy, the United States was no longer coy about the fact that China was now the top priority of US foreign and security policy. The National Security Strategy Report portrayed the next decade as the watershed moment in history that would determine whether the United States can stop China's challenge. This was tantamount to a declaration that the United States will exert maximum effort to contain China over the next ten years.

Meanwhile, antipathy toward China in the United States was at an all-time high. According to a Pew Research Center survey, more than 80 percent of Americans regarded China unfavorably.[29] The proliferation of this public sentiment transcended partisan politics.[30] Public opinion is decisive in forming foreign policies in a democratic country like the United States. That the Biden administration made a show of a hard-line stance toward China following Nancy Pelosi's visit to Taiwan in August 2022 is indicative of this reality. Russia's invasion of Ukraine in February of that year had also aggravated the public's perception of threat from authoritarian China, as borne out by the September 2022 Pew Research Center survey.[31] Americans' loathing for China had risen sharply from 47 percent in 2017 to 82 percent through 2021. This was a clear mandate that any US administration, be it either Democrat or Republican, had to show strength in dealing with China, all the more so facing the 2022 midterm elections in November of that year. Still, questions remained as to the continuity and credibility of the US confrontational strategy toward China. Where would the Biden administration's China policy go next?

Whether Europe was in sync with America was another critical link in Biden's China policy. On their part, Europeans saw Russia as their biggest security threat, but their threat perception of China was lower than that of the United States or Northeast Asian countries. According to a 2022 poll by the Pew Research Center, while more than 80 percent of people in the United States, Korea, Japan, and Australia had unfavorable public opinions about China, the figure remained at 60 percent in Western European countries, and 50 percent in Eastern European countries.[32] European governments, meanwhile, defined China as a systemic competitor in the 2022 NATO Strategic Concept and began to pursue a strong solidarity with the United States.[33] At the same time, however, they badly needed continued trade with China to maintain their respective economic stability. Facing deepening economic woes, Western Europe lacked the wherewithal to engage in ideological conflict with and decoupling from China. A case in point was German chancellor Olaf Scholz's visit to Beijing in November 2022. The visit, which the United States had advised against, came as a shock to the United States. During the visit, Chancellor Scholz spoke of mutual trust and responsibility, giving an impression of a plea from an embattled Western Europe to Xi Jinping.[34] Chancellor Scholz's visit was followed in April 2023, by the visits of President Emmanuel Macron of France and Ursula von der Leyen, president of the European Commission visited China, where they declared their support for a closer cooperation with China and in return secured sizable investments from China. Europe would go on to narrowly avert ending 2023 in a recession by a narrow margin. If the European economic crisis continues, however, the EU is more likely than not to divest itself of its ideological coalition with the United States and seek closer relations with China, despite having dubbed China its "systemic competitor."

As noted in a University of Cambridge report, Western Europe did show a remarkable degree of solidarity with the United States in the center as a result of Russia's invasion of Ukraine in 2022.[35] However, the solidarity already began showing signs of weakening in the face of spiraling global inflation. The United States did not appear capable of mitigating the economic difficulties faced by its friends and allies thus affected; in fact, the United States was ironically a beneficiary of the rising energy prices. A *New York Times* article on various countries' Russia trade following Russia's invasion of Ukraine is of particular interest. As can be seen in the following table, despite the US efforts to enforce sanctions against Russia for its unprovoked invasion of Ukraine, the majority of nations had increased their trade volumes with Russia. It is a cold reality of international politics that countries had to pursue expedient pragmatism by separating economy from security, despite

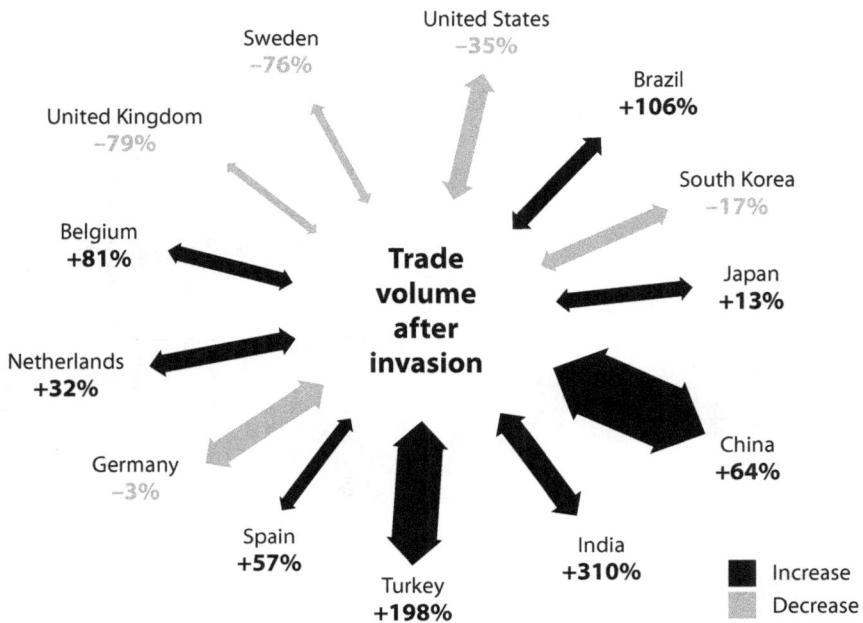

Arrows sized by post-invasion monthly trade value with Russia.
Percent change is the monthly average trade value after the invasion
compared with the monthly average in 2017–2021.

Figure 8.1 Major Countries' Trade Volumes with Russia Since the Outbreak of Russia's Invasion of Ukraine, NEAR Foundation.

the US-China competition and the Russo-Ukrainian War.[36] Thus, the world congealed into three camps: status quo states, anti-status quo states, and opportunistic states. Anti-status quo states include Russia, Germany, Iran, and North Korea. The countries that are displaying opportunistic behavior are India, Turkiye, Brazil, the Netherlands, Belgium, Spain, Germany, Japan, and others. The status quo states are by and large limited to the United States, England, Sweden, and Korea.

Thus, Secretary of State Anthony Blinken's May 26th speech at George Washington University had to show both America's resolve and circumspection. His message could be encapsulated in three key words: invest, align, and compete. America was to invest all resources and political will to increase its power and influence. America was to form a scrum of coalitions with friends and allies against the challenge to the newly emerging rule-based liberal democratic order, and America was to be prepared, militarily or otherwise, to meet any challenges from China.

Table 8.3 US-China Policy Orientation

Policy Orientation	Engagement/ Cooperation	Containment/ Conflict	Competition
Period	Obama administration	Trump administration	Biden administration
Perception of China's strategic Intentions	Unclear/ Domestic focus	Global hegemony	Regional hegemony/Long-term pursuit of global hegemony
Advocates	Henry Kissinger, Michel Swaine, Max Baucus, Jeffry Bader, Susan Shirk, David Lampton, Kenneth Lieberthal, Lyle Goldstein, Peter Beinart, Chas Freeman, Mike O'Hanlon, Robert Zoellick, Jim Steinberg.	Michael Pillsbury, Mike Pence, Peter Navarro, Matt Pottinger, Dan Coates, Dan Blumenthal, Jonathan Ward, Martin Jacques, Avery Goldstein, Aron L. Friedberg, Ashley Tellis, John Mearsheimer	Curt Campbell, Anthony Blinken, Jake Sullivan, Ruth Doshi, Joseph Biden
Think Tanks	Quincy Institutes, Brookings Institute, Carnegie Endowment, Center for American Progress	Hudson Institute Atlantic Council	Brookings Institutes Woodrow Wilson Center for New American Security
Perception of China's US strategy	Focus on domestic issues, and stability of the communist system	Pursuit of a long-term grand strategy for world domination	Securing regional influence, gradual expansion of its scope, focus on domestic issues
US' China Strategy	Hedging strategy, Engagement policy, Peaceful transition through enhanced strategic communication, Accountability to the US-centered liberal international system, Mutual guarantees, Acknowledgment of the One-China Principle, Promotion of interdependent global work breakdown structure	New cold war, Strategic struggle, Containment of China, Military preparedness, Disregard for the One-China Principle, Transformation of the Chinese system, Economic decoupling	Strategic competition, cooperation with friends and allies to contain China, primacy of diplomacy, focus on value diplomacy, military preparedness, acknowledgment of the One-China Principle, strengthening relations with Taiwan, decoupling of strategic industries, de-risking, cooperation on issues of global concern (e.g., global warming)

What transpired thereafter domestically and internationally may be indicative of the result of this shift in the US China policy. Leading up to the midterm election season in November 2022 was a challenging time for the Biden administration. It was facing much criticism, both foreign and domestic, for the US withdrawal from Afghanistan in 2021. At the time, it was facing another colossal foreign policy challenge: the Russo-Ukrainian War. The United States and Russia were demonizing each other based on dichotomous analysis of international relations. Vladimir Putin even hinted at the use of nuclear weapons. America was now facing Russia and China simultaneously, a scenario Henry Kissinger and Zbigniew Brzezinski had so gravely warned against. The Biden administration was not even benefiting much from the "rallying effect" that typically materializes in times of war. Nevertheless, the Democrats did better than expected in the midterm elections: the Democrats kept a slim majority in the Senate. This did not make it easier for the Biden administration to move forward with a consistent China policy; US domestic politics had grown savagely partisan. Nevertheless, the Biden administration appeared to have earned a little breathing room.

Soon after the midterm elections, President Biden had a summit meeting with Xi Jinping at the Indonesia G20 gathering on November 14, 2022. At that meeting, the Biden administration's subtle shift in China policy became clear: the United States would pursue managing the US-China competition, rather than confrontation. "According to Chinese media reports, the 'five nos' are promises made by President Biden that the US: Does not seek to change China's system; Does not seek to start a cold war with China; Does not seek to strengthen alliances against China; Does not support 'Taiwan independence,' 'two Chinas,' or 'One China, One Taiwan,' and has no intention of seeking conflict with China; and Does not intend to break off ties with China, impede China's economic development, or contain China."[37] This new stance appeared in part to accommodate Xi Jinping's earlier call for a "New Type of Major Power Relationship."

While the Biden administration was grappling with myriad domestic and international issues throughout 2022, Xi Jinping appeared to be enjoying much broader latitude in his foreign policy. He solidified his total control over domestic politics throughout 2022, thus paving the way for his unprecedented third term announced at the 20th Party Congress in October 2022. This came as a reprieve for the world as well in that Xi Jinping's primary focus had now turned to stabilizing China's domestic economy and social discontent. China's foreign policy direction as of 2022 can be summarized as follows[38]:

1. Stabilize China-Russia relations, but without a formal alliance with Russia;
2. Maintain the status quo with India, but bring India's neighboring countries under China's influence;

3. Stabilize China-US relations to the extent possible, but without overexpectation;
4. Strengthen relations with the Global South; and
5. Weaken the US influence on China's neighboring countries.

Characteristically reactive, China's US policy steadily oriented itself to the shifting US's China policy. Xi Jinping's successful ascension to his third term and China's worsening domestic problems made this a seemingly sensible response to the US overture.

Heading toward the 2024 presidential election, the polarization in US domestic politics has exacerbated. This unfortunate state of affairs will continue to have an onerous impact on the formation and prosecution of US foreign policy, particularly on such partisan issues as economic multilateralism. As seen during the legislative process leading to the enactment of the Inflation Reduction Act of 2022, addressing conflicting concerns and demands relating to domestic politics, investment strategies, alliance relations, and competition strategies in a toxic climate of polarization is a daunting task. This domestic polarization bodes a leadership crisis for the United States.

Moreover, the atmosphere of detente between the United States and China did not last. The unexpected Chinese balloon incident of early 2023 postponed Secretary Blinken's scheduled visit to Beijing. Nevertheless, the two nations did appear to work together to put out the fire. Secretary Blinken and the Chinese foreign minister Wang Yi met in Vienna, Austria, in April 2023 for lengthy discussions, during which Secretary Blinken reaffirmed President Biden's China policy principles outlined at the Bali summit meeting in 2022. From its perspective, China was able to identify the US red line and calibrate its US policies. Coming into 2023, China was in fact in no position to escalate the China-US conflict. The economic growth rate for 2022 had fallen below 3 percent as a result of the convergence of the Zero-COVID policy, ideology-driven socialist economic policies, and domestic political reforms.[39] The prospect of meeting the officially declared goal of 5 percent growth rate for 2023 looked grim at that time. The Chinese leadership of the newly inaugurated Xi Jinping's third term in office had no choice but to respond positively to the United States overture to manage the competition between the two countries.

"Competitive Coexistence" and Beyond[40]

Early 2023 saw an important inflection point in the U.S-China strategic competition: during a speech entitled *Renewing American Economic Leadership* delivered at the Brookings Institution in April, National Security

Advisor Jake Sullivan introduced a new "de-risking" strategy. This shift accommodated the demands of such allies as Germany, France, and Japan for the United States to adopt a more constructive approach in the US-China competition. This conciliatory message was echoed by Treasury secretary Janet Yellen in a speech delivered at Johns Hopkins University's School of Advanced International Studies: the United States did not seek "winner-take-all" competition with China and emphasized that the United States "[did] not seek to decouple our economy from China's. A full separation of our economies would be disastrous [. . .]."[41]

Starting with a meeting between National Security Advisor Jake Sullivan and Foreign Minister Wang Yi in Vienna, Austria in May, the US-China dialogue went into fast track. Secretary of State Tony Blinken visited China in June, followed by Treasury secretary Janet Yellen, Special Presidential Envoy for Climate John Kerry, and Henry Kissinger in July. In August, Commerce Secretary Gina Raimondo, widely regarded as a Beijing hawk, visited China. In September, President Biden and Premier Li Qiang had a meeting at the G20 summit in India. In October, Senate Majority Leader Chuck Schumer led a bipartisan delegation of senators to visit China, as did California governor Gavin Newsom. This flurry of visits was reciprocated by a visit from Foreign Minister Wang Yi in Washington to arrange a possible summit between Joe Biden and Xi Jinping. The climax came in the form of a Joe Biden-Xi Jinping summit meeting at the APEC summit held in San Francisco between November 11 and 14, 2023. Interestingly, Chinese diplomats—even Wang Yi himself—did not confirm Xi Jinping's attendance at the APEC summit until November 10, one day before the opening ceremony. It appears to have been a tactical move on the Chinese part to apply pressure on the Americans to secure maximum concessions in relation to the Taiwan Strait issue. In the end, although the joint communique did not expressly include the One China Principle, the United States is said to have re-acknowledged China's position on the One China Principle.

During their four-hour summit meeting, the two leaders agreed to jointly develop the "right perception" of the relationship, to effectively manage disagreements by improving mutual communications, dialogues, and consultations, to advance mutually beneficial cooperation in such areas as the economy, trade, agriculture, climate change, and AI, to jointly shoulder responsibilities as major countries to provide more public good for the world, to promote people-to-people exchanges, and to restore direct military-to-military dialogue to manage unforeseen military crises. The breadth of their agreement bespoke the new sweeping lexicon "competitive coexistence," with the meeting of the two leaders befitting the title "G2 summit."[42] It appeared the "strategy of restraint" argued in Barry Posen's *Restraint* and Ryan Hass' *stronger* had prevailed over the hawkish positions of Deputy

Secretary of State Kurt Campbell or Commerce Secretary Gina Raimondo.[43] The "competitive coexistence" strategy advocated by the likes of Henry Kissinger, John Mearsheimer, Evan Medeiros, and Richard Haass had become mainstream.

This stream of high-level contacts was indeed unprecedented. It became clear to the world that the United States and China were seeking ways to improve their relationship. In 2024, the joint efforts to restore military-to-military dialogue, cooperate in fighting narco trafficking, and stabilize the international financial sector continue at the working group levels. Although there still remains room for debate on whether this conciliatory move by the United States was motivated by strategic or tactical considerations, it appears clear that both sides saw the need for dialogue to tone down the level of their conflict.

Those who are critical of this conciliatory approach point out that nothing has changed in the fundamental structure of the US-China conflict. It is unrealistic to expect either side to raise a white flag. It appears only that the two sides opted to stand down to a degree in respect of timing and expediency. For instance, the United States was facing a presidential election in 2024. While the Biden administration had little to show for in terms of foreign policy achievement and the US economic difficulties were deepening, an intensifying US-China conflict would mean a certain defeat at the polling booth for the Democrats. The Biden administration, having promised pragmatic foreign policy for the working people of America, a continuing hardline China policy would have been untenable.

The temporary detente that emerged from the Biden-Xi summit did have its desired effect in Taiwan's presidential election on January 13, 2024. The result was exquisite. Anti-China candidate Lai Ching-te of the Democratic Progressive Party was elected president despite garnering only 40 percent of popular vote, but the opposition held on to the majority in the legislature. And candidate Ko Wen-je of the Taiwan People's Party (TPP) won 26.5 percent of the popular vote, enough to be a swing vote. The message of the Taiwanese people was clear: they wanted the status quo. Neither the United States nor China was totally satisfied, but both probably felt relieved. In place of a congratulatory message, President Biden made a point of warning Lai Ching-te not to contemplate Taiwanese independence. Detente was what the United States wanted, and he would not let Taiwan bring it into an unwanted confrontation. China, on its part, also refrained from any inflammatory rhetoric about the result of the election. Detente was what China wanted also, at least at this moment in history.

The failed attempt to assassinate Donald Trump on July 14, 2024, has brought a tremendous change in the US presidential race. Joe Biden stepped down, and Vice President Kamala Harris became the democratic party's

Presidential candidate. The outcome of the presidential race has become more unpredictable.

While the Republican Party is more anti-China than the Democratic Party, it is also isolationist. If Trump is elected again as president, his administration is expected to be more bluntly antagonistic toward China than was the case during the Biden administration. As such, a new Trump administration is likely to opt to conclude the Russo-Ukrainian War quickly and divert America's resources to a new strategy of increased pressure on China. If so, the Biden administration's "competitive coexistence" will be severely tested, if not tossed aside. Biden's Taiwan policy based on the acknowledgment of China's position on its One China Policy can be replaced by a confrontation between the United States and China centered around the question of Taiwanese independence. The question is whether a new Trump administration will formulate and implement a more systematic and consistent China policy than it managed to do during Trump's first presidency. The alliance system the United States has spent decades to build will be severely tested. More obtusely belligerent rhetoric and behaviors will only indicate the absence of a sophisticated China policy.[44]

As for Korea, Trump back in the White House is likely to pose substantial constraints and confusion on the Yoon Suk Yeol administration that has faithfully participated in the Biden administration's China policy. At a minimum, Trump will demand a sharp increase in the share of Korea's contribution to the costs of executing his new China policies. More generally, Trump's China policy is likely to be rather different in tone and form from the Yoon Suk Yeol administration's own China policy that seeks "peace based on strength."

PROGNOSIS

Four Models of the US-China Relations

With respect to the US-China relations during Xi Jinping's third term, the variables on the US side seem more determinative than the variables on the Chinese side. For China's political structure, with Xi Jinping at the top, is not expected to face much challenge in the foreseeable future. No political force or person who can challenge Xi Jinping exists. On the other hand, some argue that China has peaked, and earlier forecasts of the US and Chinese economies reaching parity by about 2030, and their military spending by 2050 are being reexamined. However, the China Peak theory estimates that China's economy will reach 90 percent of that of the United States before decreasing thereafter. Moreover, despite China's socio economic instability, the Chinese

Table 8.4 Four Models of the US-China Relations

		Security	
		Confrontation	Cooperation
Economy/ Public Goods	Confrontation	[1] New Cold War Trump administration • Systemic and ideological confrontation between strong United States and strong China • Strong and exclusionary nationalism and protectionism • Decoupling, especially in strategic and cutting-edge technology • Bi-polarization of the globe	[2] Competition within Strategic Cooperation Obama administration • US-centered liberal international order • Strong US/Rising China • Global interdependence
	Cooperation	[3] Limited cooperation within strategic competition Biden-Harris Administration • Strong US/Pursuing China • Suppression of China-Russia alliance • Shut off transfer of strategic and cutting-edge technology • Partial decoupling • Cooperation re common good	[4] Grudging coexistence through compromise Trump Administration • The U.S. is weakening, and China is not strong enough • Strong "America First" policies • Expansion of China's regional influence • Realization of 天下三分論 (Three Worlds Theory)

economy will still grow at a higher rate than the US economy into the foreseeable future. In other words, regardless of the China Peak theory, it must be assumed that China, under Xi Jinping's monolithic leadership, will continue to exert great influence on the world for some time to come. Under this assumption, the changing character of US-China relations can be understood with the aid of the following four models.

[1] The "New Cold War" model characterizes Trump administration's China policy when there existed the possibility of a military clash over Taiwan as the Trump administration began to openly challenge China.

[2] The "competition within strategic cooperation" model characterizes the previous Obama administration's China policy. His administration spanned the years when the world took notice of China's rise, something much more consequential than a mere third-world country gaining economic success. During his tenure, the United States chose to compete with China within the bounds of strategic cooperation. This model was premised upon the US superiority over China. Such is no longer the case. The United States is now in full-fledged competition with China.

[3] The "limited cooperation within strategic competition" model characterizes the US-China relations that developed through the Biden administration as the two nations engaged in limited cooperation and restraint as they actively competed. The key word still remains "competition"; the United States sees Xi's third term as a critical period in which the United States must curb China's challenge to the maximum extent possible. If Harris wins in the 2024 presidential election, this model is likely to remain the mainstay of US-China policy for the foreseeable future. If the United States fails to curb inflation and makes a breakthrough in the domestic economy during this period; however, domestic public opinion on China will worsen, driving up the probability of widening US-China confrontation. On its part, China sees Xi's third term as a turning point in Chinese history and will double down on its efforts to achieve the modernization of socialism. Chinese diplomacy is likely to be colored by ultra-nationalism, more so than before.

[4] The "Grudging Coexistence through Compromise" model refers to a situation in which both the United States and China lack the capacity for continuing clashes between them due to respective domestic problems and economic difficulties. Here, both the United States and China try to avoid clashes as each takes up a defensive posture to conserve what influence each still possesses in the international community. This model is likely to be what the US-China policy will congeal into if Donald Trump wins his second term as president in 2024. A review of Trump's first term in office reveals, however, that the Republicans

possess less capability than the Democrats to actually follow through with anti-China rhetoric, especially in lining up a coalition of like-minded nations against China. This would lead to a situation in which the US lacks the strength to curb the expansion of China's influence—hence the "grudging coexistence." If this comes to pass, the probability of the security environment in East Asia becoming a China-dominated region will increase. The US influence in East Asia will drastically dissipate, and the East Asian countries will be left to their own devices in a scramble to find their respective strategic options for survival and autonomy.

Of these four models, Korea is most wary of the "New Cold War" model. It is a "war" that runs the gamut from military, economics, value system, political system to ideology, and Korea is loath to be caught in the middle. The "New Cold War" model seemed to come to the fore toward the end of the last Trump administration and will become an imminent possibility again if Trump gets reelected as president. The new battle line thus reestablished may prompt China to change course and openly support Russia in the Russo-Ukrainian War. On its part, the new Republican administration may opt to embrace Russia in order to isolate China—a reverse of Nixon's 1972 "Opening of China." The United States considers Russia an immediate threat for the moment, but not an ultimate long-term threat. Rather, the United States considers Russia a potential source of raw material and, more importantly, the Russian military a counterweight to China's PLA. Either development, if made, will hurtle the world into a New Cold War between the United States and China in short order. Closer at home, Korea is particularly concerned that Kim Jong Un will not fail to take advantage of the arrival of a New Cold War, and try to extort concessions from either the United States or China, or both, by threatening to disrupt the precarious balance between the two. The New Cold War model being the closest to a zero-sum game among the four models, the United States and China may find it difficult to ignore North Korea's machinations—especially its demand for recognition as a nuclear state.

Short-term Prognosis

The current detente between the United States and China appears to be more of a tactical move to buy time by both sides, rather than a long-term strategic reality. Coexistence is being emphasized under the parlance "Competitive Coexistence," but competition remains the underlying reality. The world will continue to see a conflation of security with trade and economy during Xi Jinping's third term. As the global free trade order recedes into history, both the United States and China are employing trade policies as critical tools of security policies against each other. The United States, in particular, has implemented economic sanctions against China and Russia, while establishing a new supply chain among friends and allies, especially with regard to key technologies like semiconductors.

The question is to what extent the two governments can solicit cooperation from their respective business sector. Truth of the matter is that foreign policy underpinned by values and ideologies tends to be more precarious than foreign policy secured by the expectation of actual profit. This is not an easy task for the United States. China, on the other hand, does not hesitate to use coercive economic measures at the cost of its own industries to achieve foreign policy objectives. For instance, in July 2023, China imposed export restrictions on gallium and germanium—for which it accounts for 80 percent and 60 percent of the world's supply, respectively—in retaliation for the US export control on key semiconductor technologies.[45] Export controls are not limited to the United States and China: Japan had also played this card during its diplomatic spat with Korea, in the form of an export prohibition on key materials for the manufacture of chips. The conflation of national security with economy and trade is becoming an everyday occurrence around the globe.

The multilateral trade system will recede, and unilateral trade policies will become increasingly manifest in diplomatic and security considerations. The United States and China are expanding unilateral protectionist measures in contravention of the FTA conventions, as seen in the US section 232 tariffs on steel, and China's retaliatory restriction on imports of Australian beef. Competition over minilateral economic cooperative groups is intensifying. While China is seeking to join the CPTPP to expand its regional influence, the United States proposed the IPEF in 2021, with Secretary of State Blinken calling it the key pillar of the US Indo-Pacific strategy. Trade and economy is no longer divisible from diplomacy and security, as the rules of multilateral trade crumbles and cutting-edge technology increasingly dominates strategic considerations.

The supply chain realignment centered around America and its allies will accelerate, with the former global multilateral supply chain splintering into regionally integrated blocks. To foreclose the illicit export of high technology to China, the United States is establishing a "friend-shoring" supply chain block among allies and partner countries such as Korea, Japan, Taiwan, and Australia. The United States, Japan, and the EU are offering huge incentives to attract strategic industries, such as semiconductor and high-capacity battery manufacturers, onto their shores.

The dismantling of the US-led liberal international order and the multilateral trade system means the resurgence of the "rule of the jungle" in international politics and trade. Protectionism will become a new norm. The call for "strategic autonomy" by the EU nations means a reduction in over-reliance on China, but at the same time, targets overreliance on the United States as well. Seventy-six countries will hold elections in 2024. The over-riding global trend is toward the right, and this will manifest itself in terms of nationalism, national egoism, and protectionism, as if every country feels it is on its own. Geopolitical risks in the global economy, trade, and commerce are intensifying.

The most intense US-China competition, however, will be waged in the field of science and technology. With a shooting war being too risky to con-template, the United States and China have been desperately seeking a silver bullet. For the moment, the silver bullet is the science and technology sector, where the question of who will dominate the fourth Industrial Revolution will be determined. As such, the United States introduced the Endless Fron-tier Act in 2020 to integrate science and technology into national security, as part of a mammoth drive to improve its competitiveness vis-a-vis China. China reciprocated by amending the State Security Law and enacting the Law on Foreign Relations in 2023. China is making a Herculean effort to develop advanced semiconductor technology domestically. China has been feeling the pain ever since the United States imposed sweeping prohibitions on the export of high-end semiconductors—dubbed "Rice of the Fourth Industrial Revolution"—to China. This prohibition hit China's Achilles' heel as China is yet incapable of producing high-end semiconductors. The US-China competition regarding semiconductor technology is expected to get progressively more intense.

Overall, however, China has already surpassed the United States or will do so within the next five years in the fields of chemistry, engineering, energy, material engineering, AI, 5G, and quantum communications according to Prof. Baek Seoin. China has already accomplished the world's first achieve-ments in three areas: foundation, application, and commercialization, includ-ing the world's first quantum communication satellite Mozi; the world's top supercomputer Shenway; 5G; artificial intelligence with the world's No. 1 and No. 3 startups; the Baidou navigation satellite system; the construction of the world's largest particle accelerator CEPC at 100 km; the world's largest spherical radio telescope Tianyan; and the world's longest high-speed rail-way. It has also surpassed the United States in terms of patent applications, the number of academic papers in science and technology, and long-term planning and support at the national level over the past three years. Major reports from the US government and academia are ringing alarm bells about these and other Chinese advancements that threaten America's position in the world.[46] The *Hamilton Index* (ITIF) published in late 2023 reports that China has advanced ahead of the United States in seven out of the ten stra-tegic industries.[47] The *Global Critical Technology Tracker* published by the

Australian Strategic Policy Institute in early 2024 issued an assessment that China leads the world in fifty-three out of sixty-three cutting-edge technologies, with the United States doing so in eleven.[48]

The United States and China are now engaged in staking out their turfs in preparation for the real competition that will commence ten years hence. The two countries will be the two greatest global powers in the mid-twenty-first century. It will take a while for the US-China trade competition to settle into a new order, and that process will be accompanied by significant conflicts and adjustments.[49] As China made clear in the Party Congress Report, China does not want the dismantling of the UN-centered international system nor a rapid change in the global order. China just wants the world divided into three poles—the United States, China, and the Rest.

At the nascent stage of this long-term struggle, however, the US-China strategic competition has recently entered a new phase due to the Russo-Ukraine War. The war rendered China's design to divide the world into three poles no longer feasible. Russia has impressed the world that it too remains a mover of world events. This perception is relevant even though Russia has suffered a huge blow to its image and, as such, a loss of means to influence world events.

China certainly wouldn't be happy letting Russia shape the coming world order. For this reason, China remains reticent about security cooperations with Russia and yet, China is more positive about economic cooperation. Both China and Russia recognize that strategic cooperation between them will be essential in countering the United Sates. There is also a good chance that a new supply chain and financial network with China and Russia at the center may emerge.

In this line of analysis, it bears significance to pay close attention to the moves by Germany, France, and Japan. Their perceptions of world events are never black and white, nor linear. The cases in point are Germany's transfer of 24.9 percent interest in three terminals at the port of Hamburg, and Japan's decision to invest in the Sakhalin-1 and Sakhalin-2 oil and gas development projects.[50] It is by no means a bygone conclusion as to where in the three-polar world these major powers will position themselves.

However, China is facing a grave domestic crisis spanning politics, economy, and society that may hamper its competition with the United States throughout the rest of the century. The CCP built its legitimacy by developing the economy and making people's lives better. The marriage between socialist rule and capitalist market economy, which made this possible, is now under an existential threat thanks to Xi Jinping's obdurate insistence that socialist ideology should govern all economic activities. The Chinese economy thus faces a few classic traps: the middle-income trap and the deflation trap resulting from deteriorating liquidity. Of these, deflation can actually pull the Chinese economy under. As China has pursued a relentless economic development at the cost of capital accumulation, thus becoming increasingly reliant on foreign investments, it is suffocating under immense debt pressure. The fact that foreign direct investment into China fell in 2023 by 80 percent compared to the previous year does not help. The liquidity crisis will be the detonating cable if the Chinese economy is to implode.

China is engaged in a mighty struggle to escape the noose of these traps. The irony is that Xi Jinping's socialist economy may entrench itself deeper in the face of the US-China strategic competition. The United States is, of course, tracking China's progress in pulling itself out of the economic woes closely. The next three years will tell whether China's current economic difficulties are cyclical or structural. If Xi Jinping fails in economic governance during that period, China may spiral into a perfect storm of societal, economic, and political crises. If so, the world may witness China being forced to roll out a more user-friendly foreign policy to the rest of the world. More importantly, however, China's failure to pull itself out in three years will not only weaken China but also drag the entire global economy into recession with ramifications reaching far into this century.

Meanwhile, the United States is also exhausting itself in the continuing strategic competition with China. Unlike China, moreover, the United States has another domestic element to contend with: elections. The result of the 2024 presidential election will decisively determine the future US-China policy with incalculable ramifications on global security—all the more so if Donald Trump gets reelected as president.

At this point in time, both the United States and China appear headed toward a dramatic readjustment of their strategies and foreign policies due to their respective domestic political and economic problems. The resulting international structure will shape the long-term US-China competition well into the rest of the century. 2024–2025 will be remembered in history as the fulcrum on which the history of the world turned.

KOREA: STRATEGIC CHOICE

The world is mired in the US-China strategic competition. This can be viewed as a hegemonic competition or maybe even a metastasis of hegemonic power. Except that a hegemon supplanting another hegemon as in the years past is not likely. The US-China competition will be determined by who can establish an effective coalition of like-minded countries, a new global governance structure, and a collective leadership based on rules that can solicit consensus.[51] The US-led liberal international order is losing strength, but neither are Xi Jinping's "community of common destiny for mankind" and "Multiple Initiatives"—Global Development Initiative (GDI), Global Security Initiative (GSI), and Global Civilization Initiative (GCI)—gaining any traction.

The projection that the US-China relations are likely to intensify comes as a grave challenge to Korea's security and diplomatic outlook. Especially, the prospect of Donald Trump's second term as president is a cause for anxiety for the Yoon Suk Yeol administration. Korea is one of the few countries capable of large-scale production of high-end semiconductors indispensable for the fourth Industrial Revolution. As such, both the United States and China need Korea's cooperation. This state of affairs makes Korea both a lynchpin and a "pivotal state" perched on the fault line of the US-China competition. Korea is literally a battleground for the United States and China. From the Korean perspective, this state of affairs is where its national interest is wide open to risks under intense pressure from both the United States and China.

The Yoon Suk Yeol administration has established a policy of overcoming security, diplomatic, and economic difficulties through across-the-board strengthening of the Korea-US alliance. On November 11, 2022, President Yoon also declared Korea's own Indo-Pacific strategy at the G20 summit held in Phnom Penh, Cambodia, proposing to foster a "free, peaceful, and prosperous Indo-Pacific region" through solidarity and cooperation with major countries including ASEAN.[52] These policies were followed by consecutive Korea-US-Japan summits where Korea made clear that it would strengthen and play a responsible part in the trilateral pact built on solidarity of shared values. This trilateral pact is germane and timely when China's expansionism is threatening the peace and stability of East Asia, and there's an urgent need to secure effective deterrence against North Korea's nuclear ambitions.

These moves by Korea inevitably mean the deterioration of Korea-China relations. For Korea, whose trade has sizable reliance on China and whose security can never be free of China's intentions, managing Korea-China relations is a difficult and sensitive task, inevitably involving costs in terms of its national interests. China already initiated trade limitations on Korea in late 2023. It behooves Korea to find a fine balance between prudence and clarity in its execution of its pro-US policies and crisis management vis-a-vis China. Korea also needs to secure capabilities that the United States may find desirable in this complex web of diplomatic and strategic relationships. The Korea-US alliance should now transcend solidarity in values toward a balance of mutual national interests. Paradoxically, the same dictate applies to China as well.

At the moment, a comprehensive expansion and strengthening of the Korea-US alliance is essential, indeed inescapable. Korea relies on the United States not only for security and diplomacy but also for science and technology, especially high-tech equipment. In particular, Korea has no option but to rely totally on the United States when it comes to the North Korean nuclear threat, as Korea possesses little credible means of deterrence or defense. Most importantly, Korea and the United States share the values of liberal democracy, which is, in fact the very national identity of Korea.

Ever since Korea's independence in 1948, Korea-China relations have been directly proportional to the changing tides of US-China relations. This remains true today; the intensification of US-China competition and the strengthening of the Korea-US alliance necessarily mean fraught times ahead in Korea-China relations. The existential question for Korea is to what extent will the United States support Korea if and when Korea-China relations deteriorate or turn dangerous. This is the fundamental source of anxiety for Korea—all the more so if Donald Trump gets reelected as president. Korea and the United States must continue to expand their strategic dialogue, and the United States must solicit Korean cooperation by offering concrete plans to make good the inevitable economic loss that will entail in Korea's participation in US-China competition.

Korea's economic reliance on China will continue to decrease, as competition intensifies and the complementarity between the respective economic structures lessens. While this may reduce China's need or justification to interfere with Korean sovereignty and foreign policy, it behooves Korea to secure alternate means and markets to fill the growing vacuum. Korea's economic playing field should become more global, so as to secure complementarity with diverse advanced economies of the world, mostly with the United States.

Nevertheless, the Chinese market remains indispensable for the Korean economy. At the same time, China is a major power that can impose economic, trade, diplomatic, and security threats on Korea beyond its means to absorb. As was in full display during the recent urea solution crisis, Korea is vulnerable to the changing circumstances in the global work breakdown structure. For example, Korea relies on China for 80 percent of its import of over 1,800 items.[53] Add to this the security considerations, and it is plain to see how vulnerable Korea remains vis-a-vis China militarily. If Korea-China relations deteriorate, a Chinese naval or aerial encroachment in the West Sea is an immediate possibility. China also has the wherewithal to either encourage or discourage North Korean ambitions to invade Korea.

The current Korea-China relations can best be described as a "double hedging" structure. If China leans to one side between Korea and North Korea, and if Korea leans to one side between the United States and China, their counterpart will naturally lean to the other. Therefore, Korea needs to improve dialogue and work toward a future-oriented development with China as "strategic cooperative partners." At the same time, Korea must stand up and be counted as a responsible middle power in the midst of chaotic global governance and a fragmenting world order. As such, Korea should build trust assets with the United States and means of coexistence with China. Korea should also endeavor to play a part in reducing the US-China tensions. Managing the complex calculations in between alliance and coexistence, thereby securing Korea's sovereignty, right to exist, and national identity, is where all of its security, diplomatic, and economic endeavors should be focused on. This is Korea's long-term objective and strategy.

Chapter 9

Navigating the North Korean Nuclear Challenge Amid US-China Strategic Competition

Chaesung Chun

THE COMPLEXITIES OF NORTH KOREA'S NUCLEAR DILEMMA

The thirty-year failure of efforts to denuclearize North Korea is casting doubt on the viability of the goal itself. North Korea's efforts to ensure its survival in the early days of the post–Cold War era led to a crisis that exacerbated security conditions around the Korean Peninsula and the global nuclear order. At the root of the North Korean nuclear problem lies the so-called North Korean question. This question stems from the inevitable problem of survival as a divided nation, along with the challenges of ensuring the continuation of the regime under the US unipolar system, securing a sustainable international position in Northeast Asian politics, and maintaining a dictatorship amid recurrent economic crises and a lack of political legitimacy. The intractability of the North Korean question eventually led to the development of illicit nuclear weapons, posing an ongoing security threat to its neighbors and creating a crisis for the global nuclear nonproliferation regime.

The denuclearization of North Korea is a deep-rooted political challenge inextricably linked to the broader North Korean question. Efforts to denuclearize North Korea must be coupled with endeavors to determine North Korea's proper status in the international community, establish new inter-Korean relations, and shape a Korean Peninsula that serves the geopolitical interests of both the United States and China.

Skepticism surrounding the feasibility of North Korea's denuclearization has been growing in Korea and abroad. This skepticism is grounded in the advancement of North Korea's nuclear weapons program, the aggressive doctrine outlined in the Nuclear Force Policy Act of 2022, and the declining cooperation between the United States and China, which is essential for resolving the North Korean nuclear issue. North Korea has stated that its nuclear weapons serve not merely as a deterrent but could also be used "if any forces try to violate the fundamental interests of our state." North Korea has progressed too far in its nuclear development to consider denuclearization, even legalizing the arbitrary use of nuclear weapons for its own benefit rather than solely as an existential deterrent. Moreover, the United States and China are unable to agree on further sanctions despite continued provocations amid their strategic competition. The skepticism about North Korea's denuclearization has become a significant factor in the intermittently heated debate within South Korean society about the possibility of pursuing its own nuclear armament.

Is North Korea's nuclear weapons development making the country safer? North Korea's nuclear weapons advancement complicates the political survival and success of Kim Jong Un's regime, as neighboring countries adjust their deterrence policies and international sanctions against North Korea intensify. South Korea and the international community aim to make North Korea realize that its nuclear weapons will adversely affect its ability to achieve its political goals. North Korea's nuclear arsenal is a self-fulfilling prophecy, casting a dark shadow over the country's prospects for survival and development.

A nuclear war on the Korean Peninsula would be a tragedy that no nation can afford, with devastating global consequences. Conversely, the denuclearization of North Korea and the establishment of new governance on the Korean Peninsula would not only bring peace to all Koreans but also increase the potential for US-China strategic cooperation and serve as an important step forward in the global nuclear nonproliferation regime.

NORTH KOREA'S STRATEGIC SHIFT: MODERNIZING WEAPONS AND DIPLOMATIC ALLIANCES

Kim Jong Un's strategy encompasses several key components. These include the upgrading of nuclear and missile capabilities, the pursuit of the so-called New Cold War diplomatic strategy through strengthening ties with China and Russia, the institutionalization of the nuclear doctrine through the Nuclear Forces Policy Act (2022), illegal financing methods, including cyber hacking and deploying workers overseas in violation of UN sanctions, political maneuvering to heighten the nuclear threat by imposing a hostile two-state policy on South Korea, and modest economic reforms to maintain political support from the population while preserving his dictatorship and suppressing human rights.

At the 8th Party Congress in January 2021, the development of five major strategic weapons was listed as a key objective of the National Strategy. These included tactical nuclear weapons for attacking South Korea; more accurate intercontinental ballistic missiles (ICBMs) capable of striking the US mainland; hypersonic missiles capable of penetrating missile defenses; solid-fuel ICBMs capable of surprise attacks; nuclear submarines along with underwater-launched nuclear weapons; and reconnaissance satellites to spy on opponents.

North Korea has recently declared the completion of its strategic weapons development, a goal set by the country's 8th Party Congress in January 2021. According to a report by the Korean Central News Agency (KCNA) on March 19, 2024, "Kim Jong Un expressed satisfaction with the excellent completion of the development tasks in the strategic weapons sector during the five-year plan period set out by the Party's eighth congress." These comments came after the country's ground test of a solid-fuel engine for a new intermediate- and long-range hypersonic missile on September 19. North Korea emphasized that the test's success has finalized the timeline for completing a medium- to long-range hypersonic missile.

Despite Kim Jong Un's confident statements, the reality is much different. North Korea is not believed to have developed an intercontinental ballistic missile capable of reaching the US mainland. In addition, its nuclear submarines are diesel-powered rather than nuclear-powered, making it difficult to deliver any potential nuclear weapon launch for an extended distance. Therefore, North Korea does not have the means to launch an attack on the United States or to carry out a secondary attack if provoked. It also does not have warplanes capable of reaching the United States, and its air force is significantly weakened. As a result, North Korea is focusing its efforts on short- and medium-range missiles equipped with tactical warheads. At the same time, it is also developing hypersonic missiles to evade missile defenses.

These efforts are aimed at developing a full nuclear weapons system, but they have not yet been successful. In the future, North Korea seeks to make a technological leap forward and acquire the military means to credibly threaten its neighbors. This will require military and technical assistance, diplomatic backing, and economic support from China and Russia. China and Russia's diplomatic cover is essential to ensure that North Korea is not subjected to further economic sanctions while it continues to develop its nuclear and missile capabilities.

Despite North Korea's limited military capabilities to counter the perceived US hostile policy, there is another glimmer of hope in an era of great power geopolitical competition. The strategic competition between the United States and China, coupled with the heightened hostility between the United States and Russia, irreversibly exacerbated by the war in Ukraine, presents North

Korea with an opportunity to evade pressure from the United States and the international community, and may enable it to secure recognition as a nuclear weapons state and achieve economic development.

It has been four years since North Korea broke a moratorium promising to suspend its nuclear and missile tests, yet China and Russia have not imposed additional UN sanctions. Moreover, economic support from China and Russia is essential to keep North Korea's economy afloat. It is highly unlikely that North Korea will be able to revive its economy with most of its resources devoted to nuclear and missile development. North Korea has identified strengthening its centralized economy and suppressing the market as key tasks of its economic reform. Despite recently emphasizing efforts to develop the local economy, significant progress is unlikely. Therefore, Chinese and Russian support is essential to prevent North Korea's economic bankruptcy.

North Korea's development strategy of strengthening ties with China and Russia is not without its limitations. Most importantly, North Korea needs technical assistance to perfect its intercontinental ballistic missiles. However, China and Russia are reluctant to provide weapons technology that could draw criticism from the international community. Additionally, North Korea wants to develop military reconnaissance satellites to acquire surveillance assets capable of monitoring the Korean Peninsula and surrounding areas. It currently has very low-level satellites, but there is potential for future development.

The strategic challenges Russia faces in the war in Ukraine provide another opportunity for North Korea to advance its New Cold War strategy. North Korea was not only quick to give diplomatic recognition to Russia's illegally occupied four provinces in Ukraine but also has since made strategic moves to supply military arms to the Russian military. The White House reported in October 2023 that North Korea had transferred armaments to Russia in September, violating UN Security Council resolutions. In a January 4 press briefing, John Kirby, the National Security Council coordinator for strategic communications, asserted that Russia had employed North Korean ballistic missiles with a range of about 900 kilometers in attacks on Ukraine in December and January. Although Kirby did not specify the type of North Korean ballistic missile used, according to experts and Ukrainian officials, the missile fragments suggest that Russia used the short-range Hwasong-11A. Ukraine also accused Russia of using two Hwasong-11A missiles in a February 7 attack on Kharkiv. At a UN Security Council meeting on January 10, more than fifty states signed a statement condemning North Korea's missile exports to Russia. These states asserted that the "transfer of these weapons increases the suffering of the Ukrainian people, supports Russia's war of aggression, and undermines the global non-proliferation regime."[1]

However, it is premature to assume that Russia will provide North Korea with intercontinental ballistic missile technology. There is no need for Russia to directly antagonize the United States by giving North Korea a weapon capable of targeting the United States, nor is there any rationale for increasing international condemnation by transferring ICBM technology to North Korea. North Korea is well aware of these limitations for Russia. Therefore, North Korea is faced with the challenge of how to pursue its own long-term security and economic prosperity while strengthening ties with China and Russia.

NORTH KOREA'S EVOLVING STRATEGY TOWARD SOUTH KOREA

North Korea fundamentally changed its strategy toward South Korea through the ruling Workers' Party plenum late last year and early this year. In September 2022, the North released the Nuclear Force Policy Act, which stated that nuclear weapons could be used for offensive purposes, going beyond using them as part of a defensive deterrence strategy. This signifies that North Korea can use nuclear weapons at its discretion if it feels that its vital national interests have been violated.

With this strategic shift, North Korea has characterized South Korea as a hostile foreign country. The North Korean government has abandoned its previous goal of reunification with South Korea and has instead asserted its intention to achieve reunification of the country by force. North Korea's adoption of an "adversarial two-state policy" raises many issues in international politics.

However, North Korea's pursuit of reunification by force remains a major military threat to South Korea. Even in the event of a nuclear war between the two states, the notion of one sovereign state completely subjugating another is inconceivable within the framework of a sovereign state order.

Nonetheless, North Korea has adopted the two-state policy and declared that it can unify with South Korea by force. This goes beyond the nuclear threat to South Korea, embodying a strategic intention to deny South Korea's sovereignty.

Why has North Korean leader Kim Jong Un sought to alter the course of inter-Korean relations? The current situation requires that North Korea seek political deterrence in addition to military deterrence. South Korea and the United States have developed a multipronged deterrence policy to counter North Korea's growing nuclear threat. Against this backdrop, the United States specifically stated in its Nuclear Posture Review (NPR) that North Korea's use of nuclear weapons will lead to the end of the North Korean regime. Moreover, at the US-South Korea summit in April 2023, President Biden reiterated that North Korea's use of nuclear weapons will result in the end of the North Korean regime. The end of the North Korean regime means the end of Kim Jong Un's political and potentially physical existence given the autocratic nature of the regime. For a dictatorial state like North Korea, this threat is a direct challenge that is difficult to accept.

While North Korea strongly criticizes the United States, it also fundamentally condemns the South Korean government for agreeing to such a deterrence policy. North Korea cannot pursue ethnic reunification with South Korea when the South Korean government openly discusses the end of the North Korean regime. If South Korea is perceived as an ethnically unrelated foreign country, North Korea will lack any ideological incentive to refrain from military attacks, including those involving nuclear weapons.

While North Korea has stated in the past that it would not use nuclear weapons against its own people, it is now asserting that it could launch a nuclear attack at any time—not on the level of ethnicity, but on the level of two hostile nations. This is both a response to South Korea's deterrence policy and a reflection of the shift in North Korea's deterrence thinking. By explicitly mentioning a possible nuclear attack on South Korea, North Korea aims to deter both the United States and South Korea from attacking North Korea. Going beyond the military deterrence inherent in the use of nuclear weapons, North Korea seeks to strengthen its deterrence posture by also mobilizing political deterrence.

Under these circumstances, US experts are warning of the possibility of an actual war on the Korean Peninsula.[2] War could serve as an important tool for Kim Jong Un if he believes he can control the process. Moreover, if he feels that the technical and diplomatic environment is ripe for the use of tactical nuclear weapons, he may well consider escalation during a conflict, even if it starts as a conventional war.

In the end, nuclear war is indeed more likely than ever. North Korea has thus far sought to complete the development of its strategic weapons system to ensure its military deterrence, possess the capability to deploy nuclear weapons offensively if deemed necessary, and gain domestic political legitimacy.

SOUTH KOREA'S STRATEGIC APPROACH TO NORTH KOREA'S SHIFTING STRATEGIES AND GLOBAL DYNAMICS

North Korea's enhanced nuclear capabilities and the emergence of a new international context defined by the end of the post–Cold War era will require a markedly different timetable and methodology for denuclearization.

If North Korea manages to bypass international pressure for denuclearization through its New Cold War diplomatic strategy, evade additional economic sanctions with the help of China and Russia, and pursue economic development through economic exchanges with these countries, the current policy of pressure will likely prove ineffective. Furthermore, in the context of great power geopolitical competition and the increased risk of nuclear weapon deployment, the existing nonproliferation regime could be neutralized, potentially diminishing the international relevance of pressuring North Korea to denuclearize.

If the consensus among the great powers regarding nuclear nonproliferation is undermined, the pressure on North Korea to abandon its illicit nuclear program is eroded, the international community's collective stance against a new nuclear-armed state is diminished, and the international environment for denuclearizing North Korea is effectively neutralized. In this case, South Korea should focus all its efforts on strengthening its nuclear deterrence strategy and engage in concerted diplomacy to limit the international cooperation between North Korea, China, and Russia. There is no evidence suggesting a consensus among the United States, China, Russia, and other major powers regarding the characterization of the current situation as a new Cold War. For example, President Xi Jinping reiterated at the APEC Summit in San Francisco in 2023 that the current situation is not a new Cold War and emphasized the importance of cooperation between the United States and China in promoting mutual understanding. Russia, as we have seen, has also expressed its reluctance to help North Korea outside of the framework of sanctions while complying with the UN agreement on North Korea's nuclear program. While these assertions could be tentative and temporary, there is currently no indication that the consensus among the great powers regarding a rules-based order, particularly concerning fundamental issues like nuclear weapons, will be easily disrupted.

Kim Jong Un is currently at a crossroads in terms of North Korea's future national and nuclear strategy. He may be convinced that absolute dependence on China and Russia is the most viable option for North Korea's nuclear weapons advancement and economic development. Kim Jong Un could choose to use nuclear weapons as a deterrent against South Korea, the United States, and Japan while securing his deterrence through further nuclear development. However, China's and Russia's relations with North Korea are driven by their own interests, and it is difficult to assume that the great powers will continue to protect the interests of the relatively weaker party, namely North Korea. North Korea could strengthen its ties with China and Russia while ultimately negotiating with the United States and South Korea for long-term national development. In this case, even if the path to denuclearization is a protracted one, North Korea will strive to optimize its gains and extract maximum countervailing benefits for regime security and economic development throughout the negotiation process.

In such a scenario, South Korea's North Korea strategy should consist of the following components. First, it should prioritize strengthening deterrence because North Korea's nuclear military threat is imminent and real. Extended deterrence provided through the US-ROK alliance, along with South Korea's enhanced conventional force strategy, is the most important means to deter North Korea's nuclear threat. Additionally, trilateral security cooperation between South Korea, the United States, and Japan has been a key component of South Korea's security policy since the Camp David summit. Improving defense capabilities through extended deterrence, while adhering to the basic norms of the international nonproliferation regime, will ultimately provide South Korea with the legitimacy needed to pursue denuclearization.

Second, given that economic sanctions against North Korea are a long-standing and solid consensus of the United Nations and the international community, Korea should strive to uphold them. While China and Russia have devised various methods to circumvent sanctions due to their need to provide diplomatic support for North Korea, there is no doubt that economic sanctions remain the most important tool available to pressure North Korea to denuclearize.

Third, North Korea's New Cold War diplomatic strategy must be neutralized. North Korea's solidarity with revisionist states, including its growing ties with China and Russia, strengthens its incentive to seek diplomatic and economic leverage. In particular, North Korea will seek to secure economic benefits from providing munitions to Russia and diplomatic cover for its illegal behavior from China and Russia. South Korea should take the lead in actively exerting pressure on North Korea, starting with a condemnation of Pyongyang's policy of illegally supplying arms to Russia in its war in Ukraine.

Fourth, in addition to this pressure policy, South Korea should proactively develop alternatives for negotiations in the event that North Korea realizes the futility of its New Cold War diplomatic strategy. Any diplomatic engagement with North Korea must include provisions for the security of the Kim regime, the establishment of an international mechanism to ensure peace between North and South Korea, and ultimately, a democratic and free reunification. Despite the considerable challenges posed by the current situation, South Korea should develop its capacity to take a leadership role in negotiations with North Korea in the future by advocating for creative alternatives.

Finally, the North Korean nuclear issue can only be addressed through cooperation between the United States and China. Even if the US-China strategic rivalry continues to intensify, the two countries need to work together to resolve the North Korean nuclear issue. South Korea should make efforts to elevate the policy priority of the North Korean nuclear issue and develop a rationale that can convince both China and the United States that the denuclearization of North Korea aligns with both countries' geopolitical interests.

REASSESSING PRIORITIES: THE SHIFT IN US FOREIGN POLICY RESOURCES AND THE DENUCLEARIZATION IMPERATIVE IN NORTH KOREA

The United States currently has limited foreign policy resources to devote to denuclearizing North Korea. The Biden administration is allocating much of its policy resources to the war in Ukraine, now in its third year. The war in Ukraine goes beyond deterring and repelling Russian aggression; it is eroding the entire European security architecture, and NATO has been tasked with rebuilding the alliance. Russia's actions have shaken the liberal security order to its core, presenting the United States with the difficult task of encouraging European members of NATO to increase their military spending and join US security efforts to counter Russian aggression.

The strategic competition with China represents another black hole draining the Biden administration's policy resources. The United States is engaging in diplomatic and economic efforts in competition with China. China is portrayed by the United States as the only country with the capability and intent to threaten the liberal international order. In particular, China is building up its military capabilities in a way that threatens the United States and its allies. By 2027, the centennial of the Chinese People's Liberation Army's (PLA) founding, Beijing aims to fulfill its so-called Great Military Dream. It aims to modernize the socialist military by 2035 and be a world-class military power capable of challenging the United States by 2049.

Against this backdrop, North Korea's nuclear arsenal is becoming less important to overall US foreign and security policy. While the threat of North Korea's nuclear weapons to the US mainland has always been a pressing policy priority for the United States, China's acquisition of more than 1,500 nuclear warheads capable of striking the US mainland by the mid-2030s, alongside its modernization of delivery systems, has greatly increased the likelihood of a Chinese nuclear strike targeting the US mainland in the context of the US-China strategic competition.

Under these circumstances, the nuclear threat posed by North Korea has become relatively insignificant compared to that posed by China. Moreover, in the case of the war in Ukraine, Russia has declared its intention to use tactical nuclear weapons. If Ukraine joins NATO or establishes direct security ties with NATO, a nuclear-armed conflict involving NATO countries, spear-headed by the United States and Russia, could become a reality.

Given these growing nuclear threats to the United States and the lowered thresholds for nuclear use, the North Korean nuclear issue is increasingly considered a relatively lower priority within US foreign policy circles. There are also voices within the United States arguing that the complete dismantling of North Korea's nuclear arsenal, which has already reached a significant level, is impractical. As a result of this skepticism, the United States needs to abandon the unrealistic goal of denuclearization and instead focus on developing effective defensive responses to a North Korea that has already become a de-facto nuclear weapons state.

Recently, Mira Rapp-Hooper, the special assistant to the president and senior director for Indo-Pacific Affairs at the White House National Security Council, disclosed that the Biden Administration is considering "interim steps" toward the denuclearization of North Korea. This announcement was made during a speech on March 4, 2024, where she emphasized the importance of a denuclearized Korean peninsula and the commitment to explore interim steps aimed at enhancing regional and global security. She remarked,

"The United States remains committed to the complete denuclearization of the Korean peninsula. But we are also going to consider interim steps on that pathway to denuclearization, provided that these steps will make the region and the world safer. We are ready and willing to engage in discussions with the DPRK about threat reduction, especially currently in light of the situation on the Korean peninsula." She particularly emphasized "military deconfliction and de-escalation activities, and other stabilizing exchanges that could reduce the risk of misperception and inadvertent escalation on the peninsula."[3]

Given these circumstances, it is becoming increasingly unlikely that the United States will make North Korea's denuclearization a high foreign policy priority at the government level. However, can the United States advance its policy toward North Korea's denuclearization under these circumstances?

First and foremost, the proliferation of nuclear weapons poses a grave threat to the US-led liberal security order. The United States has been the hegemonic power managing the post–Cold War global nuclear order since developing nuclear weapons in 1945, throughout the nuclear monopoly period, and even after the nuclear crisis with the Soviet Union. The nuclear nonproliferation regime is at the core of the United States' ability to maintain homeland security. Although countries like India, Pakistan, and Israel have developed nuclear weapons outside the nonproliferation regime, they have not posed a direct threat to the United States nor motivated nuclear proliferation beyond their respective regions.

North Korea, however, developed its nuclear arsenal within the nonproliferation regime, thus serving as an important example of the erosion of the existing nonproliferation regime. If the United States recognizes North Korea as a de-facto nuclear state or otherwise abandons the goal of denuclearization, it cannot ignore the possibility of additional nuclear-armed states emerging within the nonproliferation regime in the future. Therefore, unlike in previous instances, it would be a major policy failure for the United States to allow North Korea to become a state that violates the nonproliferation regime, which is central to the US-led liberal security order.

In addition, the eventual proliferation of nuclear weapons would heighten the risk of other US adversaries or terrorist groups acquiring nuclear capabilities. Given these circumstances, it is necessary to convince North Korea that denuclearization is directly relevant to US security.

Second, if North Korea's nuclear capabilities continue to advance, and the United States is unable to maintain its role as the world's security superpower, South Korea will eventually have no choice but to go nuclear. Last year, Presidents Yoon and Biden took an important step toward countering North Korea's nuclear advancement by strengthening extended deterrence through the Washington Declaration.

However, during his visit to the United States, President Yoon stated at Harvard University that if nuclear disarmament talks between the United States and North Korea resulted in North Korea's recognition as a legitimate nuclear state, South Korea would be left with no choice but to develop its own nuclear arsenal. South Korea's nuclearization could lead to the nuclearization of Japan, whose security is also threatened by North Korea. This, in turn, could initiate a nuclear domino effect, prompting Taiwan to also pursue nuclear weapons. If Taiwan were to develop nuclear weapons to defend itself against a Chinese attempt at forced reunification, China could resort to preemptive military action against Taiwan.

Therefore, South Korea's potential nuclear armament would affect Taiwan's defense policy in a cascading manner, introducing a major destabilizing factor into cross-Strait relations. For the United States, which has vital security interests in both the US-China strategic competition and the prevention of nuclear proliferation among its allies, the denuclearization of North Korea is critical.

Third, the denuclearization of North Korea could constitute a major achievement for US foreign and security strategy as a whole. The United States currently frames international affairs as a battle between liberalism and authoritarianism. Yet the number of solid democracies continues to shrink, and the world is grappling with democratic backsliding. Moreover, despite solidarity among democratic countries, the number of actual liberal democracies remains quite limited. For example, a country like Saudi Arabia is considered part of the democratic coalition because it serves US interests, despite remaining a monarchical dictatorship.

If North Korea can remain a dictatorship and still be an integral part of the US-led liberal international order, the US liberal international order will receive a major boost. Regardless of North Korea's internal affairs, it would be a great boon to US global diplomatic norms if North Korea's foreign policy aligns with important US norms, such as nonproliferation.

Thus, the prospect of normalizing relations between North Korea and the United States, followed by North Korea's denuclearization and its eventual inclusion as a full member of the international community, offers a pathway for the United States to broaden its liberal solidarity and secure the legitimacy of the US-led order.

Finally, North Korea's denuclearization could ultimately benefit the US policy of balancing against China by facilitating the normalization of relations with North Korea. Historically, North Korea has maintained strong ties with China and aligned itself with the New Cold War framework in the US-China strategic competition.

However, this relationship is an asymmetrical alliance, characterized by the significant power imbalance between the two countries. North Korea places great emphasis on maintaining political autonomy amid this power dynamic, which has been a constant point of contention in its relations with China. In practice, North Korea has made various efforts to distance itself from Chinese interference in its internal affairs. In the past, North Korea has suggested that in the event of a peace agreement with the United States, it would not only tolerate the presence of US troops in South Korea but would also align itself to some extent with US policies toward China. While such a course of action would likely encounter significant resistance from China, it is not an impossible future if the United States can provide significant incentives for North Korea's development post-denuclearization.

Given that North Korea's denuclearization has become a low priority for US policy, restarting the denuclearization process within the context of US-China strategic competition—a top priority within US foreign policy—presents a compelling argument for the United States to reassess its priorities.

CONVINCING CHINA OF THE IMPERATIVE FOR NORTH KOREA'S DENUCLEARIZATION

China's policy toward the Korean Peninsula has been defined in terms of maintaining peace and stability on the peninsula, achieving denuclearization, and resolving issues through dialogue. However, amid the intensifying US-China strategic competition, coupled with the United States' narrative of exerting pressure on China, China views US-China cooperation on North Korea's denuclearization in a very negative light. China assumes that helping the United States achieve its policy objectives will put China at a disadvantage in the US-China strategic competition.

However, North Korea's nuclear weapons also pose a significant diplomatic challenge for China. As a permanent member of the United Nations Security Council, China bears a diplomatic responsibility to maintain a rules-based security order. China has traditionally pursued a policy of no alliances, with North Korea as its only ally. However, North Korea's nuclear advancement, which is in violation of international norms, poses a significant diplomatic liability for China.

In addition, North Korea's nuclear advancement has wide-ranging consequences, including the potential for South Korea to pursue nuclear armament, the strengthening of US extended deterrence, and the deepening of US-Japan security cooperation. Amid the US-China strategic competition, North Korea's nuclear advancement is adversely affecting China's security environment.

Under these circumstances, denuclearization is a crucial national interest for China, provided that North Korea's future policy orientation aligns with China's interests. Based on these points, it is necessary to make the following arguments to convince China that denuclearization is in its national interest.

First, if China is to assume global leadership as an alternative to the United States, it must create a security order that supports what Beijing calls the "common destiny of humanity." This vision was expressed in President Xi Jinping's speech at the Boao Forum in April 2022, where China announced its Global Security Initiative. The initiative proposes that all countries coexist safely together and pursue cooperative security.

In this endeavor, the nonproliferation of nuclear weapons is an important norm. Currently, China's diplomacy is being criticized as revisionist, undermining the existing international order. If China were to redouble its efforts to denuclearize North Korea and achieve some progress, it would be a major achievement in China's quest for global leadership. This is especially true for future security leadership, considering China's push to take a leading role in mediating important international disputes.

Second, a denuclearized North Korea would give China an advantage in the Northeast Asian security environment. South Korea has no choice but to further strengthen its alliance with the United States because of the North Korean nuclear issue. Through the Washington Declaration in 2023, the United States committed to provide South Korea with a more robust extended deterrent, periodic deployment of critical US strategic assets, and make efforts to increase South Korea's defense capabilities.

The strengthening of the US-South Korea alliance is an important consideration for China as it seeks to challenge the US policies of balancing and pressure. China views South Korea as the weak link in the Indo-Pacific strategy and believes it is in its vital national interest to weaken the US-ROK alliance as much as possible. However, North Korea's nuclear advancements serve to strengthen the US.-ROK alliance, further solidifying South Korea's participation in the Indo-Pacific strategy.

Despite the historical disputes between South Korea and Japan, North Korea's nuclear advancement is an important factor contributing to the growing security cooperation between the two countries. This cooperation is building the infrastructure for a security policy capable of effectively deterring China militarily. Before North Korea's nuclear advancement further enhances this East Asian security cooperation, it is worth reminding China that achieving denuclearization is vital to its security interests.

Third, North Korea's economic deterioration resulting from its development of nuclear weapons is bound to continue to strain the North Korea-China border, exacerbating China's economic burden. With North Korea's trade with China now accounting for over 90 percent of its total trade, China bears the responsibility of preventing North Korea's economy from collapsing. North Korea's nuclear program is consuming policy assets that could be used for economic development.

North Korean defectors continue to flee the country, and China's repatriation of these defectors is highly criticized on an international humanitarian level. Ultimately, North Korea's nuclear program, along with its deteriorating economy and destabilizing political situation, has become a major diplomatic and economic burden for China. If North Korea achieves denuclearization and economic development, these burdens will undoubtedly be reduced.

Fourth, China emphasizes mutual coexistence and win-win cooperation with the United States. Although it opposes US hegemony, China still recognizes the importance of cooperation between the United States and China given the significant power disparity between the two nations. However, considering the limited areas of cooperation, the North Korean nuclear issue is an important policy agenda capable of driving US-China cooperation. Cooperation between the United States and China on the denuclearization process is crucial due not only to their shared interest in nonproliferation but also to ensure close consultation on the future of North Korea after denuclearization.

Of course, it is possible that the US-China relationship could devolve into a zero-sum competition or even confrontation, in which case North Korea's geopolitical status could become a subject of contention between the two countries. However, the possibilities remain open, and the denuclearization of North Korea could provide an important opportunity for cooperation between the United States and China, and for China to coexist with the United States.

Finally, North Korea's post-denuclearization economic development could bring it into China's own supply chain. If North Korea can develop economically, China could use a stronger North Korea as an ally and an important asset in future strategic competition with the United States. This logic, of course, collides with US intentions to use North Korea as an asset in its balancing strategy toward China after denuclearization. Nonetheless, it could provide an important basis for US-China cooperation and agreement on the future of North Korea during the denuclearization phase. If China gains a stronger ally in North Korea through its denuclearization, and in turn can use it as a check on the United States, China will have more incentive to pursue North Korea's denuclearization.

TRUMP'S IMPACT ON NORTH KOREA POLICY: IMPLICATIONS FOR SOUTH KOREA'S DEFENSE AND NUCLEAR STRATEGY

If Vice President Kamala Harris wins the upcoming US presidential election, we can expect continuity in US policy toward North Korea's denuclearization. The new democratic government will seek to engage North Korea in dialogue without preconditions, with the overarching policy goal of achieving North Korea's denuclearization, while simultaneously strengthening the extended deterrence of the US-ROK alliance. However, if President Trump wins, continuity with a Biden administration is by no means guaranteed.

A potential Trump administration will have a greater impact on the future resolution of the North Korean nuclear issue than any other variable. Given his domestic political considerations and history of transactional foreign policy, Trump is likely to seek a markedly different solution than Biden. Trump is likely to prioritize burden-sharing, calling for wealthy allies to contribute more to defense costs, and if they refuse, he will likely weaken US commitments, even if it means weakening their defense capabilities.

If Trump decides that South Korea is not contributing enough, regardless of the international situation, there is a strong likelihood that he will withdraw or partially withdraw US forces from South Korea, weakening the Biden administration's existing extended deterrence commitment to South Korea. Furthermore, if President Trump were to hold a summit with North Korean leader Kim Jong Un, suspending military exercises and weakening the US military's response capabilities, this would have a profound impact on South Korea's ability to deter North Korea. Therefore, it is imperative that President Trump consult with the South Korean government before making any decisions that could affect South Korea's defense capabilities.

Regarding this, Victor Cha, senior vice president for Asia and Korea chair at the Center for Strategic and International Studies, has commented that if Trump is reelected in 2024, his "America First" posture and willingness to decouple intercontinental ballistic missile (ICBM) threats to the US homeland from short-range ballistic missile (SRBM) threats to nearby allies would undermine the credibility of US extended deterrence and hinder much of the progress made by the Biden administration's Washington Declaration and Nuclear Consultative Group (NCG) in shoring up the US nuclear umbrella over its ally. Furthermore, Trump's obsession with withdrawing troops from Korea (and other allied bases) would erode confidence in the US security commitment. The result could be increased calls in South Korea among both the public and policy elites for "going nuclear" regardless of the decreased tempo of North Korean provocations and missile exercises.[4]

The ramifications would be enormous if President Trump prioritizes the security of the US homeland in his negotiations with North Korea. If he authorizes the development of tactical nuclear weapons against South Korea in exchange for an end to the development of intercontinental ballistic missiles capable of striking the United States, the implications for South Korea would be profound. It is also unclear whether Trump will uphold global nuclear nonproliferation treaties or US nonproliferation policy if South Korea, Japan, and other Asian countries decide to build their own nuclear arsenals.

In light of these considerations, South Korea should do its best to develop a countermeasure. It should advance and institutionalize its efforts to strengthen extended deterrence with the Biden administration while also highlighting the benefits of extended deterrence to the US government. If extended deterrence can be accomplished and the US-ROK alliance can be solidified to deter North Korea, the US government and experts should continue to emphasize the importance of extended deterrence even in the event of another Trump administration.

This requires not only strengthening the NCG but also developing operational plans and conducting joint exercises to specifically respond to a North Korean attack on South Korea involving nuclear weapons. If President Trump pursues a freeze on North Korea's intercontinental ballistic missiles while disregarding a freeze on tactical nuclear weapons, South Korea should consider policy options to counter this. This could include the transfer of US tactical nuclear weapons to South Korea and, more specifically, tactical nuclear deterrence. With US troops stationed in South Korea, US intervention is practically guaranteed in the event of a North Korean nuclear attack on the peninsula.

However, if the Trump administration weakens its commitment to extended deterrence, South Korea's own nuclear arsenal would serve as a more effective deterrent. This would be an even more serious challenge if Trump were to withdraw US forces from South Korea entirely, weakening the extended deterrence commitment. South Korea cannot rely on the US extended deterrence commitment, so it must establish the rationale and conditions for the inevitability of developing nuclear weapons in the worst-case scenario. It also needs to warn of the adverse effects on the global nuclear order that such an inevitable option would bring.

If South Korea goes nuclear, it could prompt Japan and Taiwan to seek their own nuclear deterrents against North Korea and China. China would be very wary of the proliferation of nuclear weapons in Northeast Asia, and any changes in Taiwan's nuclear stance in particular would be devastating for China. Nuclear proliferation in Asia could also affect the Middle East, encouraging countries like Iran, which is on the threshold of developing nuclear weapons. The threshold for the use of nuclear weapons has been significantly lowered since the war in Ukraine, and the current situation could lead to a military conflict involving nuclear weapons in several regional hot spots. To prevent such an unfortunate outcome, the denuclearization of the Korean Peninsula and the resolution of the North Korean nuclear issue carry not only regional but also global significance.

While it is difficult to say at this point how President Trump's North Korea policy will evolve, it is important for South Korea to strengthen strategic communication with the Republican Party, as many in the Republican Party prioritize North Korea's denuclearization and advocate for restraining US expansion to its East Asian allies.

North Korea's strategy stands at a crossroads. The country is seeking recognition of its nuclear weapons status and economic prosperity in the framework of the North Korea-China-Russia triangle. At the same time, however, North Korea recognizes the limits of this trilateral alignment and is willing to negotiate its own deal with South Korea and the United States.

For South Korea, it is important to put pressure on North Korea to ensure that its New Cold War diplomatic strategy does not succeed. While strengthening deterrence against North Korea, South Korea should continue to emphasize that negotiating denuclearization with itself, the United States, Japan, and other East Asian countries is the most desirable and inevitable option for North Korea's economic development and the survival of the Kim regime.

At the same time, the United States and China, which hold the key to resolving the North Korean nuclear issue, should reaffirm their commitment to the goal of denuclearizing North Korea and strive to explore avenues for broader cooperation on this front, despite their strategic rivalry.

Chapter 10

Taiwan Contingency

Will China Invade Taiwan?

Jun-Young Kang and Young Hee Chang

HEIGHTENED GEOPOLITICAL TENSIONS IN THE TAIWAN STRAIT UNDER THE REGIME OF DEMOCRATIC PROGRESSIVE PARTY

In the cross-strait relations, there is a clear disparity between the size of territory, population, military power, natural resources, and global influence. In addition to this extreme asymmetry, the China-Taiwan relationship is fraught with danger due to the conflicting strategic objectives of the parties involved. The Chinese Communist Party (CCP) is determined to unify China by absorbing Taiwan. Taiwan's national independence movement organizations, including the Democratic Progressive Party, are determined to pursue an independent nation-state of Taiwan. In contrast, Taiwan's Kuomintang (KMT) insists on establishing a stable China-Taiwan relation to ensure the survival and sustainable economic development of Taiwan. The United States, meanwhile, maintains the "strategic ambiguity" as part of its design to manage Taiwan as a buffer at the frontline of its containment policy against China.

The world's attention has been focused on the Taiwan issue since China's 20th Party Congress affirmed Xi Jinping's unprecedented third term. It also reiterated China's determination to unify Taiwan, explicitly declaring that it would never renounce its right to use force against Taiwan during this time.

CCP leaders have repeatedly threatened the Democratic Progressive Party (DPP) administration, which seeks independence and de-Sinicization, with reunification through force, that is invasion, as early as 2020, making the Taiwan Strait the "most dangerous powder keg on earth." Since then, Chinese fighters and reconnaissance aircrafts have routinely breached the Taiwanese air defense identification zone (ADIZ), rendering moot the Taiwan Strait's median line which had served as a tacit territorial demarcation and driving the Cross-Strait tension to its highest level.

Taiwan's presidential and legislative elections were held on January 13, 2024, amid unprecedented tensions. The world saw it as a pivotal contest between the anti-China and pro-China camps in Taiwan. The Democratic Progressive Party won the presidential election and remained in power, while the KMT won the parliamentary election. The tense dialogue between President Biden and President Xi attests to this perception of Taiwan's presidential election. In a meeting of the APEC in San Francisco on November 16, 2023, the two leaders agreed to the broad principle of managing US-China relations to prevent their strategic competition from escalating into open conflict. However, while securing President Xi's commitment to resume high-level military-to-military communication between the two nations, President Biden reaffirmed the US export control regarding China, prompting expressions of deep concern from President Xi.[1]

The two leaders paid particular attention to the Taiwan issue. President Xi emphasized that the United States should "cease arming Taiwan, and support China's reunification," and "show through concrete action that the U.S. will not support the independence of Taiwan," stating that the "Taiwan issue is the most important and sensitive issue between the U.S. and China." As part of his remarks, President Biden reiterated the US belief in maintaining peace and stability, opposed any unilateral change to the status quo in the Taiwan Strait, and requested that China respect the integrity of the Taiwanese election.

President Xi affirmed that China had no plans for a military action against Taiwan for the time being, and President Biden declared following the Taiwanese election that the United States "does not support Taiwan's independence." It appears that the two leaders managed to cool down the urgency of the Taiwan issue for now, but the US-China standoff regarding the Taiwan Strait and South China Sea is expected to continue.

IMPLICATIONS OF TAIWAN'S 2024 PRESIDENTIAL ELECTION

The Democratic Progressive Party argued for "resisting China to protect Taiwan (抗中保臺)" in the 2024 presidential election, describing the election as a contest between "democracy and dictatorship." In contrast, the Kuomintang argued that a victory by the Democratic Progressive Party would heighten tensions with China, making it difficult to ensure Taiwan's security and growth. The Democratic Progressive Party put forth a relatively pragmatic centrist path, proposing to overcome the bipartisan ideological divide. China's response was "boom or bust," an implicit threat that Taiwan's future depends on the choice made by the Taiwanese voters. According to the election results, 40.05 percent of Taiwanese voters voted for the DPP candidate Lai Ching-te, ensuring that the DPP would remain in power after the administration of Tsai Ing-wen. However, the Taiwanese voters also opted for balance by choosing the Kuomintang as the largest party in the Taiwan's Legislative Yuan, while giving the Taiwan People's Party (TPP), the third largest party, the casting vote.[2]

Taiwan's presidential and legislative elections have been successfully concluded, but the US-China relations on the Taiwan issue is projected to become more complex. China has remained reticent since the election of a candidate China considered least desirable from its perspective. On the one hand, China had to a degree anticipated Lai Ching-te's victory. On the other hand, China feels that the pro-US sentiment in Taiwan has weakened somewhat as evidenced by the good showing of the pragmatic-minded Taiwan People's Party, at least in numbers. As China observed that "the election of Lai Ching-te as president cannot be interpreted as the will of the Taiwanese people," and in Taiwan itself, people's livelihood emerged as a prominent political issue, a pro-US versus pro-China framing of the 2024 election clearly has limitations. Moreover, Kuomintang's focus on the stability of Cross-Strait relations for the sake of Taiwan's security and future development is a relatively pro-China stance. The fact of the matter remains, however, that Lai Ching-te's express intention to maintain his predecessor Tsai Ing-wen's strong pro-US stance and the severance of the channels for Cross-Strait dialogue and negotiation bode further strain in the Cross-Strait relations and the US-China relations.[3]

The fundamental focus of the US policy regarding Taiwan is on its strategic value. China, by contrast, sees the preservation of sovereignty and reunification with Taiwan as a historical imperative. This sense of historical mission is also a prerequisite for the leader of China who is responsible for the "Great China." As such, China's appraisal of the "troublemaker" Lai Ching-te, more radical than Chai Ing-wen when it comes to Taiwan's autonomy and independence, is less than favorable. The president-elect Lai rejects the notion of "One China," and yet professes a desire to pursue a stable Taiwan-China relations. President Lai has rejected the concept of "one China" and promised to pursue stable relations between Taiwan and China. He also expressed his intentions through his inaugural address on May 20, 2024, to which China has largely objected and has conducted military exercises. Donald Trump, Republican candidate for the 2024 US presidential election, maintains a negative view of US military intervention in the event of a Chinese invasion of Taiwan. Regardless of the true meaning of his remarks, the outcome of the US election in November is likely to have a significant impact on China's future foreign policy toward Taiwan.[4]

The most compelling question in the current cross-strait relations is whether Xi Jinping will choose to use force to reunify Taiwan. At a ceremony marking the 110th anniversary of the Xinhai Revolution on October 9, 2021, Xi Jinping declared that he would "achieve the unification of his country at all costs." At the fifth Plenary Session of the 19th Central Committee meeting held at the end of October 2020, Xi declared that he would achieve this goal by "the 100th anniversary of the founding of the People's Liberation Army in 2027." And at the 20th Party Congress, he had it entered into the CCP Constitution that the Taiwan issue is a key point of conflict in the US-China relations and that he sternly opposes Taiwanese independence and any attempt at intervention by a foreign power in the cross-strait relations. In short, Xi Jinping has made it clear that he would not avoid or evade conflict with the United States over Taiwan. Nevertheless, China is probably not yet capable of waging a war against the United States despite Xi's resolute rhetoric. Xi cannot choose the military option lightly when China lacks the ability to carry out an all-out war against the United States, and the potential costs vastly outweigh any potential benefit.[5]

Keep in mind that 2027 will be the year when Xi Jinping will attempt to extend his rule into its fourth term. Essentially, China approaches the Taiwan issue as a matter of unification, not territorial sovereignty.[6] Some hard-liners even argue that all the conditions for the invasion of Taiwan are converging, and the time for invasion is imminent. Others argue that China's bellicose behavior toward Taiwan is but a psychological offensive[7], and overestimating China's military intention and capabilities may result in excessive military response by the United States. Richard Bush of the Brookings Institute argues that China's military threat is not an end in itself but a means, and hence should be seen as diplomatic threats.[8] There is also a view that conjuring of "Taiwan crisis" by the United States should be understood as US strategy to spread anxiety over the "Chinese Threat" in the international arena. Others even argue that this behavior is driven by the logic of the US military-industrial complex to increase the defense budget. Zhao Lizhen, a spokesman for China's Ministry of Foreign Affairs, strongly criticized the United States for "over-exaggerating Chinese threat."[9]

There is a problem in that Taiwan is exposed to China's military power and lacks the ability to resist Xi Jinping's drive toward unification. As the power gap between China and Taiwan widens, the geopolitical balance between the two has shifted. On top of that, the narrowing gap between the national powers of the United States and China, China's jingoistic nationalism, and the concentration of power on Xi Jinping are causing multiple repercussions.

Despite President Biden's repeated promise to come to Taiwan's defense, the US response, or the insufficiency thereof, to Russia's invasion of Ukraine has sown the seed of doubt in the minds of many Taiwanese as to whether the US pledge can be relied upon. Therein lies the fear of the Taiwanese people and their government.

WHAT DOES TAIWAN MEAN FOR XI JINPING?

In the October 16, 2022, 20th Party Congress Report, Xi Jinping declared, "Resolving the Taiwan question and realizing China's complete reunification is, for the Party, a historic mission and an unshakable commitment. It is also a shared aspiration of all the sons and daughters of the Chinese nation and a natural requirement for realizing the rejuvenation of the Chinese nation." Further, Xi reiterated that "[t]he policies of peaceful reunification and One Country, Two Systems are the best way to realize reunification across the Taiwan Strait"; and that it "best serves the interests of Chinese people on both sides of the Strait and the entire Chinese nation."

This report does not signal a major shift in Beijing's approach toward the Taiwan question. In line with the 19th Party Congress Report and other authoritative writings, the new report describes Taiwan's unification as "a natural requirement for realizing the rejuvenation of the Chinese nation." Since the party has laid out goals to achieve national rejuvenation by mid-century, many have interpreted this as Beijing's deadline for resolving the Taiwan issue. However, like other authoritative documents, the report does not provide any detailed timeline for reunification.

Two subtle changes in the report are worth noting, however. First, the report includes a statement that was absent in the 19th Party Congress Report that China opposes "foreign interference" in matters related to Taiwan. This reflects growing Chinese concern over the United States and international support for Taiwan.

Second, the report mentions that China has "strengthened [its] strategic initiative for China's complete reunification." The phrase "strategic initiative" is not new and has typically been associated with preventing and defusing risks, but it is the first time the phrase has made its way into a party congress report in the context of Taiwan. It represents China's desire to drive cross-strait dynamics and make progress on unification.

It is unsurprising that the report does not herald a major change in Taiwan policy. Beijing released a white paper on Taiwan in August 2022 that laid out its views and approach in much greater detail. It was unlikely that Beijing would signal a pivot on Taiwan so soon after releasing a dedicated white paper on the issue.

China declared that it would maintain the One China principle and the "1992 Consensus." Under these principles, China would push for extensive and in-depth negotiations with political parties and figures from all walks of life in Taiwan on the issues of cross-strait relations and the national unification. China urged Taiwan work together toward further development in the cross-strait relations and an eventual peaceful unification. In addition, China declared that it would maintain solidarity with Taiwanese compatriots, support Taiwan's patriotic unification activists, follow the natural flow of history, defend the cause of the Chinese people, oppose Taiwanese independence movement, and continue promoting the unification.[10] This approach reflects China's understanding that there exist differing views within Taiwan on the "One China" principle. However, Taiwan's Democratic Progressive Party denies the One China principle in the first place, and as such, considers the One Country Two System moot.

Nevertheless, there are several noteworthy changes in the language employed in the 20th Party Congress Report on Taiwan. First, the number of references to the 1992 Consensus had decreased. In Xi's oral report, the 1992 Consensus was not mentioned, indicating the loss of its significance despite the fact that it had been considered the bedrock of cross-strait exchange and negotiations. In interpreting the 1992 Consensus, while China had insisted on the unitary nature of "One China," Taiwan had dwelled on its ambiguity stating that "whether 'One China' refers to the Republic of China or the People's Republic of China should be left to each party's interpretation." However, as the Taiwanese public support for the 1992 Consensus was wavering, and even the Kuomintang called for its abolition, it had come to make little sense to emphasize the 1992 Consensus from China's perspective as well.[11]

Second, whereas the 19th Party Congress had declared the policy of "Peaceful Unification and One Country Two System," the 20th Party Congress referred to it as the favored method for achieving unification. By relegating "Peaceful Unification and One Country Two System" from a policy to a mere method, China was signaling that all options were now on the table, including unification by force.

Third, whereas the 19th Party Congress had characterized "reunification" as the *shared* interest of all Chinese people, the 20th Party Congress defined it as an essential element in the realization of the Great Revival of the Chinese People, thus emphasizing the design of China itself—a turn to a rather self-centered stance.

Fourth, unlike the 19th Party Congress, the 20th Party Congress issued an ominous statement: "we will never promise to renounce the use of force." China was trying to arouse fear among the Taiwanese public, thereby snubbing out anti-China centrifugal sentiment in Taiwan.

Fifth, whereas the 19th Party Congress had limited itself to warning against the instigators of independence movement within Taiwan, the 20th Party Congress issued warnings against the interference by external powers and the independence movement in Taiwan separately. This reflected China's perception that the Taiwan question hinges on the US course of action.

THE "ONE CHINA" PRINCIPLE AND TAIWANESE INDIGENOUS CONSCIOUSNESS

For Xi Jinping, the One China principle is the Maginot Line of the Taiwan policy. This explains the Xi Jinping regime's deliberate intensification of the anti-independence and pro-unification debates, arguing that the Taiwan issue is a "critical link in the National Development Strategy in the New Age." On the other side of the strait, Taiwan's position is well revealed in Tsai Ing-wen's "Six-points (蔡六點)." At its core is the insistence that Taiwan is an independent sovereign state. Taiwan's core argument is that two territories separated by the Taiwan Strait are each ruled by two different governments, and therefore Taiwan is an independent state. Tsai Ing-wen fundamentally questions whether there exists a consensus on the idea of One China in the cross-strait relations. Naturally, the president elect Lai Ching-te of the Democratic Progressive Party adheres to the stance that Taiwan and China are two separate countries, and Taiwan is already existing as an independent polity.

This difference in perception underpins the cross-strait relations conflict. In particular, China notes that the political landscape of Taiwan has fundamentally changed. The Democratic Progressive Party's perception of Taiwan as an independent sovereign state is founded upon Taiwanese Consciousness. The establishment of the democratic system in Taiwan and the politicization of "Indigenous Consciousness (本土意識)" led to the consciousness that Taiwanese democracy overcame the despotism at the hands of those who came over from the mainland and that the native Taiwanese became the true masters of Taiwan.[12]

Whether the Democratic Progressive Party or the Kuomintang is in power, Taiwan's political landscape has changed significantly. The most notable is that Taiwanese Identity has taken root deep in the psyche of the Taiwanese. Indigenous Consciousness has dramatically increased over the past twenty years, as the quadrupled jump from 17.6 percent in 1992 to 67 percent in 2022 of Taiwanese who recognized their identity as "only Taiwanese" shows. This trend was already evident during Kuomintang Ma Ying-jeou administration (2008–2016), during which bilateral exchanges and cooperation with China was on the increase.

The recent crystallization of Taiwanese Identity is in part due to the change in Taiwanese history education since the Democratic Progressive Party came into power. This new sense of identity is behind the recent upsurge in Taiwanese Consciousness and Indigenous Consciousness movements in Taiwan. Just as young Taiwanese are increasingly viewing the mainland Chinese as "others," increased trade and contact with China over the last few decades have only confirmed the cultural alienness they felt between themselves and the mainland Chinese. On top of this, the security threat from China is only accelerating the "otherization" process. This increase in Taiwanese Identity has led to a negative attitude toward trade and cooperation with China, despite the economic benefits from economic exchanges between the two countries.

In short, the civilizational and cultural "otherization" has already entrenched itself deeply in Taiwanese society, and there appears to be no centripetal force to reverse the course. As people who have experienced peaceful transfers of power twice already, the Taiwanese now have a national identity vastly different from the one from a previous era. This new Taiwanese identity is unlikely to acquiesce to China's assertion of nationalism among the people of Chinese origin, irrespective of the cross-strait economic exchange.

Nevertheless, it is also true that the new Taiwanese identity has certain limitations in driving Taiwanese independence. Many Taiwanese favor the status quo over independence, as the fact that those who favor maintaining the status quo has consistently remained in the high 50 percent range since 2004. It is thought that fear of military reprisal from China not only explains this trend but also does the general attitude that Taiwan already enjoys a de-facto independence.

Regardless of who is in power between the Democratic Progressive Party or the Kuomintang, China under Xi Jinping is deeply concerned over Taiwanese Consciousness driving Taiwanese Identity, which in turn may foster Taiwanese Independence movement. From Beijing's point of view, even the Kuomintang, which emphasizes "establishing a stable relationship with China to secure economic development and international diplomatic room," essentially stands on Taiwanese choice based on a full Taiwanese Consciousness when it comes to the political future of Taiwan. Therefore, the Xi Jinping regime should take steps to curb the de-Sinicization sentiment among the Taiwanese people in cross-strait relations.

NEW DIRECTION OF XI JINPING'S TAIWAN POLICY

Early in his first term as president, Xi Jinping opted to follow the Taiwan policy he had inherited from the Hu Jintao administration. The inauguration of Chai Ing-wen of Democratic Progressive Party as Taiwan's president in 2016 brought dramatic changes.

First, Xi began to strengthen the unification consciousness. The 2021 Resolution of the CCP Central Committee on the Major Achievements and Historical Experience of the Party over the Past Century declared that "realizing China's complete reunification is . . . essential to realizing national rejuvenation." Unlike the earlier stance that the reunification with Taiwan will naturally follow when China achieves its great rejuvenation, Xi Jinping now insists that the reunification is an absolute prerequisite to China attaining its great rejuvenation.

Second, Xi began to emphasize negotiations for unification. At a ceremony in 2019 commemorating the fortieth anniversary of the CCP's adoption of the *Message to Compatriots in Taiwan* at the 5th People's Congress, Xi Jinping stressed that he would seek a *Taiwan Plan* for the realization of the One Country, Two System in the cross-strait relations, and proceeded to call for dialogue with various segments of Taiwanese society. That is, he was proposing to engage in democratic negotiations to design the institutional framework for the peaceful development of the cross-strait relations.

Third, Xi instituted unification plans. The white paper titled *The Taiwan Issue and the Unification Project in the New Era*' released on August 10th, 2022, after Pelosi's visit to Taiwan, outlined the position of Taiwan after the unification—"implement high degree of local self-governance, on the condition that China's core interests in sovereignty, security and development are guaranteed." In the past, China had committed to not deploying the People's Liberation Army (PLA) to Taiwan in implementing the One Country, Two System structure. Now, however, there are "conditions," and the earlier commitment not to send the PLA to Taiwan has been withdrawn. The promise of "high degree of local self-governance" may no longer hold true.

Over the last decade, the CCP under Xi Jinping has pursued a Taiwan policy built on the key principles of (i) opposition to Taiwanese independence, (ii) promotion of political unification, (iii) promotion of socioeconomic integration, and (iv) opposition to foreign interference. Of these, the Xi administration has had high hopes of socioeconomic integration leading to political unification.[13]

Xi Jinping's first term (2012–2017) overlapped the second term of Kuomintang's (aka Chinese Nationalist Party) Ma Ying-jeou administration of Taiwan (2008–2016). During this period, opportunities for cross-strait interaction proliferated, and the two countries made substantial efforts to promote mutual exchange and cooperation. Nevertheless, the impetus behind socioeconomic and political integration began to fade, and the centrifugal force began to overpower the centripetal force in the cross-strait relation.

From 2008 to 2012, the Kuomintang Ma Ying-jeou administration had maintained a policy of gradual approach to Taiwan's exchange and cooperation with China. However, the 2014 attempt to push the Cross-Strait Service Trade Agreement (CSSTA) with China through the Taiwan Legislative Yuan sparked widespread protests among the young Taiwanese (the "Sunflower Movement)." This scandal dramatically heightening anti-Chinese sentiment in Taiwan, marking a turning point in the cross-strait relations. In 2016, the Democratic Progressive Party's Tsai Ing-wen administration took power on an anti-Chinese platform, and the cross-strait dialogue came to a halt. As the

Trump administration began implementing an aggressive containment policy against China, and the US-China strategic competition began in earnest in 2018, Taiwan turned to a robust pro-US stance and strengthened its diplomatic ties with Japan to balance the threat from China.

After a wait-and-see period, Xi Jinping began displaying bellicose attitudes toward Taiwan beginning in 2019. Xi Jinping's new Taiwan strategy was a two-pronged approach designed to drive a wedge between the Taiwanese people and their government: refusal to engage with Taiwanese authorities while the Democratic Progressive Party is in power, on the one hand, and extension of preferential economic treatment for the Taiwanese private sector, on the other.

Meanwhile, as the US-China strategic competition became entrenched and structuralized, the United States strengthened its support for Taiwan. House Speaker Pelosi visited Taiwan in August 2022, and the Senate Foreign Relations Committee overwhelmingly approved the Taiwan Policy Act of 2022, which directs the federal government to engage with the democratic government of Taiwan as the legitimate representative of the people of Taiwan—that is, a de-facto nation-state with unofficial diplomatic relations with the United States. In response, China identified Taiwanese independence and intervention by foreign powers as the most serious impediment to reunification, and embarked on a policy to block the US-Taiwan rapprochement. The third White Paper on Taiwan published in August 2022 by the Taiwan Affairs Office of the State Council stressed that "Taiwan's independence movement will not succeed" and that "foreign intervention obstructing China's total unification will inevitably fail."[14] The foreign intervention, of course, refers to the activities of the United States and Xi Jinping made it clear that the Taiwan problem is attributable to the US meddling, and is at the heart of the US-China relations.

In fact, as early as during his second term in office (2017–2022), Xi Jinping began emphasizing the reunification of Taiwan as part of the legitimization of his third consecutive term and beyond. In the process, Xi Jinping reinterpreted the reunification as something that goes beyond resolving the cross-strait issues: the reunification with Taiwan was to be the supreme achievement of the "Second 100-years" (i.e., 100 years from the founding of the People's Republic of China in 1949), and a prerequisite in achieving the China Dream (i.e., Great Rejuvenation of the Chinese People). Additionally, Xi defined the Taiwan issue as something that directly pertains to China's core national interests in sovereignty, security, and development.

The most significant structural change that took place between the 19th and 20th Party Congresses is the US-China strategic competition, which began in earnest in 2018.

The United States no longer hides its perception that China poses the greatest geopolitical challenge to the United States and is engaged in strategies to check and contain China across the spectrum. As the trade war and technology war continues between the two, the United States and China are leveraging the Taiwan issue to pressure each other. The future of cross-strait relations has become hostage to how the US-China competition will play out. We need to focus once more on the 20th Party Congress Report where Xi Jinping expressed his exasperation saying, "The Taiwan issue is a Chinese question for the Chinese to decide." He also stated that China "will never promise to renounce the use of force," but at the same time, China "will achieve the peaceful unification with the utmost sincerity and effort."

To understand these two seemingly contradictory remarks, we need to weigh the priority and weight of the two statements. Reading between the lines, Xi's default approach toward Taiwan unification will remain a peaceful one, but at such time that he concludes all peaceful approaches have been exhausted, he will be prepared to use military force.

No former Chinese leader put forth "reunification by force" as his policy toward Taiwan, for he would have had to find legitimacy and justification for such a course of action. In that vein, we should note that the targets of the above two statements are not the Taiwanese people in general, but limited to foreign intervention and Taiwanese independence movement. This shows that the CCP has made a tactical determination to employ preferential treatment for friendly elements and attacks on carefully selected targets.[15]

The 19th Party Congress report had stated, "No person, no organization, no political party, at any time, in any form, shall ever allow any part of Chinese territory to be separated from China." This represents a conceptual expansion in the opposition to Taiwanese independence from "legal independence" to all forms of "subtle and gradual independence." In addition, the conceptual scope of the term "One China" has been tightened.

The Anti-Secession Law (反分裂國家法) of 2005 defined One China as "There is only one China in the world, and both China and Taiwan belong to One China." Now, however, the white paper by the Taiwan Division of the General Office of the Central Committee of the CCP (a.k.a. Central Office) redefines One China by saying, "There is only one China in the world, and Taiwan is part of China." If the 2005 interpretation was premised on the equality of cross-strait relations, the new interpretation makes it clear that Taiwan is but a province of China.

Through his first and second terms in office, Xi Jinping came to the realization that a peaceful reunification with Taiwan will take much time and patience, and that there exists a powerful centrifugal force of de-Sinicization in Taiwanese society. In a society built on the principles and procedures of democracy like Taiwan, a political party with a de-Sinicization platform can come into power at any time. The identity politics is intensifying, and above all, Taiwanese people's distrust of the CCP and rejection of One Country,

Two System is widespread. From Xi's point of view, the United States is making the matters worse by leveraging the Taiwan question in its strategic competition with China.

As such, the key strategic objective of China's Taiwan policy during Xi Jinping's third term is to bring Taiwan to a negotiating table and force it to accept Chinese terms by completely isolating Taiwan. It follows then that the highest priority in China's Taiwan policy is to sever the line of US support for Taiwan. China recently emphasized the legitimacy of reunification by claiming that the election victory of Lai Ching-te does not represent the will of the Taiwanese people.[16] This appears to be a measured response. China probably found it difficult to intensify its pressure on Taiwan on the heels of Lai Cing-te's election victory in view of President Biden's statement after the election that the United States does not support Taiwanese independence. Nevertheless, Lai Ching-te's inauguration as Taiwan's president is likely to remain a contested source of intensifying US-China conflict.

STRATEGIC SIGNIFICANCE OF TAIWAN STRAIT AND SOUTH CHINA SEA

The strategic value of the Taiwan Strait to the United States is multidimensional. First, geopolitically and militarily, Taiwan is crucial to the United States. If China is allowed to gain control over the Taiwan Strait, China gains an upper hand in the South China Sea dispute, and acquires an ability to demand the withdrawal of the US forces stationed in Korea and Japan by choking off the sea lanes transporting energy and resources to those countries.[17] As Niall Ferguson boldly argues, the Taiwan Strait may be the lynchpin that may determine the outcome of the US-China hegemonic competition.[18] Second, Taiwan carries critical strategic value in terms of geoeconomics and economic security. As semiconductor technology has emerged as a keystone in the US effort to check China's technological rise, Taiwan's highly advanced semiconductor industry has become a valuable prize for both China and the United States. It is one of the reasons that makes it difficult for the United States to abandon Taiwan to the wishes of China. Third, Taiwan carries an enormous symbolic significance in terms of values and identity as well. Taiwan, a vibrant democracy, with western universal values, provides an example and legitimacy to the US worldview built on liberal international order.[19]

When the United States switched diplomatic recognition from the Republic of China to the People's Republic of China, the United States passed the Taiwan Relations Act in April of 1979 that expressly stipulated the extension of security guarantee for Taiwan. The United States has maintained a "strategic ambiguity" as to the Taiwan question. On the surface, the United States supports China's One China policy, but provides room for survival, thereby reaping the economic benefit such as selling arms to Taiwan on the one hand and thwarting China's ambition to become a regional hegemon in East Asia on the other. It is worth noting that Taiwan adheres to the belief that its China strategy can hold water only with the United States involved deeply in the cross-strait relations behind its back. Overall, Taiwan appears to harbor a fundamental belief that the United States' own interests will keep it from abandoning Taiwan.

Taiwan is strategically crucial for the United States. Taiwan is an island located on the borderline between Northeast Asia and Southeast Asia, straddling the sea line of communication that runs by it connecting the countries in the region including China itself, and beyond, the United States as well. Taiwan contingency is not only a driving force behind China's push to modernize its armed forces but also a critical cog in China's Anti Access strategy. From the US perspective, the Taiwan Strait figures prominently in maintaining regional stability and the United States' dominant position in the Pacific by maintaining forward deployed military bases and safeguarding freedom of navigation.[20] Referring to Taiwan as "Taiwan and other nations of the region," the Trump administration used it as a testbed for the US commitment to the whole region's security and stability.

President Biden upped the ante in the US cooperation with Taiwan. He invited the Taiwanese delegation for his inauguration in January 2021. He has spared no effort in building global support for Taiwan by making sure to include language about peace and stability in the Taiwan Strait in the joint communiques following the S. Korea-US summit, the US-Japan summit, G7 summit, and NATO summit. Abandoning Taiwan would lead to a loss of trust in the US security commitment to S. Korea and Japan under their respective mutual security alliances. Such a loss of confidence will lead to a decline of the US influence in Asia, signaling the end of Pax Americana

The South China Sea question is another key issue of contention in the US-China conflict. It is a maritime territorial dispute among China, Taiwan, Vietnam, the Philippines, Malaysia, and Brunei, each making maritime dominion and jurisdictional claims to various topographical features in the South China Sea. The dispute encompasses all 350,000 square kilometers of the South China Sea, although the world's attention has been focused on the Spratly, the Paracels, the Macclesfield Bank, and the Pratas.

The economic, security, and military significance of the South China Sea far exceeds its physical size as the second largest sea on earth. Starting in the 2010s, China began a process of militarizing the South China Sea and the artificial islands it built, prompting the United States to actively intervene in the South China Sea disputes. The Obama administration initiated the Freedom of Navigation operations, which have continued under the succeeding Trump and Biden administrations. In 2020, the Trump administration established the concept of "Free and Open Indo-Pacific" and declared China's activities in the South China Sea as "illegal." The Biden administration inherited this policy and has supported the ruling by the Permanent Court of Arbitration in favor of the Philippines ordering China to restore the "illegally reclaimed artificial islands" to their original conditions.

Already in 2013, the Politburo of the Central Committee Collective Study Session introduced a goal for China to become a major naval power in order to "guard China's maritime interests." The plan was put into practice based on the reasoning that China was not happy with the international order led by the United States and would seek greater national interests befitting its new status as a major global power. In line with this kind of thinking, China's strategic objective is to assert its sovereignty within the first Island Chain covering the South China Sea and the East China Sea. China filled the vacuum left by the reduction of the US naval presence in the South China Sea in early 1990s and has invested heavily in enhancing the size and capability of its navy since then.

However, it is not a simple matter to push the US Navy from within the first Island Chain and secure absolute superiority. For any such objective requires substantial increase in China's ability to deploy and project its military power. China' construction of artificial islands in the Spratly Islands is an obvious attempt to gain such capabilities.[21]

It is not the United States alone that is getting entangled in the South China Sea conflict in order to oppose China's aggressive challenge to the regional and international order. Apart from the traditional Pacific powers, the United States and Japan, United Kingdom, Germany, EU, and NATO have adopted Indo-Pacific strategies as well, as the geographic center of the Indo-Pacific region straddles Southeast Asia and South China Sea, a vital link between Europe and Asia.

Five lesser powers in Southeast Asia, particularly the Philippines and Vietnam, which do not possess economic and military might to stand up to China, are doing so by getting the United States, Japan, India, Australia, and Russia involved in the fray. Meanwhile, Taiwan claims—as does China for itself—that South China Sea is Taiwan's maritime territory and thus under its jurisdiction and sovereignty either historically or under international law. As part of this claim, Taiwan is beefing up its claim of effective control over the Taiping Island of the Spratly Islands, by expanding the berthing facilities, installing electric generators, deploying air-defense systems, and stationing 150–200 military personnel.

In 2010, China declared the South China Sea its "core national interest," and escalated the offensive to secure dominion over the South China Sea.

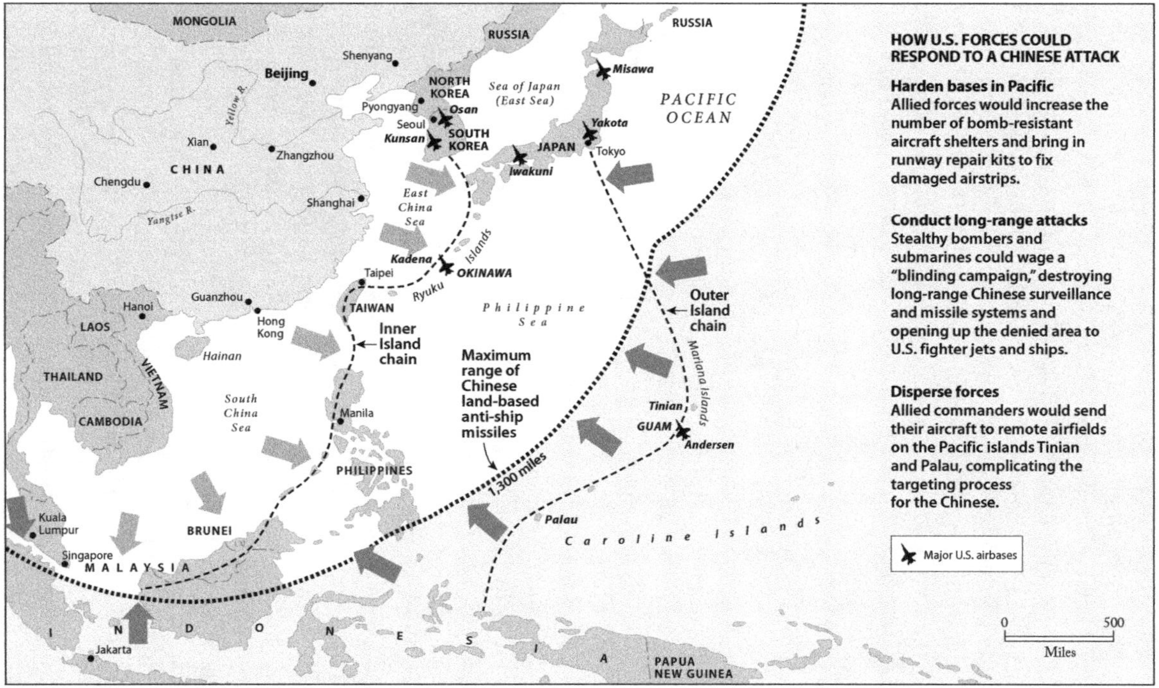
MONGOLIA
RUSSIA
RUSSIA
Shenyang
Beijing
NORTH KOREA
Pyongyang
Seoul
Osan
Kunsan
SOUTH KOREA
Sea of Japan (East Sea)
Misawa
Yakota
Tokyo
JAPAN
Iwakuni
PACIFIC OCEAN
Yellow R.
Xian
Zhangzhou
CHINA
Chengdu
Yangtse R.
Shanghai
East China Sea
Kadena
OKINAWA
Ryuku Islands
Taipei
TAIWAN
Guanzhou
Hong Kong
Hanoi
LAOS
Hainan
THAILAND
VIETNAM
CAMBODIA
South China Sea
Inner Island chain
Philippine Sea
Maximum range of Chinese land-based anti-ship missiles
1,300 miles
Manila
PHILIPPINES
Outer Island chain
Mariana Islands
Tinian
GUAM
Andersen
Palau
Caroline Islands
Kuala Lumpur
BRUNEI
Singapore
MALAYSIA
INDONESIA
Jakarta
PAPUA NEW GUINEA
HOW U.S. FORCES COULD RESPOND TO A CHINESE ATTACK
Harden bases in Pacific
Allied forces would increase the number of bomb-resistant aircraft shelters and bring in runway repair kits to fix damaged airstrips.
Conduct long-range attacks
Stealthy bombers and submarines could wage a "blinding campaign," destroying long-range Chinese surveillance and missile systems and opening up the denied area to U.S. fighter jets and ships.
Disperse forces
Allied commanders would send their aircraft to remote airfields on the Pacific islands Tinian and Palau, complicating the targeting process for the Chinese.
Major U.S. airbases
0
500
Miles

Figure 10.1 Concept Map of China's Maritime Strategy. It is not the United States alone That Is Getting Center for International Maritime Security (2014). https://cimsec.org/strategic-architectures/

This triggered an active intervention on the part of the United States in the South China Sea dispute in the name of Freedom of Navigation, leading to a widening US-China conflict.[22]

China is trying to keep the US Navy out of what it considers to be its maritime territory through arbitrary and contrived interpretation of the EEZ under the UN Convention on the Law of the Sea. China means to break through the first Island Chain by first securing control over the South China Sea. Naturally, the United States cannot allow this to happen. If the US Navy was to be barred from operating in other nations' EEZs, its ability to carry out its missions would be straitjacketed leading to the loss of the US Navy's command of the five oceans. As such, the South China Sea has effectively become a battleground between the US-led international order and China's revisionism.

Another factor that drives the South China Sea is its vast economic value. The South China Sea seabed is estimated to hold 5–200 billion barrels of oil reserves and 700–5,000 trillion cubic feet (Tcf) of natural gas. The South China Sea is also a critical transportation corridor. All Asian trade, other than those with the Americas, must pass through it. One third of the global shipment of oil and one- half of that of LNG pass through the South China Sea. Fully 80–90 percent of Korean, Chinese, and Japanese energy imports pass through it. If any one country is allowed to seal off the South China Sea, the damage to the economies of other countries in the region will be incalculable.

For now, the United States does not appear willing to share the hegemony over the Pacific with China. In view of the colossal geostrategic significance of the South China Sea, the United States is concentrating its naval power in the western Pacific to maintain its command of the seas, and strengthening cooperation with various countries in the region to isolate and encircle China. However, the US priority does not appear to be preparing for a confrontation with China but maintaining the status quo. Maintaining the status quo means the United States continued ability to carry out its military activities within China's EEZ. In line with this policy, the United States is demanding that China observe international rules and norms, rather than warning China of what the United States considers its red line.

Of course, the possibility of an actual military confrontation between the United States and China in the South China Sea is remote, but it is also undeniable that China is challenging the US hegemony for revisionist objectives—that is upend the existing international system. That this strategic standoff is playing itself out principally in the sphere of maritime order and security is more worrying than the individual territorial disputes in the South China Sea. Immediately upon inauguration, President Biden identified China as the sole state actor capable of challenging the dominance of the United States. As such, despite the ongoing Russo-Ukrainian War, the security challenge posed by China remains firmly at the center of the US national security strategic thinking.

STRATEGIC VALUE OF TAIWAN AS A BEACON OF DEMOCRACY

The United States has been supporting Taiwan diplomatically and militarily to preserve the status quo of the China-Taiwan relations. The current Indo-Pacific order is fundamentally built upon the Treaty of San Francisco framework the United States set up in the wake of World War II. Any revisionist attempt, therefore, is a direct challenge against the United States. As such, the United States faced a need to resist the challenge from the rising China before it became overwhelming. In this emerging US-China competition joined other major powers which used to stay on the sideline of the South China Sea dispute, out of the same need to stop China's revisionist ambitions. A case in point is Japan which has become increasingly vocal regarding the South China Sea dispute, under the precept of building a "free and open" Indo-Pacific order. Most disputes and controversies involving China tend to manifest themselves as gray-zone conflicts of varying degrees of intensity. This appears to reflect China's strategy of maintaining a military standoff but short of physical confrontation.

In the gray-zone conflict, Taiwan's democracy figures prominently. If the US administration focuses on the geostrategic geoeconomic value of Taiwan, the US Congress extols the democracy Taiwan has achieved as a beacon of liberal ideals and rule of law.[23] That the Senate Foreign Relations Committee so overwhelmingly approved the Taiwan Policy Act of 2022 attests to the fact that the US-China conflict is being waged on a philosophical dimension as well as those of geopolitics and geoeconomics. The act pledges 6.5 billion dollars in military aid over a five- year period for the defense of Taiwan, directs the federal government to engage with the democratically elected government of Taiwan as the legitimate representative of the people of Taiwan, bars the federal government from acknowledging Taiwan to be a part of the People Republic of China, directs the federal government to resist China's invasion of Taiwan, and confers on Taiwan the designation "major non-NATO ally."

Of course, some US strategists advocate abandoning Taiwan. At the beginning of the Biden administration, the RAND Corporation issued a report analyzing the merits of abandoning Taiwan based on the realist grand strategy of restraint. It reflected a realist assessment that a military confrontation with China over Taiwan Strait is not advantageous to the US interests, and that abandoning Taiwan would not affect the US ability to maintain its hegemonic position.[24]

The Democratic Party tends to be more pragmatic than the Republican Party in dealing with the Taiwan question, and thus can be more flexible in its approach. Still, in the midst of intensifying US-China competition and anti-China public sentiment, it appears unlikely that the Biden administration would opt to abandon Taiwan or to entertain compromises with China over the Taiwan question. With the US-China strategic competition firmly established as the overarching framework, the cross-strait relations have become a China-Taiwan-the US three-way game. In fact, the US-China strategic competition can be said to have replaced the cross-strait relations, in view of the fact that the communication channel for China-Taiwan dialogue has been severed and Taiwan has adopted the bandwagoning to the US strategy since the Democratic Progressive Party took power in Taiwan. In other words, the United States now holds the key to the cross-strait relations.[25]

The US domestic politics drives, and at times even provokes, the Taiwan Strait crisis. The Fourth Taiwan Strait Crisis on the heels of House Speaker Nancy Pelosi's visit to Taiwan is a case in point. Her Asian tour, the Taiwan visit, had the makings of a final curtain call meant to highlight her legacy as she wound down her long career dedicated to democracy and human rights. However, her tour also was an attempt to show the Taiwanese public that America was behind them, at a time less than 30 percent of the Taiwanese public trusted the US promise to come to their aid in case of an invasion by China.[26]

Unlike the United States which focuses on the strategic value of Taiwan, China regards the Taiwan reunification a historical imperative. Absolute majority of the Mainland Chinese people desire Taiwan reunification, and a significant portion of them support a reunification by military force if necessary. It is noteworthy that Xi Jinping himself is deeply knowledgeable about Taiwan and how Taiwanese think. He had extensive contact with Taiwanese industry leaders during his days as a municipal leader, and this background makes him the most perceptive (about Taiwan) among the generations of Paramount Leaders of China. Further, Xi has been personally directing the establishment and execution of the CCP's Taiwan policy for the past decade as the head of the CCP Central Leading Group for Foreign Affairs. To Xi Jinping, the Taiwan reunification is a historical mandate bestowed on him and a personal political legacy.

None of this, of course, eclipses the strategic import of Taiwan for China. If China can secure Taiwan located at the front and center of the First Island Chain, China can exert its influence not only in the South China Sea but also beyond into the blue waters of the Western Pacific. Securing TSMC of Taiwan would also make it possible for China to thwart the US scheme to restructure the global semiconductor supply chain to the exclusion of China.

TAIWANESE PERCEPTIONS ON XI JINPING'S
BELLIGERENT STANCE

Public opinion is a critical variable in Taiwan's China policy, regardless of the ruling party's political orientation. The cross-strait relations have deteriorated since the Democratic Progressive Party, which champions anti-communist, anti-Chinese, and de-Sinicization platform, took power in 2016. In response, the Xi Jinping regime has made it clear since 2019 its hard-line stance on the Democratic Progressive Party. In addition, the Hong Kong protests in the summer of 2019 and the start of the COVID-19 pandemic in January 2020, have made it almost impossible to improve the relationship. Further, the intensifying US-China competition starting with the Trump administration has heightened the tensions over the Taiwan Strait.

The cross-strait relations have entered a crisis phase as the US-China strategic competition became structuralized and the Democratic Progressive Party in Taiwan came to power. First, mutual hostility among the public on either side of the cross-strait relations is on the rise. Taiwan saw the rise of a youth group's perception that takes independence for granted as something natural and primal, while in China a youth group's perception fervently aspires for the Taiwan reunification. Every day, the internet is awash with anti-Chinese and anti-Taiwanese trolls.[27] The heightened nationalism in China is of particular concern in that the CCP broaches it whenever it needs to divert the public's attention from internal problems to external issues.[28]

According to a poll by the Election Research Center of the National Taiwan University School of Political Science in June, 2022, 63.7 percent of Taiwanese people recognized their identity as "Only Taiwanese," 30.4 percent as "Both Taiwanese and Chinese," and only 2.4 percent as "Only Chinese."[29] Over the years, the "Only Taiwanese" identity has entrenched itself ever deeper in Taiwanese society, becoming the mainstream perception, leaving the "Only Chinese" identity limited to an extreme minority. This marks a dramatic shift in the Taiwanese perception of themselves, commonly referred to as Indigenous Consciousness. When one considered the fact that Taiwanese Consciousness grew steadily even through the Kuomintang Ma Ying Jeou administration (2008–2016), it can be said that Taiwanese Consciousness is now an established fact of Taiwanese self-identity. This rise of Taiwanese identity acts like a centrifugal force driving Taiwan and China apart in any conceivable peace negotiations or political negotiations.

The same survey also indicated that the pro-independence category of the respondents (偏向獨立 [aspires for independence] + 儘快獨立 [want independence as soon as possible]), which had remained at approximately 20+ percent for nearly twenty years, recently shot up to 30+ percent. This trend obviously reflects the growing distrust and suspicion of the One Country Two Systems promise of the CCP.

These data show that Taiwanese people's sense of political identity and public opinion have supported the Tsai Ing-wen administration's bandwagoning to the United States. Founded upon a platform that Taiwan is already a de-facto independent state, President Tsai Ing-wen pushed the de-Sinification policy and strengthened diplomatic ties with the United States and Japan. Taiwan is urgently bolstering its armed forces by purchasing weapons from the United States. Taiwan is also building anti-China solidarity with the United States in defense, technology, and defense by taking advantage of the global dominance of its semiconductor industry.

Meanwhile, however, Taiwanese people's trust in the US commitment to defend Taiwan has nosedived since Russia's invasion of Ukraine. A survey conducted by the Taiwanese Public Opinion Foundation soon after the Russian invasion of Ukraine began asking the respondents whether they believed the United States would deploy its armed forces to defend Taiwan against a Chinese invasion. Only 36 percent responded in the positive. As to the question of whether they believed the United States would deploy its ground troops to defend Taiwan, 8.5 percent said they strongly believed so, 27.8 percent said they somewhat believed so, 29 percent said they generally did not believe so, and 24.8 percent said they did not believe so at all. Fully 54 percent responded negatively. As to whether Taiwan's military could resist the Chinese invasion force for more than 100 days like the Ukrainian military, only 30 percent of the respondents said yes, while 51 percent said no. The poll showed unequivocally that the Taiwanese people's confidence in its own military force was low, and their trust in the US commitment to defend Taiwan was in a freefall.

China's election meddling during the 2024 Taiwanese presidential election cycle exacerbated the Taiwanese people's distrust and loathing of the CCP. The election meddling utilized diverse high-tech techniques including AI, deep fake, and cognitive strategy. Director Tsai Ming-yen of the National Security Bureau stated, "China intimidated the Taiwanese electorate by spreading fake news under a frame 'war or peace,' and our bureau exposed 1,700+ instances of fake news production and reported the same to the Executive Yuan." Many international fake news images were produced through Russian media and disseminated online for Taiwanese consumption. Director Tsai identified further areas of China's election meddling: interference with flight and ocean transport operations, combined military exercises designed to intimidate the Taiwanese public, showcase reassessment of the Economic Cooperation Framework Agreement between Taiwan and China, showcase investigation into trade barriers, and others.

The National Security Bureau pointed out the CCP's illegal transfers of virtual goods, clandestine financial transactions through its paper companies in Taiwan, and surreptitious "black money" transfers from China's underground banking. It has also been revealed that the CCP conducted its own surveys with Taiwanese polling organizations and disseminated the reports trying to influence the Taiwanese electorates. The CCP invited a large number of influential members of Taiwanese organizations to China and entertained them to win their support and sent Taiwanese businessmen operating in China back to Taiwan to influence the election. The CCP's election meddling spanned the gamut from infiltration into Taiwanese political circles and intelligence activities to clandestine influence peddling, threatening the free and fair election and Taiwan's national security.[30]

The Democratic Progressive Party won the 2024 presidential election amid swelling anti-China and pro-independence public sentiment. President-elect Lai Ching-te's victory may accelerate de-Sinicization and exacerbate the cross-strait relations tensions. Of course, it cannot be overruled that Lai Ching-te may opt to try to reach a compromise with the CCP to keep Taiwan safe from an outright invasion. The prevalent view among the Taiwanese public is that it would be difficult for Xi Jinping to invade Taiwan in view of the myriad problems China is facing. An invasion will brand China as an aggressor in the global public perception, not an advantageous position to be in when China is staring down an economic crisis internally. An invasion would necessarily raise the very real specter of a military clash with the United States. Moreover, if Xi Jinping attempts an invasion but fails in his bid to reunify Taiwan, his political legitimacy as the Paramount Leader of China may be irremediably shaken. All things considered, an invasion at this point may be a risk Xi Jinping may not want to take.

THE FUTURE OF TAIWAN STRAIT: FROM PEACE TO WAR

In terms of military power, Taiwan is far behind China. China's military spending has been rapidly increasing of late, putting Taiwan's military in an inferior position. As a result, Taiwan's strategy has to be a combination of strengthening asymmetric military capabilities and relying on US military power.

Despite the growing disparity in military strength, several scenarios are conceivable. Richard Bush, for instance, sees the following scenarios: first, peaceful unification through persuasion; second, forced unification through war; third, nonviolent unification through threats; and fourth, unification through methods other than the One Country Two System principle. Here, the last scenario refers to an unification in the form of a loose confederation, rather than a federation.

Table 10.1   Comparison of China and Taiwan's Military Strength

	China	Taiwan
Total active forces	2,035,000	160,000
Ground forces	965,000	94,000
Navy	260,000	40,000
Air Force	395,000	35,000
Reserves	510,000	1,657,000
Tanks	4,800	750
Aircraft	3,435+	531+
Submarines	59	4
Naval ships*	92	26
Artillery	9,752+	2,0936

*Only includes ships classified as principal surface combatants, such as aircraft carriers, cruisers, destroyers, and frigates.

Source: The Military Balance 2023, IISS.

From the Chinese perspective as well, there are several scenarios of unification. First, there is peaceful unification based on the One Country Two System principle. However, this is unlikely to be accepted by Taiwan's mainstream public opinion. In particular, there is no place for a "One Country Two System" discourse in Taiwanese public opinion, having felt great alarm and antipathy while observing China's brutal suppression of Hong Kong's protests in 2019. Second is an armed invasion of Taiwan, exercising this option, however, may trigger a military response from the United States under the Taiwan Relations Act. In addition, China will also have to weather the resulting economic sanctions and a devastating impact on its global image. As options go, invasion can only be the last resort. Third, perhaps the most rational choice, China continues the present course of putting pressure on Taiwan by instilling fear of an armed invasion in Taiwanese society. This option carries with it only a small risk of actual war but will take a long time and cannot guarantee the result. Nevertheless, this option will continue to erode Taiwanese confidence and faith in their future; after all, China enjoys an irrefutable asymmetric superiority.

US POSITION: STRATEGIC AMBIGUITY 2.0

The US position on Taiwan has taken on added significance, as it vowed to support Taiwan against Chinese invasion and continues to shore up Taiwanese tactical military capabilities. As the military balance between China and Taiwan grows increasingly asymmetric and China's show of force more frequent, there arose many debates in America on whether the United States should renounce "strategic ambiguity" and adopt "strategic clarity."[31]

Over the past three decades or so, the United States has pursued a policy of "dual deterrence" under the "strategic ambiguity" doctrine: deter Chinese

Table 10.2 China's Conditions for Invading Taiwan

	Conditions
Taiwan's Ministry of Defense	① Taiwan's declaration of independence or China's interpretation of Taiwan's policies as acts of Taiwan independence.
	② Taiwan's long-term rejection of negotiations or deliberate delay in the unification issue.
	③ Major disruption in Taiwan's political and economic situation.
	④ Taiwan's "pragmatic diplomacy" has exceeded China's patience with "two Chinas, one China, one Taiwan."
	⑤ Taiwan's efforts to join international organizations such as the United Nations.
	⑥ Taiwan's development of nuclear weapons poses a clear and immediate danger to China.
	⑦ The introduction of the US MD system in Taiwan or the stationing of foreign troops in Taiwan.
Chinese military	① Declaration of independence by the Taiwan authorities.
	② The Taiwan authorities hold a referendum on independence.
	③ Deployment of foreign troops on Taiwan Island.
	④ Taiwan's resumption of nuclear weapons research and development.
	⑤ Taiwan's military attack on the mainland using military means.
	⑥ Major unrest on Taiwan Island.
US experts	① Taiwan's official declaration of independence.
	② Vague actions for Taiwan independence.
	③ Taiwan's internal instability.
	④ Taiwan's acquisition of nuclear weapons.
	⑤ Indefinite postponement of the resumption of cross-strait dialogue on unification
	⑥ Foreign interference in Taiwan's internal affairs.
	⑦ Foreign troops stationed in Taiwan

Source: Various reports compiled by the author (2024).

A limited war is possible, but even that may put China into a very difficult position internationally. A more likely form of warfare China may employ would be hybrid warfare accompanied by gray-zone tactics, hybrid warfare being a combination of cyber warfare and information warfare. Under this scheme, China would disrupt Taiwanese society through cyber-attacks and attacks on communication networks. A cyber-attack on the Taiwanese government and other key institutions, for instance, could cause serious unrest in Taiwan's capital and stock markets. China would intimidate the public through media reports intimating imminent invasion or displaying threatening military exercises. China could also advertise the incursions into Taiwan's airspace or territorial waters by its air force and naval assets or have the Eastern Theatre Command or the Rocket Force conduct live fire exercises.

aggression, and deter Taiwan's independence movement.[32] However, a serious doubt has crept in as to the utility of the Strategic Ambiguity doctrine in deterring a Chinese invasion for the following reasons: (i) there's misgivings whether the United States will intervene; (ii) the United States may not hold outright military superiority over China; (iii) the disparity between China and Taiwan in terms of military capabilities continues to widen; and (iv) China has been stepping up its pressure on Taiwan since President Tsai Ing-wen took power in 2016.[33] The Biden administration has hinted at military intervention in the event of an invasion of Taiwan and expressed support for Taiwan's participation on the international stage. While these moves may indicate a turn toward Strategic Clarity to some, the United States has also made clear its opposition to Taiwanese independence.[34]

Of course, the existing Strategic Ambiguity policy is expected to remain largely unchanged, as any changes would not benefit the US interests. However, as the balance of military power in the Taiwan Strait has collapsed and Taiwan's policy of bandwagoning to the United States is now apparent, it is clear that the existing Strategic Ambiguity doctrine needs adjustments. In some corners of America, people argue that the United States should shift to Strategic Clarity, making clear America's commitment to come to Taiwan's defense and bolstering Taiwan's confidence and determination to defend itself. However, it appears that the United States is now using Strategic Ambiguity 2.0, whereby President Biden declares his commitment to defend Taiwan while the State Depart declares the One China policy unchanged. The objective of Strategic Ambiguity 2.0 is to deter China from invading Taiwan and to prevent China from making strategic miscalculations.

Considering the growing public opinion in favor of the deployment of US forces in the event of an invasion of Taiwan, it is likely that the United States will maintain its hard-line stance on China. The Chicago Council on Global Affairs 2022 report shows that while many Americans are in favor of US support for Taiwan, they remain cautious about the deployment of US ground troops.[35] First, 76 percent of Americans support diplomatic efforts and economic sanctions in the event of China's invasion of Taiwan. Second, 65 percent are in favor of additional military aid to Taiwan. Third, 62 percent agree with sending the US Navy in response to China's blockade of Taiwan. Fourth, 40 percent support dispatching US ground troops to Taiwan. This data indicate that, while the Biden administration can and should actively support Taiwan, there may be serious reservations when it comes to deploying US ground troops.

A few clear reasons explain this reticence: the 1971 UN General Assembly Resolution adopted the One China principle, when it recognized the People's Republic of China as "the only legitimate representative of China to the United Nations." So long as this principle is upheld by the international community, the US support of Taiwan, the rise of Taiwan's stature in the international community, and the expansion of Taiwan's diplomatic domain have their built-in limitations. In fact, despite the US wholehearted support, Taiwan has found it difficult to carve out its niche in international diplomacy as many nations and international institutions remain wary of China.

Although the Biden administration is applying strong pressure on China with respect to human rights, democracy, the South China Sea, the East China Sea, and the Taiwan Strait, a complete decoupling between the United States and China is unrealistic in the long run. A dash toward frontal confrontation serves neither of the countries, and the only sensible policy direction for the Biden administration is to prevent war.

CHINA'S HIDDEN MOTIVES

Xi Jinping is escalating the threats against Taiwan in an effort to leverage the Taiwan question for his need to secure legitimacy and extend his rule. On the other side of the Pacific, despite the potential loss and possible escalation to a world war, the Biden administration has indicated America's resolve to defend Taiwan in the event of an invasion. At the same time, the Biden administration is trying to steer China away from miscalculations and to increase the uncertainty of a successful invasion through Strategic Ambiguity 2.0.[36] Although Strategic Ambiguity 2.0 is different from version 1.0, it cannot be said to be a transition to Strategic Clarity as the United States is not openly supporting Taiwan's independence. The Biden administration is focusing on repeatedly warning of a possible invasion by China and securing moral high-ground through internationalization of the cross-strait relations issue by calling for a peaceful resolution of the issue in bilateral and multilateral summits.

If the PLA starts a war in the Taiwan Strait, it is by no means certain that the PLA could overcome the numerous uncertainties and secure a clear advantage. It is hard to imagine that Xi Jinping will choose this path of uncertainty at a time when he has just confirmed his third consecutive term and is trying to lay the foundation for his fourth. In fact, Xi Jinping even lacks a clear justification for an invasion. As it stands now, neither the Tsai Ing-Wen administration nor president-elect Lai Ching-te have explicitly declared independence, and there is no strong will to pursue it either. More importantly, the United States does not support Taiwan's independence. The forecasts by US military figures are a shock therapy to prepare the nation for war in advance and should be interpreted as a means to secure more budget for the military. The United States' continued publicizing the possibility of a war in the Taiwan Strait serves two functions: to foment a crisis mentality as part of military strategy, and to create favorable global public opinion by "internationalizing"[37] the Taiwan issue.

China possesses several policy measures it can use other than an all-out war, that is legal, economic, and other means to force Taiwan to come to a bargaining table.[38] Xi Jinping is unlikely to opt for a path of uncertainty, which may destabilize his administration, without exhausting such other means. In addition, there remain important inflection points that may influence his decision whether to invade Taiwan as a last resort. The January 2024 Taiwanese presidential election was one of them, and the US presidential election in November will be another. As for the election victory by the president-elect Lai Ching-te, it is unlikely that China will commit to a course of action immediately in its wake. China needs time to observe and evaluate the position and attitude of the new president of Taiwan.

If there is no hope for negotiations with the new Taiwanese administration, China will then need to observe the attitude and policies of the new US administration following the US presidential election in November 2024. This is because what will ultimately determine the cross-strait relations is the US-China relations. An invasion of Taiwan involves deep uncertainties and risks. As such, China is unlikely to initiate any military action until the end of 2024, but instead choose to wait and see, while engaging in psychological warfare under its gray area strategy. If China is to commit to any specific action one way or the other, it will be in 2025 and beyond.

The United States, China, and Taiwan are all in a "two-level game" dilemma because of their respective domestic public opinion and political schedule. As Xi Jinping's determination to reunify Taiwan and Biden's pledge to defend Taiwan appear to be in a collision course, the two countries are locked in a "chicken game." At the same time, domestic realities affecting the leaders' prestige and election results are shaping the behaviors of both nations. Although nobody enters a war lightly because of its inherent costs and uncertainties, Xi Jinping cannot afford to appear weak. Vacillating on reunifying Taiwan will not only damage the legitimacy of his administration but also make it impossible to quash the centrifugal tendencies among the Taiwanese people. However, when one takes into consideration the weakness in the PLA (especially the lack of combined-arms operational capability and large-scale amphibious assault capability), the cost of war, the uncertainty of gain from war, the lessons from the Russo-Ukrainian War, and other options available to China, it appears that the possibility of an imminent invasion is low.

For the time being, therefore, China is more likely to focus on pressuring Taiwan to come to a negotiation table for a peaceful reunification, while continuing to bolster the size and capabilities of its armed forces.

EFFECT OF TAIWAN CRISIS ON KOREAN PENINSULA: RESURGENCE OF NORTH KOREAN FACTOR?

Although the discussions of various scenarios of the invasion by military strategists may deserve attention[39], they must be taken with a grain of salt in that they foster unwarranted fear and tend to become self-fulfilling prophecies. Military strategists and analysts tend to focus myopically on the military capabilities and preparedness instead of the historical aspect of the cross-strait relations in evaluating capabilities and willingness of a nation to engage in war. If one does not take a holistic view of the political, economic, and social factors of the cross-strait relations, one is likely to overestimate the likelihood of military confrontation, thereby stirring up a fear of war. Such an unwarranted level of fear may lead to unnecessary economic loss and political miscalculation. However, as can be seen in Russia's invasion of Ukraine, the possibility of a contingency always exists. Being prepared for such a contingency is the basics of security.

The ominous new problem for the Korean Peninsula is that the meeting of the North Korean Workers' Party Central Committee held in December 2023 declared a fundamental shift in North Korea's South Korea policy. The key changes pertain to the characterization of the South Korean regime, characterization of the North-South Korean relations, North Korea's reunification strategy, and reorganization of the structure of the South Korea relations division of the North Korean government. The most striking was the clarification that North and South Koreas were at war, and North Korea could use nuclear weapons to achieve the unification. The Central Committee deemed the concept of unification through the federation of the two governments unrealistic and defined the South Korean regime as a colonial government of the United States. The structure of the South Korea relations division, including the United Front Department—the North Korean intelligence arm responsible for espionage activities against and communist takeover of South Korea—was to be reformed and reorganized. The fundamental direction of the North-South Korean relations was to be changed to one of struggle against South Korea.[40]

It appears that the Kim Jong Un regime has decided upon a strategy of heightening the tension in order to secure recognition as a nuclear power from the United States. In order to draw out concessions from the United States and South Korea, North Korea heralded its intent to raise the military tension on the Korean Peninsula by redefining the North-South Korea relations as "at war" and carrying out missile tests one after the other. The United States appears to be deeply concerned. Deputy National Security Advisor Jonathan Finer confirmed at the Asia Society Policy Institute (ASPI) forum held on January 25, 2024, that North Korea is continuing to engage in extremely negative and dangerous behaviors. Daniel Russel, the ASPI vice president for International Security and Diplomacy and former assistant secretary of state for East Asian and Pacific Affairs, cautioned that North Korea may harbor a plan for a provocation that far exceeds the 2010 Yeonpyeong Island bombardment in scale, and advised preparedness. Same day, the *New York*

Times reported citing a number of government sources that "Kim Jong-un could take some form of lethal military action against South Korea in the coming months after" having openly proclaimed a new very hostile policy toward South Korea.

CONCERNS ABOUT CROSS-STRAIT TENSIONS IN SOUTH KOREA

Under such exigent circumstances, a military conflict in the Taiwan Strait may have enormous repercussions on the security of the Korean Peninsula. An invasion of Taiwan is likely to draw the United States and China into open military conflict, and such an event will in turn call into question the doctrine of "strategic flexibility" regarding the US Forces Korea (USFK). This doctrine means diverting the USFK forces to other theaters of conflict and was a bone of contention between the United States and South Korea during the No Mu Hyun administration. The matter was somewhat resolved by an agreement that South Korea "would not be drawn into any military conflict in Northeast Asia against the will of the Korean people," but there remains much room for interpretation in the resolution. Some military strategists argue that China may attack USFK bases in South Korea when it invades Taiwan. Moreover, if some or all of USFK is diverted to other theaters of conflict, North Korea may take advantage of the vacuum and initiate an attack on South Korea. In short, a conflict in Taiwan Strait may very well spill over to a conflict on the Korean Peninsula.

The massive Chinese military exercise during the Fourth Taiwan Strait Crisis that followed House Speaker Nancy Pelosy's visit to Taiwan appeared to have the characteristics of a dress rehearsal for an invasion, beyond mere protestation of displeasure. The PLA's blockade strategy included blocking the approaches of the US forces from the southwest and east of Taiwan, and from the northeast of Taiwan, that is, the USFK and US Forces Japan (USFJ). The live fire exercises that followed appeared to be a rehearsal for destroying the US forces embarking from the US military bases in South Korea and Japan. It was clear that the PLA considers the USFK and USFJ major factors in its plans for the blockade of Taiwan.

In the event of a military confrontation between the United States and China, the United States will demand support from South Korea as a military ally, and it is inevitable that South Korea would have to comply in some way, at least in the form of supply of military materiel. Such an involvement will give rise to Chinese anger and may even prompt North Korea to involve itself in the Taiwan conflict under the Sino-North Korean Treaty of Friendship, Co-operation, and Mutual Assistance. China's priority targets include Guam and Okinawa. Okinawa, in particular, houses 70 percent of USFJ personnel, and its proximity to Taiwan makes the USFJ forces there the most likely quick reaction force. By extension, the US bases on the Korean Peninsula can become targets of Chinese attack. In short, South Korea may very well be drawn into military conflict in the event of China's invasion of Taiwan.

A military clash surrounding Taiwan will pose massive challenges to South Korea. China remains adamantly opposed to South Korea even mentioning the Taiwan Strait issue. For instance, when the joint communique from the Korea-US summit of May 21, 2021, included "preservation of peace and stability of the Taiwan strait," China protested vehemently insisting that it amounted to interference with its internal affairs. China was clearly on edge as South Korea's pro-US leaning became clear, as demonstrated by the fact that the summit agenda included the revocation of the Ballistic Missile Range Guideline and mutual cooperation on cutting-edge technology, especially semiconductors.

North Korea, of course, did not fail to take advantage of that development and came out expressing strong support for its ally China. North Korea also made a point of warning that any conflict surrounding Taiwan is never unrelated to the peace and stability in the Korean Peninsula. A military clash in the Taiwan Strait will seriously damage the peace and stability in East Asia and force South Korea into an onerous predicament of having to choose between the United States and China.

Japan is more likely to actively engage in a Taiwan crisis than Korea, considering the US-Japan relations, its regional stature, its position in the QUAD, and its domestic elections. The difference can be read in the "US-Japan Joint Statement" of April 2022 and the "Korea-US Joint Statement" of May. The policy guideline of Japan's Liberal Democratic Party (LDP) policy guideline indicates that Japan is acutely aware of the threat posed by China's ongoing military operations in the Taiwan Strait and the East China Sea. The LDP policy guideline also notes the fast changing security environment citing China's rapid expansion of its armed forces, China's aggressive show of force around Senkaku Islands (Chinese: Diaoyudao), China's revisionism based on its economic and military might, North Korean nuclear and missile threats, and the ever-evolving role of technology in warfare. A society-wide consensus has been reached to fundamentally reshape Japan's security profile to meet these threats. Accordingly, the LDP has committed to the following measures: first, increase the defense budget to 2 percent of its GDP; second, acquire the offensive military operation capability; third, update and revise the national security strategy, attendant defense planning, and acquisition planning for weapon systems for the Self-defense Force.

If the United States and Japan get involved in the Taiwan crisis, the scope of the military conflict will encompass the South China Sea, East China Sea, and even the Korean Peninsula. The conflict will trigger a chain reaction, pulling all of East Asia into the cauldron. For South Korea and Japan which import all of their respective energy needs, the transportation costs will skyrocket. As the war becomes protracted, the sea lane to these countries itself may be severed. Such development may cripple the two countries' economies and dramatically curtail direct foreign investments into those economies.

The PLA's Anti-access/Area Denial capability is growing stronger each year. If a military clash were to happen in the Taiwan Strait, most US military installations in the region including Guam will fall within the range of Chinese offensive missile capability. If the USFK and USFJ join the battle, China will regard Korea and Japan as enemy combatants. If the North Korean factor is mixed in the fray, the situation becomes impossibly complicated.

In fact, the United States will not have the wherewithal to consider and accommodate Korea's needs. The first priority for Korea should be the defense of its home territory and the prevention of North Korean military opportunism. For this purpose, it is necessary to establish a mutual trust mechanism with North Korea to prevent clashes on the Korean Peninsula, which may in effect become a proxy war on behalf of the United States and China, respectively. As such, the most objective and pragmatic choice Korea can make would be to assist the US war effort only to the extent of providing military materiel.

The Taiwan policy during Xi Jinping's third term appears to be chiseled in stone. China will base its course of action on the "overarching strategy of the CCP for the resolution of the Taiwan question in the new age" adopted at the third CCP Central Committee on the Major Achievements and Historical Experience of the Party over the Past Century. This is the highest national strategy and as such encompasses political considerations, execution plans, behavioral guidance, and policies. Added to this, the "opposition to Taiwanese independence" and "opposition to foreign interference into the Taiwan question" adopted at the 20th Party Congress will form the core of the CCP policy on Taiwan, and China will march inexorably toward "Taiwan reunification for the Great Rejuvenation of the Chinese people."[41]

If, on the other hand, China persists in excessive military threat as a knee-jerk reaction to the election of Lai Ching-te as the new president of Taiwan, China stands to accelerate Taiwanese de-Sinicization and to further alienate the global public opinion on China. China continues to exclude semiconductors in its economic sanctions on Taiwan and has exchanged understanding with the United States to manage their relationship lest it may escalate into an open conflict, but the US-China strategic competition is now a constant—a fact of life.

South Korea has become a "Global Pivotal State" and as such should carry the mantle of promoting peace and stability in East Asia and international cooperation from a multilateral platform. The South Korean government needs to engage in strategic discussion with the United States proactively so as to identify how the various scenarios that may arise from an armed conflict in the Taiwan Strait may affect the future of South Korea. The China-Taiwan dispute may severely limit the strategic options available for the Korean businesses operating in China. China will pressure South Korea which it perceives to be the weakest link in the US-Japan-Korea trilateral cooperation, while the United States will maintain pressure on South Korea to prevent it from bandwagoning with China. As seen above, an armed conflict in the Taiwan Strait is also likely to exacerbate the security environment on the Korean Peninsula. It may force South Korea to choose between the United States and China, and act as a severe impediment to improving the South Korea-China relations as well.

PART III

A MATRIX ANALYSIS ON KOREA-US-CHINA TRILATERAL RELATIONS

Chapter 11

A Matrix Analysis on the US-Korea-China Trilateral Relations

Duck-Koo Chung

WHY TRIANGULAR MATRIX ANALYSIS?

A structured analytical tool is needed to understand the complexity of Korea-US-China relations—a triangular analytical framework that affords the user a bird's-eye view of the crisscrossing interests, conflicts, interdependencies, demands, and areas of competition and cooperation in geopolitics, geoeconomics, and geotechnology among the three nations involved. Such a tool would enable mathematical and detailed analysis while also highlighting latent conflicts and future areas of competition, thereby aiding in the proactive formulation of policies.

This chapter presents such a model—a triangular "Matrix Analysis"—and utilizes it to analyze the intersecting interests and policy directions of the three nations. This matrix analysis will include, among other factors, security concerns, economic interests, and guardrails from the perspective of each actor, and involve comparative analyses of each actor's needs, demands, strategies, intentions, and capacity, which may reveal potential points of strategic miscalculations.

This triangular matrix analysis can help overcome the error of imbalance that often results from binary strategic analysis by identifying how the binary analysis affects the third actor and preventing oversimplification of issues. The objective is to arrive at a composite three-dimensional picture of issues such as shifting alliances, emerging strategic challenges, and latent risks, thereby facilitating the formulation of proactive policies aimed at avoiding or mitigating security dilemmas, alliance disintegration, and economic catastrophes.

US strategists believe in the predominance of US power. However, this perception often leads to strategic failures due to a tendency toward oversimplification and overextension in policymaking. Effective strategy formulation requires the consideration of medium- and long-term objectives, accounting for all the complexities involved, and devising incremental approaches toward implementation. Furthermore, when a country solicits cooperation from its allies toward its strategic goal, it must maintain a keen appreciation of the costs imposed on these allies if it hopes to maintain their continued cooperation.

As China under Xi Jinping continues to pose geopolitical and geoeconomic challenges to the international order, the US-China competition is becoming increasingly structuralized and protracted. This trend magnifies the effect of the major power politics on other nations, including Korea. While the strategic significance of Korea has increased, its traditional "U.S. for security, China for economy" strategy has become fraught with risks, and its diplomatic autonomy has been compromised. The reason for this is obvious: Korea's physical proximity to China and its economic dependence on the Chinese market. Despite Korea's determination to stand by its ally in the US-China competition, the United States's unilateral pursuit of its national interests has translated into Korea's loss of its own national interests and a heightened risk of waning public opinion on the sustainability of the Korea-US alliance.

Korea is fully aware of the demands of the changing times. Moving beyond a growth model based on coat-tailing the "rise of China," Korea must adapt to the emerging economic order in the world of US-China competition. However, transitioning from a China-centric global supply chain to a US-led minilateral global supply chain requires careful balancing of interests and a gradual, long-term strategic approach. Ultimately, it is a matter of maintaining a sustainable pace and safeguarding the balance of interests.

Faced with Xi Jinping's China, Korea and the United States need to clarify between them their respective interests, delineating areas of conflict, competition, and cooperation. By openly sharing their strategic thinking, the two nations can pinpoint areas of convergence and divergence, laying the groundwork for designing a sustainable future for their alliance.

This chapter seeks to identify the intersecting demands within Korea-US-China triangular relations and the underlying conflicts that emerge as a result. Korea-US-China triangular relations consist of 3x2 dual relationships: US-China, US-Korea, China-US, China-Korea, Korea-US, and Korea-China. The objectives of this analysis are twofold: to identify the means to prevent conflicts and catastrophes, and to find pathways toward coexistence and productive competition (i.e., maximize the benefits of convergent interests while minimizing the effects of divergent interests). Utilizing this triangular matrix analysis can mitigate the risk of oversimplifying the triangular relations, thus reducing the uncertainty China may provoke and safeguarding US credibility among its allies. It is anticipated that this analytical approach will enable Korea and the United States to engage in more intricate strategic calculations and to chart a course for coexistence within the framework of the Korea-US alliance going forward.

Xi Jinping's China and the Contraints on the US China Policy

Under Xi Jinping, China's grand strategy morphed into "becoming a global power through enhancement of national power." China has set forth four objectives to realize this grand strategy.[1] The first is to maintain order and stability in Chinese society; the second is to achieve robust economic growth; the third is to resist foreign powers that threaten China's territory and sovereignty, and the fourth is to secure and expand its geopolitical influence as a major global power.

Of these four objectives, the most important is maintaining domestic order and stability.[2] To achieve this, China has maintained an authoritarian political system based on a unitary hierarchical value system. Constantly reminding the Chinese people of the "Century of Humiliation" suffered at the hands of the West, Chinese leaders have always been hypersensitive to any hints of social unrest or political division. By capitalizing on perceived threats from abroad in the era of the US-China competition, they have stoked nationalistic fervor and reinforced the legitimacy of the CCP's one-party rule.

The heightened emphasis on socialist ideology during the Xi Jinping era encompasses both political and economic aspects. Politically, Xi Jinping is solidifying his rule by emphasizing the purity of socialist ideology and the corresponding governance rules within the CCP. Xi Jinping and the CCP view socialist ideology as a means to maintain the party's monopoly on power and ensure social stability. This is achieved through the propagation of socialist ideologies and the suppression of social discourse on alternatives. Externally, socialist indoctrination and nationalism aid Xi Jinping and the CCP in resisting foreign challenges to China's sovereignty.

Economically, Xi Jinping's China is using socialist ideology as the theoretical underpinning for its state-led economic model, exemplified by the "Made in China 2025" campaign and the Belt and Road Initiative. The CCP is utilizing socialist ideology to fight against social inequality and pursue social stability through domestic programs aimed at alleviating poverty, reforming healthcare, and solving housing issues. The CCP is also tightening its grip on the private sector, demanding that private enterprises "contribute" to the "common prosperity" under socialist ideals. Measures include prohibiting excessive accumulation of wealth, regulating tech giants, and increasing the party's real-time control over private enterprises.

While the grand strategy under former Chinese leaders was to "Hide your capabilities, and bide for your time," Xi Jinping's stated grand strategy is to transform China into a global power by 2050. Under this ambitious strategy, China is to become a "moderately prosperous society" by 2020, achieve "modernization of socialism" by 2035, and become a major global socialist power by 2050.[3]

The US response has been characterized by the "decoupling" strategy. Gradually retracting from interactions with China, the United States has attempted to isolate China through initiatives such as the Chip 4, IPEF, and the Quad. China, in turn, has pursued a strategy of maximizing self-sufficiency in its economy (i.e., reducing dependency on foreign markets, capital, and technology). Though the US-China competition is unlikely to mirror the progression of the Cold War, it is becoming increasingly evident that it will be a structuralized and prolonged standoff.

The fundamental challenge in the US-China competition lies in the necessity for both nations to cooperate even as they compete for survival. Straddling the fine line between reluctant cooperation and heated competition, the two nations face the risks emanating from the complexity and uncertainty inherent in their competition. Each nation grapples with managing the potential loss, uncertainty, and catastrophic clash as they endeavor to disentangle themselves from their erstwhile economic interdependence. They also face the hurdle of internal and external limitations in weaponizing their mutual economic interdependence.[4]

The US-China competition is fundamentally different from the Cold War between the United States and the USSR. While the Cold War was waged between two ideological camps with little or no economic interactions, the US-China competition today is rooted in mutual interdependence within a globalized world.

KOREA-US-CHINA TRIANGULAR MATRIX[5]

Composition of the Demand Structure of the Korea-US-China

Korea-US-China triangular relations are characterized by complexity, the risk of collision, and economic interdependence. These relations can be better understood by employing a set of six triangular matrices that illustrate the intersecting interests and demands among these three actors.

The dynamics of US-China relations are playing out on the regional and global levels, encompassing the three elements of cooperation, competition, and conflict. While the United States and China have a high level of economic interdependence, issues such as trade imbalances, national security concerns, and technology competition push the two nations into conflict. The United States perceives China's rise as a strategic challenge to its global leadership position and is engaging in competition across military, technological, and regional domains.

Historically, the Korea-US alliance originated from security needs in the face of the North Korean threat. Under this alliance, the United States has provided security guarantees for Korea, including deterrence against and protection from a potential North Korean invasion. However, over time, this military alliance has grown into a de-facto comprehensive alliance, encompassing politics, economy, trade, investment, culture, and personal exchanges.

In Korea-US-China triangular relations, the convergence and divergence of interests between any two actors usually occur simultaneously, affecting the third actor and the structure of the triangular relationship itself. For instance, a closer alliance between Korea and the United States affects both of their relationships with China, which may perceive the alliance as a potential threat to its interests in the region. Likewise, worsening US-China tensions affect the position of Korea within the triangle, challenging Korea to strike a balance to maximize its own security and stability.

By the nature of the relationship, Korea-US-China triangular relations entail crisscrossing interactions across security issues, economic interests, societal values, and national identities. This complex interplay is an inevitable result of the simultaneous competition and economic interdependence among the three parties. The compound modality of these relations limits the possibility of cooperative development and magnifies the difficulty of devising strategies.

Needless to say, to ensure maximum efficacy of the triangular matrix analysis, each actor must remain well informed of the details of world events transpiring within the international order and maintain an updated understanding of each actor's perceptions of the others. In other words, the strategic imperatives of the actors and the discrepancies among them serve as the data to be processed through the triangular matrix analysis. When executed properly, this analysis can pinpoint and prevent errors resulting from the sheer complexity of the compound modality of the Korea-US-China triangular relations.

The world is currently witnessing the international order's descent into sweeping conflicts and uncertainties. Russia's unprovoked invasion of Ukraine was swiftly followed by the Israeli-Palestinian War. While the US-China strategic competition has not yet reached the level of a physical confrontation, it is evolving into an across-the-board competition and confrontation. The geopolitical impasses surrounding the Taiwan Strait and the Korean Peninsula are causing considerable anxiety among policy makers. Furthermore, the Korea-US-Japan trilateral security pact has engendered China-Russia-North Korea trilateral cooperation, making the security dilemma even more structured than before. This has had the added effect of making the resolution of the North Korean nuclear issue that much more remote. Given these challenges, the need is more urgent than ever for a panoramic, bird's-eye view of the complexities of Korea-US-China relations.

In analyzing Korea-US-China triangular relations, it is crucial to simultaneously consider other triangular relations: Korea-US-Japan, China-Russia-North Korea, and Korea-China-Japan. For instance, a Korea-China-Japan summit could help alleviate China's discomfort regarding the formation of the Korea-US-Japan pact. Additionally, although China-Russia-North Korea cooperation evokes memories of the Cold War, it is important to remember that this cooperation is not showing signs of evolving into a formal framework. Above all, it is essential to shed light on the strategic implications and values of the Korea-US-Japan security pact, while also examining the interdependence and elements of conflict among the three actors.

The intersecting demands among the three actors of Korea-US-China relations can be visualized as depicted in table 11.1.

Table 11.1   Conflict in the Demand Structure

	United States	China	Korea
United States		① United States' demands from China	③ United States' demands from Korea
China	② China's demands from the United States		⑤ China's demands from Korea
Korea	④ Korea's demands from the United States	⑥ Korea's demands from China	

11.1. UNITED STATES' DEMANDS FROM CHINA

[Values and Ideology Sector]

- Expects China to uphold and comply with the liberal international order, norms, and institutions.
- Demands that China respect universal values such as democracy and human rights.

[Geopolitical Sector]

- Demands that China refrain from revisionist behaviors in the Indo-Pacific region.
- Advocates the maintenance of freedom of navigation in the Indo-Pacific region.

[Economic Sector]

- Advocates for maintaining decoupling policy in advanced technology with potential military application.
- Cooperation in other areas of economic activity is expected.

[Security Sector]

- Ensures vigilance against China's emergence as a military superpower.
- Opposes China's provision of weapons to Russia.
- Acknowledges the inevitability of cooperation between the United States and China in dealing with transnational threats.
- Requires China's influence in the Global South to be contained.
- Demands the maintenance of the status quo in the Taiwan strait.
- Expects China to play a constructive role in solving the North Korea issue.
- Advocates for managed competition to prevent armed conflict between the United States and China.

In the geopolitical dimension, the United States wants stability and security in the Indo-Pacific region. This entails effectively managing South China Sea disputes, achieving peaceful resolution of conflicts, and ensuring freedom of navigation in international waters. The United States seeks to manage its relationship with China in a way that protects its interests both bilaterally and within the broader international community.

The United States aims to resolve trade imbalances and ensure fair competition in its economic relationship with China. This includes addressing issues such as intellectual property theft, barriers to market access, and unfair trade practices. The United States attributes China's rapid technological advancement to these unfair practices, expressing its intolerance toward China's rise in the sector. Amid the increasing significance of sharp power diplomacy, substantial efforts are being made to thwart China's covert infiltration into American political and social domains. This strategic goal is closely aligned with the United States' economic security policy, which aims to mitigate China-related risks through a de-risking strategy. This involves curbing China's rise in the advanced technology sector, particularly semiconductors, and weakening China's dominance in critical supply chains.

The United States' concerns about China's rise span across multiple dimensions, with "technology" emerging as the most critical domain. Considering China's advancements in technology, particularly in AI and telecommunications, the United States intends to maintain its technological superiority over China. This involves protecting critical technologies, preventing forced technology transfers, and promoting innovation domestically. The ultimate goal for the United States seems to be to prevent China from obtaining cutting-edge semiconductor technology and manufacturing capabilities.

In terms of values, the United States advocates for human rights and democracy in China, emphasizing principles such as political freedom, religious freedom, and respect for basic human rights. It hopes for resolutions to issues such as the treatment of the Uyghurs in Xinjiang, the preservation of autonomy in Hong Kong, and the protection of political and cultural rights in Tibet.

Even amid their strategic competition, the United States and China can find areas of mutual interest to pursue. First, both the United States and China seek to benefit from maintaining a stable trade relationship and economic interdependence. Bilateral trade between the two countries is significant, and they are each other's major trade partners. Cooperation in trade and investment stimulates economic growth and creates opportunities for businesses and consumers in both countries. Both the United States and China have a stake in maintaining global economic stability. As the world's two largest economic powers, their economic policies and actions have a significant impact on the global economy. Cooperation between the United States and China on issues such as financial regulation, currency stability, and economic governance can contribute to a stable and prosperous global economic system.

The United States also recognizes the need for cooperation with China to confront global challenges such as climate change, nuclear nonproliferation, and pandemic response. Addressing climate change and environmental issues requires international cooperation and coordination. Both the United States and China recognize the importance of tackling environmental challenges such as air and water pollution, deforestation, and greenhouse gas emissions. Cooperation on clean energy technologies, environmental conservation, and climate mitigation efforts can benefit both countries as well as the global community.

Additionally, the experience of the COVID-19 pandemic has underscored the importance of international cooperation in addressing global health issues. Both the United States and China share a common interest in containing the spread of infectious diseases, improving healthcare infrastructure, and strengthening pandemic preparedness and response mechanisms. Cooperation in vaccine development, healthcare provision, and disease surveillance can contribute significantly to global health security.

Thus, while the United States and China engage in strategic competition across various domains such as geopolitics and technology, there are also areas where their interests overlap, making cooperation possible. Recognizing and leveraging these shared interests can aid in managing tensions and enhancing mutual benefits in the international political and economic arenas. However, achieving meaningful cooperation requires effective diplomacy and negotiation, as well as a willingness to seek common ground despite differences and competition.

11.2. CHINA'S DEMANDS FROM THE UNITED STATES

[Geopolitical Sector]

- Opposes US containment strategies (e.g., the Indo-Pacific strategy).
- Opposes US strategy of creating blocs (No bloc games).

[Security Sector]

- Strongly opposes infringement on its core interests.
- Demands the dismantling of US encirclement of China.
- Demands respect for the "One China" principle.
- Opposes U.S. arms sales to Taiwan.

[Economic Sector]

- Opposes the politicization of economic issues.
- Opposes the United States applying pressure on China through supply chain realignment and trade tariffs.
- Expects limited competition but hopes for stabilization in US-China relations.
- Expects to maintain exchange and cooperation in science and technology sectors.
- Refrains from of US sanctions (possibility of using Foreign Relations Law).
- Opposes US interference in its internal affairs.

China opposes US efforts to contain its development through strategies such as the Indo-Pacific strategy and counters US attempts to isolate it by forming opposition blocs. However, China does not desire conflict with the United States and hopes for stability in US-China relations, seeking to manage the relationship to prevent catastrophic confrontation. Nonetheless, China recognizes that competition between the two nations is inevitable. China regards US involvement in the Taiwan issue as a violation of its sovereignty and the One China principle. It claims to oppose the politicization of economic issues and stresses the unfairness of US sanctions.

China's strategy toward the United States is complex. As China envisions a Sino-centric world order, it finds itself in conflict with the US-led liberal world order. This clash is inevitable, and the struggle for national power and international leadership between the two countries is likely to continue in the long term. However, at present, both countries prefer to engage in competition within certain guardrails, avoiding outright conflict. This preference stems from a prevailing atmosphere in both countries that prioritizes domestic politics and the welfare of their citizens.

11.3. UNITED STATES' DEMANDS FROM KOREA

[Security Sector]

- Demands Korea secure a robust defense posture against North Korea's threats.
- Requests medium-to-long term Korean participation in the strategy of countering China.

- Coordinates the complexity of convergence and divergence between Korea and the United States in the context of countering China.
- Seeks Korea's active participation in pressuring China and Russia, while calling for involvement in NATO to expand the scope of participation.

[Geopolitical Sector]

- Urges Korea's active participation and contribution to the Indo-Pacific strategy.
- Advocates for Korea's active involvement in trilateral cooperation with the United States and Japan.

[Economic Sector]

- Encourages expansion of cooperation concerning policy resources necessary for the United States' strategy to strengthen its economy.
- Expects an active role from Korea in supply chain restructuring, including participation in initiatives like Chip 4.
- Advocates for economic security cooperation between the countries.
- Applies pressure through legislation such as the Inflation Reduction Act (IRA).

[Values and Ideology Sector]

- Ensures Korea's key role in the reconstruction of the liberal order led by the United States.

As strategic competition between the United States and China intensifies, the United States recognizes the strategic importance of Korea's role and cooperation. In response to China's military expansion in the Indo-Pacific region, the United States aims to integrate Korea into a broader regional defense structure. This involves strengthening trilateral security cooperation among the United States, Korea, and Japan, as well as fostering multilateral security partnerships with other regional allies and partners. Particularly in the context of countering China's economic influence, the United States seeks to align Korea's economic policies and trade practices with its strategic interests and objectives. This includes resolving trade imbalances, enhancing market access for US companies, and promoting fair competition in key sectors such as technology and telecommunications.

Furthermore, to maintain technological superiority and competitiveness in key strategic sectors, the United States aims to strengthen cooperation with Korea in the technology and innovation fields. This entails leveraging Korea's expertise in areas such as semiconductor manufacturing, 5G communications, and advanced manufacturing to foster innovation and technological leadership for mutual benefit.

The United States also seeks to closely cooperate with Korea on regional security issues extending beyond the Korean Peninsula, including maritime security, territorial disputes, and freedom of navigation in the South China Sea. This collaboration aims to promote a rules-based order, uphold international law, and address common security challenges arising from China's unilateral actions in the region.

Ultimately, the United States aims to enhance security cooperation, economic ties, technology collaboration, and a cooperative framework for addressing regional security issues with Korea within the context of strategic competition with China. Close coordination and cooperation between the two countries are essential in advancing mutual interests, promoting regional stability, and addressing strategic challenges in the Indo-Pacific region.

11.4. KOREA'S DEMANDS FROM THE UNITED STATES

[Values and Ideology Sector]

- Advocates for an international order where "like-minded countries" and middle powers multilaterally coordinate each other's positions, rather than unilateral US leadership.

[Geopolitical and Security Sector]

- Advocates for the identification and expansion of convergent interests.
- Expects the United States to respect Korea's divergent geopolitical and geoeconomic interests.
- Seeks to strengthen security cooperation but has concerns about US protectionism in the economic sector.
- Recognizes the importance of the Korea-US alliance amid US-China strategic competition and North Korea's nuclear threat.
- Requires flexibility within the US nuclear nonproliferation framework.
- Seeks strengthened nuclear deterrence against North Korea.
- Hopes to strengthen the Korean public's trust in US nuclear umbrella assurance.

[Economic Sector]

- Seeks stronger cooperation in the fields of economic security and advanced science and technology.
- Advocates for a fair sharing of alliance benefits and costs.

[Diplomacy Sector]

- Calls for coordination of Korean Peninsula policy depending on the outcome of the 2024 US presidential election.

Korea currently faces complex challenges in both regional security and regional economic dimensions. First, the persistent threat posed by North Korea's nuclear weapons program and conventional military capabilities keeps the region in a state of geopolitical tension. Despite diplomatic efforts aimed at the denuclearization of the Korean Peninsula, North Korea's ongoing missile tests and provocative actions continue to pose security challenges. Korea's security is intricately linked with its alliance with the United States. However, the onset of US-China strategic competition has led to uncertainties regarding US strategic intentions due to doubts about its commitment to allies like Korea and potential shifts in strategic priorities, causing instability and exacerbating Korea's security concerns.

Korea finds itself in a region characterized by complex geopolitical dynamics, including competition among major powers such as the US, China, Japan, and Russia. Tensions stemming from historical grievances and territorial disputes, coupled with power struggles in Northeast Asia, pose formidable challenges to peace and security. To maintain a stable and forward-looking Korea-US alliance, careful coordination and cooperation between Korea and the United States are imperative. Differences in strategic priorities and domestic political factors between the two countries can sometimes strain the alliance and hinder effective decision-making. During the Trump administration, tensions and debates emerged regarding cost-sharing for the presence of US forces in Korea. Negotiating a fair and rational cost-sharing agreement is crucial to sustaining the alliance's viability.

As China's influence in the region expands, the Korea-US alliance faces significant challenges. From Korea's perspective, its economic relations with China and the strategic balance between China and the United States add complexity to the dynamics of the alliance. Geo-economically, the Korean economy heavily relies on international trade, particularly with China and the United States. Disruptions in global supply chains resulting from trade frictions between major economies or external shocks like the

COVID-19 pandemic significantly impact Korea's economic growth and stability.

In the era of US-China strategic competition, Korea strategically pursues several key goals in its relationship with the United States. First, Korea requires continuous security guarantees and support from the United States to counter potential threats from North Korea and maintain peace and stability on the Korean Peninsula. This entails a strong interest in sustaining the presence of US troops in Korea, conducting joint military exercises and fostering security cooperation to address regional security challenges. These goals can be achieved through strengthening the Korea-US alliance, which is considered fundamental to Korea's national security and defense strategy. This underscores the importance of enhancing interoperability, coordination, and cooperation between the two countries' militaries, as well as maintaining high-level diplomatic relations and strategic dialogues to align security interests and policies.

Korea also requires diplomatic support from the United States to address regional security issues involving North Korea, territorial disputes, and maritime security challenges both on the Korean Peninsula and across the broader Indo-Pacific region. Close collaboration includes fostering peace and stability and promoting denuclearization through multilateral forums and diplomatic initiatives.

Second, Korea aims to enhance economic cooperation and trade relations with the United States to ensure sustained prosperity and growth. This necessitates efforts to improve market access, expand investment opportunities, and cooperate on technology transfer, intellectual property protection, and innovation.

Third, Korea seeks to establish partnerships with the United States in advanced science and technology and innovation fields. With Korea's competitive advantage and technological leadership in key areas such as semiconductor manufacturing, telecommunications, and advanced manufacturing, enhancing partnerships with the United States in technology and innovation is crucial for sustaining and advancing this leadership. This requires cooperation on joint initiatives for research and development, technology transfers, innovation, and enhancing competitiveness in the global market.

In conclusion, Korea's strategic goals in its relationship with the United States in the era of US-China strategic competition center on security assurance and alliance reinforcement, diplomatic and economic cooperation, and technology partnerships. Close coordination and cooperation with the United States are essential for Korea to address regional security challenges, promote economic growth, and maintain a strategic position in the Indo-Pacific region.

11.5. CHINA'S DEMANDS FROM KOREA

[Security Sector]

- Expects Korea to exercise restraint against the United States' containment strategy toward China.
- Demands that Korea minimize its anti-China stance.
- Ensures that Korea refrains from acting in a way that provokes China.
- Expects Korea to refrain from participating in trilateral cooperation with the United States and Japan.
- Demands that Korea acknowledge North Korea's security concerns.
- Demands respect for its core interests, including the One China principle.
- Requests appropriate handling of THAAD.

[Economic Sector]

- Demands that Korea prioritize maintaining economic cooperation with China, especially in semiconductor and raw material sectors necessary for China's economic development.
- Emphasizes close cooperation in economic security sectors.
- Expects Korea to respect China's development model.

[Diplomacy Sector]

- Expects Korea to maintain cooperation in addressing transnational threats and emerging security issues.
- Expects sustained cooperation with Korea on a cultural level.
- Urges Korea to soften its anti-China sentiments.

During the Xi Jinping era, Korea and China's relationship has faced several challenges and potential threats. First, China views the Korea-US alliance as a strategic challenge to its regional influence. The presence of US troops in Korea and joint military exercises between the two countries are perceived as direct threats to China's security interests in the region. Particularly in the context of extensive US-China strategic competition, China aims to draw Korea onto its side to bolster or balance its influence. However, with growing anti-China public sentiment in Korea, Beijing recognizes the limited public support for Korea aligning with China in the US-China strategic competition. Beijing seeks to manage this situation by ensuring that Korea does not pose a significant threat to China. China's primary concern revolves around the issue of THAAD deployment. China opposes Korea's deployment of the Terminal High Altitude Area Defense (THAAD) system, viewing it as a threat to its own security interests. China argues that the deployment of THAAD could undermine its strategic deterrence and surveillance capabilities. Against the backdrop of security and defense cooperation, the enduring strategic bond between the United States and Korea presents a challenge to China's efforts to expand its influence in the region.

China perceives Korea's participation in US-led initiatives such as joint military exercises and regional security cooperation mechanisms as attempts to encircle or contain China, undermining its strategic interests. Within the framework of regional security partnerships, including multilateral security cooperation, Korea's involvement challenges China's aspirations for regional leadership and influence. By engaging in security dialogues and defense cooperation initiatives with Japan, Australia, and Southeast Asian nations, Korea is shaping a regional security architecture that diverges from China's national interests. China expects Korea to contribute to maintaining the status quo in the region and refrain from taking sides in situations that could lead to regional military conflicts or instability. However, Korea's current unfavorable view toward China stemming from domestic political factors complicates the situation. Essentially, China aims to encourage Korea to maintain a balance of strategic interests and partnerships between the United States and China. In the context of US-China strategic competition, China seeks Korea's cooperation in advancing its strategic interests and desires close collaboration with Korea in the Indo-Pacific region.

11.6. KOREA'S DEMANDS FROM CHINA

[Values and Ideology Sector]

- Demands respect for sovereignty, order, norms, institutions, and universal values.
- Demands that China uphold the principle of reciprocity.
- Opposes Korea-China relations being dependent on Korea-US relations.

[Geopolitical and Security Sector]

- Requires China's constructive role and cooperation in the denuclearization of North Korea and achieving peace on the Korean Peninsula.
- Expresses concerns over China's reduced participation in sanctioning North Korea's nuclear build-up due to US-China strategic competition.

- Emphasizes the importance of avoiding politicizing or securitizing nonpolitical or nonsecurity issues and interests.
- Hopes for stability and a peaceful resolution in the Taiwan Strait.

[Economic Sector]

- Expects China to refrain from economic retaliatory measures (i.e., no economic coercion).
- Advocates for a gradual reduction of economic interdependence.
- Requires appropriate responses to the US export controls to China and restrictions on technology cooperation.
- Expects China to ensure continued economic exchanges while engaged in economic competition.

[Diplomacy Sector]

- Highlights the common interests between Korea and China in the areas of economics, diplomacy, culture, and emerging issues.
- Advocates for expanding diplomatic dialogues to broaden cooperation opportunities in areas such as the environment, nuclear nonproliferation, health, and people-to-people exchanges to serve as a diplomatic bridge for an Asian multilateral regional order inclusive of China.

Korea faces multifaceted challenges in both regional security and economic domains. First, amid North Korea's nuclear weapons program and conventional military threats, Korea prioritizes achieving peace and stability on the Korean Peninsula. To this end, Korea continues to pursue productive economic relations with China through expanded trade ties, investment opportunities, participation in multilateral economic cooperation organizations, and other collaborative efforts. Second, maintaining peace and security on the Korean Peninsula requires China's constructive engagement. This entails addressing North Korea's security threats, promoting denuclearization and dialogue, and preventing military escalations or conflicts that could disrupt the region's stability. These strategic objectives are complemented by enhancing diplomatic cooperation with China to resolve regional security issues and enhance dialogue and cooperation on shared interests. This includes active participation in multilateral forums, diplomatic initiatives, and confidence-building measures aimed at building trust in the region and reducing tensions. Furthermore, strengthening cultural and people-to-people exchanges with China aims to enhance mutual understanding, foster friendship, and strengthen bilateral relations. This involves promoting tourism, facilitating educational exchanges, and conducting public diplomacy initiatives to deepen ties and foster goodwill.

Korea's external relations are intricately woven into a triangular dynamic centered around the United States, leading to careful consideration of its relationship with the United States while pursuing strategic objectives with China. Particularly in the context of escalating geopolitical conflicts between the United States and China, diplomatic challenges arise in maintaining the delicate balance of interests and partnerships between allies. Korea must prioritize its national interests while enhancing regional stability and cooperation and considering global interests in its foreign policy. Consequently, addressing regional security issues and promoting economic growth through relations with China are crucial strategic objectives for maintaining peace and stability not only on the Korean Peninsula but also across the entire Indo-Pacific region.

Additionally, Korea faces economic security challenges in its relations with China. When China imposes economic sanctions on Korea, vulnerabilities within Korea's supply chain of strategic materials become apparent. Given Korea's significant role in global semiconductor manufacturing and supply chains, it could suffer significant repercussions from Chinese export restrictions or sanctions targeting semiconductor-related companies. The reliance on China for semiconductor materials compounds the risks posed by these sanctions. Vulnerabilities are further highlighted in energy imports, where external dependency leaves Korea susceptible to threats to energy security and price stability if China implements sanctions on energy imports. To proactively address crises related to strategic material and supply chains, Korea must diversify its industries, effectively manage strategic inventory, secure alternative materials and sources, and strengthen international cooperation and alliance relationships to mitigate risks.

The six mutual demands and expectations derived from the trilateral relationship among the United States, China, and Korea reflect the complexity inherent in this trilateral dynamic. However, these demands represent merely the first step in the matrix analysis of the US-China-Korea trilateral relationship. A deeper exploration of mutual conflicts and dilemmas is necessary for a more comprehensive and intricate analysis.

Complexity, Collision, and Interdependence in Korea-US-China Relations

Complexity

When analyzing the intricate and complex triangle formed by the United States, Korea, and China, we cannot ignore the additional complexity introduced by the other three triangles within the Northeast Asia region. The first triangle includes Korea, the United States, and Japan, signifying the foundation of the Camp David Declaration in August 18, 2023. This development was a masterful move considering that the United States and Japan alone would not be able to stem the tide of China's expansionist ambitions in the South China Sea, the East China Sea, and with regards to Taiwan. The second triangle consists of Korea, Japan, and China. As they successfully held a trilateral summit in Seoul in May 26-27, 2024, it could significantly mitigate China's dissatisfaction with the Korea-US-Japan trilateral security pact. The last triangle is among China, Russia, and North Korea. It represents a new Cold War scenario, although relations remain tenuous.

Russia has become concerned about the balance of power in Northeast Asia, prompting it to pursue a strategy of fostering closer ties with North Korean leader Kim Jong-un. It appears that North Korea will receive missile technology, food, and energy in exchange for providing Russia with conventional weapons, bullets, and shells needed for its war in Ukraine. However, the consolidation of the North Korea-China-Russia triangular cooperation framework, which is emerging as a counterweight to the Korea-US-Japan trilateral security pact, hinges on various circumstances. If the Korea-US-Japan trilateral security pact is strengthened, the North Korea-China-Russia triangular cooperation framework is likely to follow suit. This is the current state of affairs in Northeast Asia: two triangular power blocs in opposition to each other. However, at present, the North Korea-China-Russia triangular cooperation does not appear likely to evolve into a solid alliance due to diverging interests, especially China's discontent with North Korea-Russia's illegal aspects of collaboration. China's previously amicable stance toward North Korea has gradually become more uncomfortable keeping a noticeable distance. It appears that Kim Jong-un has opted for Russia as a realistic survival partner, recognizing the practicality

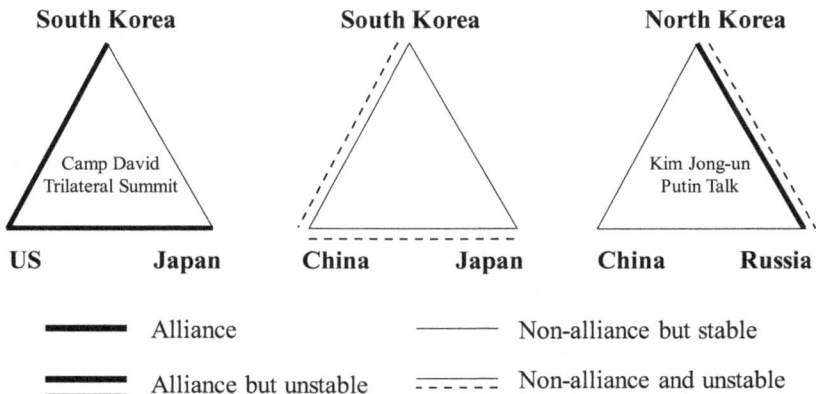

Figure 11.1   Three Triangle in the Geopolitics in Northeast Asia.

of mutual benefits over a more lukewarm China, which has been mindful of U.S. relations. The future of the North Korea-China-Russia triangle will ultimately be determined by the outcome of the Ukraine conflict and the stability of the Korea-US-Japan trilateral cooperative framework.

In addition to these, two more triangular minilateral cooperative frameworks are forming: the Korea-Japan-China triangle and the Korea-US-China triangle. However, both of these triangular frameworks involve China, and as such, have inherent elements of conflict. They require a new environment to be successful. Therefore, to fully understand the complexities of the Korea-US-China triangular relations, the remaining three triangular relationships must be factored into the calculation. Recent developments within Korea-US-China triangular relations can be attributed to the influences of these three other triangular relationships.

The Korea-US relationship has entered a belated honeymoon phase following the Camp David Declaration. Notably, the Camp David Declaration and the resulting Korea-US-Japan trilateral security framework represent the most formidable shield against China's expansionist strategy witnessed thus far. This framework places significant constraints on China's ambitions to unify Taiwan, by force if necessary. It will also affect China's stance on North Korea's nuclear weapons program. Meanwhile, it should be noted that the Korea-China-Japan triangular relationship has lost some of its momentum since Xi Jinping came to power.

The Korea-US alliance, originally formed as a security partnership, should expand its scope to encompass the cutting-edge science and technology sector. While Korea has enjoyed a mutually complementary economic relationship with China over the past four decades, it now realizes that forging a mutually complementary economic coexistence with the United States is the way forward. Korea is closely monitoring China's internal workings and its strategic maneuvers abroad with deep concern, and firmly believes that Korea and the United States share a common destiny regardless of what may transpire in the coming years.

Over the past few decades, China's share of Korea's trade-to-GDP ratio reached a high of 25 percent, reflecting the successful economic complementarity between the two countries. This ratio fell to 19.5 percent in late 2023 due to of the downturn in the Chinese economy. Despite this, Korea-China relations are still characterized by both competition and complementarity. However, this critical relationship is now spiraling down a rabbit hole.

China feels surrounded, especially in light of the US-Japan-Korea trilateral pact. This feeling is exacerbated by the ongoing strained relations between Korea and China since the 2016 THAAD crisis. Simultaneously, the United States is pressuring Korea to restrict its semiconductor exports to China, effectively expanding the scope of the Korea-US military alliance to encompass economic and technological domains. Consequently, Korea's exports to

China will see a substantial loss. On top of this, China is enacting retaliatory measures to limit imports from Korea.

For Korea, these developments signify a loss of economic complementarity with China. They will also likely lead to a reduction in China's ability to influence Korea's policymaking. China may be forced to step back from its aggressive stance vis-a-vis the United States due to domestic political instability, the demise of its market economy, and the escalating costs of strategic competition with the United States.

Points of Collision

US-China

As competition between the United Station and China intensified, their relationship transitioned from one of mutually supportive complementarity to confrontation. Ultimately, China began to challenge the United States in the capital goods market, particularly in the advanced technology and platform sectors (5G, 6G), and to engage in sharp power diplomacy, intellectual property theft, and cyber hacking.

The United States underestimated China's potential for growth. In fact, China's rise to become the world's second-largest economy was largely made possible by US-led globalization, neoliberalism, and free trade. As China's economy rapidly expanded, its market influence spread like wildfire. It was only later that the United States recognized China's expansionism as a significant threat to its national security.

Currently, the dynamics of US-China relations are showing signs of change. The two major powers have been exhausting themselves by concentrating on each other's weaknesses and vulnerabilities. Many experts assert that it is now crucial to establish a foundation for dialogue and negotiation to effectively manage tensions and conflicts. We are at a turning point where we must shift from an all-out rivalry to a managed rivalry. It is time for the United States to reassess its long-term strategy toward China to pursue coexistence while respecting the respective red lines that each country should not cross, rather than engaging in confrontation.

Korea-China

When considering the points of collision between Korea and China, it is crucial to note that Korea's industrial restructuring and highly productive manufacturing sector greatly benefited from China's economic boom. This is how the Korean economy grew increasingly dependent on the Chinese economy, and through this process, China gained more political influence over the Korean government.

In this context, China's stance on North Korea is an essential factor in Korea's national security. Korea expects China to maintain its neutral stance toward North Korea. Similarly, China demands that Korea maintain a middle ground between the United States and China. However, Korea's stance on this issue remains firm. Korea is unwilling to risk subordination to China and will not allow the Korea-US alliance to destabilize. Naturally, Korea aims to prevent collision and instead seeks a path of coexistence, thereby avoiding extreme conflicts and safeguarding strategies that protect its sovereignty, survival, identity, and national interests.

With the Camp David Declaration, which provides security assurances and promotes the benefits of coexistence, it seems that Korea has chosen the path of a closer alliance with the United States. This puts Korea on a collision course with China. At this juncture, the remaining task is to explore strategies to further reduce friction and seek coexistence with China.

Korea-US

Meanwhile, the points of collision between the United States and Korea revolve around whether the deterrence against the North Korean nuclear threat provided by the Camp David Declaration is sufficient. Likewise, there also seem to be concerns within the US Congress, as they recall the Moon administration's pro-China stance. In contrast, the Yoon administration aims to strengthen the Korea-US alliance, the Korea-US-Japan trilateral security framework, and the technological cooperation framework. It is boldly moving away from the "U.S. for security, China for economy" mindset. However, Korea's general elections in April 2024 resulted in the left-wing opposition gaining a lopsided dominance in the parliament.

The second point of collision pertains to whether the United States can avoid infringing on Korea's national interests while seeking cooperation with its policy of restricting exports of advanced science and technology to China. It is the goal of the United States to reduce China's dominance in critical supply chains and restrain China's ascent in the advanced technology sector.

However, semiconductors account for 40 percent of Korea's total exports to China, and the semiconductor industry contributes to 25 percent of Korea's gross value added. Korea's cooperation in the United States de-risking strategy might not only result in a significant reduction in Korea's semiconductor exports to China but also serious deterioration of the Korea-China relationship.

Points of Collision among Korea, United States, and China

Amid the continuing great power competition, the US-China rivalry has grown beyond conflicting national interests to mutual security threats, taking on the characteristics of a new Cold War. Although the situation has not

Table 11.2   Points of Collision among Korea, United States, and China

	Korea	United States	China
Korea		• Allow Korea's independent nuclear policy I Exercise restraint in setting defense cost-sharing amount I Avoid harming Korea's national interests through economic protectionism	• Actively participate in the efforts to suppress North Korea's provocations and nuclear weapons program I Refrain from infringing on Korea's national security and sovereignty I Uphold commitments to the separation of military and economic affairs I Exercise restraint in implementing retaliatory economic measures
United States	• Prevent close ties with China I Adopt a more accommodating stance toward cooperation with Japan I Bear an appropriate burden in defense cost sharing I Exercise restraint in promoting pro-nuclear weapons development sentiments		• Avoid any changes in the status quo in the Taiwan Strait I Address human rights issues in Xinjiang and Tibet I Uphold universal values such as democracy I Refrain from unfair trade practices
China	• Exercise restraint in pro-US policy, such as the Indo-Pacific strategy I Adhere to China's principles on the Taiwan issue I Exercise restraint in excessive closeness with the United States	• Lift trade sanctions on China I Justify decoupling and derisking strategies, especially in relation to advanced technologies such as semiconductors I Avoid infringements on core national interests, such as the Taiwan issue	

resulted in a physical war, it has heightened the uncertainties surrounding US-China relations. In the midst of these geopolitical shifts among the great powers, Korea is confronted with threats to its sovereignty and survival.

In this triangular relationship, each country has demands directed toward the other two, resulting in six crisscrossing points of collision in the intricate dance of the revolving triangles.

The United States is resolutely opposed to any changes in the status quo of the Taiwan Strait. It also opposes China's human rights violations in Xinjiang, Tibet, and Hong Kong. Furthermore, the United States feels deeply uneasy about Xi Jinping's China shunning universal values like democracy.

The United States wants Korea to restore cooperative relationships with Japan, thereby strengthening the Korea-US-Japan trilateral security cooperative framework. Before the Camp David declaration on 16 August, 2023, the United States was frequently frustrated by Korea's reluctant attitude in this matter. Additionally, the United States wants Korea to bear a more significant share of the defense costs of the Korea-US alliance. Moreover, the United States is concerned about the rising public support in Korea for the country to develop its own nuclear capabilities.

There is significant negative public opinion regarding the excessive demand by the United States for Korea to share in defense costs. Koreans want an equitable settlement on this issue. Trust in the United States is waning, as reflected in public opinion polls, which indicate that US-centric protectionist measures, such as the Inflation Reduction Act, are harming Korea's national interests.

Korean public sentiment toward China is at an all-time low. Koreans feel that China has no respect for Korea's sovereignty and national security. There is growing anger among Koreans toward China's enforcement of economic sanctions directed against Korea.

China is upset by Korea's continued alignment with the United States on the Taiwan issue, viewing it is an act of interference in domestic politics and a violation of its sovereignty.

China feels that the United States has intentionally suppressed China's development through trade wars and the implementation of the decoupling strategy. China particularly opposes the United States decoupling or derisking strategies targeting cutting-edge technologies like semiconductors.

Interdependence

By now, it is evident that all points of collision are floating on an undercurrent of extensive economic interdependence. Korea-US-China relations will continue to revolve around competition, conflict, and negotiation, paving the way for a new order. In this process, Korea finds itself in a significant dilemma. Korea stands at a crossroads.

In the past, the relationship between Korea and China had been a dependent variable of US-China relations. However, several factors are now becoming constants. The fact that Korea shares the same values and sails in the same boat with the United States is becoming a constant in its diplomacy with China. Furthermore, Korea no longer tolerates any encroachment on its sovereignty by China; this, too, has become a constant.

In terms of security cooperation, Korea is in the same boat as the United States. However, dialogue and communication with China are necessary to ensure that this cooperation does not hinder Korea-China relations. In maintaining this international posture, wedged between the United States and China, Korea is at risk of having the very foundation of its survival shaken. The United States must be sensitive to this fear within Korea. The United States must consider the national interests of its allies in its ongoing strategic competition with China.

Despite the intensifying US-China competition, the economic interdependence between the two countries has continued to expand as a result of their economic complementarity. Economic complementarity is evident between Korea and China as well as between Korea and the United States, as illustrated in the table below. These intersecting complementarities have acted as a safety valve, preventing a military confrontation despite hostility along ideological and security lines. The decoupling policy was made untenable due to the reality of existing economic complementarity, in addition to complaints from allies that it violated their respective national interests. The result was a shift to the ambiguous de-risking strategy.

Economic Competition and Cooperation

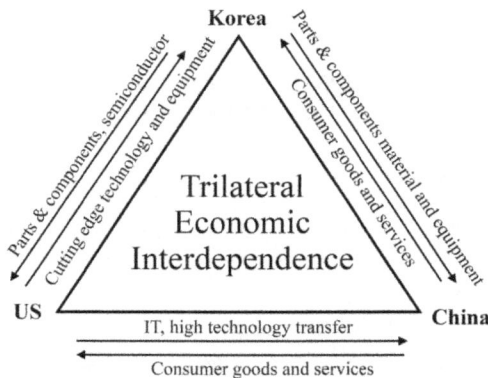

Figure 11.2 Economic Competition and Cooperation. Source: Extracted from Duck-Koo Chung's presentation titled 'Korea-China Relations Amidst U.S.-China Strategic Competition and Economic Interdependence,' which was used during a seminar at the Brookings Institution on October 10, 2023.

Korea's Economic and Industrial Complementarity with China and the US

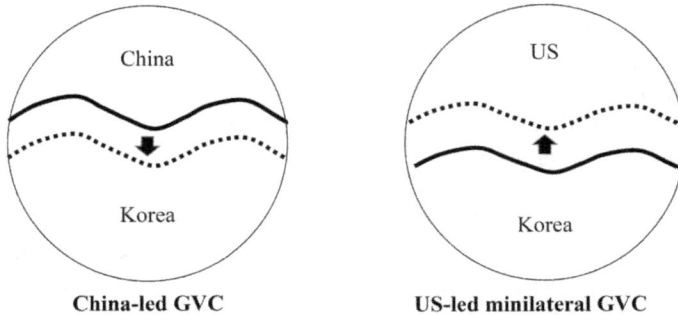

| China-led GVC | US-led minilateral GVC |

Figure 11.3 Korea's Economic and Industrial Complementarity with China and the United States. Source: Extracted from Duck-Koo Chung's presentation titled 'Korea-China Relations Amidst U.S.-China Strategic Competition and Economic Interdependence,' which was used during a seminar at the Brookings Institution on October 10, 2023.

The economic complementarity between Korea and China, which has persisted over the past forty years, is weakening due to fundamental changes in the value chain between the two countries. China's share of Korea's exports fell from its peak of 25 percent to the current 19 percent. The inevitable implication of this decline is that unless Korea develops new cutting-edge science and technology, this percentage could plummet to as low as 15 percent. Additionally, as Korea's share in the China-led global value chain diminishes, it's share in the US-led global value chain is expected to rise.

MANAGING COMPLEXITY, COLLISION, AND INTERDEPENDENCE

Future Direction for Korea

How should Korea navigate the complexity, points of collision, and interdependence among the three countries from its perspective?

Korea's traditional posture over the past couple of decades can be summed up by the dichotomy "U.S. for security, China for economy." However, with China encountering profound economic difficulties and the economic complementarity between Korea and China diminishing, Korea's dependence on China has declined as well. Consequently, a fundamental rethinking of Korea's survival strategy has become imperative.

First, it is urgent to expand the Korea-US alliance from one centered solely on security to one encompassing economic and industrial complementarity, particularly in the area of cutting-edge science and technology. Any points of collision of interests must be managed based on the principle of reciprocity.

Second, Korea must strengthen its management of the points of collision of interests between itself and China. China fears the repercussions of the Korea-US-Japan trilateral pact that emerged from the 2023 Camp David declaration, as well as the expansion of the Korea-US alliance into the areas of cultural exchange and advanced science and technology. Thus, Korea must make its red lines clear to China and manage its relationship with China by erecting appropriate guardrails. Korea must also be careful not to let the different value systems of the two countries lead to a security standoff. In the long run, it is in Korea's best interest to pursue a China policy aimed at promoting coexistence.

Third, Korea needs to position itself as an indispensable partner to both the United States and China, rather than a minor power wedged between two giants. This will require a concerted effort to further advance Korea's scientific and technological capabilities. Korea also needs to improve and expand its manufacturing capabilities in core strategic areas and manufacturing equipment essential to both the United States and China.

Future Direction for China

Meanwhile, China should refrain from utilizing economic interdependence as a means of retaliation, interference, or pressuring neighboring states. Particularly, China should stop engaging in sharp power diplomacy, intellectual property theft, and cyber hacking. Instead, by prioritizing the welfare and human rights of its citizens over its expansionist agenda, China can significantly contribute to creating a more harmonious world. China should also uphold its long-standing promise of balancing Chinese socialism and a market economy by maintaining a separation between politics and the economy. Further, China should strive to minimize conflict with other nations in pursuing Xi Jinping's China Dream. Lastly, by not breaching the United States' red lines, China can pave the way for mutual understanding, coexistence, and global prosperity.

Future Direction for the United States

The military might of the United States is incomparable to that of any other country. The US security umbrella provides Korea with a decisive deterrence effect. Furthermore, the influence of the US dollar has a significant impact on the global economy and finance.

In addition to these strategic assets, there is another essential asset crucial to the allies of the United States—the trust asset. The United States must gain the trust of its allies regardless of its domestic political situation. Only then can allies willingly and aggressively participate on the side of the United States in countering countries like China and Russia.

While the United States and its allies share values and sail in the same boat, the United States must ensure that the US-China rivalry does not jeopardize their survival. The United States must always be mindful of the economic interdependence of its allies when formulating strategies to curb China's expansionism.

CONVERGENT AND DIVERGENT INTERESTS IN KOREA-US-CHINA TRIANGULAR RELATIONS

With the aid of table 11.3 depicting convergent and divergent interests among Korea, the United States, and China, several key conclusions can be drawn.

First, the convergent interests from the Korean perspective are (1) Dialogue and cooperation in US-China relations; (2) Participation by the United States and China in resolving common international issues; (3) Restraining China on the North Korean nuclear issue; (4) Expansion of military and security technology cooperation among the United States, Korea, and Japan; (5) Expansion of NATO cohesion; (6) Strengthening and expanding the US-Korea alliance; (7) Expansion of complementary industrial relationships between the United States and Korea; (8) Enhancement of the US-Korea-Japan deterrence against North Korean nuclear threats; (9) Enhancement of Korea's capabilities in advanced technology; (10) Membership in CHIP4 for Korea; and (11) Pursuit of independent nuclear capabilities by Korea. The divergent interests from the Korean perspective are: (1) Deterioration of and conflict in US-China relations; (2) Escalation of tension over China's potential invasion of Taiwan; (3) Improving relations among China, North Korea, and Russia; (4) Failure in managing China's economic crises; (5) Economic retaliation and diplomatic pressure by China against Korea; (6) Restriction by the United States on semiconductor exports to China; (7) US isolationism and Trumpism; (8) Shifting the center of gravity in semiconductor manufacturing to Japan; and (9) Increase in defense expenditure by Korea for US forces stationed in Korea.

Utilizing the triangular matrix analysis, Korea's preferred foreign policy direction can be deduced from the convergent and divergent factors. Leveraging the improvement in US-China relations, the Korea-US-Japan trilateral

Table 11.3   Balancing National Interests among Korea, United States, and China

Nations	Convergent			Divergent			
	K	U	C	K	U	C	
Issues							
Deterioration of and conflict in US-China relations				O	O	O	Divergent
Dialogue and cooperation in US-China relations	O	O	O				Convergent
Participation in resolving common international issues	O	O	O				Convergent
Escalation of tension over China's potential invasion of Taiwan and interference with freedom of navigation				O	O	O	Divergent
Improving relations among China, North Korea, and Russia				O	O		Divergent
Involvement by China in the North Korean nuclear issue	O	O	O				Convergent
Nuclear tests by North Korea				O	O	O	Convergent
Pursuit of independent nuclear capabilities by Korea	O				O	O	Divergent
Failure in managing China's economic crises				O	O	O	Divergent
Economic retaliation and diplomatic pressure by China against Korea			△	O	O		Divergent
Expansion of military and security technology cooperation among United States, Korea, and Japan	O	O				O	Convergent
Restriction by the United States on semiconductor exports to China		O		O		O	Divergent
Expansion of NATO cohesion	O	O				O	Convergent
US isolationism and Trumpism				O	O	O	Divergent
Strengthening and expanding the US-Korea alliance	O	O				O	Convergent
Expansion of complementary industrial relationships between the United States and Korea	O	O				O	Convergent
Enhancement of US-Korea-Japan deterrence against North Korean nuclear threats	O	O				O	Convergent
Shifting center of gravity in semiconductor manufacturing to Japan		O		O		O	Divergent
Enhancement of Korea's capabilities in advanced technology	O	O				O	Convergent
Increase in defense expenditure by Korea for US forces stationed in Korea		O		O		O	Divergent
Membership in CHIP4 for Korea	O	O				O	Convergent
Membership in QUAD for Korea	O				O	O	Divergent

pact can strengthen deterrence against North Korea's nuclear threat and dissuade China from considering an armed invasion of Taiwan. Moreover, by capitalizing on the improving Chinese economy and further developing Korean science and technology, Korea can expect to see enhanced semiconductor competitiveness and expanded industrial complementarity with the United States.

Second, the divergent interests between Korea and the United States are (1) restriction by the United States on semiconductor exports to China; (2) shifting the center of gravity in semiconductor manufacturing to Japan; (3) pursuit of independent nuclear capabilities by Korea; and (4) increase in defense expenditure by Korea for US forces stationed in Korea. Korea and the United States must continue to engage in dialogues to resolve these differences.

Third, the divergent interests between Korea and China are (1) improving relations among China, North Korea, and Russia; (2) involvement by China in the North Korean nuclear issue; (3) pursuit of independent nuclear capabilities by Korea; (4) economic retaliation and diplomatic pressure by China against Korea; (5) expansion of military and security technology cooperation among the United States, Korea, and Japan; (6) expansion of NATO cohesion; (7) US isolationism and Trumpism; (8) strengthening and expanding the US-Korea alliance; (9) expansion of complementary industrial relationships between the United States and Korea; (10) enhancement of Korea's capabilities in advanced technology; and (11) membership in CHIP4 for Korea. These will be the points of contention in future strategic dialogues between Korea and China.

Fourth, the divergent interests between the United States and China are (1) escalation of tension over China's potential invasion of Taiwan and interference with freedom of navigation; (2) improving relations among China, North Korea, and Russia; (3) expansion of military and security technology cooperation among the United States, Korea, and Japan; (4) expansion of NATO cohesion; (5) strengthening and expanding the US-Korea alliance; (6) expansion of complementary industrial relationships between the United States and Korea; and (7) restriction by the United States on semiconductor exports to China. Transforming these divergent interests into convergent interests will be a difficult task. Therefore, the priority should be narrowing the gulf between the United States and China with respect to each divergent interest, thereby neutralizing the disparity between the convergent and divergent interests as points of potential conflict.

The three nations comprising the Korea-US-China triangle must clarify their red lines and erect appropriate guardrails to protect their respective core national interests. At the same time, they should engage in active dialogue and seek compromises on other interests to facilitate the restoration of the international order and contribute to the development of all three nations.

NEW BALANCING OF KOREA-US ALLIANCE WITHIN KOREA-US-CHINA TRIANGLE

Korea's National Interests within the US-China Strategic Competition

The US-China strategic competition, which began under the Trump administration, continues unabated under the Biden administration. This competition has forced Korea toward a critical juncture, and Korea must now carefully calculate the opportunity costs associated with its choices. One thing is clear, however, for Korea, situated at the crossroads of a geopolitical divide, the opportunity costs are inevitably greater than those faced by any other country. Table 11.4 illustrates a matrix of Korea's choices and the accompanying opportunity costs. If Korea chooses to align more closely with the United States, it may face China's ire, but it will gain strengthened security guarantees and science and technology cooperation with the United States. On the other hand, if Korea chooses to align more closely with China, it risks losing the benefits provided by the Korea-US alliance and may also suffer infringement on its sovereignty and identity at the hands of China. If Korea tries to strike an opportunistic balance between the two, the benefits and costs may become hopelessly muddled, leading to instability.

First, let us consider what may happen if Korea leans toward China. In terms of national security and diplomacy, Korea may experience the weakening of the Korea-US alliance, diminished national security, and diplomatic isolation. In terms of the economy and technology, Korea may be barred from technology cooperation with the United States, particularly in cutting-edge fields such as semiconductors, and its dependence on the Chinese economy will also increase. In terms of ideologies and values, Korea's fundamental value system rooted in liberal democratic ideals may come under pressure,

Table 11.4 Strategic Matrix and Korea's Choices

Target	Korea's Choice and Cost		
	Closer Alignment with the United States	Closer Alignment with China	Opportunistic Balancing
China	Collision	Infringement on sovereignty and identity/Uncertain benefits of uneasy coexistence	Unforeseeable costs and benefits
United States	Continued security assurance/Benefits of coexistence	Collision/Loss of alliance benefits	

Table 11.5 Sector-Specific Impact of Korea's Alignment with the United States or China

Korea's Position	Sector-Specific Impact		
	Diplomacy and Security	*Economy and Technology*	*Ideology and Values*
China-leaning	• Weakening of Korea-US alliance Diminished security • Diplomatic isolation	• Exclusion from US technology cooperation • Increased dependence on the Chinese economy	• Damage to and erosion of democratic ideology/ national identity, and sovereignty
US-leaning	• Escalation of tensions with China • Weakening of Chinese pressure on North Korea	• Possibility of economic retaliation, such as the disruption of supply chains for strategic materials	• Maintenance of liberal democratic ideology and national identity

thereby endangering its sovereignty. Now, what may happen if Korea leans toward the United States? In terms of national security and diplomacy, Korea will likely face the deterioration of its relationship with China. Korea may also lose any leverage it previously had through China in deterring the North Korean nuclear threat. In terms of the economy and technology, China may retaliate with economic sanctions, including restrictions on the export of strategic materials to Korea. However, in terms of ideologies and values, Korea will be able to safeguard its liberal democracy and national identity.

Among the options of coexistence, collision, and subordination, if Korea aims to strive for coexistence, it will need to persuade the United States and China of its strategic value and take on a balancing role between them to mitigate the risk of all-out confrontation.

Korea's China Policy Objectives toward a New Balance

Korea's China policy objectives should be to strengthen the trust asset with the United States, overcome the fear of China, and seek long-term coexistence without collision of interests. Korea should actively participate in minilateral frameworks as a middle power and help establish guardrails to prevent the divergent interests among Korea, the United States, and China from escalating into open conflict.

The stark geopolitical and geoeconomic reality is that Korea cannot afford to be China's enemy. At the same time, however, Korea must engage in diplomacy to stand up against threats from China to safeguard its identity, sovereignty, and right to exist. Therefore, in the short term, Korea's China diplomacy objective should be to persist in its efforts to preserve its identity, sovereignty, and right to exist in the face of the challenges posed by Xi Jinping's China. Korea must, of course, prepare to navigate China's strategies beyond the Xi Jinping era as well.

This geopolitical reality dictates that Korea is an ironclad ally of the United States. However, Korea cannot afford to be hostile toward China. Korea needs to prioritize the development of areas where it can cooperate not only with the United States but also with China. To achieve this, Korea must clearly identify China's strategic objectives and intentions in the midst of the US-China competition. By doing so, Korea can isolate the areas where it will likely compete with China as well as areas for cooperation.

The economy is one area where Korea must compete and cooperate simultaneously. In advanced technology and manufacturing, there exist complementary industrial and market structures between the two nations. In these areas of high complementarity and interdependence, Korea and China should continue engaging in negotiations to foster a sustainable economic and industrial ecosystem. However, Korea will also inevitably need to compete in this area to maintain a technological edge over China. Korea has serious concerns regarding its heavy dependence on the Chinese market, but the true danger lies in a scenario where the Chinese market no longer needs Korea (i.e., Korea becomes replaceable). This is why Korea must maintain a technological edge vis-a-vis China to remain indispensable.

China's red line that Korea should not cross pertains to China's core national interests. China's core interests, however, are ambiguous and expansive, and therefore, Korea cannot consider all aspects of China's core interests as red lines. This means that Korea's understanding of China's red line needs to be set within the bounds where China's core interests do not directly conflict with those of Korea.

Korea's China diplomacy to date has been characterized by a lack of understanding of each other's red lines, an overestimation of China's core interests, and an unreasonable fear of retaliation from China. This has resulted in an overly passive diplomatic posture. In diplomacy, a red line is established through observing the counterpart's reactions within the ongoing relationship while building consensus through negotiations. Therefore, Korea needs to clearly identify China's core interests, while at the same time, asserting its own unmistakable red lines, underpinned by clear principles, by responding decisively to any Chinese provocations.

China can threaten Korea's sovereignty and right to exist in several ways: first, through illegal entry into the Korea Air Defense Identification Zone (KADIZ); second, by conducting military activities in Korea's exclusive

Table 11.6   Assumed Red Lines between Korea and China

Red line that China should not cross	Red line that Korea should not cross
• Military activities within Korea's EEZ • Alignment with North Korea's threat and aggressive acts toward South Korea • Illegal entry into KADIZ, incapacitation of KADIZ • Illegal fishing within the territorial waters of Korea • Denial of freedom of navigation in the South China Sea and East China Sea • Intervention in Korea's national security sovereignty • Distortion of Korea's national identity • Behaving in a contradicting way to Korea's national values and ideologies	• China's core national interests(Taiwan, human rights, etc.) • Participation in overt military encirclement strategy toward China • Participation in the US-Korea-Japan military alliance • Deployment of offensive weapons targeting China • Possible military intervention in the Taiwan Strait and South China Sea due to ROK-US strategic flexibility • Inclusion of China as a defense target in the US-South Korea alliance • Resorting to preemptive strikes as a means for the denuclearization of North Korea • Promotion of US-Korea-Japan military alliance

economic zone (EEZ); third, through the distortion of Korea's national identity and history, and infringement on its ideology and values; fourth, via activities by Chinese nationals in Korea that disrupt social stability; and fifth, through China's indiscriminate actions against Korea's security interests.

China's provision of offensive military equipment or economic assistance to North Korea in violation of the UN sanctions also poses a significant threat. Moreover, when China imposes harsh and unfair restrictions on Korea's key industries or businesses, Korea should regard such actions as challenges to its sovereignty and right to exist, and respond firmly. Conversely, Korea should also acknowledge and respect China's red lines.

Korea's stance on the points of contention between itself and China remains firm. First, adopting a pro-China posture not only risks putting Korea's interests subordinate to those of China, thereby destabilizing the Korea-US alliance, but also contradicts Korea's national pride and ideology. Second, Korea has opted for a pro-US posture by aligning itself with the US-led technology alliance and the Korea-US-Japan trilateral security framework, making conflict with China inevitable. However, such a conflict is not what Korea desires. Third, Korea desires to avoid conflict and pursue a path of coexistence, thereby safeguarding its sovereignty, way of life, identity, and national interests. Coexistence with China should be the ultimate objective in Korea-China relations. The tasks that remain are to reduce friction with China, clearly identify each other's red lines, and pursue a strategy of coexistence.

Meanwhile, a point of contention in Korea-US relations pertains to whether the nuclear deterrence against North Korea reaffirmed in the Camp David declaration is indeed sufficient. Likewise, it appears that some members of the US Congress have expressed reservations about the former Moon Jae-in administration's pro-China posture. In contrast, the Yoon Suk Yeol administration's strategies include strengthening the Korea-US alliance, participating in the Korea-US-Japan trilateral security framework, and expanding Korea-US technology cooperation. This administration has boldly shed the "U.S. for security, China for economy" mindset of the past. Nevertheless, the influence of the liberal left in Korean politics remains strong. Another point of contention between Korea and the United States is whether the United States will sufficiently accommodate Korea's need to compensate for its losses resulting from US restrictions on exports of cutting-edge science and technology to China. The United States aims to diminish China's presence in key global supply chains and impede its advancement in science and technology. However, the United States needs to be reminded that semiconductors comprise 40 percent of Korea's total exports to China, and the semiconductor industry accounts for 25 percent of Korea's total value added. Korea's participation in the United States de-risking strategy may drastically reduce Korea's semiconductor exports to China and severely strain Korea-China relations.

These points of conflict underscore the economic interdependence among the three nations. The dynamics of Korea-US-China relations will help define the future international order through competition, conflict, and negotiations. In this process, Korea stands at a crossroads, knee-deep in a profound dilemma. In the past, Korea-China relations were often viewed as a by-product of US-China relations. Now, however, several factors are becoming constants in the triangular relationship. For instance, the shared values and aligned interests between Korea and the United States are now widely acknowledged within Korea-China relations. Moreover, China can no longer infringe upon Korea's sovereignty—this too has become a constant. However, Korea needs to engage in ongoing dialogue and communication with China to prevent these constants from boiling over into conflicts. These very constants can threaten Korea's existence due to its dependence on overseas markets.

The world's economies are intertwined, and most of America's allies have developed deep economic interdependence with China due to their own unique geopolitical and geoeconomic reasons. Korea, for instance, has heavily relied on the Chinese market over the past forty years. Despite sharing liberal democratic values with the United States, the EU has also developed deep economic interdependence with China. The United States must prioritize this reality in its China strategy. However, can the United States adequately compensate its allies for the losses incurred in the US-China competition? The United States must exercise caution so as not to undermine Korea's economy as a result of its containment policy against China. How, then, should the complexity, conflict, and interdependence among Korea, the United States, and China be effectively managed?

Korea must clearly articulate the following principles to China:

(1) China should cease regarding Korea as its vassal and refrain from imposing economic sanctions as it did during the THAAD controversy. The closer Korea leans toward the United States, the more effort China should commit to maintaining a friendly relationship with Korea.

(2) Korea rejects unfair demands from China that contradict the principles of the Korea-US alliance. This is a fundamental aspect of Korea's China policy. In view of this principle, Korea and China must respect each other's red lines.

(3) Korea will strongly resist any attempts by China to ignore or cooperate with North Korea's nuclear weapons program. China should maintain a neutral stance on this matter and fulfill its responsibilities as a responsible member of the UN Security Council in promoting peace on the Korean Peninsula.

(4) China must refrain from weaponizing Korea's economic dependence on and complementarity with the Chinese economy through diplomatic and political pressure. China should keep its promise to maintain separation between politics and the economy. Korea will pursue economic and industrial complementarity with the United States while reducing its economic dependence on China.

(5) Korea will resolutely protect its sovereignty, identity, and right to exist and will strongly resist any attempts by China to infringe on these core national interests.

(6) Korea will strive to maximize convergent interests with China, thereby aiming to form a special partner relationship with China that contributes to the common goal of peace and prosperity in Northeast Asia.

How should China manage the complexity, points of collision, and interdependence in today's world? Above all, China must cease the use of sharp diplomacy, intellectual property theft, and cyber hacking. China can contribute to global harmony not by pursuing expansionist ambitions but by prioritizing the welfare of its citizens, bolstering social safety nets, and upholding human rights. China should also keep its promise of maintaining a balance between socialism and a market economy. Finally, China can forge a path toward global prosperity by carefully observing the red lines that exist between itself and the United States.

The United States, Dominant Power with Like-Minded Allies

As previously noted, the United States has become now "the largest minority shareholder of the world." It cannot be part of the majority unless it consolidates its shares with those of its allies and partners. As such, the United States has no choice but to rely on its friends and allies in its foreign policy endeavors. Conversely, it also bears the burden of leading such a coalition, given its status as the most powerful nation among them. This book has explored many of the conflicting points of interest that exist between the United States on the one hand, and its allies and partners on the other. As such, US policymakers and think-tankers must move away from the usual oversimplification of crisscrossing interests and demands borne out of global interdependence, and resist the urge to solve problems solely through the United States' sheer power as exemplified by the Office of the United States Trade Representative's (USTR) aggressive trade policies during the 1980s. The United States must now shift its approach toward the default mindset of persuading its friends and allies to come on board by sharing in the balance of interests with them. Unfortunately, many US policymakers still cling to the perception of being the largest shareholder. However, this perception does not reflect the current reality, and the United States should recognize the many difficulties it is asking its friends and allies to bear, as a fellow, albeit the largest, minority shareholder. This means that the United States should adopt a more open and positive attitude in its dialogue with its friends and allies. While many US policymakers and think-tankers may not agree with this observation, there are undoubtedly some who would.

How should the United States manage the complexity, points of collision, and interdependence in today's world? No other military power rivals that of the US military. The US security guarantee provides a decisive deterrence against North Korean aggression on the Korean Peninsula. The US dollar overwhelmingly influences the global economy and finance. However, beyond these strategic assets, lies another critical strategic asset the United States must not take lightly: the trust asset. The United States must carefully nurture the trust between itself and its allies and partners. This means that the United States must be keenly aware of and accommodate the needs of its friends and allies to compensate for any losses they may incur by aligning with the United States in the US-China strategic competition. Preserving the trust asset requires the United States to maintain maximum flexibility in managing tensions and conflicts. Only then could its friends and allies readily participate in United States strategies to meet the challenges posed by China and Russia.

How should the United States balance the differing interests between itself and its allies? While the United States and its allies sail in the same boat sharing common values, the United States must actively earn their trust by assuring them of their right to exist. This can only be achieved by taking into consideration the economic interdependence of its allies when formulating its strategies to oppose Chinese expansionism. Of particular concern is the economic interdependence among Korea, the United States, and China.

The United States must earnestly engage in talks with Korea to address the losses that will inevitably result from the US containment policy or de-risking strategy toward China. Through such dialogue, the Korea-US alliance, will become a beacon among all US alliances.

CONCLUSION

Korea, the United States, and China must continue to engage in dialogue to identify and address the points of collision among them. Through such dialogue, the three countries should strive to establish a strategic matrix to minimize divergent interests and maximize convergent interests.

The United States and China must establish clear guardrails to prevent their competition from escalating into open conflict. Moreover, they should share such guardrails with their respective allies and partners. By establishing clear and balanced guardrails, the United States can encourage its allies and partners to align their interests with its own.

Many nations witnessed a decline in trust in the United States during the Trump administration due to its pursuit of unilateral protectionism, often at the expense of the interests of its friends and allies. The United States neglected opportunities to engage in dialogue and cooperation with its allies and friends, failing to create channels to rally the collective energy of like-minded countries in addressing common challenges, particularly from China. The friends and partners of the United States in the Indo-Pacific region place greater trust in the United States than in China and desire the continuation of United States leadership in the region. However, if the United States persists in unilateral policymaking solely in pursuit of its own interests, its allies and partners in the Indo-Pacific region may lose their strategic bearings.

Korea must pursue unwavering cooperation with the United States in national security matters, while adopting more conditional cooperation in the area of economics. If the Korean government engages in cooperation with the United States at significant costs to Korea's national interests, this risks eroding the trust that the Korean people place in the United States. Such a development could weaken the Korea-US alliance, giving China room to exploit what it perceives as a "weak link" by employing a divide-and-rule strategy.

Korea and the United States should build a sustainable alliance based on mutual respect by maximizing the convergent interests and minimizing the divergent interests between them. If the United States insists on pursuing unilateral protectionism without regard for Korea's interests, it could diminish US leadership, ultimately weakening its position in the US-China strategic competition. A case in point is the recent deterioration in the Korean public's perception of America, as the losses borne by allies like Korea became apparent. Therefore, the United States must consistently pursue a balance of interests with its allies and partners.

Korea's involvement in the Taiwan Strait issue may damage its relations with China. However, the truth of the matter is that peace and stability in the Taiwan Strait directly affect the freedom of navigation in the Western Pacific, and by extension, the sea lines of communication vital for Korea's continued existence. Therefore, Korea must work toward a peaceful resolution of the Taiwan Strait issue through employing appropriate rhetoric in its communications with China and the international community.

The United States must pursue a foreign policy that does not infringe upon the national interests of its allies and partners amid the US-China strategic competition. European countries have pointed out the limitations of the decoupling strategy and proposed the de-risking strategy as an alternative. The United States reluctantly embraced this approach, recognizing that it could not bank on European support if the damages resulting from the decoupling strategy continued to accumulate. However, challenges persist in establishing clear guidelines under the de-risking strategy. The United States' friends and allies require a shared strategic map for implementing the de-risking strategy to avoid fragmentation and erosion of trust among themselves. If this were to happen, they risk becoming a prime target for China's divide-and-rule strategy. In short, the United States has a responsibility to support its like-minded friends and allies in their efforts to preserve and protect their sovereignty, development, identity, and right to exist. What the United States and its friends and allies cannot afford is a loss of trust in US leadership.

Notes

INTRODUCTION

1. NEAR Foundation, *The Impact of Xi Jinping's New Era on Korea and the World* (21st Century Books, 2023), 40–42. https://product.kyobobook.co.kr/detail/S000201234436.

2. NEAR Foundation, *The Impact of Xi Jinping's New Era.*

3. "Henry Kissinger Explains How to Avoid World War Three," *The Economist,* May 17, 2023. https://www.economist.com/briefing/2023/05/17/henry-kissinger-explains-how-to-avoid-world-war-three.

4. Richard N. Haass, "Promoting Order in a Disorderly World" (Special Address Presented at the 2023 NEAR Global Survey Report Conference on the World Order, December 6, 2023, Seoul, Korea).

5. Choi Yoo-sik, "The Decline of the Chinese Economy," *Chosun Ilbo*, March 2, 2023. https://www.chosun.com/international/china/2023/03/02/R62B3XHG3JGXPKJSQNPYB7FTHE/?utm_source=naver&utm_medium=referral&utm_campaign=naver-news.

6. Tepperman, Jonathan. "China's Dangerous Decline." *Foreign Affairs*, December 19, 2022. https://www.foreignaffairs.com/china/chinas-dangerous-decline. (Accessed February 11, 2024).

7. Paul Gewirtz, "Words and Policies: Derisking and China Policy," May 30, 2023. https://www.brookings.edu/articles/words-and-policies-de-risking-and-china-policy/ (Accessed February 11, 2024).

8. 程大为, 从"脱钩"到"去风险"：看美国战略意图的本质, <光明日报>, July 26, 2023. https://www.chinanews.com.cn/gj/2023/07-26/10049699.shtml (Accessed February 11, 2024).

9. Jung Jae-heung and Kim Kyu-beom, "The Derisking Policy of the US and China's Response," Sejong Policy Brief, No. 2023–12, September 5, 2023. https://www.sejong.org/web/boad/1/egoread.php?bd=3&itm=4&txt=%EC%A0%95%EC%9E%AC%ED%9D%A5&pg=1&seq=7314,

10. "Searching for Sustainability of the Korea-US Alliance Amidst the US-China Competition." Keynote Speech at Korea Economic Institute (KEI) by Duck Koo Chung in Washington, DC, September 2023.

11. This section is extracted from Kimyoungsa, "Korea's Strategies to Overcome Chinese Expansionism" pp. 50–51, ed. by the NEAR Foundation, August 2020.

OVERVIEW

1. "2023 Munich Security Conference Report," in *Munich Security Conference*. https://securityconference.org/en/publications/munich-security-report-2023/ (Accessed March 18, 2024).

2. "2023 NEAR Global Survey Report on the World Order," NEAR Foundation. https://nearfnd.imweb.me/57/?q=YToxOntzOjEyOiJrZXl3b3JkX3R5cGUiO3M6Mzo iYWxsIjt9&bmode=view&idx=17467467,325&t=board (Accessed March 18, 2024).

3. Cheng Li is a nonresident senior fellow in the Foreign Policy program at Brookings. He was a senior fellow at Brookings from 2006 to 2023 and served as director of the John L. Thornton China Center from 2014–2023.

4. "A Conversation with Henry Kissinger," *Economist*, May 17, 2023. https://www.economist.com/kissinger-transcript

5. 2023 NEAR Global Conference on the World Order was held in Seoul, South Korea from December 5–6, 2023.

6. Richard N. Haass, *Foreign Policy Begins at Home: The Case for Putting America's House in Order* (New York: Basic Books, 2013).

CHAPTER 1

1. 中共国家民族事务委员会党组, "以铸牢中华民族共同体意识为主线加强和改进党的民族工作," 求是, March 2024.

2. China National Bureau of Statistics announced on July 17, 2023, that the youth unemployment rate for 16–24 year olds in urban areas was 21.3 percent in the 2023 Q2 major economic indicators. However, they did not announce the youth unemployment rate for unclear reasons.

3. The 15th BRICS Summit was held in Johannesburg, South Africa, in August 2023, and six emerging countries (Argentina, Egypt, Ethiopia, Iran, Saudi Arabia, and the United Arab Emirates) were invited. Among them, Egypt, Ethiopia, Iran, and the United Arab Emirates officially joined BRICS on January 1, 2024, and became members.

CHAPTER 2

1. "思想旗帜引领方向　实干笃行开创新局——深入学习贯彻习近平总书记重要指示和全国宣传思想文化工作会议精神," 新华社, October 10, 2023.
http://www.news.cn/politics/leaders/2023-10/10/c_1129907758.htm (Accessed March 14, 2024).

2. 王滬寧 著, 政治的人生』(上海: 上海人民出版社, 1995): 51–52.

3. 习近平, "在文化传承发展座谈会上的讲话,"『求是』, August 31, 2023. http://www.qstheory.cn/dukan/qs/2023-08/31/c_1129834700.htm (Accessed March 14, 2024).

4. For example, if several conditions are the same or similar, age, party membership duration, and work duration are used as important indicators. These indicators provide relatively objective and quantified information.

5. Gap-yong Yang, Kyung-seok Ha, "China's 'Global South' Strategy and Implications under the U.S.-China Competition," National Security Strategy Institute No. 246, December 20, 23. https://www.inss.re.kr/publication/bbs/js_view.do?nttId=41037044&bbsId=js&page=4&searchCnd=100&searchWrd=.

6. Guoguang Wu, "Li Qiang Versus Cai Qi in the Xi Jinping Leadership: Checks and Balances with CCP Characteristics?," *China Leadership Monitor Fall 2023, Issue 77,* September 1, 2023. https://www.prcleader.org/post/li-qiang-versus-cai-qi-in-the-xi-jinping-leadership-checks-and-balances-with-ccp-characteristics (Accessed March 15, 2024).

7. 2024年2月5日外交部发言人汪文斌主持例行记者会," 中华人民共和国外交部　版权所有, February 5, 2024. https://www.mfa.gov.cn/fyrbt_673021/jzhsl_673025/202402/t20240205_11240693.shtml (Accessed March 14, 2024).

CHAPTER 5

1. The Advanced Research Projects Agency (ARPA), established in 1958 under the Department of Defense and renamed the Defense Advanced Research Projects Agency (DARPA) in 1972, has played a key role in the initial and critical stages of the development of semiconductor industries in the United States. "Federal funding for semiconductor-related research and development (R&D) has for decades spurred industry breakthroughs that have led to everyday commercial innovations that have grown our economy, propelled U.S. technology leadership, and contributed to our national security"—SIA, "The Importance of Federal Semiconductor R&D Funding." https://www.semiconductors.org/wp-content/uploads/2020/06/Importance-of-Fed-Semi-RandD-Funding.pdf

2. Robert Noyce would later have a huge impact on the development of the semiconductor industry as the founder of Intel.

3. 2023 Factbook, Semiconductor Industry Association (SIA).

4. 2023 Factbook, Semiconductor Industry Association (SIA).

5. McKinsey & Co, "Exploring New Regions: The Greenfield Opportunity in Semiconductors," January 2024. https://www.mckinsey.com/industries/semiconductors/our-insights/exploring-new-regions-the-greenfield-opportunity-in-semiconductors

6. Trendforce, "NAND Flash Market Landscape to Change?" March 14, 2024. https://www.trendforce.com/news/2024/03/14/news-nand-flash-market-landscape-to-change/#:~:text=As%20per%20a%20research%20from,the%20previous%20quarter%20to%2021.6%25.

7. Therefore, there are rumors circulating about a potential merger between WDC and Kioxia as a strategic move to expand market share and leverage economies of scale.

8. The market share numbers by company are from Kyung-Hui Kwon and Sang-Hoon Kim, "World Non-Memory Semiconductor Market Landscape and Policy Implications," Monthly KIET Industrial Economy (Issue August 2023) (requoted).

9. The market share numbers by company are from Kyung-Hui Kwon and Sang-Hoon Kim, "World Non-Memory Semiconductor Market Landscape and Policy Implications," Monthly KIET Industrial Economy (Issue August 2023) (requoted).

10. Counterpoint, "Global Semiconductor Foundry Market Share: Quarterly," November 30, 2023. https://www.counterpointresearch.com/insights/global-semiconductor-foundry-marketshare/

11. Lee, Jeong-ah and Do, Won-bin, "US and EU Semiconductor Industry Development Strategies and Implications," KITA Trade Report, Vol. 8, 2023 (requoted).

12. Lee and Do, "US and EU Semiconductor Industry Development Strategies and Implications" (requoted).

13. While water supply is a crucial area, it was excluded as it is not considered a point of strategic conflict between nations. Water supply involves two main aspects: the ability to receive an adequate water supply, which varies by country and region, necessitating strategic site selection within a country. Another aspect is the timely supply of high-quality water in large quantities. With ongoing climate change, ensuring a stable water supply is a critical issue for each country to address. However, this is unlikely to become a point of policy conflict between nations, as exemplified by the fact that the competition for semiconductors with the water supply issue is not that kind of water competition between China and countries along the Mekong River in Indochina.

CHAPTER 6

1. "习近平:我人生第一步所学到的都是在梁家河," *China Central Television*, June 27, 2018. http://news.cctv.com/2018/06/27/ARTIZ5xlYR6riAfsqxtedCxc180627.shtml (Accessed February 22, 2024).

2. "习近平自述:永远是黄土地的儿子," *People's Daily*, February 14, 2015. http://politics.people.com.cn/n/2015/0214/c1001-26567403.html (Accessed February 22, 2024).

3. "Functional/Structural Domains," The Millon Personality Group. https://www.millonpersonality.com/theory/functional-structural-domains/ (Accessed February 22, 2024).

4. "The Personality Profile of China's President Xi Jinping," Unit for the Study of Personality in Politics. http://personality-politics.org/china (Accessed February 26, 2024).

5. As a reporter and later senior editor for JoongAng Ilbo, I have been covering China since 1988. As such, I have covered Xi Jinping ever since he began to emerge as a key political figure in the Chinese Communist Party (CCP).

6. You Sangchul, *Into the Mind of Xi Jinping* (Seoul: Lisa Publication, 2023).

7. Although I cannot reveal the exact source, this article is based on the content of the following books and my experience and knowledge. (白信. 『習近平是如何成爲一位超級政治强人的?』, 台北: 新銳文創, (2018)., 鄧聿文. 『不合時宜的人民領袖: 習近平研究』, 台北: 獨立作家., (2023)., 洪耀南. 『中共百年, 看習近平十年』, 台北: 新銳文創 (2018)., 劉明福. 『中國夢』, 北京: 中國友誼出版公司 (2013)., 習近平. 『之江新語』, 杭州: 浙江人民出版社 (2015)., 梁家河 編寫組編. 『梁家河』, 西安: 陝西人民出版社 (2018)., 楊中美. 『習近平』, 台北: 時報出版 (2015)., 吳玉山·寇健文·王信賢 主編. 『一個人或一個時代: 習近平執政十週年的檢視』, 台北: 五南出版 (2022)., Kang Kyung-gu, et al., *In the Xi Jinping Era, the Process of Religious Sinicization* (Seoul: Shin-A Publishing, 2021). KimKi-su, *Xi Jinping's Leadership and China's Golden Time* (Seoul: Seoktap Publishing, 2015).

8. Harrison E. Salisbury, *The New Emperors: China in the era of Mao and Deng* (Boston, MA: Little Brown, 1992).

9. Brown Kerry, *The World According to Xi* (London: I.B. Tauris, 2018).

10. Salisbury, *The New Emperors.*

11. Source: https://lyricstranslate.com

CHAPTER 7

1. 周晓蕾, "人类命运共同体与"中韩命运共同体":对韩国舆论的分析," 国际论坛 (January 2021): 120; I analyzed articles on the Community of Common Destiny for Mankind and the Korea-China Community of Common Destiny in ten Korean newspapers from September 6, 2011, when the Chinese government first proposed the Community of Common Destiny, to May 31, 2020.

2. Joo-young Jang, "Young-min Noh, Chinese Ambassador to China, Says 'Korea and China Are Neighboring Cousins,'" *Seoul Economic Daily*, October 10, 2017. http://v.daum.net/v/20171010171806371.

3. Seung-woo Lee, "Mi-ae Choo, Self-Defense Reasons Cannot Tolerate Threats to Other Countries. . .The Restoration of Korea-China Relations is a Great Force in Maintaining Peace," *Segye Ilbo,* December 3, 2017. http://v.daum. net/v/20171203185615704.

4. Je-pyo Hong, "Did Moon Jae-in Really Say 'Korea-China Community of Common Destiny'?," *CBS Nocut News*, February 23, 2020. http://v.daum. net/v/20200223164206946.

5. Gap-yong Yang, "Why Xi Jinping's Ideology Is Titled So Long," *Kyunghyang Shinmun*, October 26, 2017. http://v.daum.net/v/20171026161142808.

6. Young-shin Lim, "Korea-China Relations 'Turning Point' . . . Need to Break through the Private Sector," *Maeil Business Press*, October 25, 2017. http://news. mk.co.kr/newsRead.php?year=2017&no=706300.

7. He Yafei (何亞非), translated by Kim Do-hoon, *Choice, China and Global Governance* (Seoul: Dong-A University Press, 2017), 9–10.

8. 何伟文, "一带一路和江东区的历史机遇," *2015 中国(宁波) 海商文化国际论坛 (China (Ningbo) Maritime Culture International Forum,* June 18, 2015.

9. "習近平在周邊外交工作座談會上發表重要講話強調 爲我國發展爭取良好的周邊環境 推动我国发展更 多惠及周边国家," 人民日報, *October* 26, 2013. https://www.baidu.com/link?url=NPJZrdhFCGXm4s7ckRPCj gFtkbJsmvvlWcnpgYFyOVkX5ws1JzYZLGeNLZAFGsLEev0FosP8Qt_Fzf58y-CFWiTwzzpK6jAo7usKTn_Y0zHq&wd=&eqid=fe9553db013a316a0000000666 af87c2.

10. 郑必坚, "世界热议中国:寻求共同繁荣之路," *中信出版社* (2013): 5.

11. 国务院新闻办公室, "中国的和平发展," *人民日报,* September 7, 2011.

12. 徐进·郭楚, "命运共同体概念辨析," *战略决策研究* 第6期 (2016年): 14.

13. The author referred to 王海东·张小劲, "新时代中国国际战略: 以"命运共同体"论述为重点的解读," 国际论坛 第6期 (2019年): 73.

14. 习近平, "加强和改进国际传播工作展示真实立体全面的中国," *人民日报,* June 2, 2021. https://www.baidu.com/link?url=zJ1dRiyjrxTADspFZkPLIsRMj6gpu sAkhckTuafX15z0qThR4AaCaEUs5yd2nvtE8-KnBpSI1xdICi-F0gtj-vgyFWGiUYt 73LGpfGHoFGe&wd=&eqid=a6379b3e0142c05e0000000666af8a6d.

15. 胡锦涛, "坚定不移沿着中国特色社会主义道路前进 为全面建成小康社会而奋斗," *中国共产党第十八次全国代表大会上的报告,* 人民出版社 (2012): 47.

16. 王海东·张小劲, "新时代中国国际战略:以"命运共同体"论述为重点 的解读," 国际论坛 第6 期 (2019年)*:* 72.

17. "习近平 携手构建合作共赢新伙伴同心打造人类命运共同体-在第 七十届联合国大会一般性辩论时的讲话," *人民日报,* September 29, 2015. https:// www.baidu.com/link?url=C6HpIWU6UOSfcPsR7ECKpCe1V6O6jQHy8jRMVuZV spZGTJgndHIlcrUK6JuoSuzecssH0H6nxh1brA5mNVxM4C9KdOA1y6DSdd98aBl fvUa&wd=&eqid=a83e0fc5000ab2850000000666af94dd.

18. "践行人类命运共同体理念的中国担当," *光明网-理论频道,* January 26, 2022. https://www.baidu.com/link?url=ezD-iDSI_xH2JazRmT9tFf3N4xImza_piI_ BGhOqT7zKjdkcVSxp_0QCgJsWUL3KdVWfo_lm4z_oJ45v9teVKXJSSAsG3PB Ah1QwIOb0nXy&wd=&eqid=a12865a70142834b0000000666af8bb2

19. 中華人民共和國憲法修正案 第35條 March 11, 2018.

20. 习近平, "论坚持推动构建人类命运共同体," *中央文献出版社* (2018): 5–6.

21. "外交部:中国的发展是全世界的机遇, 不是任何人的威胁," *新华网,* April 11, 2022. https://www.baidu.com/link?url=pxtavfBXgbem2xu4Jp6WptE2fh12tu_1 uBf79_rrVYbqjkAkPxfX9Vh-fW07hjuiNIh6noCZFhqfL3UjElBjiF9wcoT5vL_QaIo KxrIPGCG&wd=&eqid=fa42d27e0064293a0000000666af8bf5.

22. 胡鞍钢·李萍, "习近平构建人类命运共同体思想与中国方案," *新疆师范大学学报(哲学社会科学版)* 第39卷 第5期 (September 2018): 7–8.

23. 胡鞍钢·李萍, "习近平构建人类命运共同体思想与中国方案," 10.

24. 张海鹏, "从世界历史进程看人类文明新形态," *中国社会科学网, 中国历史研究院,* March 2, 2022. https://www.baidu.com/link?url=5pEDZQpF fvofbu7h01Cf1v2UkRhHyNQdMCg6cFyzmQLlEwSl7FbQLC1xn49cKH5v9ium

AeoavJL26nhipKLhPogZxFCpqDtGxYTNZPMkdJO&wd=&eqid=82b8f16500cdb
19a0000000666af8cb5.

25. 习近平, "在中国共产党与世界政党高层对话会上的主旨讲话 (Xi Jinping's Keynote Speech at the High-level Dialogue between the Communist Party of China and World Political Parties)," December 1, 2017. https://www.baidu.com/link?url=V9PRIeArKtNqWTl3Zrlf5oMa8kfl6WaKHNag6LKeL56c4l4lBaS0ZC4Yu ljRv0gp2FX3S-MwETmrnY0fNcGT70PfHRg5AzoxrVhOPccGXoW&wd=&eqid=d d64178d014f1d440000000666af8d2e.

26. 禮記 "禮運" "大道之行也 天下爲公. 進賢與能 講信修睦. 故人不獨親其親 不獨子其子. 使老有所終 壯有所用 幼有所長. 矜寡孤獨廢疾者皆有所養. 男有分 女有歸. 貨惡其棄於地也 不必藏於己 力惡其不出於身也 不必爲己. 是故謀閉而不興 盜竊亂賊而不作 故外戶而不閉. 是謂大同."

27. 卡尔 马克思·弗里德里希 恩格斯, "马克思恩格斯文集," 人民出版社 第1卷 (2009): 53,7.

28. 李雪, "人类命运共同体的理想性与现实性," 探索 第5期 (2017年): 10,6.

29. 高奇琦, "全球共治:中西方世界秩序观的差异及其调和," 世界经济与政治 第4期 (2015年): 67–87.

30. 习近平, "加强和改进国际传播工作展示真实立体全面的中国," 人民日报, June 2, 2021. https://www.baidu.com/link?url=i4bXZYC6_IEUnk_ PBlFVLl8WP22rBpK1DY5DOuRFpBe62Aw7Gi5JKYFRPdf-uGWknaseClYL_ oP0Gp2HUneu0DunlEz3qtMJvxhcfS0ijby&wd=&eqid=d048f6c6014d09c30000000 0666af8dab.

31. 罗海兵·史元丰, "柯乐山:何为"世界伦理"的文明基础?," 中国新闻网, April 11, 2022. https://www.baidu.com/link?url=Cply1zxeXXuLOKX_DsGGYfwQSBLl- hY2qV4Q-ZejtxZ3HIXYSJyKeMuzSSxvAK8YzBpmUPwLWr6L7A8nMY7duFa& wd=&eqid=eced682d00008f890000000666af8e5f.

32. 周信言, "文化全球化视域下中国文化世界传播的探索与策略研究," 新闻文化建设 (2020): 38.

33. "探索后疫情时代国际中文教育实践路径," 中国社会科学网-中国社会科学报, September 25, 2021. https://www.baidu.com/link?url=btEZqwquS6CH2 CWwOIpHe57248RlukUFEOH-Drs8GtvWqSh3-UxRdF5ROBMCmGJy0CvRcghy GIUSwH4ITZC1Fq&wd=&eqid=8de3a8880002d87c0000000666af8ead.

34. 朴現圭·朱剛君, "Analysis on the Content of Korean Confucius Institute Text-books," 中國文學研究 85 (2021): 27,7.

35. Louisa Clarence-Smith, "Ban on Chinese Institutes at U.K. Universities Drawn Up After Rishi Sunak's Pledge to Scrap Them," *Telegraph,* October 25, 2022, https:// www.telegraph.co.uk/news/2022/10/25/ban-chinese-institutes-uk-universities-drawn -rishi-sunaks-pledge/ (Accessed March 7, 2024).

36. PRAMESINIKHAMTAB, "文化软实力思想与弘扬中国传统文化— 基于孔子学院的文化传播工作," 华南理工大学博士学位论文 (2018): 82.

37. Euidal Song, "Xi Jinping Data Center, Seoul National University and Yonsei University, Why Are They Helping China's Infiltration into Korea," *Chosun Ilbo*, October 9, 2022. http://v.daum.net/v/20221009103246987.

38. "为世界和平与发展作出更大贡献," 人民日报, January 3, 2022. https:// www.baidu.com/link?url=NUyzZxHsDM-BE7pJYNStodfFS7F4qPnLEcrZw_Ndnl-

GKxBXYXU_yxuXDfbS9BXE2wNTIyXhh8MpgrbefRqWcWJ1Lf0unhl65zm-lmK
4pcp_&wd=&eqid=cda3265c00006bad0000000666af910f.

39. "向世界传播中国传统文化正能量(国际论坛)," 人民日报, April 5, 2022. http://paper.people.com.cn/rmrb/html/2022-04/05/nw.D110000renmrb_ 20220405_2-03.ht.

40. 刘旭, "韩国学者:中国外交智慧将为全球治理作出更大贡献," 中新社, October 23, 2022. https://www.baidu.com/link?url=lK7jDHiY4PlsU34JWlmTozJLX gYhB6k3WviXe-8GlYFgYsLRDBT1p26QQP01sXHAONh9-YdSi8phSLgpT0a6N EXmu7eUXAfooELHGpl4Q4y&wd=&eqid=cbc68a1f000bee6f0000000666af9384.

41. 郑永年, "中国国家间关系的构建:从"天下"到国际秩序," 当代亚太 (2020).

42. 周信言, "文化全球化视域下中国文化世界传播的探索与策略研究," 新闻文化建设 (2020): 38.

43. 徐梦, "人类命运共同体理念的世界秩序观意蕴-兼论"天下主义"与"世界主义"的当代价值," 国际观察 第1期 (2020年): 7–9.

44. 徐进·郭楚, ""命运共同体"概念辨析," 战略决策研究 第6期 (2016年): 10.

CHAPTER 8

1. Roberto S. Foa, Margot Mollat, Han Isha, Xavier Romero-Vidal, David Evans, and Andrew J. Klassen, "A World Divided: Russia, China and the West," *Cambridge: Center for the Future of Democracy, Cambridge University*, October 2022. https:// www.bennettinstitute.cam.ac.uk/wp-content/uploads/2022/11/A_World_Divided.pdf (Accessed March 2, 2024).

2. White House, National Security Strategy, 2022. https://www.whitehouse .gov/wp-content/uploads/2022/10/Biden-Harris-Administrations-National-Security -Strategy-10.2022.pdf; Department of Defense, National Defense Strategy (NDS), 2022. https://media.defense.gov/2022/Oct/27/2003103845/-1/-1/1/2022-NATIONAL -DEFENSE-STRATEGY-NPR-MDR.PDF (Accessed Feburary 12, 2024).

3. Graham T. Allison, *Destined for War* (New York: Mariner Books, 2017).

4. Kim Heungkyu, "The United States' China Policy Transformation and the Start of a New Cold War?" *International Political Review* 58(3).

5. Rush Doshi, *The Long Game* (New York: Oxford University Press, 2021), 6.

6. PEW, "How Global Public Opinion of China Has Shifted in the Xi Era" (September 2022). https://www.pewresearch.org/global/2022/09/28/how-global-public -opinionof-china-has-shifted-in-the-xi-era/ (Accessed December 12, 2023); PEW, "Negative Views of China Tied to Critical Views of Its Policies on Human Rights" (June 2022). https://www.pewresearch.org/global/2022/06/29/negative-views-of -china-tied-to-critical-views-of-itspolicies-on-human-rights/ (Accessed December 12, 2023).

7. The World Bank is assessing China's superiority at about 18.8%, and the CIA at about 16%, "The World's Biggest Economy America or China?," *World Economics,* February 2024. https://www.worldeconomics.com/Thoughts/ The-Worlds-Biggest-Economy.aspx#:~:text=An%20alternative%20measure%20of

%20country,be%2023%25%20larger%20than%20America (Accessed February 4, 2024).

8. The White House, "National Security Strategy of the United States of America," 2017 (Accessed October 26, 2023). https://trumpwhitehouse.archives.gov/wp-content/uploads/2017/12/NSS-Final-12-18-2017-0905.pdf.

9. Mike Pence, "Remarks on the Administration's Policy Towards China." https://www.hudson.org/events/1610-vice-president-mike-pence-s-remarks-on-the-administration-s-policy-towards-china102018 (Accessed March 27, 2024).

10. David Barboza, "Ken Lieberthal on Washington's Major China Challenges," *The Wire China,* April 24, 2022. https://www.thewirechina.com/2022/04/24/ken-lieberthal-on-washingtons-major-china-challenges/.

11. This perception was first raised in an editorial in the People's Daily by Zhang Yunling(张蕴岭), "人民日报人民要论：在大变局中把握发展趋势," *People's Daily,* March 15, 2019. http://opinion.people.com.cn/n1/2019/0315/c1003-30976769.html (Accessed March 22, 2024); Xi Jinping's speech at the Central Party School is Xi Jinping, 2019. http://www.xinhuanet.com/2019-09/03/c_1124956081.html (Accessed March 22, 2024).

12. Katharina Buchholz, "U.S.-Chinese Trade War: A Timeline," *Statista,* August 17, 2020. https://www.statista.com/chart/15199/us-chinese-trade-war-escalates/.

13. Idid. And Kinling Ko, "US Watchers in Beijing Urge Closer Look at Biden's Tough New "China Hands'," *South China Morning Post,* March 20, 2022. https://www.scmp.com/news/china/diplomacy/article/3171116/us-watchers-beijing-urge-closer-look-bidens-tough-new-china.

14. Kurt M. Campbell and Jake Sullivan, "Competition Without Catastrophe," *Foreign Affairs* 98 (September/October 2019): 96–110.

15. The White House, "Interim National Security Strategic Guidance," March 2021. https://www.whitehouse.gov/wp-content/uploads/2021/03/NSC-1v2.pdf (Accessed December 11, 2024).

16. Hal Brands et al., *COVID-19 and World Order* (Baltimore, MD: Johans Hopkins University Press, 2020).

17. Kurt M. Campbell and Jake Sullivan, "Competition Without Catastrophe," *Foreign Affairs*, August 1, 2019. https://www.foreignaffairs.com/articles/china/competition-with-china-without-catastrophe (Accessed November 20, 2019).

18. Daniel Strieff, "America Must Heal Itself First," Chatham House, Feburary 2021. https://www.chathamhouse.org/publications/the-world-today/2021-02/america-must-heal-itself-first (Accessed March 1, 2024).

19. Kinling Ko, "US Watchers in Beijing Urge Closer Look at Biden's Tough New "China Hands'," *South China Morning Post,* March 20, 2022. https://www.scmp.com/news/china/diplomacy/article/3171116/us-watchers-beijing-urge-closer-look-bidens-tough-new-china (Accessed March 15, 2024).

20. Financial Times, "The Three Pillars of U.S. Foreign Policy under Biden." October 19, 2020.https://www.ft.com/content/6f85ae61-2e16-4272-8974-a38123ed994f (Accessed May 10, 2022).

21. The description of the meeting is from Wikipedia about United States-China talks in Alaska, https://en.wikipedia.org/wiki/United_States%E2%80%93China

_talks_in_Alaska. An article from china is based on "Alaska Talks: Officials' Take on 'One-China' Reveals Two Opinions on Taiwan," *South China Morning Post*, March 21, 2021. https://www.scmp.com/news/china/politics/article/3126288 /alaska-talks-officials-take-one-china-reveals-two-opinions (Accessed November 15, 2021).

22. Biden, Joseph R. Jr., "At UN, Biden Pledges New Era of "Relentless Diplomacy' to Tackle Global Challenges," *The United Nations News*, September 21, 2021. https://news.un.org/en/story/2021/09/1100502 (Accessed March 15, 2024).

23. 孙水岩, "拜登的外交政策團隊與對華政策認知," *iGCU报告*, November 13, 2020. https://www.thepaper.cn/newsDetail_forward_9986227 (Accessed March 15, 2024).

24. 习近平, 中国共产党第二十次全国代表大会报告全文, October 19, 2022. https://mp.weixin.qq.com/s?__biz=MzU3NDAxNDY3OA==&mid=2247517993 &idx=1&sn=1a13f55cb56e7093542aa362678b8fb7&chksm=fd3a1290ca4d9b86804 c89c43db20d64ce6c41aa91004410cf997893316c130973b3e98d05b3&scene=27 (Accessed March 15, 2024).

25. Lazaro Gamio and Ana Swanson, "How Russia Pays for War," *New York Times*, October 30, 2022. https://www.nytimes.com/interactive/2022/10/30/business/ economy/russia-trade-ukraine-war.html (Accessed March 15, 2024).

26. Xi Jinping uses 坚定 and 谨慎 interchangeably; "永远保持 "赶考"的清醒和谨慎," 人民日报, November 3, 2022. https://www.163.com/dy/ article/HL8OMFR005560N26.html; "永葆"赶考"的清醒和坚," 人民日报, August 4, 2022. https://baijiahao.baidu.com/s?id=1740178247994843492&wfr=spider&for =pc (Accessed March 16, 2024).

27. White House, "National Defense Strategy," October 2, 2022. https://www .whitehouse.gov/wp-content/uploads/2022/10/Biden-Harris-Administrations -National-Security-Strategy-10.2022.pdf (Accessed March 16, 2024).

28. White House, "National Defense Strategy."

29. LAURA SILVER, CHRISTINE HUANG, et al., "Americans Are Critical of China's Global Role – as Well as Its Relationship With Russia," *Pew Research Center*, April 12, 2023. https://www.pewresearch.org/global/2023/04/12/americans-are -critical-of-chinas-global-role-as-well-as-its-relationship-with-russia/

30. The US Senate has already passed the bipartisan Strategic Competition Act to contain China in 2021. This is shown in the China Briefing (2024) Day 92.

31. Pew Research Center, "How Global Public Opinion of China Has Shifted in the Xi Era," September 28, 2022. https://www.pewresearch.org/global/2022/09/28/how -global-public-opinion-of-china-has-shifted-in-the-xi-era/ (Accessed March 15, 2024).

32. Pew Research Center, "How Global Public Opinion of China."

33. NATO, "NATO 2022 Strategic Concept," June 29, 2022. https://www.nato.int /nato_static_fl2014/assets/pdf/2022/6/pdf/290622-strategic-concept.pdf (Accessed March 25, 2023).

34. "What to Take From German Chancellor Scholz's Visit to China," *RANE*, November 9, 2022. https://worldview.stratfor.com/article/what-take-german-chancellor-scholzs-visit-china; The Prime Minister Scholz's stance is from "German's Scholz Defends China Trip Amid Controversy," *Deutsche Welle*, November 3, 2022.

https://www.dw.com/en/germanys-scholz-defends-trip-to-china-as-car-industry-signals-support/a-63634777 (Accessed March 15, 2023).

35. Roberto S. Foa, Margot Mollat, Han Isha, Xavier Romero-Vidal, David Evans, and Andrew J. Klassen, "A World Divided: Russia, China and the West," University of Cambridge, Cambridge (Accessed October 2022).

36. Lazaro Gamio and Ana Swanson, "How Russia Pays for War," *New York Times*, October 30, 2022. https://www.nytimes.com/interactive/2022/10/30/business/economy/russia-trade-ukraine-war.html (Accessed February 5, 2024).

37. China Briefing, "U.S.-China Relations in the Biden Era: A Timeline, Day 664." March 12, 2024. https://www.china-briefing.com/news/us-china-relations-in-the-biden-era-a-timeline/ (Accessed February 5, 2024).

38. This is the summary of the author's discussions and interviews during his visit to China in 2023.

39. IMF, "Global Recovery Remains Slow, with Growing Regional Divergences and Little Margin for Policy Error," October 2023. https://www.imf.org/en/Publications/WEO/Issues/2023/10/10/world-economic-outlook-october-2023?cid=ca-com-compd-pubs_belt (Accessed February 5, 2024).

40. This concept is one of the five scenarios for the future presented in Global Trends 2040 by the National Intelligence Council, "Renaissance of Democracies, A World Drift, Competitive Coexistence, Separate Silos, and Tragedy and Mobilization," 2021. https://www.dni.gov/index.php/gt2040-home/scenarios-for-2040/renaissance-of-democracies

41. China Briefing, "Day 821: U.S. Treasury Secretary Janet Yellen Calls for a "Constructive and Fair" Relationship with China," March 20, 2023. https://www.china-briefing.com/news/us-china-relations-in-the-biden-era-a-timeline/ (Accessed February 5, 2024).

42. China Briefing, "Xi-Biden Meeting: "Productive" Talks Lead to Increased Cooperation in Key Areas," November 16, 2023. https://www.china-briefing.com/news/us-china-meeting-productive-talks-lead-to-cooperation-in-key-areas/ (Accessed February 5, 2024).

43. Barry R. Posen, *Restraint: A New Foundation for U.S. Grand Strategy* (Cornell University Press, 2014). http://www.jstor.org/stable/10.7591/j.ctt5hh0db; Ryan Hass, *Stronger: Adapting America's China Strategy in an Age of Competitive Interdependence* (Yale University Press, 2021). https://doi.org/10.2307/j.ctv1fx4hnj

44. Kenneth Lieberthal. Daved Barvoza. "Ken Lieberthal on Washington's Major China Challenges," *The Wire China,* April 24, 2022. https://www.thewirechina.com/2022/04/24/ken-lieberthal-on-washingtons-major-china-challenges/ (Accessed February 5, 2024).

45. China Briefing, "Day 895: China's Ministry of Commerce Places Export Restrictions on Key Metals for Production of Chips," July 3, 2023. https://www.china-briefing.com/news/us-china-relations-in-the-biden-era-a-timeline/ (Accessed February 5, 2024).

46. Graham Allison, Kevin Klyman, Karina Barbesino, and Hugo Yen, *The Great Tech Rivalry: China vs the U.S.* (Belfer Center, December 2021). https://

www.belfercenter.org/sites/default/files/GreatTechRivalry_ChinavsUS_211207
.pdf; US STAR Subcommittee on U.S.–China: Winning the Economic Competition
(S. HRG. 116–385, July 22, 2020). https://www.govinfo.gov/content/pkg/CHRG
-116shrg42704/pdf/CHRG-116shrg42704.pdf; Robert D. Atkinson, "Is the United
States Really One of the Most Competitive Economics in the World? No." *ITIF,
Hamilton Center on Industrial Strategy,* July 2022. https://itif.org/publications
/2022/07/18/is-the-united-states-really-one-of-the-most-competitive-economies-in
-the-world-no/

47. Robert D. Atkinson and Ian Tufts, "The Hamilton Index, 2023: China Is Running Away with Strategic Industries," *Information Technology & Innovation Foundation,* December 2023. https://www2.itif.org/2023-hamilton-index.pdf (Accessed
February 4, 2024).

48. Robert D. Atkinson and Ian Tufts, "The Hamilton Index, 2023: China Is Run-
ning Away with Strategic Industries," December 2023. https://itif.org/publications
/2023/12/13/2023-hamilton-index/; Original Source: Jamie Faida, Jennifer Wong
Leung, et al., "ASPI's Critical Technology Tracker – Sensors & Biotech Updates,"
Australian Strategic Policy Institute, September 2023. https://www.aspi.org.au/
index.php/report/critical-technology-tracker; And according to the 2023 report The
Deglobalization Myth by the Hinrich Foundation, a China-focused research institute,
China's trade with the United States is declining, but its influence in trade with other
countries is expanding.; "The Deglobalization Myth: How Asia's Supply Chains
Are Changing," *Hinrich Foundation,* January 9, 2024. https://www.oxfordeco-
nomics.com/resource/the-deglobalisation-myth-how-asias-supply-chains-are-chang-
ing/#:~:text=19%20Jan%202024-,The%20Deglobalisation%20Myth%3A%20How
%20Asia's%20supply%20chains%20are%20changing,year%20between%20
2018%20and%202022.

https://www.hinrichfoundation.com/research/wp/trade-and-geopolitics/how
-asia-supply-chains-are-changing/ (Accessed February 4, 2024).

49. Melissa Cyrill, "How Will the US-China Trade War End? We Explore Three
Scenarios," *China Briefing,* June 25, 2019. https://www.china-briefing.com/news/
how-will-us-china-trade-war-end-3-scenarios/

50. "Japan, Which Is Sanctioning Russia, Invests in Putin's Oil Business," *Han-
kook Ilbo,* November 1, 2022. https://www.hankookilbo.com/News/Read/A202211
0110230002446?did=DA (Accessed March 1, 2024).

51. Extracted from a presentation by Professor Chaesung Chung of Seoul National
University at the Plaza Project meeting held on November 19, 2023.

52. Presidential Office Announcement, "Yoon President Implementing the Indo-
Pacific Strategy with Three Visions of Freedom, Peace, and Prosperity." November 11, 2022. https://www.korea.kr/news/policyNewsView.do?newsId=148908196
&pWise=main&pWiseMain=A1 (Accessed March 1, 2024).

53. Extracted from Professor Jeon Byung-seo (Joongang University)'s presentation from Plaza Project in Seoul, South Korea (2021), "China's Economic Outlook
and Korea-China Economic Relations."

CHAPTER 9

1. Kelsey Davenport, "Russia Uses North Korean Missiles Against Ukraine," Arms Control Association, March 2024. https://www.armscontrol.org/act/2024-03/news/russia-uses-north-korean-missiles-against-ukraine (Accessed March 21, 2024).

2. Robert L. Carlin and Siegfried S. Hecker, *"Is Kim Jong Un Preparing for War?"* January 11, 2024. https://www.38north.org/2024/01/is-kim-jong-un-preparing-for-war/ (Accessed March 25, 2024).

3. "Biden Administration's North Korea Policy – Mira Rapp-Hooper's Featured Conversation with Victor Cha," CSIS Transcript, March 3, 2024. https://www.csis.org/analysis/biden-administrations-north-korea-policy (Accessed March 25, 2024).

4. Victor Cha and Andy Lim, "Slow Boil: What to Expect from the DPRK in 2024," CSIS Commentary, January 16, 2024. https://www.csis.org/analysis/slow-boil-what-expect-dprk-2024 (Accessed March 25, 2024).

CHAPTER 10

1. US Mission China, "Readout of President Joe Biden's Meeting with President Xi Jinping of the People's Republic of China," *US Embassy & Consulates in China,* November 17, 2023. https://china.usembassy-china.org.cn/readout-of-president-joe-bidens-meeting-with-president-xi-jinping-of-the-peoples-republic-of-china-2/ (Accessed February 19, 2024).

2. Kang Jun Young. "Taiwan's Presidential Election Results: Don't Get Caught Up in the Pro-US vs. Pro-China Paradigm," Aju Economic Daily, January 14, 2024. https://www.ajunews.com/view/20240114133908099 (Accessed Feburary 20, 2024).

3. Jeongmin Ha, "Global Scholar Interview <4> Cross-Strait Relations Expert Zhao Chunshan, Honorary Professor of Taiwan's Tamkang University," *Dong-A Ilbo*, January 9, 2024.
https://blog.naver.com/nymphmk408/223316843572 (Accessed February 19, 2024).

4. Kang Jun Young, "Continuation of Cross-Strait Tensions and the Importance of 'Principled Diplomacy,'" *Munhwa Ilbo*, January 15, 2024. https://www.munhwa.com/news/view.html?no=2024011501073111000002 (Accessed February 19, 2024).

5. "解析共軍實彈軍演背後缺陷 前艦長：夜間防空戰力不足 (Analyzing the shortcomings behind the Communist Army's live-fire military exercises: Former captain: Insufficient night-time air defense capabilities)," 自由時報*(Liberty Times Net),* April 15, 2021. https://news.ltn.com.tw/news/politics/breakingnews/3500285 (Accessed January 12, 2024).

6. Kang Jun Young, "Reality of Armed Conflict between China and Taiwan -Focusing on the Scenario of US Support and Conflict in Taiwan," *Journal of Korean-Chinese Social Science Research* 20(1) (January 1, 2022): 9–32.

7. Benjamin Jensen, et al., "Shadow Risk: What Crisis Simulations Reveal about the Dangers of Deferring U.S. Responses to China's Gray Zone Campaign against

Taiwan," *Center for Strategic and International Studies*, February 16, 2022. https://www.csis.org/analysis/shadow-risk-what-crisis-simulations-reveal-about-dangers-deferring-us-responses-chinas-gray (Accessed February 20, 2024).

8. Richard Bush et al., "Don't Help China by Hyping Risk of War over Taiwan," *National Public Radio,* April 8, 2021. https://www.npr.org/2021/04/08/984524521/opinion-dont-help-china-by-hyping-risk-of-war-over-taiwan (Accessed Feburary 20, 2024).

9. "外交部发言人赵立坚主持例行记者会(Foreign Ministry spokesperson Zhao Lijian hosted a regular press conference)," *Ministry of Foreign Affairs of the People's Republic of China,* March 10, 2021. https://www.fmprc.gov.cn/ce/ceus/chn/fyrth/t1859958.htm (Accessed February 1, 2024).

10. "习近平：高举中国特色社会主义伟大旗帜　为全面建设社会主义现代化国家而团结奋斗—在中国共产党第二十次全国代表大会上的报告," *Xinhua News Agency,* October 25, 2022.
    http://www.news.cn/politics/2022-10/25/c_1129079429.htm (Accessed Feburary 19, 2024).

11. "受权发布）习近平：高举中国特色社会主义伟大旗帜　为全面建设社会主义现代化国家而团结奋斗—在中国共产党第二十次全国代表大会上的报告," *Xinhua News Agency*, October 16, 2022. http://www.news.cn/politics/2022-10/25/c_1129079429.htm (Accessed February 19, 2024).

12. 李登輝(Lee Teng-hui), "中嶋嶺雄,駱文森.楊明珠譯,『亞洲的智略," 臺北:遠流圖書公司 (Taipei: Far East Book Company) (2000): 35–36. Chinese scholars argue that this perception is the root of the so-called Taiwan independence consciousness. For details, see Qu Congwen, "Interpreting the Three Forms of 'Taiwan Consciousness,'" *China Review (Hong Kong)*, July 2005, 91.

13. "對照中國對台白皮書新舊內涵 學者：反外力干涉將成北京主軸 (Scholars Comparing the Old and New Connotations of China's White Paper on Taiwan: Opposition to External Interference Will Become Beijing's Main Focus)," *Central News Agency*, August 11, 2022. https://www.cna.com.tw/news/acn/202208110379.aspx (Accessed February 19, 2024).

14. "台(Taiwan Issue and China's Unification Cause in the New Era)," Taiwan Affairs Office of the State Council of the People s Republic of China, August 10, 2022. https://www.gov.cn/zhengce/2022-08/10/content_5704839.htm (Accessed Feburary 20, 2024).

15. Young Hee Chang, "The 20th Party Congress and the Change in the Chinese Communist Party's Taiwan Policy," IFES Research Report, Kyungnam University Far East Research Institute, Seoul, November 7, 2022.

16. Tang Yonghong, "2024 年台湾"大选"结果及其影响刍议,"华夏经纬网, January 19, 2024. https://baijiahao.baidu.com/s?id=1788455130803924677&wfr=spider&for=pc (Accessed Feburary 20, 2024).

17. Chris Horton, "Taiwan's Status Is a Geopolitical Absurdity," *The Atlantic*, July 8, 2019. https://www.theatlantic.com/international/archive/2019/07/taiwans-status-geopolitical-absurdity/593371/.

18. Niall Ferguson, "A Taiwan Crisis May Mark the End of the American Empire," *Bloomberg Opinion*, March 21, 2021. https://www.bloomberg.com/

opinion/articles/2021-03-21/niall-ferguson-a-taiwan-crisis-may-end-the-american -empire.

19. Shelley Rigger, *Why Taiwan Matters: Small Island, Global Powerhouse* (Lanham, MD: Rowman & Littlefield, 2013).

20. Kim, Tae-ho, "Four Reasons Why Taiwan Is Still Important," *Pressian*, April 6, 2016. https://www.pressian.com/pages/articles/135021#0DKU (Accessed Feburary 20, 2024).

21. Lee, Dae-woo, "South China Sea Territorial Dispute and US-China Relations," *KINU Unification Journal* (Fall 2016). chrome-extension://efaidnbmnnnibpcajpcgl clefindmkaj/
https://www.kinu.or.kr/pyxis-api/1/digital-files/366661a5-4ca4-4d16-a71a -af3117218d60 (Accessed February 20, 2024).

22. Kang Jun Young, "China's South China Sea Territorial Dispute Observation Method," *E-daily*, July 18. https://www.jsd.or.kr/?c=1178&uid=18491_(Accessed Feburary 20, 2024).

23. Jocelyn Coffin, "Rhetoric and Reality: Taiwan's Democratization and its Effects on US-Taiwan Relations," *American Journal of Chinese Studies* 24 (2017): 1–12.

24. Miranda Priebe, et al., "Implementing Restraint: Changes in US Regional Security Policies to Operationalize a Realist Grand Strategy of Restraint," Rand Corporation (2021). https://www.rand.org/pubs/research_reports/RRA739-1.html.

25. William M. Arkin, "Is China the New Threat?," Washington Post, February 8, 2006. http://blogs.washingtonpost.com/earlywarning/2006/02/is_china_the_ne.html (Accessed February 20, 2024). The Pentagon's new Quadrennial Defense Review takes the first formal step in designating China this country's number one enemy. . . . a clear message: The United States will seek to ensure that "no foreign power" will develop "regional hegemony" or "disruptive capabilities"—and China is the only nation with capacity to do both.; Nancy Bernkopf Tucker, "War or Peace in the Taiwan Strait?," *The Washington Quarterly* 19.1 (1996): 171-187. Nancy Tucker, a professor at Georgetown University, also emphasizes that the United States should avoid interfering or mediating in China's affairs.

26. Bonnie S. Glaser, "Nancy Pelosi's Taiwan Visit, With Bonnie S. Glaser," Council on Foreign Relations, August 2, 2022. https://www.cfr.org/podcasts/nancy -pelosis-taiwan-visit-bonnie-s-glaser (Accessed February 20, 2024).

27. 鄭文翔, "從「天然獨」到「小紅書」世代，不想被統的台灣與拒絕文化 的距離," *The News Lens*, May 24, 2021. https://www.thenewslens.com/article /151253/fullpage (Accessed February 20, 2024)

28. 王信賢, "Taiwan's Security Strategy and Challenges in the Era of US-China Competition," East Asia Institute EAI Special Report, June 17, 2021. https://www.eai.or.kr/new/ko/project/view.asp?code=97&intSeq=20562&board= kor_special&keyword_option=&keyword=&more= (Accessed February 20, 2024)

29. A research from a Journal of Electoral Studies, *Election Research Center of the National Taiwan University School of Political Science*, June 2022.

30. 黃 秋 龍 (H u a n g , C h i u - L u n g), "中共介入我2024年總統與立委選舉動向研析,展望與探索月刊 (An Analysis

of PRC's Interference in 2024 R.O.C. Presidential and Legislative Elections),"第22卷第1期 (January 2024). chrome-extension://efaidnbmnnnibpcajpcglclefindm-kaj/https://www.mjib.gov.tw/FileUploads/eBook s/87a26af7eb974891abdb8679d435182f/Section_file/a1f43fe8083c4b1396501bd363c020ee.pdf (Accessed February 20, 2024)

31. Alastair Iain Johnston, et al., "The Ambiguity of Strategic Clarity," *War on the Rocks – National Security for Insiders*, June 9, 2021. https://warontherocks.com/2021/06/the-ambiguity-of-strategic-clarity/ (Accessed February 20, 2024).

32. David Keegan, "Strengthening Dual Deterrence on Taiwan: The Key to US-China Strategic Stability," *Stimson Center Issue Brief*, July 6, 2021. https://www.stimson.org/2021/strengthening-dual-deterrence-on-taiwan-the-key-to-us-china-strategic-stability/ (Accessed February 20, 2024).

33. K. S. Charles, et al., "Why the US Should Ditch Strategic Ambiguity Toward Taiwan," *The Defense Post*, December 1, 2021. https://www.thedefensepost.com/2021/12/01/us-strategic-ambiguity-taiwan/. https://www.justsecurity.org/82912/strategic-ambiguity-isnt-working-to-deter -china-on-taiwan-it-will-invade-anyway-its-time-to-commit/. (Accessed February 20, 2024).

34. Diana Glebova, "Kirby Says U.S. Doesn't "Support Taiwan Independence' as China Threatens Pelosi ahead of Expected Taiwan Trip," *National Review*, August 1, 2022. https://www.nationalreview.com/news/kirby-says-u-s-doesnt-support-taiwan-independence-as-china-threatens-pelosi-ahead-of-expected-taiwan-trip/ (Accessed February 20, 2024).

35. Dina Smeltz, et al., "Americans Favor Aiding Taiwan Against China," Report on Public Survey Based on 2022 Chicago Council Survey, The Chicago Council on Global Affairs (August 2022). https://www.thechicagocouncil.org/research/public -opinion-survey/americans-favor-aiding-taiwan-against-china (Accessed February 21, 2024).

36. Jang, Young-hee, "The Continuity and Change of Cross-Strait Relations in the Biden Era," Korea National Diplomatic Academy (KNDA), Asia-Pacific Studies Series, Seoul (July 2022).

37. Based on the reading from Opinion, *China Times,* May 1, 2021.

38. Quoted an analysis conducted by Li Mingjiang, a professor at Nanyang Technological University in Singapore, *Singapore* 联合早报, October 24, 2022.

39. Based on a comprehensive review of several articles, including *Financial Times* on October 22, 2022.

40. Kang Jun-young, "The World Will See a More Provocative North Korea," *Thinkchina* 9 (January 2024). https://www.thinkchina.sg/world-will-see-more-provocative-north-korea (Accessed February 21, 2024).

41. Jang, Young-hee, "The 20th Party Congress and the Change in the Chinese Communist Party's Taiwan Policy," IFES Research Report, Kyungnam University, The Institute for Far Eastern Studies, Changwon, November 7, 2022.

CHAPTER 11

1. Khan, Sulmaan Wasif, *Haunted by Chaos: China's Grand Strategy from Mao Zedong to Xi Jinping, With a New Afterword.* (Cambridge, MA: Harvard University Press, 2022)

2. Swaine, Michael D., Sara A. Daly, and Peter W. Greenwood, *Interpreting China's Grand Strategy: Past, Present, and Future.* (Washington, DC: Rand Corporation, 2000).

3. Shin Bong-su, "China's Grand Strategy and Xi Jinping's One-Man Rule System," *China Experts Forum*, September 19, 2018.

4. Lee Seung-joo, "Economic and Security Nexus and the Evolution of US-China Strategic Competition," *Korean Journal of International Relations (KJIR)* 61(3) (2021): 121–156.; Henry Farrell and Abraham L. Newman, "Weaponized Interdependence: How Global Economic Networks Shape State Coercion," *International Security* 44 (2019): 42–79.

5. A preliminary analysis of this triangular matrix was published by Duck-Koo Chung and his team in August 2024 by the Korea Institute for International Economic Policy (KIEP).

Index

www.ingramcontent.com/pod-product-compliance
Lightning Source LLC
Chambersburg PA
CBHW032342280326
41935CB00008B/417